# BAD WATER

**Asia-Pacific** CULTURE, POLITICS, AND SOCIETY
Editors: Rey Chow, Michael Dutton,
H. D. Harootunian, and Rosalind C. Morris

# BAD WATER

Nature, Pollution, and Politics in Japan, 1870–1950

**Robert Stolz**

Duke University Press  Durham and London  2014

© 2014 Duke University Press
All rights reserved
Printed in the United States of America on acid-free paper ∞
Typeset in Arno Pro by Westchester Books
Designed by Courtney Leigh Baker

Library of Congress Cataloging-in-Publication Data
Stolz, Robert, 1970–
Bad water : nature, pollution, and politics in Japan, 1870–1950 /
Robert Stolz.
Pages cm — (Asia-Pacific: culture, politics, and society)
ISBN 978-0-8223-5690-5 (cloth : alk. paper)
ISBN 978-0-8223-5699-8 (pbk. : alk. paper)
1. Environmental protection—Political aspects—Japan.
2. Pollution—Political aspects—Japan. I. Title.
II. Series: Asia-Pacific.
TD187.5.J3S76 2014
363.730952'09041—dc23     2013050759

STUDIES OF THE WEATHERHEAD EAST ASIAN
INSTITUTE, COLUMBIA UNIVERSITY

The Studies of the Weatherhead East Asian Institute
of Columbia University were inaugurated in 1962 to bring
to a wider public the results of significant new research
on modern and contemporary East Asia.

CONTENTS

## ACKNOWLEDGMENTS

*Bad Water* is the result of a project over a dozen years in the making. Over this time I have benefited from the help and support of numerous teachers, friends, institutions, and family. I apologize in advance to anyone I failed to mention but who nonetheless deserves my thanks.

I must express my deepest gratitude to Tetsuo Najita and James Ketelaar for their insistence on the importance and intellectual stakes of historical investigation. Both deserve special thanks for teaching me to be a better reader, writer, and thinker. Their passion for sustained, deep thinking not only, I hope, informs this book but is also a model I have tried my best to emulate in research and the classroom. With them, Harry Harootunian has also intervened at key points of this process, helping me to try to combine theoretical analysis with daily practice. Needless to say, any stumbles in this area in the pages that follow remain mine alone.

Brett Walker and Julia Thomas kindly read the entire manuscript when it was at its roughest. Carol Gluck graciously took on this project at the Weatherhead East Asian Institute at Columbia University, and she and Daniel Rivero stuck with it through all the ups and downs. I am also thankful to the readers from both the Weatherhead Institute and Duke University Press, whose substantial and thoughtful comments surely improved the final version. Others who read parts include Prasenjit Duara, Norma Field, Anne Walthall, Douglas Howland, Gregory

Golley, William Sewell, Dan Magilow, and Chad Black. I also want to thank Ken Wissoker, Jade Brooks, and Liz Smith of Duke University Press for their enthusiasm and support in bringing this book to press.

In Japan I am forever grateful to Anzai Kunio, who welcomed me to Waseda on two occasions. Together with Kanai Takanori, he shared his immense knowledge of Meiji history and the *jiyūminken undō*. Kanai was also incredibly patient in walking me through the finer points of *sōrōbun* starting from scratch. Igarashi Akio at Rikkyō University, Nakahara Jun'ichi and the staff at the Kurosawa Torizō Kinenkōdō at Rakunō Gakuen daigaku, Komatsu Hiroshi at Kumamoto daigaku, Eto Shigeyuki of the Tekireikai, the JR East union members who let me join them in replanting the hills around Ashio in 2002, and members of Tanaka Shōzō daigaku in Tochigi and Tokyo, especially Fukawa Satoru and Akagami Takashi, all welcomed me and gave me access to their collections and expertise.

Federico Marcon deserves special thanks for not only reading and commenting on large sections but also being willing to debate nearly every piece of the project. With Federico, others who were always ready to organize meetings and panels to discuss and argue over the finer points of capitalism and ecology include Ken Kawashima, Katsuya Hirano, Gavin Walker, Katsuhiko Endo, Ian Miller, Brett Walker, and Julia Thomas. Many more colleagues in Chicago, Tennessee, Virginia, and Japan contributed and deserve special thanks here: Jim Bartholomew, Celia Braves Jeremy Butler, Julie Christ, Alon Confino, Daniel Corl, Bruce Cumings, Chris Hebert, Iwasaki Masaya, Patti Kameya, Sho Konishi, Fabio Lanza, Maezawa Bin, Makihara Norio, Tanya Maus, Trent Maxey, Jeri McIntosh, Christopher McMorran, Allan Megill, Christopher Oakes, Brian Owensby, Albert Park, Sam Perry, John Person, Zac Pessin, Rob Sklenar, Sugai Masurō, David Tompkins, Alberto Toscano, Umemori Naoyuki, Michael Wert, and Mikael Wolfe.

Resources and time to complete this project were provided by a Japan Society for the Promotion of Science (JSPS) and Social Sciences Research Council (SSRC) Fellowship at Waseda, a University of Virginia Arts, Humanities, and Social Sciences Research Grant, the UVa East Asia Center, a University of Tennessee Professional Development Award, a Fulbright (IIE) Graduate Research Fellowship, and a University of Chicago Center for East Asian Studies Writing Fellowship. The final version has also benefited from comments from faculty and students at Amherst College, the University of Toronto Department of East Asian Studies, and the Department of Japanese Studies at National University of Singapore. Earlier versions of parts of chapter 3 were published as "Nature over Nation: Tanaka Shōzō's Fundamental River Law," *Japan Forum* 18, no. 3 (2006): 417–37.

Lastly, I would like to thank my family for their support and understanding over this long process. For all their help, I thank my parents, Robert and Claire Ann Stolz, my sister Suzanne, my brother Peter, nieces Nicola, Pippa, Riley, and Katrina, and finally and most importantly Kimberly, who not only read and helped with the manuscript and images but also, for better or worse, was there from the very beginning.

*the quality of having strong moral principles. honesty + decency*

Questions like Where is nature? or What is nature? have long lost any residual probity or innocence they may have had (or pretended to). . . . The point here is not that nature has become cultural; one might as well argue that culture has become feral. . . . Rather, the point is that nature has become political.

—PETER VAN WYCK, *Signs of Danger*

*adj. in a wild state, especially after escape form captivity or domestication*

## Nothing to Fear Here

In the eighth lunar month of 1868, amid the collapse of the Tokugawa samurai government—even as civil war raged in the North—a pamphlet appeared in Edo (modern-day Tokyo) assuring its readers that Benjamin Franklin had made them safer: "In the past, devoid as it was of scientists (*shikisha*), it was endlessly repeated that lightning was the scolding of an angry god, an object of awe, something to be feared. But ever since a man named Franklin came into the world there is no one who would explain lightning this way. He has even built the device by which this disaster may be avoided—people's joy is truly boundless." So begins *Tenpen chii* (*The Extraordinary Workings of Heaven and Earth*), by Obata Tokujirō (1842–1905). An eleven-page work divided into eight chapters, *Tenpen chii* was dedicated to "subdu[ing] the strange (*ki o osaeri*), . . . showing that neither does Heaven act strangely nor Earth go mad." One by one Obata attacks the false wisdoms of the past and explains the true principles at work behind seemingly strange natural phenomena. In turn, lightning, earthquakes, comets, rainbows, sunspots, lunar haloes, "shooting stars and fireballs," and "cold fires" (*inka*)[1] are revealed as wholly knowable, predictable, and avoidable.

For Obata, Franklin's discovery means that lightning, rather than a form of divine punishment is nothing more than the same electricity (*ereki*) that exists "in more or less amounts within all substances." To prove this to his readers, Obata invites them to rub a few pieces of paper together in a darkened room, producing their own spark of static electricity. After establishing this safe, mundane essence of lightning, Obata declares atmospheric lightning to be the mutual stimulation of heaven and earth, the *yin ereki* of one meeting the *yang ereki* of the other. Having reduced lightning from divine punishment to a parlor trick, Obata produces a Kantian separation of this natural phenomenon from politics and morality, assuring his readers that all the lightning and thunder they see and hear acts according to its own independent principles, with no relationship to their personal situation. Obata lays out the mechanics that keep them at a safe distance: because the gap between the lightning flash and the thunderclap is the result of the differing speeds of light and sound, if they can "count to three or four between the flash and the clap," they may safely conclude the bolt struck some "700–800 ken"[2] away. In fact, "if you do not immediately hear the thunder following the flash, you have absolutely nothing to fear."

In contrast to its title, then, *Tenpen chii*'s opening sentence makes clear that Obata's project is to prove that the "extraordinary workings of Heaven and Earth" are, in fact, quite ordinary. Only the false wisdom of the past has obscured this liberating insight. The first sentence of the Franklin chapter denies the past any "scientists" (*shikisha*) whatsoever, making no allowance for the wisdom some past "sage" (*seijin*) may have had. Each section of *Tenpen chii* begins with a repetition of common wisdom linking natural phenomena to the gods, followed by a survey of Western scientific breakthroughs that reveal nature's true, earthly principles. And each section culminates in an assurance that, with the true workings known, there is nothing to fear. In Obata's text, previous knowledge of the workings of nature was not only flawed but also caused people to fear the wrong things. Worse, people's vague understandings of the underlying principles (*ri*) behind phenomena rendered their outdated knowledge useless for avoiding future disasters. For Obata, Franklin's greatness is not his discovery that lightning is electricity but his invention of the lightning rod. Franklin

not the principle
but the function
of the truth

showed that the way to protect oneself from lightning was not to hope and pray to avoid it, but to attract it with a copper rod placed at the highest point of a building. (The accompanying illustration in Obata's text shows a churchlike European structure with six rods, one on each gable.) People, not gods, would now have the power to make lightning go where they want.[3] According to this new worldview, no longer would natural phenomena such as earthquakes and comets foretell Heaven's political dictates, as they had from the *Mencius* to the recent Ansei earthquake (1855). Obata's comets exchanged their political roles for scientifically predictable and stable orbits with a periodicity "wholly determined by themselves" (*mawari kuru jikoku wa mizukara kimari ari*). In sharp contrast to the politically active nature of the 1850s and 1860s, the nature of the 1870s existed outside politics.[4]

Tenpen chii appeared just months after restorationists seized control of the court in Kyoto and issued the five-point Charter Oath, point 4 of which read, "Evil practices of the past shall be broken off and everything based upon the just laws of nature." Throughout the 1870s and 1880s, all inherited thought was ruthlessly scrutinized and brought into agreement with a regime of knowledge known as "civilization and enlightenment" (*bunmei-kaika*). Civilization and enlightenment was an optimistic intellectual, social, and political reorganization that sought to bring Japanese practice into alignment with those "just laws of nature" most often defined as the Western, rational, scientific worldview.[5] According to this new regime of knowledge, humans, armed with absolute scientific principles, stand outside their environment and are able to manipulate a material nature operating according to knowable laws. In other words, human manipulation of nature based on knowledge of true principles can remove the unpredictability, randomness, and fearsomeness from nature itself.

It is important to notice that the epistemological and physical separation of humans from nature in Obata's text is also the construction of the individual, autonomous, modern Japanese subject. The indifferent comets and lightning of *Tenpen chii* echo the equally disinterested Heaven of Meiji natural rights theory (*tenpu jinken*), in which Heaven neither played favorites nor chose anyone to be lord or master over another. Here we need look no further than Obata's Nakatsu colleague and founder of Keiō gijuku (*Tenpen chii*'s publisher), Fukuzawa Yukichi, whose hugely influential *Gakumon no susume* (*An Encouragement of Learning*, 1873) opens with the famous lines "Heaven makes no person superior to another, nor does Heaven make any person inferior to another. All are born of Heaven and, as such, all are

*[handwritten margin note: branch of philosophy that involves the origin nature & methods + limits of human knowledge]*

alike."[6] Under natural rights theory, the Meiji subject was a world unto him- or herself, entering only consciously chosen, voluntary relations with the outside world. Freely chosen contracts, either economic or social varieties, were the liberal model of interaction. Obata's separation of nature from politics was in no way a simple Japanese story. As we shall see in chapter 1, this separation of the individual from nature and nature from politics was, and is, fundamental to the theory of the liberal subject, making a repoliticization of nature explored in this book a point of particular concern for liberal political theory. Indeed, in the European context, Marx had already noted sarcastically how "remarkable" it was that Darwin "rediscovered" his own bourgeois society at work in nature in *The Origin of Species*. We could say something similar of Obata, who in investigating the extraordinary workings of Heaven and Earth "discovered" self-determining comets to be the complement to natural rights theory's bourgeois social relations of discrete, equal individuals operating and interacting according to their own inner principles.[7] *Tenpen chii*'s radical attack on superstition and tradition metaphorically, and as we shall see in some cases literally, cleared the ground for a Meiji subject separated from its surroundings.

To be sure, when the true principles of nature were themselves quite dangerous (as in the case of a comet striking the earth), Obata could not completely separate the Meiji subject from nature. Nonetheless, in these instances he was still able to subdue the real powers of nature by resorting to rational calculation of the enormous odds that any individual subject would ever be so unlucky as to have nature intrude on his or her life: "The universe is an enormous place; as for something as incredibly small as the earth moving through it, even though there are countless comets, there should be no fear that there would ever be a collision. It is like a few leaves floating on the enormous expanse of the ocean."[8] Earthquakes and volcanic eruptions, too, are fearsome and destructive, but the forces that might destroy any given town or village (*ikka kuni wa ikka mura no nangi*)[9] are the same forces that produced the land, mountains, and islands that form the basis of human life.[10] "When viewed from this perspective, truly thinking and feeling people (*kokoro aru hito*) cannot bear any grudge against Heaven for these [localized tragedies]."[11] In Obata's world, there really is nothing to fear. For in this new understanding of the human-nature relationship, rational calculation proves powerful enough to erase even actual, lived disasters. *idea of rewriting the past - personal + political*

But by 1900, just thirty years after Obata had banished them from modern experience, disasters once again seemed to be everywhere. Seemingly understood, accounted for, and controlled in the 1870s and 1880s, nature's power reasserted itself in the 1890s, most spectacularly in the massive amounts of copper, arsenic, mercury, and a host of other pollutants unleashed into the Watarase and Tone watersheds by the Ashio Copper Mine. With Ashio, Japan's first experience with industrial-scale pollution, the certainty, optimism, and ambition characteristic of the natural and social sciences during the first two decades of Meiji began to falter and fail. Unfortunately for Obata, by 1900 it seemed the earth could indeed go mad.

In one of the first responses to the emerging environmental crisis in 1890, Kawashima Isaburō, writing in what would be the first and last issue of the journal *Ashio Mine Pollution*,[12] warned the residents of the Watarase and Tone watersheds that the mine had fundamentally changed their world and that they could no longer rely on the natural laws that had sustained the life of the valley for generations.[13] Across the polluted regions, Obata's separation of nature and politics was coming undone as rural liberals feared that the growing environmental crisis was eroding the political gains of the popular rights and liberty movement of the 1870s and 1880s. By 1902, writing at the height of the Ashio Incident, the former Progressive Party (Kaishintō) member Tanaka Shōzō anticipated the current concept of "ecocide" and signaled a breakthrough in environmental thought when he openly expressed the fear that Japan was creating a "second nature" of "foul rocks and polluted soil that wholly penetrates the [river] water. . . . Once this process is complete," he warned, "there will be no saving anyone."[14] Later, fresh from battles in the Ashio Incident and the slaughter of World War I in Belgium, the anarchist Ishikawa Sanshirō used the reciprocal relation of humans with their environment to formulate a critique of industrial society and Darwinian natural selection, even developing a dispersed social ecology based on the rhizome. Another Tanaka disciple, Kurosawa Torizō, fearful of the corruption of the environment wrought by money and politics, fled to Hokkaido in search of a social model that explicitly did not "rely on [polluted] distant mountains and rivers."[15] Convinced that only family-operated dairy farms could save Japan from simultaneous ecological and social degradation, he founded Japan's original "green company," a producers' cooperative that became Snow Brand Dairy (Yukijirushi)—until a 2003 merger Japan's largest dairy company. By the time postwar thinkers took up Minamata disease (methylmercury poisoning), it seemed that no discussion of human freedom was even possible without considering the environment. As all of them asked in their different ways, "Just how free can one be in a toxic landscape?" Clearly something greater than a literary nostalgia for a lost agrarian past or an Orientalist environmental ethic was at work in the decades following Japan's first experience with industrial pollution.

So what had changed? Put simply, in the 1890s nature became political again. After Ashio, Japanese thinkers and activists came face to face with the reality of modern nature: that for the first time in history, human practice had the capacity to transform nature itself into something antithetical to human health and freedom. Industrial-scale pollution showed how easily and often nature permeated liberalism's supposedly autonomous, self-contained, individual bodies, and the environmental degradation of the Watarase and Tone watersheds showed how vulnerable nature was to modern human practice. By forcefully reasserting the mutual penetration of humans and nature, industrial pollution not only eroded Meiji ideologies of a nature indifferent to human practice, it *biologically and politically* contaminated the autonomous liberal subject on which Meiji political philosophy was built. The emergence of industrial pollution revealed that nature and society, which Meiji neo-Kantian ideology had considered to be two separate systems, were in fact a poorly understood, indeed ignored, totality. Put another way, Ashio's pollutants mapped Japanese society in ways political philosophy had not yet grasped. As the growing links between the body, society, and nature were revealed in the 1890s, thinkers and activists from Popular Rights and Liberty leaders such as Tanaka Shōzō to socialists like Kōtoku Shūsui, and radical journalists like Matsumoto Eiko, realized that a significant part of human health and freedom existed outside the individual subject. As the subject was penetrated by an increasingly toxic material nature leading to sickness, poverty, pain, and sometimes death, it became clear to many that even if nature had lost its autonomy, it clearly had not lost its agency. The discovery in the 1890s of an inescapable ecological part of the abstract liberal subject set off a frantic search for a reintegration of the environment into Japanese social and political theory. In the following decades, Confucian benevolence and moral economy, socialism, anarchism, and even fascism were marshaled in the search for new theories of a modern political subject and for a social organization adequate to the environmental crisis. This book is about that search for what might be called an "environmental unconscious" at the base of modern political and social thought; more specifically, it is about Japan's environmental turn, a broad historical moment when Japanese thinkers and activists experienced nature as alienated from themselves and were forced to rebuild the connections.

## The Politics of Permeable Bodies

To say that environmental politics emerged in Japan only after 1900 is not to say that pollution itself was new—it was not. Nor was pre-Meiji exploitation so small that there was no ecological damage—there was. The Ashio mine itself had been exploited since at least the late sixteenth century. In the Ashikaga and Tokugawa Eras, farmers downstream from Ashio, Kamioka, and other early modern mines frequently drafted petitions complaining of "bad water" (*akusui*) from the mines that damaged their crops.[16] There were also many other peasant protests against other environmental problems, such as those caused by the opening up of new areas to cultivation and numerous large Tokugawa River projects, including those on the Tone River supervised by the Confucian scholar Kumazawa Banzan in the eighteenth century. There were even petitions and protests against garbage and food poisoning.[17] Further, Conrad Totman, Brett Walker, and David Howell have shown the significant changes that took place in the early modern period in forestry, fishing, and the ecology of Tokugawa trade with Ainu.[18]

To say that an environmental politics emerged around 1900 is also not to say that Japanese discovered that nature is finite, that its fertility may be exhausted. This had already been grasped by Tokugawa forestry.[19] More broadly, it is also obviously true that humans have always and everywhere been altering their environment. To say that an environmental politics emerged is to say that it was not until the development of industrial capitalism's terrifying nature-altering capacity that basic material practice became an urgent political, even existential issue. This confluence of the ecological and the political in pollution, means much more than that the concept of the environment was discovered in its moment of crisis. It means the environment was discovered *as crisis*.

What drove this urgency was only partly the scale of the problem. In other words, the environmental problem in 1890s Japan was much more than a case of "bad water" becoming "really bad water." Such a quantitative understanding of the problem might suggest a purely technological fix. Instead, the 1890s activists' emergent understanding of the human body as permeable to an increasingly polluted environment undermined the self-contained, autonomous, individual subject of Meiji liberalism. Contrary to Kurosawa's hopes, it turns out that human health and freedom do rely on distant mountains and rivers. And this realization required a much deeper and wider examination of the whole of nature-body-society interactions and mutual penetrations. Under the early Meiji rationalist (neo-Kantian) model, nature was the study of *fact* left to the materialist methods of natural science, while history was the creation of *value*, especially as manifested in morality, politics, and culture. But nature could not fail to be deeply transformed in complex interplay of new power relations arising from capitalist production and the making of the Meiji state, both of which created the material and ideological networks that allowed industrial pollution to contaminate social, cultural, and political realms in unprecedented ways. The poverty, the disease, and the loss of suffrage due to tax relief for poisoned fields that seemed to follow in pollution's wake reestablished nature as an active force in human history.[20] With the environmental crisis, nature and history needed, once again, to become a totality. Built as it is on the necessity of the complete autonomy of the individual body, the liberal Meiji subject—and, because we inhabit the same political imaginary, our own subjectivity as well—is deeply vulnerable to anything that insists on an involuntary interaction. The materiality of the air, food, and water that may have been adulterated or even poisoned by negligence, accident, or politics located far away and in some other time only to be later taken in to the human body is perhaps the most basic blind spot of liberal political philosophy.[21] This vulnerability of the liberal subject was noticed by Marx in the *1844 Manuscripts*: "[External] Nature is man's inorganic body, that is to say in so far as it is not the human body. Man lives from nature, i.e. nature is his body, and he must maintain a continuing dialogue with it if he is not to die. To say that man's physical and mental life is linked to nature simply means that nature is linked to itself, for man is part of nature. Estranged labour not only . . . estranges nature from man. [It also] estranges man from himself, from his own active function, from his vital activity."[22]

As we shall see in chapter 1, the attempt by Meiji liberalism to completely transcend nature led to the massive project of building physical and metaphorical boundaries between the human body and the environment. Brett Walker's recent work on industrial disease in Japan, *Toxic Archipelago* (2010), tracks the permeability of the human body to its environment and subsumes all of the incredibly complex interactions between Japanese bodies and nature under the most notable and most personal concept of industrial production: pain.[23] As such the Meiji project of separation was immediately threatened by the discovery of the porousness of the human body to outside agents as the modern Japanese subjects ate, drank, and inhaled their new world. Building on Walker's work, I will show how the pain suffered by the permeable bodies of nineteenth- and early twentieth-century pollution victims became the signal that the neo-Kantian separation of nature (fact) from society (value) that underwrote the liberal model of bodies and the environment, however elegant, was missing something important.

The particular political addition to the environmental problem I want to explore in this book came with a realization by Japanese antipollution activists that the nature of modern Japan was both alienated *and alienating*. By this I mean that the original severing of the majority of the population from their means of subsistence—their connection to the land—was now combined with the new problem that nature had been so altered by industrial capitalism that a simple reconnection with a now polluted nature was problematic. In other words, Meiji Japanese had discovered that permeable human bodies are always already embedded in what Linda Nash called "inescapable ecologies." Being part of an inescapable ecology also meant that humans were not only the *subject* of evolution but also its *objects*. As the radical ecologist Gregory Bateson put it,

> Let us now consider what happens when you make the epistemological error of choosing the wrong unit [of the survival of the fittest]: you end up with the species versus the other species around it or versus the environment in which it operates. Man against nature.... When you narrow down your epistemology and act on the premise "What interests me, or my organization, or my species," you chop off consideration of other loops of the loop structure. You decide that you want to get rid of the by-products of human life and that Lake Erie will be a good place to put them. You forget that the eco-mental system called Lake Erie is part of your wider eco-mental system—and that if Lake Erie is driven insane, its insanity is incorporated in the larger system of your thought and experience.[24]

Bateson's own preference for psychological feedback loops likely needs to be better grounded in the material relations and processes discovered by the sciences. But the impulse is correct and important, and I will follow something of this method.

While not specifically concerned with environmental politics, Julia Thomas's *Reconfiguring Modernity* (2000), on the ideologies of nature in modern Japanese political philosophy, identified the 1890s and early 1900s as a key period for developing a political theory of the environment. After her examination of natural rights theory and social Darwinism in the 1870s and 1880s, Thomas reports a sudden lack of invocations of nature in Meiji political documents beginning in the 1890s.[25] I have already suggested that this is no coincidence, for it was precisely in the 1890s that nature, altered by human practice, began behaving in strange and unprecedented ways. Nature's loss of normative status in the 1890s is therefore the key point of contact between Walker's bodies in pain and Thomas's history of modern Japanese political philosophy. In what follows I will combine environmental history with political philosophies of the subject in order to explore the extremely rich and still urgent search for a form of political subjectivity and social organization adequate to the environmental crisis of capitalist modernity.

What Tanaka Shōzō and his followers realized was that because of humans' new relation to nature, not all contact with material nature could be seen as beneficial. Any contact must be carefully chosen and organized. What Nash, Thomas, and Walker's work shows definitively is that nature is never transcended, only reconceptualized. So what sort of conception of nature can be the basis of a new politics adequate to the environmental crisis? This is the question the thinkers examined in this book have asked. And their question remains our question. While the thinkers examined here had diverse understandings of the cause and solution to the problem of an alienated and alienating nature, they are united not only by a connection to the crisis of the 1890s, but also by a belief that when attempting to reintegrate nature into a theory of human health and freedom, it was the specific *practices of nature* that mattered. For these thinkers, an external nature outside politics simply didn't exist anymore.

### Throughline and Structure

One trend in environmental history, a way to talk about the nature-society metabolism historically, is to periodize based on different modalities of that relationship. In *Humanity and Nature: Ecology, Science and Society* (1992), Yrjö Haila and Richard Levins use the concept of "eco-historical periods" to explain the complex, changing specificity of the human coevolutionary relation to nature.[26] Beginning in the 1980s with *The Green Archipelago*, Conrad Totman has increasingly made the human-nature relationship the basis of his periodization of Japanese history. Echoing Haila and Levins, his *A History of Japan* (2000) and *Pre-Industrial Korea and Japan in Environmental Perspective* (2004) takes the nature-society metabolism as a method of periodization.[27] So if we were to follow these examples and look at Japan's modern transformation after the fall of samurai rule in 1868 from the perspective of humans' relationship to nature in the 1870s and 1880s, we would see that the dominant way thinkers and policy experts described that relationship was in the language of *separations*, of barriers not only between the body and miasmas, sewage, and (later) germs, but also between the modern subject and the superstitious past, between Enlightened, rational Meiji and the Tokugawa dark ages. But with the outbreak of industrial-scale pollution in the 1890s, the language of separation is replaced with the language of *leaks*. After 1900 it becomes the language of *connections*, or, better, mutual penetrations. Once activists started looking, they found mutual penetrations everywhere: in the river, in the soil, in the indigo dyes, in breast milk, and in politics. After Ashio, the question is no longer the stable "What *is* nature's relation to humans?" In the wake of humanity's new capacity for complete alteration of the environment, the question becomes the practical "How do we *build* healthful human-nature relations?" I use this periodization as a way to explore the history of the metabolic rift, to follow how it has worked in thought and practice in modern Japanese history, and, ultimately, as a way to think through its implications for our own struggles on an increasingly toxic planet.

Pollution's very materiality makes it seem straightforward, even ahistorical. But it, too, has a history, and this history depends on more than (natural) scientific and technological narratives. While retaining its materiality and therefore being somewhat more resistant to politics than traditional political philosophy or literary naturalism, pollution is nonetheless deeply embedded in the social, moral, and political networks through which it spreads.[28] The particular material history of the Watarase watershed was the foundation of the Ashio pollution. And it was on this material environmental base that the pollution was deployed. But it is also true that the ideologies of private property and laissez-faire individual rights, not to mention the Meiji policies "encouragement of industry" and "rich nation, strong army," played an equal, and in some cases defining, role in how and where pollutants moved through space and time.

Actor-network theory (ANT) and science, technology, and society studies (STS) have long been arguing for a move from the analysis of discrete objects to the analysis of a relations obtaining between them. I will make much use of this work in arguing for the agency of the nonhuman world and its implications for our own bodies, communities, and politics. But while I think ANT-inclined readers will find much familiar in what follows, I intend to remain within an explicitly Marxian analysis. It seems to me that, particularly with the main tradition of ANT seen in Bruno Latour's work, Marx's concept of subsumption does more to address the historicity of the relations between the organic and inorganic, nature and society; and it is the specific historicity of the environmental crisis that I am after. For without a strong historical analysis and historical sense, the environmental crisis is too often universalized, leading either to the fatalism that it has always been thus and therefore nothing can be done or, just as unhelpfully, to the conclusion that what is needed is a return to a premodern or even prehistoric hunter-gatherer society seen in much recent radical ecology.[29]

Still I believe there are connections with ANT and STS, especially in work such as Michelle Murphy's Marx-inspired readings of technology.[30] As I will develop throughout the book and argue explicitly in the conclusion, I believe that Marx's concepts of subsumption (both formal and real)[31] of labor and nature under capital accumulation provides one of the best theoretical apparatuses for unpacking the current problem—that industrial capitalist production represents a specific social technology with immense implications for understanding the environmental crisis. Throughout the text, and more theoretically in the conclusion, capital's, or capitalism's, attempt to render both human labor and the environment as a wholly abstract base of infinite accumulation not only makes it hugely interventionist into bodies and nature, but also dooms it to fail precisely because of the inescapability of both the materiality of the laboring body and the finite environment that are the necessary base of its expansion. Like Obata's depoliticized nature, a nature subsumed under capitalist production, too, is one that may have lost its autonomy but, given the "inescapable ecologies" of life itself, can never lose its agency. Thus to say that an environmental politics emerged in Japan only after 1900 is to say that the environment cannot become the basis of a new politics until it has first been "discovered"—which is to say that it must be experienced as a discrete object, or, following Lukács's thoughts on labor in capitalist society, it must first be alienated and reified.[32] The commodification of human labor-power achieves this for Lukács. In Japan I argue something similar happened to the environment in the 1890s with the irruption of modern pollution at the Ashio Copper Mine. What was new in the 1890s was not only the sudden realization that humans were alienated from nature—something that was grasped by political economists in the destruction of traditional usufruct (*iriaiken*) and the establishment of absolute property rights and the land tax reform in 1873.[33] New was the realization that with the emergence of a "second [toxic] nature," nature is not only alienated, but also alienating—thereby highlighting its role in human health and freedom. In many ways this book is an exploration of environmental theory's insistence that, in the words of David Harvey, all social choices are at the same time environmental choices, and vice versa.³⁴ Starting from the initial moment of realization in the Ashio crisis, this book is about detecting the often veiled environmental basis of modern Japan's seemingly abstract social, cultural, and political ideologies.

A further benefit of the Marxian approach to the emergence of environmental politics is that it suggests ways of grounding the famous culturalist (and Orientalist) discourse of Japanese culture's "special relationship" to nature. By focusing on the subsumption of nature and labor in the specific relations of capitalist production, the Marxian approach possesses tremendous theoretical and analytical resources for exploring the implication of the simultaneous deployment of multiple temporalities. It thus has the potential to undo the absolute opposition of premodern nature and modern industry that is the culturalist theory's very condition of possibility. After Ashio, nature was never more ideological than when it was being invoked as outside history, capable of serving as a norm for society. At the same time, my approach points the way to integrating Japan's environmental turn into a global history of modernity. Wherever capitalism has been established across the globe, the separation from nature in the creation of the liberal subject veiled that inherently ecological side of human existence. But in Japan, because there was a readily available tradition of nature as an ethical norm—neo-Confucianism, nativist studies (*kokugaku*)—the post-Ashio discovery of the interconnections between the human and the environment meant that any reconnection, though taking place across the industrialized world, *could appear to be* an especially *cultural* move. This is to say, in giving an account *of* the culturalist turn toward nature as outside capitalism, a Marxian attention to simultaneous temporalities can also account *for* this move.

In other words, cultural nationalists (and contemporary radical ecologists) grasped modern nature's inability to adjudicate human social and political disputes—both capitalism's contradictions and the negotiations and compromises of political liberalism—only to re-reify it by once again separating it from those struggles in a return to an imagined stability of premodern nature. Unlike the attempt of the Meiji theory of civilization and enlightenment to separate human culture from a dangerous nature, later theories of the human-nature metabolism, from Taishō vitalism (*seimeishugi*) to agrarian fundamentalism (*nōhonshugi*), followed the reverse course, identifying nature as a separate realm where the parasitic effects of cities, money, and class war did not obtain.

Chapters 1 and 2 explore the relationship of the Meiji liberal subject to the material environment, from the early attempt by Meiji liberals to separate the two to the growing difficulty in maintaining that separation in both thought and practice during periods of industrial pollution. In chapter 1 I explore the establishment of the autonomous individual as the unit of politics based largely on a neo-Kantian division of fact and value, or science and politics. But with the emergence of toxic flows that repeatedly penetrated this body, the separation of nature and politics that had been essential for the "civilization and enlightenment" attack on superstition became a weak point of Meiji liberalism, because liberalism had also removed the modern political subject from the space it occupied. As the chapter moves from the 1870–80 invention of the autonomous individual subject to the growing leaks between this subject and the material exterior, the autonomy of the individual became harder and harder to maintain. The first significant attempt to deal with the new toxic threat came from *within* Meiji liberalism. As Ashio toxins revealed hidden connections between people, places, and things, liberals would try to augment the autonomous subject with voluntary associations between individuals in an effort to grasp the social-level problem of industrial pollution, but without discarding the hard-won popular rights. The chapter ends with perhaps the most important investigation of the pollution problem—works by the journalist Matsumoto Eiko. Her 1901–2 exposé on the ravages of pollution in Gumma, Tochigi, and Ibaraki was a key moment in the abandonment of the liberal model of the subject on the cusp of Japan's environmental turn.

Chapter 2 includes a major reconsideration of Japan's famous "first conservationist," Tanaka Shōzō (1841–1913), especially the invocation of the seventeenth-century peasant martyr Sakura Sōgo in Tanaka's appeal to the emperor in 1901. Chapter 2 sees Tanaka not as Japan's lost agrarian consciousness, but as a dedicated Meiji liberal whose environmental thought only developed *after* the exhaustion of Meiji political philosophy in the Ashio Incident. This reconsideration of Tanaka is necessary because the iconic narrative of Tanaka as a residual peasant martyr is not only inaccurate (he was deeply involved in liberal and utilitarian politics for decades), but the peasant narrative also reconstitutes the ideological continuance of premodern agrarian consciousness in modern Japan at the level of biography. I argue that what is actually going on beneath the seeming continuity of Tanaka's use of peasant imagery and tactics is a major rupture between preindustrial and industrial society. To do so, I focus on Meiji liberals' extremely interesting and extensive use of Sakura Sōgo as a model of a *modern* Japanese subject. Nonetheless, as the initial optimism that the ideology and tactics of liberalism could be applied to the pollution problem waned, and as the early trouble in the Watarase River turned into "the social problem," the uses and connotations of Sakura also morphed into a contradictory image of free individual subjects who nonetheless had need of Confucian benevolence from their government. In an extended examination of Tanaka and Kōtoku's dramatic appeal to the Meiji emperor (*jikiso*) in 1901, I argue that this contradiction was pushed to its limits and finally broke—a move that I argue signaled Tanaka and Japan's environmental turn.

Chapter 3 takes up Tanaka's post-jikiso lament: "I have finally awakened to the folly of appealing to this government. There is nothing left but to appeal to Heaven (*ten*, nature) itself." From 1902 on, Tanaka threw himself into an investigation of the multiple interactions between humans and nature through what he called "river pilgrimages." It was on these pilgrimages that he developed his theory of the "real powers of the land and water" (*chi no ikioi, mizu no ikioi*), which cannot be transcended, only managed. The real powers of the land and water acknowledge the existence of a material nature external to humanity that is nonetheless still implicated in human practice by the concept of "flows" or material exchanges, a metabolism of humans and nature, building from these exchanges to a monistic ecological philosophy of (beneficial) "flow" (*nagare*) and (harmful) "poison" (*doku*). From here, I argue, Tanaka made a key breakthrough in environmental thought when he argued that humans could neither transcend nature nor completely control it. Worse, attempts to do so would result in the formation of a "second, toxic nature" of doku, a system of matter in motion that, like a cancer co-opts the body's own capacity for growth but now distorts it, leading to an accumulation of death instead of life. Tanaka's move to Yanaka in 1904 was an attempt to thwart the Meiji state's plans to reengineer the Kanto plain according to its (in Tanaka's view) false belief that the environmental problem was solvable through engineering. Instead Tanaka developed a socioecology he called *Yanakagaku*, which he believed pointed the way to a "true civilization" of material flows that fostered human health and freedom.

Modernization theorists and many others have located Tanaka's life and work within a period of transition from traditional to modern—an exciting time, to be sure, but one that has largely passed and has resolved into our still difficult, but largely stable, relationship between civil society, politics, and nature. Of course, the idea that the environmental crisis was caused by incomplete modernity is pure fantasy; I write this introduction on the one hundredth anniversary of Tanaka's death and during the continuing crisis in Fukushima. As I will show throughout this book, both Meiji Japan's environmental crisis and our own are located precisely in the fully modern categories of the subsumption of nature in industrial capitalist production. Thus, thinking in terms of subsumption not only allows a criticism of both Meiji rationalism and Japan's special relationship to nature: it also, in a final advantage of a Marxian analysis of the environmental crisis, will allow us to acknowledge and account for the environmental practices and damage of actually existing socialist regimes from Stalin to Mao.[35]

Nearly all works in English and Japanese depict Tanaka as a lonely crusader whose fate it was to be ignored. In chapters 4 and 5 I argue that this premise is simply untenable. Tanaka may have been one of the most spectacular and celebrated antipollution thinkers, but he did not invent the environmental crisis, and as everyone would agree, the crisis did not end with him. Of course, many others took up the complicated and urgent question of the nature-individual-society relationship after Tanaka's death in 1913. In the last two chapters I focus on two thinkers, the anarchist Ishikawa Sanshirō and the founder of Snow Brand Dairy, Kurosawa Torizō, both of whom had deep, direct contact with Ashio and Tanaka. Nonetheless, in exploring the ways these two took up the challenge after Tanaka, we glimpse many other attempts, from Second International socialists to Taishō life philosophers (*seimeishugisha*) such as Mushakōji Saneatsu or the members of the Shirakaba group to fascists like Tachibana Kōzaburō and Gondo Seikyō, who were also working out their own theories of the problem of bodies, subjectivities, and social organization under industrial capitalism. In this way, I try hard to avoid the fate of popular history (*minshūshi*) and some women's history in becoming merely one more voice heard from, adding to a familiar national narrative. Instead I try to show environmental history's potential for a larger political and cultural critique. Ishikawa's attempt to inject ecological concerns into socialism led him to develop an extremely interesting social ecology of liberation of all living things (one that is very close to Murray Bookchin's Social Ecology). It also allowed him the intellectual space to launch an illuminating critique of the agrarian fundamentalism of the divine soil of Japan (*nōhonshugi*) during the 1930s and 1940s.

Likewise, Kurosawa Torizō's attempt to find a mode of production and political economy that would follow and not fight nature's cycles led him to develop what I call the original green company. Though beset by theoretical and political problems that brought it close to the wartime state and participation in the Greater East Asia Co-Prosperity Sphere, Kurosawa's grasp of the problem as located in production, what Marx called "the real relation of man to nature," meant his urgent problematic survived the war. Even here, it is the soundness of Kurosawa's initial diagnosis of the problem of relying on distant mountains and rivers that allows us to see the deep continuities between Snow Brand's collaboration in the 1940s and the recent tainted milk and beef scandals of 2002–3, while still giving credit to its penetrating insight.

By the end of chapter 5, I argue that the real problem that began with Ashio is revealed to have been the real subsumption of nature under capital— or that, in the need to accumulate units of surplus value, capital is driven to remake a nature that is more conducive to future accumulation, without regard to any other possible valuations or temporalities, whether biological, ecological, political, or even ethical. In the conclusion I explore the implications of this argument for the relationship between ecology and capitalism and look for possible beginnings of a future theory of the subject and an environmental politics adequate to our own global environmental crisis.

# ONE

# A DECADE OF LEAKS

Thought lags behind nature.
—GILLES DELEUZE AND FÉLIX GUATTARI,
*A Thousand Plateaus*

The third decade of Meiji, the 1890s, is supposed to have been a time of consolidation and control.[1] It was the decade of the constitution and the Diet, the end of the violence of the popular rights and liberty movement (*jiyūminken undō*, 1874–84). It was the departure from Asia, military victory over Qing China, the replacement of foreign experts with highly trained Japanese, the extension of sovereignty over Okinawa and Hokkaido, and the beginning of the end of the unequal treaties. At worst, the 1890s are seen as having been a transitional period, the last gasp of the Tokugawa Era before the "traditional" finally gave way to the "modern." In short, the 1890s are supposed to have been the end of the irrationality of feudalism and the beginning of the enlightened institutions of modern life.[2] In the first decades of Meiji, nearly every aspect of life was judged against modern, rational, scientific standards and, when necessary, reformed. Central to this project was the production of a new Japanese subject unbound by the "backward, feudal" practices of the past, an idealized, autonomous individual who identified with the new nation. Doubly liberated from the feudal past by national revolution and from enslavement to nature by capitalist industrialization, the new Japanese subjects joined together and worked to build a nation of "civilization and enlightenment," a "rich nation [with a] strong army."[3] By 1895, the new nation had defeated the long-venerated Chinese, established a colonial presence in Korea and Taiwan, obliterated distance with the beginnings of a national rail and telegraph network, and banished night with the new gas lamps of Tokyo. To all the world, Japan and the Japanese seemed on the cusp of the long-promised rational modernity. Things seemed so secure that even a previously terrifying nature was readmitted into modern life, this time as (national) landscape, to be gazed upon and internalized as Japaneseness itself.[4] But with the emergence of industrial-scale pollution at the Ashio copper mine northwest of Tokyo, the material nature and material bodies that Meiji ideology had worked so hard to transcend returned and started causing new problems. It soon became clear that nature had been transcended only in thought.

If we consider what was happening in *material* nature, in the environment, in the 1890s, the entire narrative of stability and control breaks down. There nothing was certain. Nothing could be taken for granted. If we include the environment in our narratives of modern Japan, the dislocations and instability of the third decade of Meiji put the struggles of the 1880s and even the chaos of the *bakumatsu-ishin* period to shame. Despite the way Obata Tokujirō and his colleagues struggled to rationalize every aspect of life, and despite most Meiji historiography, the 1890s stood witness to a return of the strange. It is surely no coincidence, then, that in the 1890s historians have found few political appeals to a normative nature, though such appeals had been common during both the recent periods of natural rights theory and the social Darwinism of the 1880s.[5] How could there have been many appeals to a normative nature, when nature was behaving in ways never seen before?

After the fifty-year, toxic floods of August 1890, and again after even larger flooding in 1896, antipollution activists got back to basics to try and find out what was going on. Across the Watarase and Tone watersheds they set up investigative committees, volunteer associations, new journals, and fact-finding groups. Their dogged pursuit of the Ashio pollutants eventually took them into nearly every corner of Meiji society, finding industrial effluent and its effects everywhere: from fish, to levee failures, to soil chemistry, to breast milk, to disease and poverty, and even to representative politics. In contrast to the attempted separation of humans and nature begun by Obata and friends in the 1870s and 1880s, the 1890s was a decade of leaks. The decade of leaks culminated in the muckraking journalist Matsumoto Eiko's ethnographic *Sufferings of a Mine-Poisoned Land* (*Kōdokuchi no sanjō*, 1901–2), in which she documented the total breakdown of the legal, conceptual, and even physical walls built to separate the Meiji subject from a now-toxic environment. In Matsumoto's text the leaks became a flood and then an undifferentiated sea of toxins and misery. We shall see in the next two chapters that as the countless mutual penetrations of humans and nature grew harder to ignore, the autonomous subject independent of the environment of Meiji liberalism became harder to maintain. By 1900, the stage was set for a move away from the autonomous individual as the cellular form of society toward new forms of social organization that began with the environment. The growing doubts on—and later rejection of—the separation of humans and nature during the decade was at once a social, scientific, conceptual, and political move that signaled Japan's environmental turn, and the beginning of an environmental politics.

### The Pure Bodies of Meiji Rationalism

In order to appreciate the urgency and importance of the environmental crisis of 1890s Japan, we must understand the extent to which the modern, liberal subject depended not only on the stability of Heaven in Fukuzawa's *Gakumon no susume*, but also on the stability of Earth in Obata's *Tenpen chii*. The environmental crisis of the 1890s was able to politically contaminate the Meiji subject precisely because that subject was an idealized and reified individual, imagined as an autonomous actor divorced from outside corruption, whether from the state, other actors, or the natural world. In most historiography, from Fukuzawa's "trends of the times" (*jisei*) to Katō Hiroyuki's evolutionary schema, the dominant view of the first two decades of Meiji has privileged time: linear development and modernization. In this rush to escape the Tokugawa dark ages and join the Western powers in modernity, Meiji thinkers sought a temporal rupture with the traditions of the past. But they sought a spatial rupture as well. Recent work on the ideologies of time and space in the Meiji period have explored the abandonment of the ethico-epistemological status of nature in the Tokugawa period in favor of "the acculturation of nature"[6] in social Darwinism and the "emptying" of the "spaces of experience"[7] that characterized the rise of the scientific approach to space in Meiji Japan. Further, recent Japanese environmental historiography by Julia Thomas and Brett Walker has shown that the age-old question of overcoming nature—from the Frankfurt School to Maruyama Masao to the Lecture School (*Kōza-ha*) of Japanese Marxism—is the wrong question. Thomas's work on the multiple ideologies of nature in Japanese political philosophy, and Walker's examination of the inversion of attitudes toward the Japanese wolf in the Meiji period, show that nature is never transcended, merely reconceptualized.[8]

If we adopt Henri Lefebvre's claim that each form of society constructs its own kind of space, we need to find out what the space of Meiji rationalism was and what sort of subject inhabited it. In the 1870s and 1880s, across the Meiji intellectual and ideological spectrum—including positivism, neo-Kantianism, social Darwinism, the abolition of usufruct (*iriaiken*) and the alienation of land,[9] and the ambitious anticholera campaigns in the new discipline of public health—we can clearly see how in "health, wealth, and thought"[10] Meiji rationalism constructed an idealized Japanese subject alongside an alienated nature. In exploring the role of the environment in Meiji rationalism, I want to supplement the period's numerous appeals to a normative (metaphysical) nature (social Darwinism, natural rights theory, natural law) with what historian of medicine Warwick Anderson has called "the transcendence of the natural body."[11] By transcending the natural body, liberal political philosophy sought to create an ideal body with no (or only voluntary) relations with the outside world. This transcendence was accomplished through the epistemological, discursive, and (as much as possible) physical separation of the new political subject from the material environment. The reduction of an active nature to inert space cleared the ground, in some cases literally, for the production of the abstract, sterilized space of modern Japan that would serve as mere resources for accumulation, the raw materials for the production of a "rich nation [with a] strong army."

Though it is tempting to see Meiji Japan as some radical ecology does, as a tragic break from a premodern organic community to an anthropocentric and inherently destructive Western modernity, this view is very difficult to maintain. Further, as we shall see in later chapters, adopting this view sets up a politically dangerous dichotomy that sets a "naturalized" Japan against a "mechanistic" West. Although much good work has been done on the emergence of modern medicine in Japan and Asia, I will not focus on the history of medicine and the major breaks between the Tokugawa, miasma, and germ theories of disease. Although these clearly are important disciplinary ruptures within medicine, focusing on the differences veils a much longer, deeper process of alienation and reification of nature and humans that begins well before the Meiji Era. Despite their differences, both miasma and germ theories of disease represented a break from medicine as a neo-Confucian *ethical* practice in the Tokugawa period.[12] Rather than studying this rupture as only a change in medical paradigms, I will look at the politics and the implications for political subjectivity that came of this rupture. The result, I argue, is that just as capitalist private property is the apotheosis of earlier partial alienation from the land, Meiji rationalism should be seen as the industrial capitalist apotheosis of a long trend that had been secularizing and reifying the natural world for over a century.[13] Conrad Totman has shown the fundamental break with the metaphysical Tokugawa discourse on nature as infinite (*shizenron*) in his study of Tokugawa forestry. In Totman's work the *infinite* nature of *shizenron* is replaced with a *finite* nature of forestry management, making the Tokugawa discourse on the economics of forests a function of their scarcity.[14] Federico Marcon's excellent recent study has further shown the clear reification of the natural world in the field of *honzōgaku* (*materia medica*), beginning with the national surveys done under Yoshimune from 1735 to 1736. Already here we can see the process of commodifying individual species as they are ripped from their network of social and ecological relations to be idealized as discrete "species" existing in glorious isolation on the pages of lavishly illustrated natural history encyclopedias, ready for buying and selling. Some of this tradition came to influence Meiji policy directly from the Satsuma agronomist and theorist of national economic power, Satō Nobuhirō.[15]

In religion numerous environmental ethics celebrate the Shinto—and therefore indigenous Japanese—intimacy with nature. But in fact, more often than not, Shinto conceived of nature as a horrifying realm of rot, decay, and disease—*kegare* and *yomi*—a place to be avoided at all costs. Indeed, if not ritually constrained, kegare can consume a kingdom, and great care was taken to protect the court and the capital from contamination.[16] Well before the Meiji period, Shinto and folk medicine understood epidemic disease as the intrusion of "that world" (*ano yo*) into "this world" (*kono yo*). Contemporary rituals aimed at controlling and preventing epidemic disease (*ekibyō matsuri*) do not enact a philosophy of balance or harmony between worlds. Ekibyō matsuri were organized to prevent the forces of "that world" from entering the body and home. This included placing charms or *shimenawa* at the boundaries between inner and outer, especially doors and gates, to prevent infiltration across the thresholds. In short, far from an intimate connection to nature, ekibyō matsuri show clearly that "that world" and "this world" were two realms *meant to be separated*. Priests, geomancers,

FIGURE 1.1. An 1880 image from an anticholera manual published by the *Tokyo shintō jimubunkyoku*. The manual uses the pre-Meiji imagery of *ekibyō matsuri*, in which disease in the shape of demons is cast out of "this world" (*kono yo*), back into "that world" (*ano yo*). Source: Kakimoto Akihito, *Kenko to yamai no episuteemee* (Kyoto: Mineruba shobō, 1991).

and people themselves made huge efforts to police these frontiers. Further weakening the hard break between a premodern Japanese nature and a modern Western one, ekibyō matsuri and kegare have much more in common with the similarly reductive miasma and germ theories of disease than with modern environmental thought or ethics.[17] The "inescapable ecology" of the body-in-environment examined in later chapters was simply not part of this pre-Meiji discourse.

Nor should the long tradition of discourses on health, the countless *Yōjōkun*, be considered an early version of environmental politics. Contrary to an Orientalist environmental ethics that assumes an Asian intimacy with nature, the overwhelming majority of the *Yōjōkun* do not show a simple Taoist trust in nature's healing capabilities. Like the policing of boundaries by the *shimenawa* charms, most of these texts preach strengthening the individual body against external harm. Hashimoto Hakujū's *Dandokuron* (1810) explicitly called the body a battleground where health and disease fight, and if the body has been made strong through proper habits, the external, invading disease will be defeated. Another text warned that sickness-causing demons entered the body through the gap between finger and fingernail; it advised constant care of this area.[18] The most famous *Yōjōkun*, too—Kaibara Ekiken's—was a guide to strengthening the individual body against the various poisons, dangers, and ill winds that lurked outside. Tellingly, in texts that focused on the relation between the body and nature, as in the neo-Confucian *shizenron* tradition, nature was an imagined and idealized realm, an infinitely fecund source of nourishing life, never the source of pollution and harm.[19] Of course the nature of these shizenron texts was not the material environment of the *Yōjōkun* and kegare, but the wholly abstract, *immaterial* nature of metaphysics. As we have seen, it was this metaphysical nature that was adopted by Meiji natural rights theorists.[20]

To sum up, Meiji "civilization and enlightenment" was less a clean break with an imagined premodern harmony between Japanese society and nature than the apotheosis of all these previous, partial reifications of humans and nature. In Henri Lefebvre's terms, we could say Meiji rationalism was the moment of inflection when the production of *things in space* gave way to the production of *space itself*—both internal and external. This means, of course, that the separation of the body from the environment in the creation of the modern subject was by no means limited to medicine or ritual practice. In fact, the separation of the human from the natural is the condition of possibility of the liberal subject, essential for it to carve out an autonomous, individual conscience protected from outside interference, first from nature and then from the state. This atomistic individual is what others have called the "bourgeois body," an enclosure that polices itself, maintaining a constant internal purity.[21] Just as in the West, in Meiji Japan this separation was expressed as a new regime of knowledge centered on the individual psychological subject. Like the Tokugawa medical texts, the Meiji liberal metaphors are spatial and militarized. Indeed, defending the fortress of the individual conscience from state incursion is the explicit goal of Uemura Masahisa's *General Psychology* (*Shinri ippan*, 1884).[22] Nishi Amane's even more ambitious *Encyclopedia* (*Hyakugaku renkan*, 1870) systematized all disciplines centered on the psychological subject. Though heavily influenced by Auguste Comte's *Cours de philosophie positive* (1830–42), Nishi broke with Comte's privileging of biology and the body as the basis of all science, replacing them with Mill's *Logic* and psychology (Nishi had discovered both Comte and Locke as a student in

Leiden from 1862 to 1865).[23] As a result of this substitution of psychology for biology, the natural sciences take up a very small and relatively unimportant part of the *Encyclopedia*, in which the natural world and the material body as the starting point of a system of knowledge is replaced with a mind-centered system.[24] Nishi repeated Obata's Kantian separation of nature and politics by severing the material (*butsuri*) from the mental (*shinri*), preserving the latter for the realm of politics and values. He illustrated this separation by insisting on the qualitatively different and unrelated principles (*ri*) behind (subjective) good government and (objective) falling rain.[25] Likewise, Meiji ethicists and moral philosophers Nishimura Shigeki, Nakashima Rikizō, and Inoue Tetsujirō followed a similar division of (natural) fact from (human) value in the construction of a national ethics.[26] This Kantian divide was popularized in texts such as Nakamura Keiu's translation of Samuel Smiles's *Self-Help* (*Saikoku risshi hen*, 1870), a runaway Meiji best seller that had a deep impact on Tanaka Shōzō. *Self-Help* was a series of biographies describing such self-made men as George Washington, Benjamin Franklin, the Duke of Wellington, and other individuals who were not only politically free subjects but also, through constant frugality, not beholden to anyone else through debt.[27] Nakamura's introduction preached that it was one's attitude or spirit alone that defined one's relationship to the world and determined one's success or failure.[28]

Even those interested in what were considered the mysteries of the universe, such as "the Monster Professor" (*yōkai hakase*) Inoue Enryō, preserved an epistemological human/nature divide. Like Nishi, Inoue relegated the study of nature to the relatively insignificant and wholly knowable realm of natural science. Though he elevated "the mysterious" (*fushigi*) to the highest level of human knowledge, Inoue's "mysterious" was a category of the human mind alone, best dealt with by religion. Resorting again to a spatial metaphor, Inoue sought to wall off the mind, the "castle keep," from its environment.[29] Like Obata's lightning and Nishi's rain, Inoue's method began with the separation of ethics from natural phenomena, creating two independent systems from something "the benighted folk (*gumin*)" had incorrectly considered a single system. Inoue believed that the false theories of nature held by the ignorant had to be eradicated so that the natural realm of "finite and relative phenomena" would not contaminate the "realm of the infinite and absolute mind"[30]—a fear that mine pollution would realize in cruel and unexpected ways a few short years later when fushigi returned, but this time in the supposedly knowable realm of nature.

The separation of the subject from the space it inhabited was at work in sociology, too. In 1881 Katō Hiroyuki famously renounced natural rights theory (*A New Theory of Human Rights* [*Jinken shinsetsu*]) in favor of Herbert Spencer's "survival of the fittest" (*yūshō reppai*). To highlight the nature/society divide, Katō split competition into two registers: a lower Hobbesian form in which humans were indeed in thrall to their environment, and a beneficial, higher register where competition was governed by the rules of international and domestic—constitutional—law. Even though based on an anti–natural rights theory, Katō's theory of civilizational progress was similar to Fukuzawa's three-stage taxonomy of civilizations in *Outline of a Theory Civilization* (*Bunmeiron no gairyaku*, 1875), in which failure to transcend nature relegated human groups to the lowest strata, often represented by Native Americans or Australian aborigines. Even outside such explicitly rationalist theories, this view of transcending nature prevailed. Both Inoue and the folklorist Minakata Kumagusu, the former influenced by Spencer, doubted the applicability of Darwinian evolution to human history, believing that at some point humans diverged from animals by means of their intelligence, freeing themselves from being ruled by nature.[31] Of course, by the very nature of the modifier "social," social Darwinism was already opposed to one of Darwin's central insights: the coevolution of organisms and their environment. Though in Japan social Darwinism through Spencer was popularized prior to Darwinism itself, the denial of the coevolution of nature and humans was not an effect of this accident of Japanese engagement with Western theory. It is part of the ideology of nature characteristic of liberalism everywhere, at least since Descartes separated the inner world of thought from the outer world of material science in the sixteenth century. We would do well to remember that even J. S. Mill, like most other nineteenth-century liberals, denied the coevolution of organism and environment. While allowing for variation *within* species, Mill viewed species themselves as a natural type, a metaphysical essence that served as a barrier both to the emergence of a new species and to humanity's complete subsumption into the world of nature and evolution. Indeed, Meiji sociology drew less on Darwin than on the much more liberal-friendly popularization of neo-Lamarckian theory, self-help (*risshin-shusse*), where (as we saw with Nakamura) the human subject is not the *object* of natural selection but rather its own *subject* of evolution and progress.

Though clearly these evolutionary anthropologies and sociologies describe a temporal sequence, they could hardly have avoided affecting the physical space these new bodies were meant to inhabit. In fact, it would not be saying too much to conclude that the major urban renewal and public health campaigns of the 1870s and 1880s were designed to produce an abstract, civilized space as the site of practice for the newly posited modern subject. This new understanding of the human-nature relationship was inscribed in the physical space of Tokyo as early as 1873, when a *Dajokan* edict converted the sacred spaces of the Tokugawas—Sensōji, Kan'eiji, and Asukayama—from functioning politico-religious sites into public parks under the secular administration of the governor of Tokyo. In 1879, three years after the site of the Tokugawas' last stand at Ueno hill became a temporary imperial residence, the *Chōya shinbun* declared that Ueno had finally been "cleansed of ghosts."[32] But beyond exorcising ghosts through renaming sites, Meiji rationalism was also reflected in the complete remaking of the physical space of the city across multiple spatial scales, from urban planning, to commercial and residential architecture, to clothing—part of the process that historian Ruth Rogaski has called "hygienic modernity."[33] Ernst Tiegel, the disciple of the Munich miasmist Max von Pettenkofer,[34] brought his teacher's methods to Tokyo Medical School, where as a hired foreign expert he taught the new science of public hygiene in the 1870s. Tiegel, together with the founder of the Home Ministry's Department of Public Health (*Naimushō eiseikyoku*), Nagayo Sensai, strove to separate, and when possible transcend, Meiji rationalism's body. As a miasmist, Tiegel held that a body, while vulnerable to outside influences, maintained a vitalist core unto itself that needed to be protected and separated from harmful vapors, winds, temperature extremes, and other external conditions. In fact, like the Tokugawa *Yōjōkun* before it, Tiegel and Nagayo's strove to shore up the individual body against penetration by a dangerous natural world.[35] Tiegel's collection of lectures, *Eisei hanron* (1879), is a blueprint for a "miasma-free Tokyo," following his mentor Pettenkofer's miasma-free Munich. In it, we can see the goal of evacuating a central point—whether the individual body or the new imperial capital—of all wastes and impurities, leaving a pure, rational space, a clean slate with an unlimited possibility for expansion.

From the macro reimagining of Tokyo Tiegel moved to the micro level of the individual body in a series of experiments on the relative hygienic merits of Japanese and Western clothing. The experiments, commissioned by Nagayo, were meant to determine the relationship of Japanese clothing and footwear to the "established principles of the science of hygiene."[36] The official Home Ministry report, *Ifukuryō shinkensetsu* (1881), sought to duplicate the purified center of the capital at the level of the individual body. As mentioned, for Tiegel, the human body had its own internal temperature that was

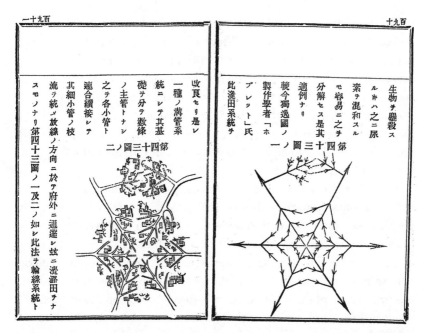

FIGURE 1.2. Ernst Tiegel's plan for a "miasma-free Tokyo," from *Eisei hanron* (1879).
Source: Ernst Tiegel, *Eisei hanron* (1879), vol. 3, translated by Ōi Gendō, Eisei hanron maku 1–2, *Kindai Nihon yōjōron eiseiron shūsei* (Tokyo: Ozorasha, 1992).

largely independent of the environment in which it was located. But it was not completely separated from the outside. While largely independent, the body was healthy only within a very limited temperature range and was adversely affected by extreme changes, both higher and lower. The task of public health was thus building and maintaining barriers between the body and the hostile exterior as a matter of life and death:

> Clothing to us is as fur and feathers are to the animals. In fact, clothing is an essential part of our daily lives, something we are not without for a moment from waking in the morning to retiring at night. The question of sickness and health returns to the question of clothing. . . . In short, does it maintain and protect the body? We have here subjected several articles of clothing to experiments. The published results show each article's relation to physiology, that is to say, for example, an article's capacity to be permeated by the air, or to insulate the skin.[37]

Civilized, scientifically vetted clothing was essential to ensure that the body possessed its own portable environment that would keep it within the narrow healthful parameters it required as it moved through the dangerous and corrupting outside world.[38] Tiegel, a hired foreign expert and a confident man of science, took time at the end of his report to point out that any suggestion of historical coevolution of humans and environment was purely coincidental: "To those who ask why bother [with these experiments] when people have designed clothing, food, and housing appropriate to their climate over millennia? [To them I say] I speak from the science of hygiene (*eiseigaku*) and the principles of physiology ... not from random or uninformed opinion (*mugaku mushiki*)."[39]

But just as Obata was unable to completely separate humans from nature in the case of earthquakes and comet strikes, Meiji rationalism was similarly unable to completely sever the connections between humans and nature in practice. The devastating waves of cholera that hit Meiji Japan in the 1870s and 1880s made sure that the discourse on public health kept focusing on what went in and what came out of the individual body.[40] Yet even this obvious penetration of the body by nature—through water and food—did not result in the abandonment of the autonomous subject. As we shall see below, the Meiji discourse on epidemic disease instead displaced the etiology of cholera, plague, and typhus from material body-environment relations to the social practices of what were increasingly being coded as unenlightened or backward social groups.

Though it signaled a major break in the history of health and biology (in terms of the relationship of the body to its environment), as in the West, the germ theory of disease merely accelerated the separation and individuation of bodies already under way in miasma theory. According to germ theory, health or disease could be epistemologically contained within the pathogen's presence or absence in the body.[41] And just as Linda Nash found in her excellent study of disease and landscape in California's Central Valley, in practice the pure body imagined by the germ theory of disease complemented the previous work of (miasmist) sanitary engineers to sterilize and separate the body from the environment. Bruno Latour, too, has found that the germ theory merely subsumed the hygienic practices begun under the earlier and now discredited public health officials.[42] Kitasato Shibasaburō, the discoverer of the plague bacillus and the father of the germ theory in Japan, followed this pattern of reducing disease to the isolated bacillus of the laboratory cultures while at the same time calling for more effective and extensive quarantine.[43] Consistent with the imagined pure liberal body, the germ theory allowed for health to be recast as the absence of impurities. With germ theory and the bacteriological revolution, the already weakened links between humans and

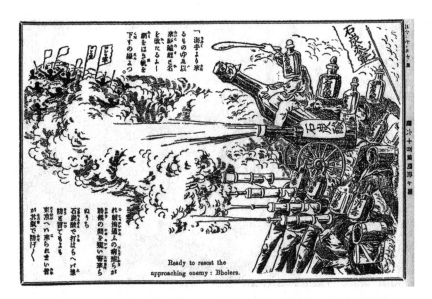

FIGURE 1.3. Editorial cartoon from the July 12, 1879, tabloid *Maru maru chinbun*. The "Phenol [石炭酸, Carbolic Acid] Army" defends Japan against the advance of the "Cholera Army," represented as indistinguishable dark masses that "come from the sea (*umite yori kitaru mono*)." Source: Kakimoto Akihito, *Kenko to yamai no episuteemee* (Kyoto: Mineruba shobō, 1991).

nature were finally broken and the relational, metabolic interaction of nature and society was no longer seen as the source of disease. As the cholera bacillus became the sole cause of the disease, the germ theory allowed health experts to reduce disease to the presence or absence of pathogens in individual bodies, while paradoxically at the same time insisting on the social roots of epidemics. The cause of cholera was increasingly identified with the hygienic practices of the impure, unenlightened, backward classes and races even as the material environment was sterilized by the massive application of carbolic acid (phenol) in military-like campaigns.

This move to the pathology of groups, too, had begun in the Tokugawa period. Initially chapters on epidemic disease were merely grafted onto the long tradition of *Yōjōkun*. Already in Hashimoto Hakujū's *Dandokuron* (1810) the spread of epidemic diseases such as smallpox and measles were mediated by groups.[44] It is from *within* the *Yōjōkun* tradition that we can even see the emergence of the creation of the self-surveilling subject as a rational, decision-making individual within society. In texts such as *Tsuzoku yōjōkun mō* (1880), the individual is said to be guided by an interior sense of right and wrong. The individual is also warned to be aware of how his or her behavior may affect the health of the group.[45] Likewise, the Public Health Bureau's 1880 memorandum "Koreri yōbo ronkai" instructed people that every cholera victim was also the possible source of future victims[46] and should therefore be isolated and reported to the police, who under the Prussian model adopted in Japan were responsible for enforcing hygiene codes—a responsibility they held until 1945. The police, and later citizen groups themselves, were required to report victims of cholera or of any other epidemic disease. Victims were then required either to stay home or to enter one of the newly created quarantine hospitals (*hibyōin*), mocked as "houses of death" (*shibyōin*) by the populace.[47] The police were popularly believed to be so good at finding victims that it was rumored they could hear the discharge (vomit and diarrhea) of a cholera victim as they patrolled a neighborhood. This meant that villagers—sick and well alike—were in turn forced to self-discipline their own bodies.[48] Japanese subjects were therefore instructed to internalize the gaze of both the police and doctors— two of Foucault's modern disciplinary practices for the price of one. These and other forms of police and self-surveillance were so wrenching that literary critic and historian Komori Yōichi labels the anticholera campaigns of the 1870s and 1880s such a major advance in daily control of the body as to be a form of "self-colonization."[49]

It is surely no coincidence that it was also at this time that Meiji psychology began to become interested in "the social mind." Aided by the recent use of statistics and urban geography, unhygienic practices were increasingly identified with certain groups: the poor, the uneducated (*kyakubun*, *gumin*), the *buraku* minority, and foreigners (especially the Chinese, who were seen as the source of plague).[50] This view that disease was the result of insufficient state supervision and lack of self-control led to a redoubling of the civilizing mission: increased policing of troubled areas and the creation of local, self-surveilling citizen hygiene boards.[51] This anticholera discourse thus marks the unification of social and physiological pathologies in a nationalized theory of the subject.[52] Using the new hygienic language— diagnosis, treatment, prevention, quarantine—it sought to prevent dangerous, occasionally "poisonous" ideas, from socialism to women's sexuality, from contaminating the increasingly idealized individual mind of the Japanese national subject.[53] The full displacement of the etiology of disease onto groups lacking in self-control later resulted in the creation of physical and legal boundaries—customs, immigration, and quarantine—around the national body, the *koku-tai*.[54] But public health's condemnation of "backward" or "unenlightened" groups was in many ways an attempt to once again shift the etiology of disease from complex and highly politicized spatial relations to questions of time and development.

By the 1890s, paralleling moves in epistemology and political philosophy, the Public Health Bureau had created a modern science of medicalized hygiene combined with the dominant social ideological production of the national community. Displacing Japanese health and safety from a body's interaction with its environment into an idealized social realm of self-surveillance and modern sanitary practices produced a pure Japanese subject separated from all foreign bodies. This is the familiar narrative of consolidation and control of the 1890s. But, of course, it was also right here, at the moment when Obata's promise seemed about to be fulfilled, that these physical and conceptual walls began to leak.

### The Return of the Strange

In the mid-1880s, residents of the Watarase valley noticed a strange (*fushigi*) disappearance of fish in the river. An undated report from Shibata county, Asakura village, reported that neither dace (a member of the carp family) nor *ayu* (sweetfish, a kind of freshwater trout and staple of the fishing industry) had been seen in substantial numbers since 1882.[55] The August 12, 1885, issue of the *Chōya shinbun* ran a story reporting that ayu were so weak that children were able to catch them by hand. By January 27, 1890, when the *Yubin hōchi shinbun* reported a local mining study group's (*kōgakkai*) ongoing experiments on the effects of blue vitriol (*tanban*, copper sulfate) on fish, almost none of the over seven hundred families once engaged in full-time fishing remained.[56] The newspaper suspected copper from the Furu-kawa zaibatsu's Ashio Copper Mine as the cause of the damage to the fish populations. As the pollution grew over the 1890s, the destruction caused by the Ashio floods would prompt residents to rename the previously bountiful Watarase "the river of death."[57]

Located some one hundred miles northwest of Tokyo, just over the ridge from the Tokugawa mausoleum at Nikko, the Ashio mine sits at the headwaters of the Watarase River. From there the Watarase of the 1880s and 1890s flowed through agricultural, fishing, sericulture, and indigo centers in Gumma, Tochigi, Ibaraki, and Saitama prefectures. As it left Saitama and entered Tokyo, in those days the Watarase changed names, becoming the Edogawa. Near the borders of Tochigi, Saitama, and Ibaraki, the Watarase joined the Tone River, which emptied into the Pacific at Zushi in Ibaraki. Ashio, which had been a functioning copper mine since at least the seventeenth century, was acquired by Meiji success story Furukawa Ichibei (1832–1903) in 1877 as part of the Meiji state's policy of selling off former Tokugawa assets to a new industrial elite (*haraisage*). In 1882 and again in 1884, increasingly rich veins of copper were discovered, and Furukawa went to great efforts to introduce cutting-edge extraction technologies imported from Montana. He also signed a lucrative deal to supply huge amounts of copper to the British trading firm Jardine-Matheson that both made him rich and obligated him to a rapid increase in output beginning in the 1880s. By 1890 the Ashio mine produced nearly 42 percent of Japan's copper, an export responsible for 9.5 percent of Japan's export earnings that year.[58] Boasting Japan's first electric railway, first hydroelectric plant, compressed-air drills, electric lighting, and centrifugal fans for ventilation, by the late 1880s the remote mountain town of Ashio was "one of the most technologically advanced centers of the country," a partial fulfillment of the success that "civilization and enlightenment" promised.[59]

The low-lying Watarase and Tone River valleys were naturally flood prone. But whereas previous floods had brought green fertilizer for both the wet paddy fields and the dry mulberry and barley fields (*hatake*), after the summer of 1890 floods were bigger and more destructive than in the past; they also brought a host of pollutants, including copper sulfate, chlorine, arsenic, sulfur, aluminum oxide, magnesia, iron, and mercury, as well as nitric and phosphoric acids. Flowing down from the mine to the watersheds, Ashio pollutants not only killed fish and plant life in the river but also ravaged the willows and bamboo planted on the extensive system of levees, some dating to work done by Tokugawa neo-Confucian scholar Kumazawa Banzan in the seventeenth century. The loss of plant cover led to erosion and weakened the levees at precisely the same time that floods were increasing in intensity and frequency. Deforestation due to toxic smoke and clear-cutting the mountains surrounding the Ashio mine for fuel and shaft support further exacerbated the problem: the destruction of the forests at the Watarase's headwaters destroyed the soil's ability to hold water, not only increasing the volume of water that reached the river but also silting the riverbed, raising it several feet relative to the levees and thus guaranteeing continued and increasingly severe flooding. Through silting, flooding, and the use of river water for irrigation, Ashio pollutants infiltrated the rice paddies, settling into the mud. (The still ponds of rice paddy agriculture are perfectly suited to letting heavier pollutants like copper and other metals precipitate and settle into the soil.) The increased floods meant that even the fields of mulberry trees, whose leaves are the only food of the silkworm, withered and died. The new chem-

ical composition of the water also damaged the famed indigo industry surrounding Ashikaga and Kiryū as Ashio pollutants in the water reacted with
the dyes, ruining the deep blues for which the area was famous. Like radio-
active tracers sent into an ecosystem to map its invisible relations, the
changed hues of the indigo industry showed that, contrary to popular and
expert opinion, there was in fact exchange of water and pollutants far upstream on several Watarase tributaries, a dynamic hydrological relation first
described in the dyers' antipollution petitions—an early instance of countless previously unknown ecological connections that would be discovered
over the decades.[60] In short, during the 1890s the production methods that
had long sustained the region's inhabitants ceased to work.

A sense of generalized social and ecological breakdown prompted Kawashima Isaburō to lament in his journal *Ashio Mine Pollution* (1891),
"What is it that humans cannot go a day without? Is it not clothing, food,
and shelter? And upon what are these built? Is it not agriculture and its
products? . . . Do not the essentials of human life then depend on the un-
changing natural laws? But for the residents of seven counties of Ryōmō
along the banks of the Watarase, these laws may no longer be relied on
(*[tensoku] o fukuyō sezarumono naran ya*)."[61] The unprecedented scale of the
destruction of the 1890 flood also caught the attention of the local liberal
salons (*enzetsukai*) and village associations.

After the floods of 1890, liberal activists in Ashikaga, Sano, Kiryū, Tatebayashi, and countless other towns along the banks of the Watarase realized
that Ashio effluent threatened to erode the political victories of the previous decades. With liberal activists perhaps still flush with their recent victory over the government in the constitutional battles in the 1880s, the decade of leaks that ended with Matsumoto's horrifying pollution exposé and
Tanaka and Kōtoku's despairing appeal to the emperor began in the pages of
the *Shimotsuke shinbun* with a rousing call to arms for local popular rights
group the Shimotsuke Liberal League (*Shimotsuke jiyū kōdōkai*) to join the
battle against blue vitriol.[62]

### Blue Vitriol versus the Shimotsuke Liberal League
Though later in the late Meiji and Taisho periods the Ashio Incident became a story of "modern" pollution invading and destroying a "premodern"
agrarian idyll, in fact Ashio's effluent bubbled and coursed through a region
that had already seen two decades of largely successful, occasionally violent,
political organization and struggle.[63] Throughout the 1870s and 1880s both

the Liberal Party (Jiyūtō) and Tanaka Shōzō's own Constitutional Progressive Party (Rikken Kaishintō) had clashed with the Meiji state and with each other in the Fukushima, Gumma, and Kabasan Incidents. Not only were early popular rights activists successful in arguing for a constitution; in the 1880s they had also succeeded in establishing local village (*mura*), town (*chō*), and county (*gun*) assemblies that brought the rural population into national politics. These local assemblies continued to function even after the famous dissolution of the national parties in 1884, so that by the flood of August 1890 these local assemblies had been practicing participatory politics through elections, debates, and petitions to the Meiji state (*kenpakusho*) for nearly a decade. Thus, contrary to the popular romanticized story of peasant resistance, given the strong liberal traditions in the afflicted counties, these groups were constituted by, and therefore had a stake in, the autonomous subject of Meiji liberalism and all that entailed. Meiji liberalism's understanding of rights and nation ensured that the initial fight over the Ashio pollution would take place in the arena of political inclusion, negotiation, compromise, and economic compensation for damage to property. Pollution in these early years was merely an effective means for criticizing the narrowness and selfishness of the government.[64]

In the April 8, 1891, issue of the *Shimotsuke shinbun*, a Shimotsuke Liberal League member scolded his fellow members for shirking their "true calling." He believed the league's job must be to protest the problem of blue vitriol, which was fundamentally changing the Watarase River and threatening life and livelihoods in the valley. He urged the league's secretaries (*kanji shokun*) to call an extraordinary session "to hear the many opinions, to consult." Given the later scale and scope of the Ashio disaster, the appeal to the membership showed an unexpected optimism and faith that the mere expansion of participation, tactics, and rhetoric that had succeeded in painting the Satchō oligarchy as a tyranny during the popular rights and liberty movement would prove just as effective against mine pollution:

> To the members! Assemble the volunteers from the banks of the Watarase in Gumma; draft your measures. To facilitate this, at the general [county] assembly, select one or two members as representatives, trust their policies, form a consensus with the volunteers from Gumma. Accordingly, carry out a full investigation of the effects of blue vitriol on the various things. This is a fight over rights. Once that is acknowledged . . . there is no reason for shame. Spread the light of the Shimotsuke Liberal League. This will lead to the happiness of

those on the banks of the Watarase. It will be welcomed. We dare summon to action the Shimotsuke Liberal League![65]

The previous autumn in Ashikaga, Chō Sukeyuki, one of the earliest and most vocal antipollution activists, had used similar language to rouse the residents to use both the law and their intense dedication (*kesshin*) against mine owner Furukawa Ichibei and the pollution he had unleashed into the Watarase. Chō also invoked the legitimacy of the town and village council system: "Article 35 section two of the Town and Village System allows for town and village assemblies to petition the authorities when the matter touches on the public good. . . . Already last autumn, Sangamo village called an extraordinary council and made public their protests and their reasons for opposing the mine." Chō adds, with a note of hope, "Ah, perhaps Heaven's decree (*tenmei*) is not yet extinguished, perhaps men of virtue and dedication (*jinjin soshi*) have not died out." Chō urges these men of high purpose to combine forces with the inhabitants to press Furukawa to clean up the mine pollution or to change the location or refining process at Ashio. Should he refuse, Chō hinted, there is the possibility of direct action, of violence, "as a last resort in the battle for our rights."[66]

Kawashima Isaburō's journal, *Ashio no kōdoku*, also extended the language of public and private interests of 1870s liberal protests to the pollution problem by suggesting that the destruction caused by the powerful over the weak is more appropriate to the Edo dark ages than to enlightened Meiji: "In our enlightened age of Meiji (*Meiji shōdai*) . . . the destruction of the laws of nature for the benefit of a single individual . . . cannot be allowed (*hitostu shinin no tame ni tensoku o yaburan . . . suru koto atawazu*)." The journal itself is a four-paragraph report on the difficulties of the valley's farmers and fishermen. This is followed by five much longer congratulatory notes from local and Tokyo-based liberals predicting that, like Chō's report, this journal too will be banned by an autocratic and selfish government, but that other patriots (*tenka shishi jinjin*) will step up to take his place after he himself is likely arrested and forbidden from publishing. The final salutation urges members not to sit idly by while all benefits of the enlightened age are monopolized by a single individual.[67]

### The 1897 Pollution Prevention Order
The liberal attack on the narrowness of the Meiji state continued in Tanaka Shōzō's famous questions to the government in the first and second meetings

of the Diet in 1891–92. Though, as we shall see, volunteers were discovering countless complex interactions between nature and society in their pollution investigations, from roughly 1890–96 those relations were largely subsumed under a utilitarian and natural rights logic hardly modified from the popular rights struggle to establish a national assembly during the 1870s and 1880s. Though Kenneth Strong and traditional Tanaka historiography see this as the beginning of environmental politics in Japan, the questions actually appeal to the sanctity of the farmers' property rights enshrined in article 27 of the Meiji constitution. Both of Tanaka's questions are expressed in public and private language, with an emphasis on property rights. They question the government's motives in not moving to protect those residents' rights as they seemed to be protecting Furukawa's. In these Diet questions there is none of Tanaka's later social ecology of poison and flow (see chapter 3). After a long speech detailing the toxic effects of the flood of 1890—using materials gathered by local volunteers—Tanaka suggests the narrowness of the government:

> Article 27 of the Constitution recognizes the sanctity of private property and article 10 paragraph 3 of the Mining Act says that "if the method of extraction or prospecting is harmful to the public good" (*kōeki ni gai aru toki*) the Minister of Agriculture and Commerce may revoke permission to exploit the mine. Yet poison from the Ashio mine in northern Shimotsuke has flowed down the Watarase and caused hugely expensive damage in Tochigi and Gumma since 1888. It has ruined wet and dry fields and destroyed the levees and bamboo on the banks.
>
> Question: What is the reason for the government's inaction and foot-dragging? What is its plan for dealing with and rescuing this situation? What are its plans for preventing this in the future?[68]

The government responded, rather artlessly, that the cause of the damage was unknown *and* that they had already taken steps to prevent it in the future. This prompted another, longer and more sarcastic question from Tanaka in the second Diet, in which he framed this obvious obfuscation as proof that the government was selfishly taking sides with the mine. These two questions are hardly different in content or form from Tanaka's, or, for that matter, from any other Liberal (Jiyūtō) or Progressive Party (Kaishintō) members' opposition to the Hokkaido land transfers in sweetheart privatization deals to friends of the oligarchy (*haraisage jiken*) or military contractor scandals in the 1880s. (As party politics became more integrated with the government itself with the opening of the Diet, eventually entering the cabinet in the 1897, this tactic was robbed of much of its potency.) This time the government's response was to stall whenever possible, but also to encourage the private resolution of the competing property claims through contracts between the Furukawa zaibatsu and the victims for condolence payments (*mimaikin*) that did not acknowledge legal responsibility on the part of the mine. The majority of the Ashio protest from the second Diet question to the floods of 1896 are concerned with the inadequate amounts of the payments, the perception that the government was on Furukawa's side, and other issues regarding the *haraisage jiken*, such as the selling of the forests around Ashio to Furukawa for less than the cost of replanting with seedlings. Further proof that pollution was not yet an issue unto itself, Tanaka, Shimada Saburō, and others voluntarily refrained from bringing the growing pollution problem before the Diet while it was in session in Hiroshima during the Sino-Japanese War (1894–95)—to be physically and symbolically closer to the fighting taking place in Korea. Here, too, the logic is the liberals' logic of a larger (national) public over a narrower (local) private characteristic of Utilitarianism's mantra: the greatest good for the greatest number.

A turning point in the antipollution discourse came with the floods of 1896. In extremely poor timing for the Furukawa zaibatsu, the initial condolence contracts expired in 1896, during some of the worst flooding in memory, beyond even the fifty-year floods of 1890. As in 1890, the 1896 flood breached levees in Ibaraki, Saitama, Chiba, and even Tokyo, eventually damaging 136 towns and villages and over 46,723 hectares of farmland.[69] The 1896 flood carried so much mine pollution that faith in Furukawa's ability to ever prevent Ashio pollution from escaping into the valley was in doubt. In response, the activists reassembled at the Buddhist temple near Tatebayashi, Unryūji, which became their headquarters for the antipollution campaigns for the next few years. They quickly collected petitions from ten towns and villages, demanding tax relief, levee repair, and closure of the mine. In November enough pressure had been brought to bear on the government that agriculture and commerce minister Enomoto Takeaki visited Gumma and Tochigi, and by December the ministry established a pollution investigation commission.

The Pollution Prevention Order of 1897 represented the high-water mark of Meiji liberalism. Though it did mark the beginning of the state's direct involvement in the pollution problem, the state intervened only in an attempt to preserve existing property relations. The order was issued directly to Furukawa Ichibei, "owner-operator of the Ashio Copper Mine." Furukawa was ordered to complete the measures at personal cost and was made wholly responsible for overseeing the retrofitting of his operation. Slag heaps, precipitation ponds, and "smoke scrubbers" (a mist of lime-water) to remove sulfur from the refinery's smokestacks were the order of the day—projects designed not only to separate cross-contamination of discrete, competing property interests, but also to police the boundary of human and natural systems. See, for example, the attempted isolation of waste and rainwater:

> Item One:
> None of the wastewater from the pits Ariki and Kotaki at Ashio is to be allowed to wash away. After being washed with live lime, all mine waste is to be collected and directed to precipitation ponds and filter beds that will be newly built [by the owner] ...
> Item Three:
> New construction must be undertaken to completely prevent the mixing of rainwater with any of the copper found at the smelting site. ...
> Item Five:
> ... So that no rainwater will get into [and overflow] the precipitation ponds, a roof will be constructed over them. ...
> Item Thirty-Two:
> The preceding projects listed in this order are to be completed within the time given in this order. Until the precipitation ponds and filter beds have been constructed, the mine is to be closed.
> The ponds at Ashio are to be completed within fifty days.
> The ponds at Kotaki are to be completed within forty-five days.[70]

Despite this attempt at separation, as Brett Walker has recently shown, the industrialization of nature requires the simplification of complex systems,[71] a process that undermines the ability to maintain the separation of natural and social systems. So it should be no surprise to learn that despite this major effort, one of the world's first attempts at regulating a polluting industry, the 1897 order did not have the desired effect. Pollution kept flowing, and it even seemed to be increasing. The environment had not yet become the specific *political* problem it would be in the years to come.

But already in the early 1890s, as the Shimotsuke Liberal League was organizing along popular rights lines, beneath the surface of existing political categories the ground was shifting. There was a growing crisis and a growing sense of the inadequacy of current knowledge and methods for dealing with the still-growing environmental crisis. Paralleling the activities of the Shimotsuke Liberal League's rallying of the councils, activists and local party members mobilized the local press, volunteer groups, and lecturers; organized mine study groups (*kōgakkai*); established five experimental monitoring stations; began to study the effect of "bad water" (*akusui*) on fish; and started investigating the extent of the pollution in the fields.[72] These investigations were racing ahead of the simplified language of cause and effect, public/private, and even victim/victimizer of Meiji rationalism, as thought lagged behind nature.

### Meiji Soil Science and the Pollution Problem

In 1891, Chō had said that all of the area's problems "returned to blue vitriol." But even as Chō wrote, investigations in the natural and social sciences were discovering that things were not so simple. After the floods of 1890, antipollution activists enlisted the help of Kozai Yoshinau and Nagaoka Shūkō, assistant professors of agricultural science at Tokyo Imperial University. In February 1892 Kozai and Nagaoka reported on one of the experiments they had conducted on behalf of the Watarase farmers over the course of 1891. While they definitively proved that Ashio pollutants were present in the river and soil, they were startled to discover that causes of crop damage due to Ashio pollutants were so diffuse and complex that the investigators were hard pressed to come to any conclusions other than that significant damage coincided with the exploitation of the mine. In many ways they were able to do little more than express in a scientific vocabulary of uncertainty the lay observers' repetition of "the strange" (*fushigina mono*) that was a hallmark of early antipollution investigations.[73] Unlike with the nature of the 1870s, when Inoue Enryō and Obata Tokujirō were writing, when *fushigi* returned it returned in the least likely place—right in the middle of the supposedly knowable and predictable realm of natural science. Unlike Obata's lightning, which he claimed operated according to its own principles, pollution's harm was a result of politics, policy, soil chemistry, lifestyle, and livelihood, therefore it was related to one's personal situation. Despite Obata and civilization and enlightenment's claims to the contrary, it now seemed the earth itself was indeed going mad.

The numerous uncertainties in Kozai and Nagaoka's first report meant it started and ended with more questions than answers. After presenting a table of the measurements they took in Tochigi and Gumma, Kozai and

Nagaoka were distressed to see that there did not seem to be any pattern to the damage. In Tochigi it was the dry fields that were harmed more than the paddies. In Gumma it was the rice paddies. Even within these areas it was impossible to talk about an "average level of damage," because there wasn't one. Every variable they looked at seemed to have some effect on the existence or degree of damage: "Investigation as to the causes of the damage to fields along the Watarase shows that the cause is in the physical makeup (*rigakuteki soshiki*) and chemical composition (*kagakuteki sosei*) of the soil. [It is therefore] not merely a question of farming, but includes questions of wet and dry weather, [which has a] relationship to cracking of roots and stalks. . . . But even this is an insufficient explanation of the causes of the withering and dying of the plants. . . . That is why we had to inquire into the chemical composition of the soil."

While their measurements did show Ashio copper present throughout the region, Kozai and Nagaoka also discovered that the copper found in the soil was insoluble in water "and thus was not a direct cause of damage to crops." But although not soluble in water, it was soluble "in a solution of diluted acetic acid (*sakusan*)." This sent them back to the field, where they discovered that the soil of the Watarase and Tone watersheds contained 5 percent naturally occurring iron oxide. When this soil was mixed with the Ashio copper, the result was cupric oxide, a compound that was directly harmful to plants. Further, they found that damage was not directly proportional to the amount of copper in the soil. In one place copper levels could be large without causing significant damage, but in other situations the damage could be great even if the soil contained only small amounts of sulfuric acid or iron sulfide. All this depended on reactions with other pollutants and naturally occurring soil acids, and it was further influenced by the vagaries of weather and variable human practice.[74]

Consulting recent German soil science, the report outlined a further problem: that soil itself "breathes," interacting with "its" environment:

All soils have the ability to absorb materials. This is called their absorption ability (*kyūshūryoku*). It is the reason that soil is not stripped of applied fertilizers and elements of cultivation by rain or irrigation water. So, when copper salts are dissolved in water and thus make their way into the fields, they form associations with the elements in the soil and are transformed into copper hydroxide (*suisankadō*) and alkaline copper salts (塩基性銅塩). The cast-off acids combine with the alkaloids potassium, lime, and magnesium in the soil, and these are eventually washed away. This means that though the amount of copper dissolved in the irrigation water may be small and cause no direct harm to the plants, gradually the elements of growth will be washed away. It is not only this loss of fertility, but the copper accumulating in the sludge will increase over time to a point at which it will cause direct harm to plants. . . . Our experiments show that as the amount of dissolved copper increases, the amounts of potassium, lime, and magnesium that are dissolved in phosphoric acid also increases. But the amounts dissolved differ depending on the conditions. Insoluble copper present in the soil can become soluble according to the variation of moisture and dryness, and this can affect the absorption ability of the soil. These relations, too, have not yet been fully worked out by Western scientists.[75]

What is being described here is the discovery of the historicity of the soil, both as accumulation of nutrients and toxins over time and, more fundamentally, in its capacity to be altered through complex processes and interactions both material and social. This coevolution, of course, threatened to undo the separation of natural disasters and politics promised by civilization and enlightenment. It threatened in turn to make the soil political in a way it had never before been. The report even begins the leap beyond a narrowly defined soil science to a much broader nature-society metabolism by including a necropsy on cattle living downstream from a brass utensil factory reported in *Die Landwirtschaftlichen Versuchsstationen, 38*. According to the report, though the cattle had not drunk from the stream, they had nonetheless died of copper poisoning from grazing on grass that had become increasingly toxic as the level of copper in the soil increased, likely through irrigation. With this expansion of the relevant variables to include soil chemistry, weather, bovine biology, hydraulic systems, and brass-utensil production processes, the German report was forced to conclude (if that is the word) that the myriad mediations were not well understood.

It was just these sorts of diffuse and startling connections between nature and society that antipollution activists were increasingly discovering on their own investigations in the years after 1896. Despite the extremely complicated causal relations revealed by the investigation, the 1892 report recommended only the liberal application of lime and "deep farming" to reach down to pre-Ashio, unpolluted soils. Thus, with a growing sense of panic in the years immediately after the ineffective Pollution Prevention Order of 1897 the frustrations born of the hybrid causality of environmental problems led to increasingly desperate and urgent searches for solutions at a more fundamental level. This crisis of mapping the problematic relations of the inescapable ecology of human life would eventually mark the emergence of the environment as the site of a new politics.

### The Sufferings of a Mine-Poisoned Land

After the floods of 1896, I suggest that what was being discovered both ecologically in Meiji soil science and socially in antipollution protests was the historical, social, and political specificity of modern pollution. Modern ecological threats are political not only because they are caused by human technological and industrial practices but also because they are so pervasive, simultaneously occurring at enormous and intensely intimate levels.[76] As a result, it necessarily becomes an issue of society as a whole, calling into question national goals and the social contract itself. As historian of risk and insurance François Ewald puts it, "Ecological risk divides society against itself at its most intangible, least measurable, and perhaps most essential point: it divides society on what is supposed to unite it, on its values, on the definition of its collective interest."[77] It is surely, then, no coincidence that as the antipollution activists deepened their investigation into the social effects of the Ashio pollution, they increasingly appealed to broader social goals and began questioning the direction and basis of Japanese modernity itself. Ashio pollutants escaped not only the precipitation ponds, levees, and slag heaps designed to isolate them; they also escaped the economic, scientific, and legal categories of victim/victimizer and public/private meant to contain them.

Modern ecological risk is characterized as acting both above and below normal thresholds of classic risk that harmed, maimed, even killed an individual body. As Ewald argues, classic risk was accounted for through compensation, something he calls "compensation for the body-as-capital." By contrast, the new forms of ecological threats act both below this level—by compromising the integrity of the individual body itself over time, as through the ingestion of polluted food, water, air, and so on—and above it in the unprecedented scale (temporal and spatial) of the damage they cause. They do so to the point that it is less and less adequate to talk about these new threats as having easily identifiable individual victims[78]—a problem that continues in the constant battles over certification of victims of Minamata disease and the *hibakusha* of Hiroshima/Nagasaki and will no doubt continue with the Fukushima meltdowns of 2011. As compensation and the assignation of legal responsibility becomes problematic, in place of the body-as-capital comes the much more intractable problem of the body-in-environment.[79] I am arguing that the years after the floods of 1896 and the failure of the Pollution Prevention Order (which together with tax relief and Furukawa's condolence monies are a classic case of definable risk resolved by compensation) signaled the historical moment in Japanese modernity when the risks associated with the body-as-capital gave way to those of the body-in-environment. In place of the clear causal language of liberal ideology the damage seemed to degenerate into "lines of causality so multiple and overlapping that the cause gets lost in a general chain of effects." Early activists constantly talked about the invisible nature of the threat, a toxic process that worked in the dark, a creeping, unseen disaster masking the enormity and urgency of the threat, one that could be hidden from the gaze of visitors and touring Diet members; Tanaka Shōzō's writings are full of warnings and fear of the "invisible" (*me ni mienai*) nature of the problem.

In place of Obata's knowable laws of action and reaction between discrete subjects there was an unsettling indeterminacy of what Brett Walker called "hybrid causality," and what Deleuze and Guattari called an unending network of conjunctions and articulations: in place of clear causality there was now only the seemingly occult "and . . . and . . . and."[80] It was, in other words, the return of the strange.

Paralleling the disturbing discoveries of the soil scientists, the pollution victims, too, began tracing the mutual penetrations of humans and nature. And like the soil scientists, they found countless interactions and mutual penetrations both direct (sickness, sores, and loss of eyesight) and indirect (poverty, inability to marry, loss of suffrage, and despair). One of the most dramatic and tragic examples of the porousness of Meiji bodies came in 1899, when activists began months of study into birth and death rates and low-breast-milk problems in the Watarase watershed. The study revealed an extreme example of the breakdown of walls separating the modern subject from the now increasingly polluted environment. At Unryūji, organizers formed twenty teams of researchers for a village-by-village, house-by-house canvassing of the entire area. In a letter to canvass organizer Oide Kōhachi, Tanaka wrote,

> Drop everything! Concentrate all effort on the life-death survey.
> Break down by location [all the way to] hamlet and subhamlet
> (*koaza*). Be sure you break down the degree of damage and make a

full accounting. If you do not record the victims' occupations, we will not know [if they are eating] purchased rice or grow their own—do not be vague on this. The most important are deaths before age three from 1890 to 1898. These too must be broken down by hamlet. People must realize we are talking about a question of life or death. . . . Struggle through your tears and do not give up on this urgent task.[81]

The results of the survey (see table 1.1) were perhaps worse than even the investigators had suspected.[82]

In the winter of 1901, after these investigations and as Tanaka and Kōtoku were preparing their appeal to the emperor (see chapter 2), a series of articles on mine pollution was commissioned by Shimada Saburō and edited by Kinoshita Naoe. In this series a journalist for the *Mainichi shinbun* and member of the Mine-Polluted Lands Women's Salvation Society (*kōdokuchi kyūsai fujin kai*) named Matsumoto Eiko tracked the mine pollution through every corner of life—plant, animal, and human. These articles by Matsumoto were later published as a collection, *Sufferings of a Mine-Poisoned Land* (*Kōdokuchi no sanjō*), a prescient and eerie text in which there is seemingly no barrier at all between the body and the toxic environment. Matsumoto's ethnography of industrial pollution was a monument of "muckraking" journalism in the tradition of urban ethnographies such as Matsubara Iwagoro's *Saiankoku no Tokyo* (1893), Yokoyama Gennosuke's *Nihon Kasō shakai* (1899), and even Engels's *The Condition of the Working Class in England*. By extending this tradition to the environmental problem, it also suggested how difficult, and likely futile, the Meiji attempt to quarantine pollution, to separate humans from nature, might be. Her accounts of communities completely eroded by industrial effluent pointed the way to a new recognition of the inescapable ecologies that flowed through the ecological, social, and political life of the valley. *Sufferings of a Mine-Poisoned Land* is in many ways the social equivalent of the diffusion of causality discovered in soil ecology by Kozai, Nagaoka, and the Pollution Prevention Committee investigations. But unlike those official reports, Matsumoto emphasizes the return of the strange (*fushigi*). In the first of fifty-nine installments Matsumoto immediately calls attention to the novelty of the problem, noting that unlike most things, the pollution problem grows stranger the more one learns about it. Worse, it seems to be an active force itself. Writing under her pen name, Midoriko (literally, "green child"), in her first report she showed how the strange would not be contained—how it moved freely from bodies, to fields, to politics:

TABLE 1.1 **Results of the Pollution Activists' Survey, 1899–1900**

|  | Unpolluted Tochigi | Polluted Tochigi |
|---|---|---|
| Births per 100 people | 3.44 | 2.80 |
| Deaths per 100 people | 1.92 | 4.12 |

SOURCE: Uchimizu Mamoru, ed., *Shiryō Ashio kōdoku jiken* (Tokyo: Akishobō, 1971), 361–84. See also Komatsu Hiroshi, *Tanaka Shōzō: Nijū isseki e no shisōjin* (Tokyo: Chikuma shobō, 1997), 47.

> In this world, there is this strange thing (*fushigina mono*) called the mine pollution problem. . . . And though it was long taken up by the Diet, though so many months and years have passed since its outbreak, after countless newspaper articles and speeches illustrating the situation, and despite the many volunteers, this problem is still not fully grasped or given the attention it needs. . . . No one stands against the victims, nowhere has a contrary voice been raised. And yet the problem has receded into the background, operating now in the shadows. Truly, this gives rise to a sense of the strange (*fushigi no kan*).[83]

The stricken counties in Gumma, Tochigi, Ibaraki, and Saitama that Matsumoto chronicles are bereft of any economic base, citizenship rights, or community ties—what Tanaka Shōzō called "national death" (*bōkoku*). Mine pollution has eroded all economic, social, political, familial, and generational bonds. The metabolic rift opened up by the pollution is reflected in countless ways: mortgaged farms, dysfunctional families, stomach illnesses, blindness, and a near doubling of the infant mortality rate. In Takayama from 1882 to 1887, out of a population of 3,709, Matsumoto records 19 deaths before age one, plus another 3 stillborn. In the next seven years, out of a population of 4,810, there were 65 deaths plus another 18 stillbirths.[84]

Once she started looking, Matsumoto found the strange everywhere. Sixty years before Rachel Carson's *Silent Spring*, Matsumoto notes in her second report of November 23, 1901, the eerie silence that envelops the polluted lands: while reporting on the disappearance of fish and eels from the marshes, she realizes it has been days since she heard a bird or insect's song.[85] She describes shacks without doors or even roofs, schools without floors, starving children, crime, women left alone by the death of a husband or the exodus of children in search of work as day laborers or rickshaw men. One particularly heart-wrenching story tells of an old woman, nearly blind, whose children have been forced to leave for work and whose home has been lost. She now lives in the forest near an abandoned shrine, sleeping under its broken roof and spending her days sweeping the dirt floor. But Matsumoto's text is more than another litany of the poverty and misery of a certain dark corner of Japanese modernity seen in the urban ethnographies. Extending to the social the complex network of ecological relations found in the soil science investigations, Matsumoto finds that in just twenty years, as the land changed from a fertile plain (*yokuya*) to a wasteland of reeds (*yoshiya*), the life and lives, even the language, of the valley has been transformed. *Sufferings of a Mine-Poisoned Land* chronicles the complete destruction of community. Here Matsumoto's reporting has anticipated what Rob Nixon has called the "slow violence" of environmental degradation and the political neglect that seems to plague the victims of attritional disasters, in which, as opposed to spectacular disasters such as volcanic eruptions, typhoons, or earthquakes, "life-sustaining conditions incrementally—rather than suddenly—erode."[86]

As a toxic nature invaded the biological and social bodies of the valley, the most stable aspects of human life were now in doubt; the problem was not only of a new scale, but also of a new kind. In this way, *Sufferings* documents something worse than the mere loss of previous ties, something more than just a major change in daily life in the region. In chronicling the complete absence of community, *Sufferings* describes what the disaster sociologist Kai Erikson calls a "new species of trouble," a diffused, chronic social trauma often found in communities that have suffered toxic events both slow (methylmercury poisoning in Grassy Narrows, Ontario) and sudden (the dam failure in Buffalo Creek, West Virginia, 1973).[87]

Pollution was even enough to change the everyday language of the people. On arriving in the valley, Matsumoto and her companions were confused by the constant repetition of the ominous-sounding word *akuto*. After some questioning she learns that this is a play on the word *akuta*: the term that formerly referred to the fallen leaves that made up the green fertilizer but now has been transformed, as the river and nature themselves have been, to suggest damage, destruction, and even evil. Just as she prefigured *Silent Spring*, in many ways Matsumoto prefigures Erikson and the recent discipline of disaster sociology when in her report on *akuto*, she chose 悪戸 as the characters (*ateji*) for *akuto*, a construction that with only a bit of license can be translated as "broken home."[88] With this linguistic move Matsumoto cuts right to the heart of the new species of trouble and describes its central characteristic, what Michael Edelstein has called "the inversion of the home."[89] The inversion of home marks a major shift, the complete loss of faith in a stable ground for practice and even ontology, a spatial and temporal rupture from "what ought to be a hearth, a safe haven, a source of pride, a place of comfort, [yet] now becomes something spoiled, dangerous, and even hateful."[90]

In Matsumoto's text, pollution emerges as more than a physical agent of destruction, though it is that too. It emerges as the way people relate to each other and to the land, as a social mediation between discrete entities: mother-daughter, farmer-field, and infant-breast milk. The invisible forces of Tanaka's and early activists' reports reach their apotheosis in *Sufferings*. Just as in the *Grundrisse*, where Marx describes how money slowly erodes feudal and tributary relationships until money itself becomes the new community, the communities Matsumoto describes are not attacked from without, as in the classic Meiji and liberal model of the nature-society relationship. Pollution here actually constitutes the community. In *Sufferings*, pollution is the universal social mediation, the one thing that structures daily life and creates a community in its own dark image. By Matsumoto's final entry, all other social relations are either gone or mediated by a polluted environment. The afflicted land is thus more than a *poisoned* community; it is a *poison community*.

In her last two reports Matsumoto returned to Ashikaga, to the scene of the 1896 floods that had first revealed the extent of the changed relation with nature. This time she finds none of the previous enthusiasm of the Shimotsuke Liberal League and Meiji liberalism. Gone too is faith that property rights, Diet politics, compromise, and compensation are adequate to the crisis. Instead, despite the decade of unprecedented activism, she finds at the home of early activist Nagashima Yōhachi a large mound of poisoned earth (毒塚). This was the result of the topsoil being removed by hand from the poisoned fields in the hope of getting down to pre-Ashio soil, a process the inhabitants called "inverting the soil" (*tenchigaeshi*). Her final submission suggests ominously that this "poisoned mound" is matched by an equally strong accumulation of resentment (恨の塚)—a need for vengeance, for revolution.[91] Matsumoto follows this thought to socialism, but not in Shimotsuke. In 1903, shortly after *Sufferings* was published, Matsumoto moved to San Francisco. There she attended several universities and became active in labor issues within the Japanese community in California, where she remained until her death from ovarian cancer in 1928.

Back in the winter of 1901, as Matsumoto was beginning her reports, Tanaka Shōzō, Kōtoku Shūsui, and radical attorney Ishikawa Hanzan were also pushing the limits of liberalism, in one last, desperate attempt to cut through the maddeningly complex relations of "and ... and ... and" and find an immediate solution to the problem, by means of a dramatic appeal directly to the Meiji emperor.

# TWO

# POLLUTION AND PEASANTS AT THE LIMITS OF LIBERALISM

> It is, in reality, much easier to discover by analysis the earthly kernel
> of the misty creations of religion than to do the opposite, i.e. to develop from the
> actual, given relations of life the forms in which these have been apotheosized.
> —KARL MARX, *Capital,* vol. 1

At 11:20 on the morning of December 10, 1901, moments after having convened the sixteenth session of the national Diet, the Meiji emperor was in his carriage making a left turn out of the Diet building in downtown Tokyo when a great commotion erupted up ahead. An old man rushed toward the imperial carriage waving a piece of paper above his head and screaming something about a petition. As one policeman on foot scrambled to get hold of the man's sleeve, a second mounted officer whirled his horse around in an attempt to block the man's path to the emperor, whereupon both officer and horse fell to the ground with a crash, causing the old man to stumble. The man was quickly arrested and the imperial carriage passed safely. Police and onlookers alike recognized the man as the recently retired Diet member from Tochigi, Tanaka Shōzō. Still in his hand was an extraordinary scroll, written by radical journalist Kōtoku Shūsui (1871–1911) and edited by Tanaka, which read in part,

Respectfully, forty *ri*[1] north of Tokyo lies the Ashio Copper Mine. For some time, the exploitation of this mine has caused poisonous waste to fill the valley and flow in its waters, joining the Watarase River and continuing downstream so that nothing living along the banks escapes its disastrous effects. . . . Last year forests at the river's source were recklessly felled by toxic emissions so that now the river runs red with the poisoned earth of the bare mountain. . . . Entire species of fish have died out and the countryside lies ruined. Tens of thousands have lost their health and livelihoods. . . . In this way, in the last twenty years, as far as the eye can see the once fertile land has been reduced to a wretched sea of withered yellow reeds and white rushes.[2]

Like Matsumoto in *Sufferings of a Mine-Poisoned Land,* Tanaka and Kōtoku went on to describe the poverty, disease, and death—the complete breakdown of society—that seemed to follow in the wake of the mine pollution.

In the December 20 issue of the *Kokkei shinbun,* Tanaka declared that he acted "not merely [as] one born and raised in the poisoned fields," but as "a duly elected representative" who "sacrifices himself" by "single-handedly" forcing a redemption of unbearable misery, in this case, Japan's first experience with industrial pollution.[3] Continuing his defense, Tanaka concluded that this "criminal act" was undertaken neither because he loved violence nor out of madness, but rather because he wished "to be the present-day incarnation of Sakura Sōgo."[4]

The Sakura Sōgo of legend was a village headman (*nanushi*) from Sakura domain, Shimōsa (present-day Narita city, Chiba prefecture).[5] According to many versions of the tale, in 1652 Sakura and other village headmen traveled to Edo to present an appeal for relief from new, excessive taxation assessed by their lord, Hotta Masanobu (1632–80). When their appeal to domainal authorities in Edo was rejected, Sakura took it upon himself to appeal directly to the shogun, which constituted a direct, out-of-channels appeal, or *jikiso*—a crime that carried an automatic death sentence. Tried and convicted, Sakura and his wife were crucified and their four sons beheaded.[6] Despite the guilty verdict against Sakura, the taxes were reviewed by the shogunate and found to be excessive. The house of Hotta was ordered to restore the levy to the previous levels demanded in the peasants' petition. In versions of the Sakura tale prepared for the kabuki stage, the ghosts of Sakura and his wife return to terrorize Lord Hotta for the cruel and unjust execution of their sons, eventually bringing ruin to the house of Hotta, who are dispossessed of the Sakura lands and enfiefed in inferior lands outside Shimōsa. In 1736 the Hotta clan itself constructed a shrine to the "great august deity" (*dai-myōjin*) Sakura in order to placate the angry spirits.[7]

In more than one respect Tanaka had failed to reenact this legend, not least of which, his stumble meant he had not succeeded in getting the appeal to the emperor.[8] As he sat in jail that night, things were unbearably unsettled. He had not expected to survive the day. The peasant who perpetrates a jikiso is supposed to trade his life for the fulfillment of his appeal. Yet the police brought in a doctor who declared Tanaka sane,[9] and when morning came he was released—it turned out that a jikiso wasn't even illegal in 1901.[10] Despite the flurry of front-page stories and editorials on the "jikiso scandal," the copper and pollution at Ashio kept flowing. As far as Tanaka and the antipollution movement were concerned, absolutely nothing had happened. This was not the stuff of legend.

IN ONE TELLING, the traditional story of the emergence of an environmental consciousness in Japan is straightforward: Tanaka's lonely protest against the ravages of the Ashio mine culminated in the jikiso, a dramatic expression of a fading peasant consciousness. Beginning with the *Gijin zenshū* (1925–28) and continuing with "people's historians" (*minshūshi*) of the 1960s,[11] Tanaka's failure to close the Ashio mine and his later retreat to the village of Yanaka (where he died of stomach cancer in 1913) stands as a constant reminder of the dark side of Japan's modern experiment. Like Tanizaki Jun'ichiro's later elegy for the lost shadows of traditional Japanese art and architecture, Tanaka's fight is a measure of what Japan had lost in its encounter with modernity.[12] Kenneth Strong's *Ox against the Storm* (1977) reproduces this enduring peasant past at the level of biography when he follows Tanaka's autobiography, *Tanaka Shōzō mukashibanashi* (1895), from Tanaka's days as a village headman (*nanushi*) up to the outbreak of the pollution problem in 1890, at which point Strong leaves Tanaka's text to concentrate on the Ashio case. He does this even though Tanaka's autobiography, written five years after the toxic floods of 1890 and four years after his first pollution questions to the Diet in 1891, makes no mention of the pollution problem.[13]

Alongside this romantic narrative centered on Tanaka is modernization theory's treatment of the Ashio case as an example of Meiji Japan's incomplete modernity. Historiography from the 1975 symposium in the *Journal of Japanese Studies*[14] to more recent scholars[15] has located the

Ashio drama—indeed, the pollution problem itself—in the tension "between tradition and modernity."[16]

There are several problems with both of these traditional narratives. First, presenting Tanaka as an unproblematic extension of his peasant identity requires erasing his decades of organizing and politicking as a dedicated member of the Progressive Party (Rikken Kaishintō), which we discussed in chapter 1 and will explore further below. Even more importantly, the incomplete modernity thesis completely ignores just how vulnerable the pillars of liberalism (perfectly autonomous individual subjects and inviolable property rights) are to the complex and hybrid causal relations of ecological threats. Indeed, in the tradition/modernity narrative, the completion of liberalism is seen as the universal solution to the pollution problem. Accordingly, the trauma of industrial pollution is safely contained within a transitional period that is left behind with the emergence of fully modern (liberal) politics.

But as we saw in the preceding chapter, those classic liberal forms were already under tremendous strain with the emergence of an ecological threat that worked at thresholds both above the individual body (at the social level) and below (inside the body at the physiological level).

This chapter explores how the growing uncertainties and ambiguities of the social and natural worlds examined in chapter 1 found expression in Meiji politics. In contrast to both traditional narratives, I will argue that Japan's environmental turn was a move *beyond* Meiji liberalism, with the realization of its inadequacy to the pollution problem. The emergence of the environment as a possible basis for politics came only after years of effort to expand and stretch Meiji liberalism to accommodate the major changes in nature-body relations. An effort that eventually failed. The jikiso, then, is not the last gasp of a fading peasant sensibility, but the final, failed attempt to make liberalism adequate to the pollution problem.

As such, the best example of ambivalent politics of pollution in Meiji Japan can be found in the text of the jikiso itself. I will argue that the jikiso is not a blast from the past, but is in fact likely *the* document most attuned to the uncertainties of the historical specificity of Meiji politics. That it is also a contradictory text shows not that it is an oddity belonging to a transition to modernity period that has since passed, but that the decidedly modern contradictions of the environmental crisis at the collective level were also expressed in the contradictory logic and political symbolism of the text itself. Multiple genres of remonstration, each with their own political logics and subjectivities, sit uneasily together in the jikiso text, making it the political equivalent of the ambivalent conclusions reached by the Meiji soil scientists assigned to study the Ashio pollution. In other words, the ambivalence in the social and historical context was reproduced in the text.[17]

The jikiso was a failed appeal. Ironically, its very failure is also the source of its subversiveness and the point of departure of the environmental turn. For all its criminality, the jikiso form is in fact a conservative genre. Its goal is a return to the status quo ante. But with the myriad changes in the natural environment effected by industrial pollution, a return to the status quo is precisely what seemed most unlikely. Indeed, it was the failure of the jikiso genre and, in turn, the failure of Meiji political categories to respond to the environmental crisis that prodded Tanaka to abandon those categories and begin a fundamental rethinking of nature-society relations.

In short my argument, like the more traditional narratives, has a lot to say about Sakura Sōgo and the jikiso. But in my telling, the jikiso's seemingly straightforward identification with Sakura and peasant moral economy in fact veils a historical rupture in the politics of nature in Japan. In response to the chimerical nature of the pollution problem, individual liberalism was increasingly supplemented by new groups and associations with concepts of charity, private relief, Christian socialism, and others. Appeals to benevolent government and moral economy were part of this larger project to supplement classic liberalism with social-level correctives. Before arriving at a close reading of the jikiso, we must reconsider the peasant narrative (and Tanaka's own peasant identity) by examining the seemingly most straightforward peasant aspect: the invocation of Sakura Sōgo himself.

### The Meiji Sakura

Tanaka was by no means the first Meiji liberal to invoke Sakura Sōgo. In fact, in addition to being the model of Edo Era peasant protest, by 1901 Sakura had also been the image of Meiji liberalism for over two decades. Using Sakura as a barometer of good or bad government was in fact common from very early on in the Meiji period. One of the first invocations of Sakura by a liberal came in 1878, when the *Osaka Daily News* (*Nippō*) enshrined a recently acquitted early popular rights activist, Mori Tōemon, involved in the basket weavers' disturbance (*wappa sōdō*, 1873). Mori was celebrated as a Meiji Sakura for appealing on behalf of the people of Tsuruoka (in present-day Yamagata). The Osaka editorial denounced Edo Era ideology for condemning Sakura Sogorō, further contrasting the Tokugawa past with an enlightened Meiji, a new age that could recognize the worth of individuals such as Mori. In the *Osaka* editorial, selfishness is identified with the Tokugawa Era's lineage-based allegiances, and "public-ness" with the new nation of Japan: "Even though [Mori] protested on behalf of the people of Tsuruoka, if he had done so but eleven years earlier [in 1867—i.e., before the Meiji revolution], he could not have escaped martyrdom in a death sentence. Both Mori and Sogorō championed the public and rejected the selfish (*kōhai-mushi*, 公拝無私). How awful for Sakura Sogorō, yet how wonderful for Mori Tōemon."[18] Though he or she must always be prepared to die, the Meiji national martyr was one who did not deserve to. Good government was supposed to reduce and ultimately remove that threat.

Beyond the creation of the autonomous actor explored in the last chapter, another major concern of early Meiji liberals was producing a Japanese subject who would support and identify with a strong and modern Japanese nation. Living in constant fear of Western imperialist powers, early Meiji liberals instead saw nothing but servility and eventual colonization in the superstitious, inward-looking rural masses. Both the "Tokyo nichi nichi shinbun" and the Liberal Party's broadsheet, the *Lantern of Liberty* (*Jiyū no tomoshibi*), feared that if provided with three meals a day their compatriots would gladly submit to foreign domination by the "swaggering, red-bearded foreigners."[19] Leading liberal thinker Fukuzawa Yukichi claimed that Japan had no more than one thousand enlightened citizens and suggested that if the country were forced into war with a foreign power, the masses (*kyakubun*) would see sacrificing themselves as unreasonable, thus the number of deserters would be high: "It is very difficult for a country to gain independence this way."[20] Itagaki Taisuke, founder of the Liberal Party (*Jiyūtō*), supposed Japan had no more than five thousand patriots, all of whom were former samurai, believing commoners invariably flee from all hardship.[21] Even the famous Osaka conference on the establishment of a National Assembly in 1875 had settled on representative government because it had concluded that an assembly was the best way to foster a patriotic consciousness in the masses.[22]

Recent work has further explored this tutelary and conservative trend in Meiji ideology.[23] In the early years, Meiji liberals, Tanaka included, searched for and eventually found an ideology by which to produce a subject both conscious of his or her self-worth and still willing to sacrifice him- or herself for the nation: Utilitarianism.

The 1870s and 1880s saw an explosion of treatises and translations of Mill and Bentham: Mill's *On Liberty* (*Jiyū no ri*, trans. Nakamura Keiu, 1871); *Utilitarianism* (*Rigaku*, trans. Nishi Amane, 1877); Bentham's *Principles of*

*Legislation* (*Rippō ronkō*, trans. Shimada Saburō, 1878), *Introduction to Utilitarianism* (*Rigaku nyūmon*, trans. Ono Azusa, 1879–80), and *In Praise of Utilitarianism* (*Rigaku masamune*, trans. Mutsu Munemitsu, 1883–84) all date to this period.[24] As we saw, Nakamura Keiu (1831–91) also translated Samuel Smiles's *Self-Help* (*Saikoku risshi hen*, 1870). As editor of the *Tochigi shinbun*, Tanaka, too, was instrumental in introducing Utilitarianism to Tochigi readers, publishing translations of Mill's *On Representative Government* and Bentham's *Principles of Legislation*.

For Meiji liberals who wished to recruit the former commoners to the national project, Utilitarianism's preference for larger and larger groupings, inherent in "the greatest good for the greatest number," made even local interests amenable to co-optation by the national agenda. The choice of Chinese characters for the translation of "utility" also contributed to this trend. In an early Meiji neologism, Ono Azusa, a Progressive Party member, translated "utility" as *kōeki* (public good). The *kō* of *kōeki* was the Japanese *ōyake* (public). The etymology of *ōyake* shows not only that it indicated a sort of *Gemeinschaft* (*kyōdōtai*) quality but also that it was originally a relative term. Traditionally, *ō-yake* was related to *wo-yake*, a community smaller than the larger *ōyake*.[25] It should also be remembered that in Japanese political terminology the term *ōyake* was commonly identified with the largest administrative unit. Though Japanese historiography refers to the shogun's government as the *bakufu* (literally, "tent government"), it was known to contemporaries as *kōgi* (public/official realm).[26]

Positing themselves as the ideal of a new, modern Japan, Meiji liberals saw themselves as both above a backward peasantry and untainted by participation in an autocratic Meiji state. Armed with the vocabulary of Utilitarianism, they called for a national assembly by attacking the current administration as being too narrow and therefore not public enough—in their terms, "selfish" or "private" (*watakushi*), the traditional opposite of ōyake in Confucian ethics. In Meiji liberalism, it was not a question merely of individual private interests opposing the state, for public and private both had their role to play. Private became a problem only when it prevented the public aspect from operating effectively. This meant that a smaller ōyake (public) becomes watakushi (private/selfish) when confronted with a larger, greater grouping. As in Rousseau's thought, where free individuals combine to form the general will, Fukuzawa Yukichi's *Tsūzoku minkenron* (1878) outlines a series of rights that build from the individual to the general: "Rights are tied to each person's body, and if there are rights in each person, then there are rights in each village and town and there are rights in each district and prefecture and if each nation is a collection of prefectures, each nation has rights."[27] During the 1870–80s, Utilitarianism's notion of nested rights building from individual to national formed the basis of Meiji liberalism's simultaneous attack on the narrowness of the Satsuma-Chōshū clique and the production of modern, patriotic Japanese subjects.

It was through this liberal self-image as in between an autocratic government and above a backward peasantry that the peasant defender of traditional rights, Sakura Sōgo, became the explicit point of contact between Tokugawa commoners and Meiji liberalism. In the search for indigenous analogues to Western liberals such as the American and French revolutionaries, and as a mediation for the awakening of patriotism among the common people, Meiji liberals used the self-sacrificing Sakura Sōgo as a heuristic device to both spur the people on to "enlightenment" and bind their hearts to the nation.

Two important texts that brought Sakura into the Meiji Era and installed him as the national liberal ideal were the seventh installment, "The Role of the Citizen," of Fukuzawa Yukichi's *Gakumon no susume*, the same text we saw earlier, which begins with the famous lines "Heaven makes no man above another." The other text was Komurō Shinsuke's *Tōyō minken hyakkaden* (*An Encyclopedia of Japanese Popular Rights Advocates*, 1883–84).[28] Though Fukuzawa was not himself a party activist, his text outlines the precarious position of popular rights activists searching for a way to remain patriotic while resisting an unelected, autocratic Executive Council dominated by former samurai from Satsuma and Chōshū.[29] After establishing that citizens must obey the law and that the people of a nation are the foundation of its government, Fukuzawa examines three courses of action that citizens could take in the event that their government oversteps its bounds and becomes tyrannical: do whatever the government says, become a confederate and take up arms, or sacrifice oneself in the name of defending just principles. Fukuzawa easily dismisses the first as slavish, blindly obeying the government to the point that it "destroys one's role in life," and the second, taking up arms, as anarchic, stating, "There is nothing more anathema to human compassion than internal discord (*nairan*)." Clearly, Fukuzawa prefers the third way: to pressure the government with "repeated proclaiming of just principles" (*tadashi ri o tonaeru*),[30] no matter how much one suffers. "In the West," Fukuzawa says, "this is called 'martyrdom.'"[31]

When it comes to Japan's prospects for resisting Western imperialism and emerging as an independent nation equal to the great powers, Fukuzawa believes there is one critical question: does Japan have its martyrs? He explains that although Japanese history is full of examples of people sacrificing themselves in battle, in service to their lord, or in acts of revenge, none of these qualifies as martyrdom: "When looked at from today's vantage point of civilization and enlightenment, these people did not know where or when to sacrifice themselves." For Fukuzawa this is as true of the legendary forty-seven *rōnin* (masterless samurai who in 1701 were ordered to commit suicide after avenging the death of their lord) as it is of Gonsuke, the servant who hanged himself after losing one *ryō* of his master's money. Though the rōnin are celebrated for their loyalty and Gonsuke is ridiculed for killing himself over such a small sum, Fukuzawa warns, "We should debate neither the amount of money nor the number of people but only, is there a benefit to civilization? . . . Even had the rōnin killed ten thousand, from neither them nor from Gonsuke is there any benefit to civilization— neither knew how to [properly] give up one's life—this is not martyrdom."[32] Was there anyone in Japanese history who did know how to sacrifice himself, stressing popular rights and challenging the government by the repeated invoking of just principles? Fukuzawa believes "there is but one" who could stand together with the Western martyrs: Sakura Sogorō.[33]

The process of nationalization and abstraction of Sakura is pushed further in Komurō Shinsuke's *Tōyō minken hyakkaden*. In her study of the semiotics of Tokugawa Era peasant anthologies, Anne Walthall states, "[In] the modern period, some editors have deliberately and explicitly omitted what they considered to be wild exaggerations, falsifications of facts, and irrelevant material, precisely the kinds of fictive elements I find most fascinating." The footnote attached to this passage directs us to Komurō's text.[34]

Komurō's *hyakkaden* contains forty-nine biographies of peasant martyrs and leaders of peasant protests. Komurō saw no reason why Sakura alone should receive all the credit, taking pains to include as large a geographical distribution as possible in order to show that there were past, and still are potential, Sakura Sōgos throughout Japan. Many commentators take Komurō's apparent focus on the regions as evidence of sensitivity to localism and agriculture.[35] But Kanai Takanori's work shows that what is really happening is a complicated process of abstraction that actually lessens the weight of the local and particular on the Meiji martyr.[36] This should not be surprising, as Komurō's explicit goal was to modernize the early modern (*kinsei*) martyr anthologies while addressing the prickly question of Japanese history and popular rights: "In our nation's past there is no theory of liberty or rights. These have come since the Meiji revolution, being imported from the West. So, prior to Meiji, those in the past whom we call popular rights activists (*minkenka*) were motivated by loyalty, chivalry, filial piety, and chastity. There are none who did not incorporate these qualities in some way. Rather than call them minkenka, we should remember the appropriate name for them is benevolent and righteous loyalists (*jinjin gishi*, 仁人義子)."[37]

Komurō's use of the peasant martyr shows an even more complicated relationship of "enlightened Meiji" to its near past (here called the Edo "dark ages" [*ankoku jidai*]), than in Fukuzawa or the Osaka editorial. In the *hyakkaden* the qualities that Fukuzawa dismisses as private are not so much condemned as neutralized by showing that all past "benevolent and righteous loyalists" shared a partially understood common ethic to sacrifice themselves "for the nation, for the people, and for just principle" (*kuni no tame, tami no tame, ri no tame*). The phrasing for "sacrifice oneself, for the nation, for the people, and for just principle" in this passage is adapted from the *Analects* of Confucius, where it reads, "Shishi wa tami no tame, kuni no tame, ri no tame, mi o korosu jin o nasu" (this last phrase, *mi o korosu, jin o nasu*, is also read *sasshin jōjin*, 殺身成仁, "give up one's life in the enacting of benevolence").[38] However, in the *Analects*, the subject of the sentence "gives up one's life in the name of benevolence" is not the peasant *gimin* but the aristocratic *shishi* (patriot, man of high purpose), the ideal of the previous revolutionary generation.[39] Here Komurō has made a conscious choice to expand the pool of possible patriots and martyrs beyond the former samurai class. In Komurō's imagining, it is the gimin that fights for these principles. Writing in 1873, Fukuzawa clearly wished to end the years of bloodshed that ushered in the revolution, and Komurō may very well have had Saigo Takamori's antigovernment samurai rebellion (1877) in mind in making the switch from samurai to peasant, something Kanai calls "shishi inflation." Still, it must be remembered that all this was a didactic endeavor aimed at former peasants.[40]

In Komurō's work, self-sacrifice in the name of just principles and the national cause (*sasshin-jōjin*) becomes a mediating general imperative linking the historically impaired Edo Era peasant protester and the self-consciously enlightened Meiji people's rights activist. Abstracting this martyr ethic from varied and complicated peasant rebellions removes the weight of the local and homogenizes the gimin, further preparing him for mobilization in the national project of building a "rich nation, strong army" (*fukoku-kyōhei*). By criticizing the "private motivations" (lord-retainer loyalties, filial piety, etc.) of traditional Japanese heroes "laboring under the Edo dark ages," while at the same time elevating the public sensibilities of the peasant Sakura, Fukuzawa's and Komurō's texts at once consolidate the Meiji revolution against the Tokugawa *ancien régime* and attempt to channel that revolutionary energy into the building of a modern Japanese nation-state. Another factor contributing to the focus on Sakura Sōgo as a "self-starter" (*jihassei*), in the tradition of Samuel Smiles's *Self-Help*, was the Meiji liberals' view of the American and French Revolutions as spontaneous expressions of liberty from the bottom strata of society. In 1880, activist Ueki Emori wrote of the American Revolution, "The people of the thirteen colonies got together with a common purpose in mind and waged war against England for seven years. They finally won the war and liberated themselves from English rule. This was a war for Liberty."[41]

In addition to these texts, liberals frequently used Sakura Sōgo used as a provocation against the government throughout Japan during the popular rights and liberty movement. A major tactic of popular rights protest was the "memorial service" for past peasant martyrs (*gimin*). The services were combined with political lectures and salons (*enzetsukai*) and usually took place at local temples or shrines. The authorities were well aware of the ideological implications of such "memorial services": hearing a popular rights activist invoke Sakura's name at a political rally was usually enough for the police to disperse the crowd. In 1883 a full production of the kabuki drama *Sakura gimin den* (*Tale of the Righteous Martyr Sakura*) was performed in Tokyo, with Ichikawa Danjurō (Ichikawa IX) playing Sakura, as Ichikawa Kodanji had done in the original 1851 production. Liberals even carried Sakura talismans (*mamori*) to protect their freedom of speech. Not only did Sakura become a liberal, but the Meiji liberals also embodied Sakura.[42]

Douglas Howland's linguistic history of the period claims that "the concepts supplied by liberalism and its enlightenment project separated both politics and epistemology from the hereditary forms of the Tokugawa [Edo] regime and placed them in new categories of Western knowledge."[43] The image of the gimin was undergoing precisely this kind of great transformation. As such, the defender of local village rights was nationalized and rationalized, becoming a liberal paragon along largely American and British models. From now on the nation, not the native village, would be the source of identity and the stage of operations for both the Meiji Sakura and the new Japanese subject.

## Tanaka Reconsidered

A close reading of Tanaka's antipollution activities in the early 1890s reveals that the "last peasant protest" view of Tanaka and the Ashio protest is historically inaccurate. Tanaka was a committed liberal, and like other Meiji liberals, he was deeply suspicious of the backward ways of the rural masses until at least 1895—a full five years after the toxic flooding of the Watarase and Tone Rivers. Materials made available by the publication of Tanaka's *Collected Works* from 1977 to 1980 confirm that he was wholeheartedly a part of Meiji liberal discourse, and they challenge Tanaka's status as a repository for Japan's lost environmental past.[44] According to Komatsu Hiroshi, "Prior to the *zenshū* (*Collected Works*), Shōzō was seen as an unproblematic figure situated comfortably in an early Meiji nationalism centered on the imperial house."[45] For more recent Tanaka and Ashio scholars, the discovery of volumes of political correspondence and early diaries has disrupted this narrative arc and promoted Tanaka from tragic hero (*gijin*) to intellectual (*shisōka*).[46] Previously, the eminent "people's historian" (*minshūshi*) and Tanaka scholar Hayashi Takeji had identified Tanaka's *ōyake* with "the people" (*jinmin*), where the people are invariably the rural masses.[47] But as we saw in his antipollution questions in the Diet, rather than an automatic identification with the village against modern industry, until at least the floods of 1896 Tanaka's understanding was more in line with the Meiji liberals' public-private dualism (*kōshi*), in which both public and private have their roles to play. This dualism is perfectly illustrated in Tanaka's criticism of Saigo Takamori's samurai rebellion against the Meiji government in 1877: "Saigo's error was that while practicing one public identity [his domainal loyalties in Kūyshū], he failed to recognize the larger one [the nation] and thus slipped into watakushi."[48]

In the early years Tanaka was in fact critical of the small rural villages he was later identified with. In the 1870s and 1880s he favored larger, rationalized public identities. His "greater good" bias is shown in a letter to fellow Tochigi activist Kawamata Kyūhei in which he praises the consolidation of Edo Era administrative divisions, especially the hamlet (*ōaza*) and the sub-village (*buraku*), into towns and districts (*machi*): "The incorporation of Tochigimoto village into Tanuma town will have a great effect on the future of national autonomy (*kokka jichi*). I can only hope that your work here will become a model of successful consolidation for others to follow. [Of all the other proposed consolidations] none of them think big enough. I would combine all of the individual plans into one grand design."[49] There are even instances of Tanaka complaining of the unenlightened, backward nature of the mountain villages and towns he was forced to visit as part of his popular rights lecture circuit.[50]

As we saw, Tanaka was an early popularizer of Bentham's and Mill's Utilitarian theories as publisher of the *Tochigi shinbun*. In September 1879 he published his own position paper (*kenpakusho*) calling for a national assembly, the first of its kind in Tochigi. The position paper shows some of this regional *minken* democratic potential:

1   The aim of the government is the welfare of the people; a national assembly is necessary to reduce the burden on the emperor and grant the people their right of political participation.

2   Because the people pay taxes and submit to military conscription, they must be given a say in both taxation and government spending.

3   The current government has not been able to provide economic stability, nor has it succeeded in renegotiating the unequal treaties with the Western powers.

4   The excuse of 1874, that a national assembly was premature because the people were unprepared to govern, can no longer be used as the people have progressed through prefectural assemblies and have shown their sense of autonomy in the land tax disputes.[51]

5   A national assembly is the will of the majority of the people.

6   A national assembly is necessary to bind the people's hearts to the nation and avoid colonization by England or Russia.

Articles 1, 2, 3, and 6 are found in nearly all popular rights petitions. Tanaka's progressivism lies in articles 4 and 5, which show more democratic tendencies than the rest of the petition does. In fact, these articles were not in the published version—they were removed in editing for publication.[52]

Given this indisputable liberal activism, Tanaka's autobiography (*Tanaka Shōzō mukashi banashi*), serialized in the *Yomiuri News* from September to November 1895, presents serious problems for those who would cast him as an ersatz peasant fighting a losing battle against the might of industrialization. This traditional interpretation rests on an uncritical reading of the famous first line: "I am a peasant of Shimotsuke [present-day Tochigi prefecture] (*Yo wa Shimotsuke no hyakusho nari*)."[53] The *Gijin zenshū* (1925–28), Hayashi Takeji's *Tanaka Shōzō* (1974), and Kenneth Strong's *Ox against the Storm*, together with countless popular books on Tanaka—a minor industry in Japan—all take this first line as declaration of a peasant consciousness, albeit to varying degrees. Strong's paraphrased translation of Tanaka's autobiography makes up the first five chapters of his text.[54] But recent Tanaka scholarship has shown much of the autobiography to be rhetorical, anachronistic, or the result of artistic license.

In my reading, the Tanaka that emerges in the autobiography is suspiciously close to the aphorisms of common wisdom and thrift found in Nakamura Keiu's translation of Samuel Smiles's *Self-Help* (*Saikoku risshi hen*), especially those of George Washington and the Duke of Wellington. It is no secret that Tanaka thought highly of the text after having read it in prison in Esashi prefecture (present-day Iwate) from 1870 to 1873. As in the biographies of *Self-Help*, lack of debt and business success is actually something Tanaka boasts about in his autobiography. Yui Masaomi and Shoji Kichirō have separately shown that Tanaka not only made considerable money in land speculation through 1884 but also worked as an official inspector of rural values during the tax rationalization program and had access to inside information. Shoji definitively demonstrates that Tanaka used this information to buy the choicest plots of foreclosed land from farmers unable to adjust to the economics of cash-based taxation. The famous "3,000 yen" used for his "devoted leap" (*hasshin*, 発身) into public service, cited by many biographers as Tanaka's commitment to "the people," came from this money. In the autobiography this commercial success is at once a spur to an entrepreneurial spirit and a lesson on the importance of individual success combined with public service consistent with bourgeois mentalities elsewhere.

Further, Akagami Takeshi has shown that the autobiography's famous "household constitution" was clearly an apocryphal didactic device invented for the Yomiuri readership. Lessons like those in *Self-Help* can be seen in the household constitution's insistence on the avoidance of debt, the decision to rest on Sundays, and the use of liberal democracy to supersede familial relations:

1  Notice of any debts to be posted in the family eating-place, so as to keep every member constantly in mind of them.
2  All household articles to be used for at least three years. Nothing new is to be bought unless it is unavoidable.
3  All members of the family to rest on Sunday.
4  A family council to be held whenever there is a question of any extra expenditure.[55]

My reading is that the autobiography was meant to be a Japanese edition or chapter of *Self-Help*, a "civilization and enlightenment" tale to awaken docile citizens, not a paean to rural values. This makes the irruption of mine pollution in Tanaka's thought (after the floods of 1896) all the more traumatic, as he had formerly been a rural elite supporter of the official civilization and enlightenment project. As such I read the autobiography's first line not as complete praise of the Japanese peasant but as an example of modern potential inherent in *even a mere* "peasant of Shimotsuke" if he or she would cast off the past, awaken to the larger concerns and identities of citizenship, and actualize his or her personal and public autonomy ( *jichi*).[56] Tanaka's 1895 autobiography, then, is far from a simple extension of peasant consciousness and easily fits within the tutelary function of popular rights imagery. Like other Meiji autobiographers, Tanaka berates his sister for trying to heal his sickness by walking around a Shinto shrine, one of several practices he considers backward and unenlightened, a story that when combined with his indigo entrepreneurial efforts is very close to the autobiography of Shibusawa Eiichi, another rural trader who rose to great heights in Meiji Japan.[57]

It is also clear that the immediate context and the target of the autobiography is the contemporary struggle between the Diet and the government over sweetheart land deals in the selling off of public lands to friends of the oligarchy (*haraisage*), especially in newly settled Hokkaido. The bulk of the autobiography describes Tanaka's struggle against the misappropriation of public assets by government (不正), both in the wasteful spending of the house of Rokkaku in the 1860s, and later with a larger fight against the autocratic methods of taxation in the road-building projects of Governor Mishima Michitsune in the 1870s and 1880s.[58] Tanaka's text is an attempt to get the people to care about national politics and protest the narrowness of the government. An interesting quotation from the autobiography taken from the middle of his fight against the house of Rokkaku supports reading the autobiography as tutelary text, showing both the impatience of a teacher and that teacher's belief in the students' potential:

> Here I would like to digress a bit and complain to the reader. . . . I am
> reminded of something regarding the people of Kanto. . . . They
> believe all creation to be tiny and only work to enhance this small
> sphere. They make personal convenience their highest law of living,
> leaving no room for interaction with others from the outside . . . so
> they spend their lives in small spheres, tiny hamlets, forming small
> unions. . . . Such are the people of Kanto—trivial personal concerns,
> weak, feeble, characteristically shallow, falling easily into temptation,
> swept by rumors, captive to cowardice.[59]

The Tanaka that emerges from the autobiography and the zenshū is a loyal member of the Rikken Kaishintō. Like most liberals, he is committed to Japan's modernization along only slightly more democratic lines than those followed by the Meiji state. As we shall see, neither his faith in the local peasant village nor even his environmental thought comes from the pre-Meiji peasant past. Tanaka is not the key transitional figure that enables a mature liberalism to emerge. He is one that highlights the limits of liberalism and its autonomous, private individual to deal with the unprecedented horrors of industrial pollution.

### Pollution's "Wrongfully Dead"

Tanaka's autobiography should be famous for what is not in it. Despite its 1895 date (five years after the first antipollution volunteer groups and four years after Tanaka's questions to the Diet), there is no mention of mine pollution in the text's fifty-four chapters.[60] As we saw in the last chapter, the floods of 1896 were the turning point, as they began to erode faith in liberal politics and the language and ideology of individual compensation. The same floods that led to the ending of the "condolence payments" (*mimaikin*) and the move toward government action in the 1897 Pollution Prevention Order also marked a retreat from the language of laissez-faire individualism in Meiji liberalism. As the scale and scope of the pollution problem crossed Ewald's thresholds of the body and the local, activists began stretching the categories of Meiji liberalism to express the increasingly social and national issues forced into everyone's consciousness by the environmental crisis. Already in Chō Sukeyuki's appeal in 1891 there had been a hint that the pollution problem suggested new links between the masses, the state, and the activists: "The people of the villages and towns of the Watarase[,] are they not Japanese subjects possessing the right to safety and prosperity?" He continues, "With no disparities between us, as humans we are all equal . . . yet strangely we allow a small group of us to be harmed. . . . But this is not something that is happening to 'other people,' because all of the fish in the Watarase below Ashio are dying."[61] As the early Meiji mechanistic theories of discrete causes and effects were replaced with the seeming occult powers of "and . . . and . . . and," it was this linking of people with each other and with nature that, after 1896, became harder and harder to suppress.

In an attempt to account for this complexity, the rhetoric of Meiji liberalism was increasingly supplemented with social (i.e., supra-individual) concepts such as charity, Christian socialism, and Confucian benevolent government. In response to the novelty of modern ecological threats we saw in the last chapter, after 1897 there was a change in the politics of pollution away from a question of public and private distinctions founded in the protection of property rights toward a more holistic understanding of "human life" (*seimei, jinmei*) in all of its material and social aspects.

In his comparative study on the nearly simultaneous emergence of the social question (*sozial Frage*) in Japan and Germany, Erik Grimmer-Solem writes, "'Liberalism,' as defined in the context of Bunmei kaika[,] was in essence the ideal of laissez-faire."[62] This laissez-faire doctrine had taken extreme forms in the early phases of Meiji state building and forced tutelage of the "backward classes," especially during the period of engineered deflation under finance minister Matsukata Masayoshi (1835–1924)—the "Matsukata defure" of 1882–85, a policy of capital accumulation in preparation for industrialization through the transfer of wealth from agriculture to industry. The immediate result of the Matsukata deflation was a spike in the cost of rice: exorbitant rice prices quickly put that staple out of reach for most of the rural population. In the Tokugawa Era, economic distress would have been accompanied by the distribution of *okimai*—rice handouts provided by suppliers and transporters to prevent social unrest. But during the Matsukata deflation, okimai was expressly forbidden as an example of the irrational economics of the Edo period. During the deflation crisis, laissez-faire economic policy was identified with "Enlightenment" itself. As Makihara Norio puts it, "The consequent hardship of free markets was used as a tool to force the people into Enlightenment."[63]

Japan's experience of industrialization was similar to the contemporary experience of Britain and the United States, and so too were the consequences of that industrialization, consequences Grimmer-Solem describes as leading to the "international demise of laissez-faire liberalism": "With that sameness [of Britain and the United States] came common problems: scarce or inadequate housing, large-scale migrations of people, structural and cyclical mass unemployment, industrial accidents and sudden indigence, pollution, toxins and the new diseases they generated, as well as massive trusts and monopolies. In short what emerged was a clash between the individual rights of private property and public welfare. Associative liberalism was revealing its limits everywhere."[64] In Britain this problem led to the rise of "welfare economics." Founded by Alfred Marshall of Cambridge University, welfare economics was designed to "curb the excesses of competitive individualism associated with the rise of urban, industrial civilization."[65] In Japan the search for new social knowledge begun in this period would eventually lead to the establishment of the Ōhara Institute for Social Research, based largely on similar studies in the West, most notably by the social policy experts of the German historical school of economics, whose members included Gustav von Schmoller, Lujo Brentano, Werner Sombart, and Max Weber.

These excesses of liberal capitalism, and the Ashio Incident in particular, were also the motive for countless private charity and relief organizations, many of which grew out of Christian socialist temperance and antiprostitution movements. Others spontaneously formed in relation to specific problems of modern Japan, such as urban poverty, pollution, orphans, and countless others.[66] One such group was the Ashio Incident Society (Ashio jiken enzetsukai), organized by Tsuda Sen and Diet member Shimada Saburō, which was attended by Abe Isoo, Kinoshita Naoe, and a young Kawakami Hajime. Kawakami reportedly donated his coat after being moved by one speech. Though the exact reason is not known, the wife of Ashio owner Furukawa Ichibei committed suicide by jumping from a bridge into the Kanda River in downtown Tokyo after attending one of these lectures. Matsumoto Eiko herself had traveled to the polluted lands as part of the Mine-Polluted Lands Women's Salvation Society, whose members included Shimada Saburō's wife, Nobuko. The group also organized clothing and fund-raising drives in Tokyo and recruited a nurse to treat over twenty patients on a day-trip to Tochigi in winter 1902. Within these and other new relief groups, there also appeared increasing invocations of benevolent government as part of a larger trend of trying to soften the edges of industrial modernity—a trend also seen in a move away from the early optimism of the Shimotsuke Liberal League to more urgent, mass protests, directed at Tokyo, arguing for the closure of the Ashio mine.

According to the traditional ideology of benevolent government (*jinsei*), when the lord was unable or unwilling to control greed from harming the body politic, peasants would enact benevolence on their own through uprisings (*ikki*) and even occasionally house smashings (*uchikowashi*). In the late 1890s, the pollution victims did in fact begin mass marches on Tokyo. Starting out from a "pollution headquarters" at the Buddhist temple Unryūji, near the confluence of the Watarase and Tone Rivers, these marches were less a peasant remnant than political theater, consciously deploying the pre-Meiji symbols of benevolent government as a rebuke to the damage to the public good caused by private industry. There were four of these marches beginning in 1897, and the largest (nearly ten thousand strong) turned violent and bloody when marchers were attacked by civil and military police at the Watarase crossing at Kawamata on February 12, 1900. For this fateful last march in 1900, protesters dressed in Edo Era peasant clothing and carried *ikki* banners. The performative and symbolic nature of the peasant tropes used is especially clear in planning documents in which Tanaka insisted on having precisely 1,064 marchers who would stand in for the exact number of victims identified by the mortality surveys examined in the last chapter. To see the change in the ideology of protest and Tanaka's own thought, we should compare this march with an earlier march in 1898, when Tanaka persuaded marchers to turn around by arguing that fellow Progressive Party member Okuma Shigenobu was in the government and thus the chance for peaceful, political compromise was high. It is likely also no coincidence that the Kawamata march, by exceeding the accepted ideology of social protest, not only led to a deepening of despair and urgency on the part of the victims but also turned very violent.

Indeed, not all liberals were pleased with this turn toward moral economy symbolism in the antipollution protests. Fukuzawa Yukichi explicitly denounced the use of "straw raincoats" and "ikki banners" in an editorial in May 1897. He insisted that the only legitimate way to protest was to sue for monetary compensation in court. Fukuzawa remained firmly committed to the categories of liberal political philosophy, seeing the Ashio crisis as a question of property rights and therefore a matter of civil society, not politics. From this formal perspective he declares the end of the Ashio affair:

> The disposal of the matter of the Ashio mine mineral poisoning [the 1897 Pollution Prevention Order] was published yesterday. . . . Since the method of preventing the damage and so forth are the result of studies of committee men appointed by the government and are drafted by technological specialists who are responsible for measures to prevent the pollution and are approved by the government as proper, the matter now ends, being unable to be changed at all. . . . The government can be said to have carried out its responsibility because the government has done what it could within its jurisdiction. Accordingly, if the people of the afflicted area could not leave the damage as it stands and would ask compensation, they should only sue in court. And if the proprietor of the mine could not obey the instruction, he should also appeal to the law and ask for justice. . . . It is all permissible if there is no illegal behavior, but if the speech meeting were not peaceful *or if there were a certain type of atmosphere leading to instigating a demonstration with bamboo spears and straw mat*

*flags,* or if there were behavior threatening others by the power of the mob, the government should disperse them decisively and unsparingly.[67]

The narrowness and inadequacy of the standard categories of Meiji ideology are here forced into the open—and into a dead end. A dead end Fukuzawa explicitly acknowledges. But, of course, in announcing the end of the matter, Fukuzawa was not only wrong in the legal, political, and economic sense that he intended. His retrenchment of classic liberalism in the face of a new crisis already lagged behind the understanding of environmental crisis as a more fundamental existential threat held by Tanaka and the Ashio activists. As the Ashio Incident worsened in the last years of the nineteenth century, it was not Tanaka's social protest but Fukuzawa's formal liberalism that was revealed as antiquated and exhausted. Fukuzawa was, however, correct in his prediction of increasing state violence against the Ashio protesters in the years to come.

But if activists such as Matsumoto Eiko had already grasped pollution as a social-level problem, why do Tanaka's letters and speeches of this period show what seems at first glance to be a classic liberal fixation on single, private individuals harming the public, such as in his focus on mine owner Furukawa Ichibei as the sole instigator of their suffering? In a memorandum (*chūigaki*) to all protesters on February 6, 1897, Tanaka wrote:

> Every day the mine pollution destroys both property and rights. One must surely realize that many people are being robbed of their Heaven-granted lives (*tenpu seimei*) by a single merchant. Anyone observing this [sad state] cannot merely stand by and do nothing. Indeed, just last autumn, once the victims finally awakened from their bewilderment and petitioned as one for the closing of the mine, it caused a great stir and not a little distress to Furukawa. That is when he started bribing politicians and even some of the local people. This is not to mention that his money pollutes even the journalists' newspapers. That said, the needs of a single merchant cannot be allowed to make victims out of a large number of citizens.[68]

The overdetermined nature of the phrase "a single merchant" conceals tensions and possibilities of this language of benevolent government in light of the environmental crisis. For example, "the needs of a single merchant," part of the Ashio protest vocabulary since at least 1890, could be seen as merely a naive peasant refusal to recognize the benefit of Furukawa copper to Japan's industrial development. Modernization theorists would say—and have said—just that. "The needs of a single merchant" could also be assimilated to a crude utilitarian calculus that saw the many harmed by the few. This, too, is part of it. But this phrase is also code for Tokugawa Era benevolent government, where the sovereign had a responsibility not only to avoid tyranny but also to regulate the merchants so they would not damage the public good through hoarding, price-fixing, or usury.[69] When the government was unable to control a merchant, the peasants would attempt to censure him themselves.[70] But a redeployment of this vocabulary in the 1890s, especially in light of its coincidence with charity work, relief organizations, and Christian socialism, should not necessarily be seen as an antimodern move to premodern forms, or a retreat to an indigenous nonmodern culture. It should, I argue, be seen as an attempt to use and adapt the resources of the past to confront a rapidly changing present. Raymond Williams called this use of the past the "residual," in which "certain experiences, meanings, and values which cannot be expressed or substantially verified in terms of the dominant culture, are nevertheless lived and practised on the basis of the residue."[71] Before ascribing the eruption of peasant moral economy in industrializing Meiji to an Orientalist identification of premodern Japan with nature, we would do well to remember that Alfred Marshall called his new school of welfare economics "chivalrous capitalism."[72]

Controlling the excesses of runaway capitalism with the Confucian concept of benevolent government is the central tenet of Tanaka's "national death" theory (bōkokuron, 亡国論), developed in his famous Diet speeches, which Strong famously summarized as "To kill the people is to kill the nation!" For Tanaka the death of the public is the result of the prevalence of bribery (wairo) or the dominance of private property (money) that prevents the actualization of the democratic promise latent in both the popular rights movement and the Meiji constitution. In Tanaka's "national death," "Japan" has ceased to exist because the government has been completely overrun by the private power of the Furukawa zaibatsu. The Kawamata Incident and subsequent trials and convictions of the marchers for "riotous assembly" were evidence of this. In the middle of one of his speeches, Tanaka denounced the police as servants of private gain and dared them to come and arrest him for treason, telling them that if they were reluctant to break legislative immunity by arresting him on the Diet floor, he would give them the address of the place where he would be staying that night. At the end of his speech, faced with proof of the deadly nature and source of the pollution but prevented from legally protesting because of the selfishness and corruption of the government, Tanaka asked, only partly rhetorically, "What are we supposed to do?"[73]

For Tanaka, the rot and corruption of bribery had penetrated into the people's very hearts and killed the promise of a public Japan, replacing it with formal structures that exploited the rhetoric of freedom but actually ruled by selfish, private gain (kanemōkeshugi, 金儲主義 or kairakushugi, 快楽主義). Because of this, the polluted lands, which now included parts of Tochigi, Gumma, Ibaraki, and Saitama, were "lawless regions" outside the reach of the constitution. Far from meaning "unruly," here "lawless" meant they were not afforded the rights and privileges of the constitution, and in this sense the "national death" speeches of 1900 were the equivalent of the total breakdown of law and community seen in Matsumoto's Sufferings. In a letter to antipollution activist Kawamata Kyūhei dated February 12, 1900, Tanaka included a poem on bōkoku, complete with a sketch of a dancing skeleton near a pile of corpses set upon by dogs and demons (fig. 2.1). Tanaka titled the drawing "The Mark of National Death" (bōkoku no ato).[74]

It was from within these "lawless regions" of the poisoned villages of the Watarase and Tone watersheds, when he moved into the doomed village of Yanaka (see chapter 3), that Tanaka would eventually rethink the relationship of nature, rights, and practice. As with the English radicalism and social reform movements in Europe, Tanaka's "national death" speeches show a groping search for new articulations of modern community, justice, and "publicness" (kōkyō, 公共). The increasingly desperate search for a solution to the pollution problem pushed two largely incompatible vocabularies further toward their final aporia in the jikiso, which tried and failed to bridge conceptual gaps between individual laissez-faire and the social problem–inspired corrective of benevolent government. The resulting collapse in the failure of the jikiso led the way to reconsideration of nature and rights not captured by Meiji natural rights theory.

By 1900, the growing existential threat of the Ashio crisis was producing frantic experimentation in political rhetoric and tactics in an attempt to redeem the suffering. In what should be considered a Confucian analogue to Engels's "social murder," the activists began calling pollution victims himei no shisha. This term, hi-mei, is a negative form signifying the opposite, or absence, of the Confucian ten-mei, or "Heaven's decree," meaning something akin to "fate." The concept of tenmei developed in the Analects and the Mencius says that life and death are regulated by tenmei. Occasionally the concept is equated with a hard fate that cannot be changed, as when the Mencius says, "That which is done without man's doing is from Heaven. That

FIGURE 2.1. A *bōkoku* sketch from Tanaka's diary: "The spirit in the hearts of governance, justice, and law has died / There are those eaten by dogs / and those reduced to dancing skeletons / All that remains for the starving survivors is death / The mark of bōkoku." *Bōkoku* (亡国) means "national death" and is also a satiric pun on "motherland" (母国, *bokoku*). Source: Tanaka Shōzō, *Tanaka Shōzō senshū*, edited by Anzai Kunio, Kanai Masanao, Komatsu Hiroshi, Sakaya Junji, and Yui Masaomi (Tokyo: Iwanami shoten, 1989), 3:256.

which happens without man's causing is from the decree of Heaven."[75] But more often tenmei represents a higher "natural" process or fate, in contrast to a lower, "artificial" one. At the level of the temple schools (*terakoya*), which produced the leaders of the antipollution movement, the Confucian tenmei was often mixed with Taoist principles that say human activity should not be allowed to interfere with what Heaven has granted. It is also clear that this *ten* is also the *ten* of natural rights theory, translated into Japanese as "Heaven-granted rights" (*ten-pu jinken*).[76] The implication of referring to pollution victims as *himei no shisha* is clear: Meiji policy, by allowing the continued polluting of the Watarase by "a single merchant," had robbed the people of something that had been decreed by Heaven, something supposed to be above governmental policy. For this reason I translate *himei no shisha* as "the wrongfully dead" and further mark it as the beginning of Japan's environmental turn. As such, "the wrongfully dead" of the mortality surveys point toward a new politics that links the concept of rights to the instability of the environment and reintegrates material nature and its complex relations into a new theory of human health and freedom.

### At the Limits of Liberalism

In the ideology of the peasant protest, the final move to self-sacrificial, direct, out-of-channels appeal (jikiso) can come only when the system has failed. It is a last-resort, desperate attempt to restart the system. Throughout 1901, following the guilty verdict of "riotous assembly" against the farmers who marched in the Kawamata Incident, the mood turned to deep despair for Tanaka, Kōtoku, and activist attorney Ishikawa Hanzan. Ishikawa's diary records a meeting with Tanaka and Kōtoku in which he reportedly suggested to Tanaka, "There is nothing left but for you to become Sakura Sōgo."[77] It was around this time that Tanaka's diary also records a sense of a dead end for the antipollution movement and a strong martyr self-image at work. Perhaps the decision had already been made:

> *Normal governance of the villages and towns has been destroyed. . . .*
> Before the power of [Furukawa] Ichibei there is no Ministry of
> Agriculture, no Home Ministry. And so the mountains are lost, the
> rivers ruined; [he] is handed the rivers and destroys them. At the same
> time, the fields and land are quickly ruined and the people murdered.
> The Home Ministry does not prevent this; rather, it makes it worse.
> How do we preserve the constitution? That is the question.
> Shōzō alone speaks; what to do? Am I to do it?[78]

A key Tanaka diary entry shows a conflicted Sakura consciousness not only reaching new heights but also clearly exceeding the ideological constraints of Sakura's civilization and enlightenment representation. In a typically disjointed diary entry in February 1900 we find,

> Sakura Sogorō achieved his goal through death—although he did not
> become a spirit (*rei*) [haunting others]. Looking around at the poisoned

villages where even the women are killed [I go] in place of Sōgo's [*sic*] life and even his death to appeal [on behalf of] the people.

18,400 victims. 1,064 poisoned to death. These people have souls (*rei*). Among the victims there are probably even those who do not know they are being poisoned; yet they too have souls. Could this wretched state ever be redeemed even if [Sōgo] were to be born and sacrifice himself seven times? One thousand dead does not seem to have been enough. But these one thousand whom we have killed with pollution, their ghosts (*yūrei*) will surely haunt us. In place of Sakura Sōgo's life, and death.[79]

The beginning of this entry shows early Meiji liberals' uneasiness with the "fictive elements" of vengeful spirits characteristic of the more theatrical productions of *Sakura gimin den*. Like Fukuzawa and Komurō, Tanaka prefers the rational Sakura. Yet the mine pollution had already produced 1,064 martyrs to the national cause, with no redemption. By the end of the entry, Tanaka reveals profound doubt that this sanitized, national Sakura of representative Diet members is up to the task of redeeming the unprecedented suffering of the Watarase valley farmers dying from industrial poisoning. The ghosts of the past have not been completely purged. There is a sense that something of this tragedy will remain behind and haunt the survivors, as the 1,064 victims become a kind of ghost or spirit (*yūrei*) in the present.

A textual analysis of the jikiso document itself reveals the deep contradictions of Meiji society and illuminates the crisis in post–popular rights ideology in the face of the late Meiji crisis of relationship between public and private brought on by the pollution problem. We can actually see this aporia in the jikiso text itself. As a text, it includes two literary forms of remonstration, each with its own internal logic, rhetorical devices, and political subjectivity: the "petition" form (*seigantai*) and the "appeal" form (*aisotai*)—the Edo Era form of a pure jikiso. A petition, by far the more popular form of Meiji remonstration, is wholly written in Chinese characters (*kanbun* or *kakikudashibun*) and takes the liberals' natural rights as its internal logic. The appeal, by contrast, is written in the person-to-person *sōrōbun* literary style reserved for letters and individual correspondence. As such, it is a much more emotional and personal form of writing. The internal logic of the appeal is the personal benevolent government of the "people's emperor" (*ikkun-banmin*). Though not written in the epistolary *sōrōbun* (the most obvious quality of an appeal), the jikiso includes other elements characteristic of the appeal. One is the quality and quantity of honorific speech (*keigo*). Both forms, the natural rights petition and the benevolent government appeal, are used in Tanaka's appeal, which means the nature of rights, the perceived locus of sovereignty, and the subject position of the petitioner are unstable and ultimately untenable. Like mine pollution, sovereignty seemed to exist between the categories of Meiji political philosophy.

The hybrid quality of Tanaka and Kōtoku's text is clear if we compare it to ideal examples of both the petition and the appeal. Comparing Kōno Hironaka's 1879 (*seigantai*) petition for the opening of a national assembly with Matsuzawa Kyūsaku's 1880 (*aisotai*) appeal for the same shows the different use of honorific speech at work. Both texts were submitted to the Executive Council but were addressed to the emperor. Matsuzawa's appeal begins: "As representatives of over 21,530 deeply faithful citizens, your subjects Matsuzawa Kyūsaku and Kōedo Sadanosuke, in fear and reverence, in fear and humility, respectfully, obediently (*tonshu tonshu*), under pain of death, face death and prostrate ourselves below the imperial palace, we courteously request our esteemed, sagely, powerful and lettered (*bunbu*) Imperial Majesty to permit the establishment of a national assembly."[80] Kōno's petition simply reads: "Japanese citizens Kataoka Kenkichi and Kōno Hironaka, *fearing not the august dignity* (*songen o osorezu*), respectfully and reverently make a request of our imperial majesty."[81]

Kōno's text uses the polite speech for making a general request, not the emperor-specific *keigo* of Matsuzaka's appeal. The extensive use of honorific speech in Matsuzawa's piece highlights an important ideological difference between the two forms. In the petition, the word "government" may be substituted for "imperial majesty" without disrupting the meaning of the text. To do this in the appeal would be strange at best and nonsensical at worst— especially given the phrase *bunbu*.[82] This, together with its epistolary sōrōbun style, emphasizes the difference in the relation of the emperor to the government. The petition addresses the emperor as an organ of the government, whereas the appeal addresses the individual personality of one in a succession of Japanese emperors. Kōno's text uses the logic of natural rights, placing the imperial will secondary to the general will and therefore rendering it as something not to be feared. Kōno's petition continues: "The citizens of Japan have wished for a national assembly for some time. They are born of Heaven, grasping the liberty that Heaven has granted them; it has given them enormous abilities, and through it they enjoy the greatest joys." The petition builds from individual natural rights that are ultimately expressed in the general will. Sovereignty is based in the people, and the emperor is obligated to comply. This is more a demand than a request.

In Matsuzawa's appeal the imperial will takes center stage. In comparison to the petition based on natural rights, the appeal seems an anachronism guaranteeing servility, but there is much more going on in the political philosophy and rhetorical strategies of the appeal.[83] The imperial will in an appeal is not that of the current emperor alone, but the will of the imperial institution manifested in the succession of emperors (*ressei*) since the legendary founder Jimmu (660–585 BCE). The will of these emperors is further known to be "the happiness of the people." This is the "people's emperor" (*ikkun-banmin*) theory developed in Tokugawa nativism (*kokugaku*), where it was used as a subversive ideology in opposition to the Tokugawa shogunate's division of society into ruler and ruled. In "people's emperor" ideology, all are equal before the emperor, and all are due the great happiness flowing from the imperial house. This egalitarian impulse also figured in early popular rights salons in Tanaka's Tochigi, where the nativism of the Hirata Atsutane school was especially influential.[84]

In Matsuzawa's text the imperial will is specified further by reference to the founding document of the Meiji Ishin, the Charter Oath of 1868, in which the emperor proclaimed that "deliberative assemblies will be established." The Charter Oath makes the imperial will a matter of public record that may not be revoked, something along the lines of the pope speaking ex cathedra. As a contemporary expression had it, "The Emperor's words are like sweat: once out they are impossible to put back in."[85] So the rhetorical strategy of Matsuzawa's appeal is to show that the emperor has bad advisers (the oligarchy) who are blocking the actualization of the imperial will, which is a known quantity—the safety and happiness of the people.

Matsuzawa's emphasis on actualizing the imperial will also appears in the jikiso.[86] Though not written in sōrōbun, the jikiso is in many ways an appeal. In the address it is clear that the addressee is not an official organ of the government but an individual and personal emperor (*jinkakuteki tennō*):

Your lowly and humble subject, Tanaka Shōzō, in fear and trembling, reverently and respectfully submits this appeal. Humbly, even though a mere commoner, this subject dares to transgress the boundaries and break the law by approaching the imperial carriage, a crime punishable by death. Yet, resigned to this, and mindful only of the plight of the nation's people, it is suddenly clear that the current state of affairs can no longer be endured.

Humbly, I beseech you, in your majesty's profound benevolence and boundless compassion, have pity on this subject's great transgression, and deign to grant (*tamonau*) the reading of this appeal.

The use of the verb "deign to grant" (*tamonau*), a sense of criminality, the inevitability of death, the personal feeling, and the use of honorifics only used when addressing the emperor (少く乙夜の覧を垂れ給はんとを) all mark this text as an appeal to the personality of an individual emperor.

After describing the misery brought on by the mine pollution, Tanaka and Kōtoku invoke the obligation of the emperor to ensure the happiness of his people. They also reproduce the "bad advisers" thesis used in Matsuzawa's text:

Ah, must we not say that this suffering is a stain on your enlightened rule? But in truth it is the government officials who have neglected their office as leaders.

The land of these four prefectures, is it not of your majesty's house? The people of the four prefectures, are they not your majesty's children? The government officials have cast your majesty's land and people into this horrible condition. Though falling into this sad state, the government has not even begun to reflect on this matter, and so, this subject can no longer remain silent.

But the jikiso's proposed solution to this problem is an impossible juxtaposition of people's-emperor benevolence and Heaven-granted, rights-based constitutionalism. In short, the jikiso concludes by calling on the transcendental sovereign of the people's-emperor ideology as a means to actualize natural rights theory:

I believe the government officials carry the blame for this, and so *there is nothing left but for your majesty to unleash the great blessing and morality of the imperial house*. The water of the Watarase River must be made pure again; that is first. The damaged areas of the river must be repaired and the river itself must be restored to its former state; that is second. The severely poisoned earth must be removed; that is third. The bountiful living things of the riverbanks must be restored; that is fourth. The many degraded towns and villages must be rebuilt; that is fifth. The polluting mine must be closed so that the issuance of poisoned waste and poisoned water may be once and for all stopped at its source;[87] that is sixth. In this way countless souls will be saved from a death sentence; their populations restored, the villages may escape extinction by death and emigration.

*Only then shall we see the full realization of the laws and constitution of our Japanese empire.*[88]

This construction, "that is first," "that is second," is from the *seigantai* petition form. It appears verbatim in Kōno's petition for the establishment of a national assembly, and as such the petition makes those demands from the subject position of free citizens possessing natural rights. These items are not requests—they are demands for the realization of constitutional protections, and clearly not "strict constructionist" ones at that. The fact that the Meiji constitution was "handed down" from the emperor to the people actually works with the appeal's logic, whereas it works against the petition's logic, which is based on the sovereignty of the people. Even so, the demands here cannot be said to be fully compatible with the imperial will in the specific historical moment of late Meiji. This is especially true given that the Meiji emperor was publicly identified with the "encouragement of industry" and the "rich nation, strong army" ideologies that needed the Ashio mine's copper. An anti-mine appeal to the imperial will does not work if the emperor is publicly aligned with the very ideology that led to the pollution deaths. At best the jikiso, in explicitly calling for the mine's closure, pitted two incompatible expressions of the imperial will against each other, merely creating yet another contradiction in Meiji ideology, one that installed the emperor as simultaneously a vehicle of "restoration" and "modernization."[89]

Though the liberals' calls for a constitution in the 1870s and 1880s did use the language of inalienable natural rights, the Meiji constitution used the language of conferred rights and a sacred and inviolable emperor. The ambiguity of Tanaka's appeal is the ambiguity of the constitution and of Japanese modernity. The appeal is so far from a last peasant protest, or even the signaling of a final "tectonic shift" from early modern to modern social or political forms,[90] that we must entertain the possibility that neither Tanaka nor Kōtoku Shūsui is misrecognizing the situation. In fact, we could say that they saw, or at least unconsciously expressed, better than anyone the ambiguities of Meiji political philosophy and the lack of a vocabulary to talk about systemic problems (such as industrial pollution). A year after the failed appeal, Kōtoku abandoned his emperor-based socialism in favor of a Marxist understanding of society, and Tanaka made his break with Meiji liberalism to develop a radical environmental politics (see chapter 3). But in

December 1901, neither was able to find the space within the Meiji framework to make his point.

## The Search for New Social Forms after 1901

This search for new social forms can be seen in reactions to the jikiso as well. In an editorial in the Christian socialist paper *Rikugō zasshi* on January 15, 1902, Tanaka's friend and later biographer, Kinoshita Naoe (1869–1937), condemned Tanaka's jikiso for its acknowledgment of a coexistence of constitutional government and a transcendental emperor. Kinoshita was concerned that the emperor might indeed have this much power and that using it was not something to be encouraged. "I am not certain if Shōzō's appeal is illegal or not. Nonetheless, I must say that it is clearly a fearful threat to our constitutional system."[91] Kinoshita was alarmed to see the great display of sympathy for Tanaka's actions. For him it indicated that the transition to modernity was incomplete—that Edo Era sensibilities remaining in the Japanese people were preventing social advancement and improvement along Christian socialist lines.[92] Kinoshita calls for a "true democracy" of participatory politics, suggesting that Japanese citizens need to take back the government in the same way (as he saw it) that New Yorkers had recently eliminated corruption from Tammany Hall.[93]

While Kinoshita's article criticizes the Edo ideology at work in the jikiso as a premodern handicap that needs to be overcome, the *Nihonjin* editorial on the jikiso by Tanaka's future friend and Meiji Swedenborgian thinker Arai Ōsui on January 1, 1902, "Seeing the Crime, Knowing Its Benevolence," criticizes modern society with the resources of the past.[94] Arai's piece praises Tanaka's sense of benevolence and community in attempting to take it upon himself to redeem the polluted land and save its people. But there is also a partial quotation of a famous passage from the *Mencius* that has some interesting possible interpretations. Arai quotes, "Mencius said, 'Here is a man who receives charge of the cattle and sheep of another, and undertakes to feed them for him. Of course he must search for pasture and grass for them. If, after searching for those, he cannot find them, will he return his charge to the owner? Or will he stand by and see them die?'"[95]

On the face of it this quotation is another instance of the "bad advisers" attack on the government, and there is no question that this is part of it, but there is also a strong potential for an oblique criticism of the emperor. Readers of this piece would have been familiar with the rest of this story and could easily have supplied its conclusion on their own. The unquoted portion continues when the governor, K'ung Chü-hsin, confronted by Mencius with the inadequate care of the flock, takes responsibility for his failure to provide for them. He responds, "Herein I am guilty." Then the story concludes: "Another day, Mencius had an audience with the king, and said to him, 'Of the governors of your Majesty's cities I am acquainted with five, but the only one of them who knows his faults is K'ung Chü-hsin.' He then repeated the conversation to the king, who said, 'In this matter, I am the guilty one.'"[96] The unquoted but readily available portion chastises not only the emperor but also the very path and practice of Japanese modernity. (Matsumoto Eiko recounted a similar story, written in December 1901, of a king entrusted with the care and feeding of his flock. Her story, titled "A Child's Tale," was included in the 1902 reissue of *Sufferings*: "a certain wise king of England" successfully provides for his constituents, leading to happiness and prosperity.) Like Kinoshita's editorial, Arai's article ends with a call for a new society of benevolent individuals imbued with a social conscience.

Arai's piece, like Matsuzawa's before it, shows how the seemingly irrational and anachronistic logic of the people's emperor ideology can become subversive. Unlike the natural rights–based petition of formally held, abstract rights, there is an emphasis on the actual performance of safety and happiness in the people's emperor political philosophy, which judges the current emperor against an ideal.[97] Both Kinoshita and Arai decry the lack of a functioning society, and both end their pieces with vague calls for the establishment of a genuine community of human beings against the rot of pleasure-seeking profiteers who have created pockets of extreme misery and distress. And not coincidentally, both articles are occasioned by the jikiso's failed attempt to resolve the pollution crisis.

Still, the logic of a successful jikiso does not contain such a subversive outcome—but a *failed* jikiso does. The ideal type of the jikiso's cultural form is not exactly the same as either the petition or the appeal. It belongs to the Confucian ideology of Edo Era benevolent government and historically specific structures of political economy. In response to an unbearable situation, peasants would select a martyr who would illegally appeal out of channels to a transcendental outsider for redress, bypassing local officials and appealing either to the domainal officials in Edo or, in the extreme, directly to the shogun. The goal of the jikiso is conservative. It is meant to return things to the *status quo ante*, usually meaning the repeal of new taxes or edicts, as in the Sakura legend. The goal is also to restore the harmony between "benevolent lords and honorable peasants,"[98] ensuring a smooth functioning of village life. Restoration of a village's lost harmony is the ideo-logical complement to political-economic structures behind the recurring phrase "[granting this request] will allow us to continue as peasants," which Stephen Vlastos highlighted in his study of peasant protest.[99] The jikiso form is therefore severely handicapped in dealing with new and emerging problems. Like the emergence of mine pollution in the valley, the irruption of the martyr necessarily ruins this harmony, even as he is trying to restore it. His very existence becomes anathema to his goal, hence the requirement that the martyr be put to death, and coconspirators banished, even when the complaint is just and the appeal successful in restoring benevolent gov-ernment to the village. This is also the reason that help must come from outside the immediate lord-peasant relationship. Help must come from one who may return to absence.

In all of these requirements, Tanaka failed to reproduce the ideal cultural form of a jikiso. That he stumbled and never reached the imperial carriage is perhaps a perfect metaphor for the entire event. Not only did he fail to hand over his appeal, but he also was not killed. He was certainly unable to re-store benevolent government, as there was none to restore. Instead there was a constitutional monarchy governed by the abstract and formal rule of law. Tanaka's being declared sane and his anticlimactic release the follow-ing morning are further proof of this. Perhaps most damning, a jikiso was not even illegal in 1901. The only possible crime Tanaka could have been charged with was *lèse-majesté*, or "lack of respect." Even those hostile to Tanaka could not deny that this was not the case. Indeed, as Kinoshita's editorial warned, the jikiso actually accorded more power and respect to the emperor than he legally held according to the constitution.[100]

Despite occasional invocation of a transcendental emperor to bypass the Diet in fiscal matters, the Meiji emperor was a constitutional monarch of specific privileges and duties enshrined in the constitution. Thus he could not fulfill the role of transcendent guarantor of social harmony demanded in the jikiso. Despite Tanaka's statement in the December 20 *Kokkei shinbun*, the gimin is not able to "single-handedly" force a resolution—the gimin re-quires a partner. The ambiguous position of both petitioner and emperor in the jikiso text itself precludes this mutual determination. The emperor did not fulfill his role.[101] Tanaka, the would-be martyr, lacked a transcendent outsider who could complete the equation. Accordingly, after six months of waiting for an imperial rescript closing the Ashio mine, Tanaka planned an-other jikiso, this time to the foreign embassies in Japan, to tackle pollution as a "crisis of humanity" (*jindō*), one which "through rot and immorality our government and Furukawa Ichibei have failed to address."[102] Tanaka was still looking for that transcendent outsider who could redeem modernity.

In the end, Tanaka did not make an appeal to the foreign embassies. Instead he made a different move, one that marginalized both emperor and nation: "I have finally awakened to the folly of appealing to this government—there is nothing left to do but to appeal to Heaven itself."[103] It is surely no coincidence that this radical turn to nature (*ten*) itself comes at precisely the moment in a kabuki play when the vengeful spirits appear and effect a final resolution to the crisis. But just as Tanaka feared in his diary musings on the spirit of Sakura and the ghosts of the pollution victims, no divine judgment arrived. In the end, the solution was neither simple nor supernatural. Liberal political protest gave way to a new practice of aligning human life with an active nature (*tennen*), an environmental turn in which a nature existed as the ultimate guarantor of human freedom, above the nation and beyond industrial capitalism.

# THREE

# NATURE OVER NATION

*Tanaka Shōzō's Environmental Turn*

Levels of a *human consciousness of nature* are wounded and awakened which undermine the dualism of body and spirit, or nature and humankind. In the threat, people have the experience that they breathe like plants, and live *from* water as the fish live *in* water. The toxic threat makes them sense that they participate with their bodies in things—"a metabolic process with consciousness and morality"—and consequently, that they can be eroded like the stones and the trees in the acid rain.

—ULRICH BECK, *Risk Society*

Matsumoto Eiko left Japan for San Francisco soon after publication of her exposé of the horrors of industrial pollution in the Watarase and Tone watersheds. In 1902, shortly after the failure of his appeal to the emperor, Tanaka Shōzō began documenting what he called "river pilgrimages" (*kasen junshi nikki*), a series of his own exhaustive investigations of the polluted landscapes. Reconstructing his travels from his letters and diaries, it is estimated that by his death in 1913 Tanaka and his assistant, Yanaka village resident Shimada Sōzō, had walked or floated the entire Watarase, including its tributaries—a distance of over 1,900 kilometers, roughly the distance from Aomori to Kyūshū or Dallas to Los Angeles. These investigations confirmed and expanded his understanding of the mutual penetration of humans and nature and transformed Tanaka from a Meiji liberal to an environmental activist. Tanaka based his new political thought on "the real powers of the land and water" (*chi no ikioi, mizu no ikioi*), eventually developing a monistic philosophy of poison (*doku*) and flow (*nagare*) that took free-flowing water as the model of health and freedom. Though expressed in the neo-Confucian vocabulary of principles (*ri*) and essences (*sei*) reminiscent of the Tokugawa *shizenron* tradition, Tanaka's thought broke from that tradition by denying the infinite fecundity of nature and identifying doku as a conceptual and historical intervention in the relations between humans and nature. In the process, like nature itself, the older Tokugawa thought was fundamentally transformed with the inclusion of doku. In Tanaka's modern version of the Tokugawa tradition, complete trust in nature is abandoned in favor of a mutual relation—a nature-society metabolism—that must be constantly managed in order to prevent the accumulation of poison and to ensure an accumulation of freedom.

From the beginning Tanaka's environmental philosophy was developed and given material expression in his fight against the Meiji state's second Pollution Prevention Committee of 1902. Unlike the largely reactive and defensive First Committee of 1897, the second committee's proposals sought no less than the complete reengineering of the Kanto plain. In what was to become the centerpiece of Tanaka's thought and activism, the Second plan called for the purchase and destruction of Yanaka village to clear the way for the construction of a flood-control reservoir near the confluence of the Watarase and Tone Rivers. As he increasingly linked humans and nature as two moments of a material economy of flows, Tanaka documented how the state's projects inevitably spilled over into and flowed through the social world. In fighting the committee, Tanaka theorized that the state's attempt to restrict what he considered an inherently active nature was not only doomed to fail. It also would lead to further violence against nature and eventually people in a series of increasingly costly, autocratic, and ultimately disastrous engineering projects. In Tanaka's view, both tendencies—bad environmental policy and political repression—came together in the state's destruction of Yanaka village in 1907. For him, Yanaka represented the ecological and social metastasizing of the environmental crisis.

Tanaka's investigations in the wake of the failed *jikiso* show a turn toward an active nature as the necessary source of human freedom, a basis for politics different from both the state and capitalism. He rejected the state's environmental engineering projects as merely a new, higher form of Meiji rationalism's separation and containment of humans and nature. Instead Tanaka proposed a new practice of nature, *Yanakagaku* (Yanaka studies, literally Yanaka-ology), based on a new model of the human body. Tanaka's new political subject was built on the acceptance of a permeable body open to

nature and in constant congress with its flows. Yanakagaku sought a new organization of nature, body, and rights designed to ensure the reversal of the
destruction and oppression caused by the reengineering of nature. He
would later call the state's forced rationalization of nature a "civilization of
roads." In its place the new model of the subject as an "unleasher of flows"
would practice "natural water management" (*chisui*), leading to a new social
organization, an ecologically sound and egalitarian "civilization of rivers."

## The Second Pollution Prevention Committee of 1902

Despite the unprecedented mobilization of private and state power in the
late 1890s, the pollution problem only seemed to worsen and spread. As
toxic flooding reached even Tokyo, the environmental crisis was causing
problems the state could not afford to ignore, including the problem many
Meiji leaders found most alarming: the number of rural youths who failed
their physicals for military service.[1] In response to the continuing crisis in
1902 the state commissioned a second Pollution Prevention Committee to
have another try at dealing with the environmental crisis. The massiveness
of this new attempt is nothing less than the state's move from a reactive *containment* nature to an active *production of* nature.[2] (From 1900 to 1930 the
dams, levees, and concrete river bottoms built in Japan would displace more
earth than the contemporary Panama Canal.) In producing its own nature,
a nature that would behave, the committee was anxious to simplify and rationalize the complex causal nexus that had successfully resisted the 1897
committee's attempts to isolate and contain.[3] As we saw, the first Pollution
Prevention Committee in 1897 had issued an "order" directly to the individual Furukawa Ichibei, "owner-operator of the Ashio Copper Mine." It focused on technological improvements to the mine's infrastructure designed
to police the boundaries of the industrial and natural environments as well
as the boundaries between competing property rights. The second Pollution Prevention Committee was altogether different. Far from an order to
an individual, in 1902 the state took responsibility for the administration of
the entire watershed. In taking control of the Tone and Watarase Rivers, the
committee drew its authority from the 1896 River Law, which allowed the
Home Minister jurisdiction over any river that "had a strong effect on the
benefits or harm to the public good" or "when such riverine/riparian construction's harms or benefits do not coincide with any one prefecture's
boundaries; when the construction is especially difficult; or when the construction is especially urgent" (*Kasenhō* 1896). With the 1902 committee it

is clear that liberal laissez-faire models were as extinct in state circles as they were in the ideologies of protest. Just as the river and its fish had been the measure of ecological change in the 1880s, after 1902 the river marked the move from liberal capitalism to its state-centered, administered form.

Much historiography on Tanaka and Ashio treats the 1902 committee as an example of governmental fraud or cover-up, a bait-and-switch (*surikae*) meant to protect their friend Furukawa from further scrutiny. There is no doubt that the ties between the Furukawa zaibatsu and the government were deep and intimate; Meiji statesman Mutsu Munemitsu's son Junkichi was adopted by Furukawa.[4] Likewise, there is no doubt that flood control, not pollution, became the main focus of the committee's attention. But a look at the language used to discuss the environment and pollution in the committee's reports shows that there was much more going on here than a cover-up. This in turn means that the pollution problem is in no way explained, let alone solved, merely by pointing out the corruption of powerful officials. In fact, one of the lead scientists of the 1902 committee was the same Kozai Yoshinau who had written the original soil chemistry analysis that served as the basis of the Watarase farmers' early protests (see chapter 1). Again in 1902, despite the growing complexities and uncertainties in the new fields of soil chemistry and ecology documented by Meiji liberals and activists throughout the 1890s, the committee's approach to nature remained the older reductionist model of constant causal relations. But in contrast to 1897, in 1902 it attempted to intentionally produce a (second) nature that would behave according to simple causal relations.

The committee's work was more than a cover-up, then. The particular conceptualization of nature seen in its reports allowed for absolving industrialization as a "cause" of pollution and authorized the massive reengineering of nature itself. In the final report published in March 1903, the committee defined pollution narrowly as the presence of copper in the river, soil, or human body above specific levels. By adopting the language of specific levels or thresholds, the committee was able to absolve the first few parts per million of harmful effluent as acceptable levels of toxicity. But beyond this setting of acceptable levels, the committee also broke down the damage into that directly traceable to soluble or insoluble copper. Arsenic, mercury, and other pollutants received less coverage. So while the committee found that Ashio effluent did contain soluble copper that reached the river, irrigation works, paddies, drinking wells, and even the breast milk of local women, "the amount was not sufficient to cause harm in humans." It even went on to add that copper was a necessary dietary mineral in certain small doses, the unspoken conclusion apparently being that the inhabitants of the Watarase valley merely had a rather unorthodox way of receiving their recommended daily allowance.

While the committee did not find large amounts of soluble copper, it did find insoluble copper in "huge amounts in the area immediately around Ashio and downstream in the river bed." But based on rather thin evidence it also declared that the 1897 measures (precipitation ponds, slag heaps, retaining walls) seemed adequate, which meant the dangerous insoluble copper in the riverbed must predate 1897.[5] Therefore the only pollution-specific recommendation was to complete any unfinished measures ordered in 1897.

Thus for the committee insoluble copper in the riverbed was considered the great danger to crops, drinking water, health, and livelihoods in the valley. The huge majority of this insoluble copper had settled into the mud of the riverbeds and banks. Therefore, because they had concluded that only safe amounts of soluble copper were still reaching the rivers from the mine, the committee held that the cause of current suffering was not mining, but flooding that agitated the polluted mud, allowing the embedded insoluble copper to escape and cause damage. It was thus not the mine's waste but the river—nature itself—that was identified as the culprit. The committee's assumptions also meant that toxic floods would continue to harm fields even if Ashio were closed, so closing the Ashio mine was taken off the agenda.

The great "discovery" made by the committee, then, was the general poverty of nature itself: "We find that the generally poor quality of public health in the region is largely due to the lowness and meanness of the land itself . . . and cannot be directly traced back to mine pollution."[6] It continued: "Through flooding, drinking wells are infected with parasites and contagions [causing the inhabitants' ill-health and poverty], all of which for decades now the inhabitants have misnamed mine-pollution sickness (kōdokubyō)."[7] It further noted that some Ashio miners were in fact afflicted with chronic copper poisoning, but the farmers were victims of the land.

The general poverty of nature in the countryside became the central metaphor and operating assumption for the proposed solution, which argued that the Watarase and Tone valleys, historically Japan's most fertile, were compatible with mining, yet "completely unsuited to agriculture"— indeed, "physically unsuited to cultivation"![8] A massive engineering project transforming the river system to make it flood-proof therefore promised not only a solution to the pollution problem but also an "improvement" of the land. This clearly marks a major change from the politics of mine pollution during the Tokugawa period, when the focus was on regulating access to nature's productive capacity, as when mines were moved or temporarily closed during agriculturally sensitive seasons.[9] Instead the committee found that the Kanto plain was best suited for modern industrial production of copper rather than the agriculture of the Tokugawa period. In 1902, it was the older, agrarian base that would have to be reengineered in order to be made compatible with industrial production.

Despite these real differences with the pre-Meiji past, given what we have already seen of the reification of nature in the pre-Meiji period, should we be surprised that the committee's recommendations, too, were the culmination of a long process of commodification and industrialization with antecedents in the early modern era?

The major reworking of the Kanto plain begun by the 1902 committee was an extension of earlier plans to build a realmwide, Edo-centered commodity network that could capture the national product, a wish of Tokugawa Era mercantilists such as Honda Toshiaki.[10] In his *Secret Plan for Ordering the Realm* (*Keisei hisaku*) Honda called for putting nature into the service of political economy by building a national water transportation network that could turn agricultural production into monetary wealth through trade. Honda's plans for reengineering the whole topography of Japan to make it more amenable to capital accumulation through easier transportation and trade, and therefore strong enough to take on the Western imperialist powers, was based on overcoming Japan's inconvenient mountainous terrain through the liberal application of dynamite.[11]

Honda's plan was never explicitly put in place, and he himself was arrested for violating the ban on unauthorized travel abroad. Nonetheless, his mercantilist vision of a militarily and economically strong Japan did become widespread in the Meiji period. In many ways, a version of Honda's plan was revived in the 1870s by the Meiji oligarch Okubo Toshimichi. Okubo's "Position Paper for the General Encouragement of Industry and to Provide Work for Former Samurai" (1878) argued for the construction of commodity network similar to Honda's to be built by draining marshes and rerouting rivers to create a contiguous network of navigable rivers from Tokyo to Niigata Bay.[12] Even so, both Honda and Okubo's plans were exceeded by the 1902 proposals. Honda and Okubo had based their economic visions on river transport (*mizu hakobu*), which called for a low-levee system like those in northern Germany and Holland. River transport also required a softer, more permeable barrier between the river and the surrounding area, as easy access to docks and piers meant tolerating occasional overtopping and flooding. That concession was no longer necessary with the emergence of railroad transport beginning in the 1890s.[13] As trains replaced boats in circulating the national product, docks and piers were no longer essential to economic growth. This in turn made possible a corresponding shift to "high-levee" engineering and a complete rupture between the river and the land beyond its banks. High-levee engineering also allowed the committee to aim for a "zero-tolerance" policy toward flooding without harming commodity circulation. In turn, high-levee construction enabled the expansion of agricultural land into traditional floodplains, the rationalization of agriculture, and the promotion of industry.

The 1902 committee's adoption of high-levee construction was the beginning of Japan's now infamous wholly engineered river system of concrete banks and bottoms, what the riparian engineer Jeremy Purseglove calls the difference between a river and a drain.[14] Just as invoking the 1896 law nationalized the rivers (removing them from the local communities and prefectures that had used them), the river reform projects drafted the Watarase and Tone into the service of national policy goals. We must not lose sight of the fact that the committee delivered its recommendations just one month before the government's decision to prepare for a war with Russia. As we shall see below, Tanaka, too, made this link between the rationalization of nature and war in his protests against the committee's recommendations.

The goal of the committee's flood-control plan shows an abstraction to a completely rationalized nature: the fetishized nature of the laboratory, a nature the committee would try to reproduce in the field. This is clearly seen in the committee's proposals to "completely control access to irrigation waterways, [for it] is during floods that pollution enters the fields so *we must be able to restrict the flow to only that necessary under ordinary conditions.*" Achieving total control of the river's flow meant building new levees along the entire length of the rivers, wherever "there is nothing now blocking the current."[15] When, as in flooding, the flow itself was the problem, the river needed to be stilled completely. Thus the key to this whole plan was the creation of a flood-control reservoir that could absorb nature's energy, an engineered zero point that could still the water before allowing it to rejoin the Watarase-Tone system in a controlled manner. Yanaka village, near the confluence of the Watarase and Tone Rivers in Tochigi, was ultimately chosen as the site of the new reservoir. Despite all the complex relations discovered by the activists since the outbreak of the pollution problem in the 1880s, the committee's belief that it could completely control the river betrays its mechanistic bias toward singular causes and effects that exist in a one-to-one relationship that may be completely known and predicted. But even in those cases when simple causal relations proved elusive, the committee's final report suggests that such a nature should be actively produced.

In contrast to the committee's assumptions, Tanaka believed the committee dangerously confused the agent (flooding) with the cause (mining, industrial capitalism). It is in Tanaka's 1902 petitions and position papers, some of which were submitted to the committee, that an inherently dynamic nature (*tennen*) begins to emerge as an active and essential element in human health and freedom in Tanaka's thought and activism. Perhaps most important for our investigation of Tanaka and later environmental thinkers such as Ishikawa Sanshirō and Kurosawa Torizō, Tanaka completely rejected the committee's assertion that motion is external to nature, something to be imparted from without (by engineers, bureaucrats, businessmen). For both the committee and their Tokugawa and Meiji mercantilist predecessors, nature was a source of only *inanimate* power, a power that was tapped or valorized only when set into motion by humans according to the demands of political economy. But Tanaka insisted that motion was an inherent property of all things. This meant nature was an *animate* power and an active force that contained its own value—but only if humans understood this and acted accordingly. Though Tanaka had studied the Confucian classics, especially *Mencius*, his choice of a neo-Confucian language of essences (*sei*) and principles (*ri*) to describe nature is explained, I argue, not merely as a premodern holdover, but by the fact that neo-Confucianism was one of the only languages in which he could link social and moral values with nature. His language of nagare (flow) and doku (poison) was an attempt to describe a different relationship of agents and causes that was, to him, more accurate and always already deeply political. Bruno Latour's idea of "networks," whether personal, social, organic, or inorganic, is helpful here, for we could say that the rivers themselves were being, in his terms, "recruited" to the national cause. But Latour also reminds us that "permanences" do not exist. Networks are assembled only for certain durations and are tremendously costly to maintain.[16] For Tanaka and the farmers, nature was an active force that could not be contained without "tremendous cost" in the form of ecological and social doku.

### Tanaka's Environmental Turn: The Philosophy of Nagare and Doku

Before she left for San Francisco, Matsumoto Eiko had documented the sufferings of the Watarase and Tone watersheds and linked them to the major changes in the landscape since the intense exploitation of the Ashio mine.

But she had been unable in the pages of the *Mainichi shinbun* to go beyond a phenomenological accounting of the inescapable ecologies of human existence. Tanaka and Yanaka resident Shimada Sōzo's extensive studies of the watersheds were an attempt to pick up where Matsumoto's reports left off, to get to the principles of mine pollution. As the committee was meeting and occasionally touring the polluted areas, Tanaka and Shimada made their own tours in an attempt to fully understand the interaction of water, land, and humans in the valleys. Tanaka's finished report, submitted to the committee in 1902, marks his emergence as an environmental thinker. Like Matsumoto, he refused to define pollution narrowly, seeking it out in all its manifestations and mediations and eventually finding it everywhere. In expanding the notion of pollution to social processes, he anticipated what François Ewald and Ulrich Beck identify as the aporia of classic notions of risk in the face of the modern environmental crisis. Because they operate above and below classical thresholds—which is to say, above and below classical theories of the body and politics—modern "ecological threats" are impossible to eradicate or fully compensate for under liberal political philosophy. If one does not abandon that concept of the body and that form of politics, the only way to deal with toxic events is by determining minimum levels of acceptable poisoning: "If one permits toxicity at all, then one needs an acceptable level decree. But then that which is *not* contained in it becomes more important than what is in it. Because what is not in, not covered by it, *is not considered toxic*, and can *freely be introduced into circulation, without any restraints.* The silence of the acceptable level decree, its 'blank spots,' are its most dangerous statements. What it does not discuss is what threatens us the most."[17] The seemingly occult ability of mine pollution to creep into the spaces between the legal, social, economic, and political structures of Meiji society is a problem of the social basis of the environmental crisis that we saw in the examination of the Tanaka and Kōtoku's jikiso in chapter 2. What Kōtoku and Tanaka had likely sensed but were unable to express in their appeal in 1901, Tanaka made explicit in 1902. His fight against the state's plan seeks both to shine a light on the "blank spots" that the massive engineering projects deemed unworthy of consideration and to push back the scope of acceptable levels of toxicity.

While the state saw nature as a passive object to be manipulated by humans, Tanaka's law argued for an active nature in constant motion. Here his thought was partially grounded in Tokugawa agronomy, a monistic tradition that conceived of nature as the constant motion of an infinite material energy. But Tanaka's encounter with industrial-scale pollution taught him to doubt that nature was indeed infinite. To the more optimistic eighteenth-century belief in the eternal motion of material energy, nagare, he added another category: doku. In Tanaka's thought, and unlike in the reductionist theory of disease or pollution as the presence of an outside element, doku represents the flow of nature's energy in harmful, destructive ways. Doku begins to emerge as a new category of social thought in Tanaka's letters, diary, and petitions during his investigation of the watershed in 1902. Doku also signals Tanaka's break from liberal politics. In fact, Tanaka never adopted the contemporary and current word for pollution: kōgai (literally, "injurious to the public [interest]"). In many ways pollution considered as kōgai belonged to the liberal political philosophy of public and private that collapsed in the failed appeal to the emperor. Kōgai also allows for a debate on acceptable levels of poisoning and a cost-benefit calculus based on the current definition of public interest. Tanaka's second question to the Diet in 1892 had been rejected by the government on precisely these grounds, and we already saw that the 1902 committee spent time establishing acceptable levels of toxicity. The language of kōgai thus leads to the calculation of who and what are part of the main thrust of the public interest. As we shall see, the Yanakans who refused to move to make way for the reservoir became "remainders" (zanryūmin) left behind by modernity and progress, as Yanaka became one of the forgotten places that activists and thinkers such as Mike Davis have called "national sacrifice zones."[18] In contrast to kōgai, doku literally means poison, and it retains an elemental quality that expresses its irreducibility and resists the utilitarian calculus.

In Tanaka's theory nagare and doku took many forms, moving easily from the material and ecological to the social and political—so much so that it is often easier to talk about doku and nagare without reference to distinct social or ecological realms. Nagare and doku express two possible organizations of the dynamic processes of Heaven-humans-Earth, the classic Confucian categories describing the universe. (In the classic understanding "Heaven" is synonymous with a material "nature," and "humans" have a crucial role to play.)[19] As descriptions of the universe, both nagare and doku simultaneously operate on multiple levels and are therefore open to multiple levels of "knowing." Both exist as *material, biochemical* processes such as river hydraulics, agronomy, and mining; as *sociological* expressions of the organization of human society in relation to "Heaven" and "Earth"; and as *epistemological* understandings of the ground of human knowledge and practice. Finally, both require an *existential* choice in aligning one's thought, practice, and being with one of the processes, whereby one becomes an embodiment of either nagare or doku.

Because motion was inherent in nature and human intervention could create the beneficial nagare or harmful doku processes, for Tanaka the state's policies of control through constriction and manipulation of the rivers' currents would not have the desired effect of wholly controlling the river. On the contrary, they would result in a harmful "backflow" or "regression" (*gyakuryū*) as the river confronted the concrete banks, sluices, and reservoirs and then reversed itself, breaking though levees and bursting its banks in unexpected places, resulting in flooding upstream. (This is precisely what happened.) Whereas human practice based on the state's policy of stopping and reversing flow would lead to an accumulation of harm in larger and larger artificial and toxic floods (doku), Tanaka's fostering of flow or nagare— what he would later call "natural water management" (*chisui*)—would lead to an accumulation of life, health, and freedom by encouraging the multiple interactions of ecology.[20] Nature thus served as the battleground, the seemingly universal category used by both sides that hid the power struggles of modernity and the construction of the modern Meiji state.

In his extensive tours, Tanaka showed that the floods of 1890 and 1896— along with two more massive floods in 1902 and 1907—were caused not by the *lack* of engineering projects, but *by* such engineering projects. Tanaka thus declared these floods "artificial disasters" (*jin'i saigai*) created by human projects. Tanaka stuck with this theme until his death in 1913. His *River Pilgrimage Diary* (*Kasen junshi nikki*) and the pamphlet *Not the Work of Nature* (*Tennen ni arazu*, 1910) were part scientific, part anthropological investigations into the 1907 flood. In the pamphlet, Tanaka and Shimada declared: "The government's preventive projects are contrary to Heaven's time (*ten no toki*) and Earth's features (*chi no ri*), and so absolutely no good can be expected of their completion."[21] In these works he clearly demonstrated that the rains of 1907 had not been particularly heavy; the 1907 flood was the result of backflow (*gyakuryū*) caused by the measures recommended by the 1902 committee, such as narrowing sluices as Sekiyado and heightening concrete levees, actions that restricted flow and therefore accelerated and channeled the river.

While in 1903 the committee announced its stunning conclusion that the Watarase and Tone watersheds, despite centuries of agriculture and sericulture, were in fact "incompatible with cultivation," as we saw in chapters 1 and 2 based on his own research on the reduced crop yields, infertile fields, increasingly violent flooding due to deforestation, low birth weights, low breast milk, and pollution everywhere, Tanaka had already concluded that nature had ordered the closing of the mine, even though the government had not: "Even if we are not saying the committee's measures are totally useless, we can say that they are planning only for the best-case scenario. . . . But over time, slag heaps and tailings acidify and during heavy rain this washes into the river. Copper suspended in the marsh ice in the winter quickly delivers a great deal of poison during the spring thaw—this is not caught by the prevention technologies. Nor should it be called a flood. Due to the real powers of the land and water (*chi no ikioi, mizu no ikioi*), if we are to swear off useless pollution prevention projects, clearly we must do nothing at all—such are the limits of nature."[22] The phrase "the real powers of the land and water" here describes not only the material base, but also the limits of human agency. What Tanaka's vision of the environment required was for humans to learn the real powers of the land and water so that they could be careful to "foster, not fight" its flows. If they could do that, they could consciously arrive at what fish seem to instinctively know: "Observe. Fish have no [legal] protection and though they live in the dark polluted waters [of the Watarase] do they not avoid total extinction? The reason why the polluters (*kagaisha*), with all their power, are unable to destroy these fish is this: though no law protects them, the fish instinctively rely on nature (*tennen*) and follow a path out of danger to unpolluted smaller streams, and, happily, save themselves. This is the way to use nature. The fish follow it. Why not all the more for people?"[23]

The need to rely on "natural" (rather than human) law is taken further as Tanaka shows that, like the fish in the polluted Watarase, the pollution victims will save themselves not through appeals to the Diet, but only through the power of the land and water:

It is said [by the 1902 committee] that this great misery is caused by the lay of the land. But it is also the land that will save them. In Saitama recently people were able to find refuge in the shrine [on the other side of the river] in Ibaraki. The law did not then save them. The law does not save the people during a disaster. The land does. Far from saving, the law augments the power of the polluters; it rejects the people's petitions and increases the mine-poisoned floods that ride upon the power of the land. Yet what saves the victims is another power of the land.[24]

In this understanding "the real powers of the land and water" form a solid basis for human health and freedom. But this was not an eternal truth. The critical lesson of the Ashio crisis was that this window of opportunity to "rely on nature" was closing; the nature that saved the Watarase fish was rapidly disappearing.

The key insight is this: while Tanaka held that nagare was nature's ultimate principle, human action contrary to nagare not only thwarted nagare but actively created doku. This is altogether different from the older notion in which pollution, *kegare*, was identified with discrete sites and objects, as "matter out of place."[25] In other words, because motion is not imparted from without but inherent in nature, some kinds of human intervention will not neutralize nature. Instead, the system will continue to move, but now it will produce the harmful doku cycle:

> The mine-poisoned floods *borrow the great power of the land* and thus make it all the way into the Home Ministry. The ministry's civil engineering department is destroyed by the mine pollution— dooming it to a cycle of destruction, rebuilding, and further destruction. Poison *runs on the lay of the land* and *rides the river's currents* to the welfare bureau, eventually felling people. The police are powerless to stop death by poisoning, and the local authorities cannot stop the destruction of local autonomy (*chihōseido*). They merely watch as it is destroyed by huge amounts of pollution invading the villages and towns, killing the people.[26]

There is great deal going on here, even beyond the important conceptual linking of material contamination of an environment to the social contamination of rights, safety, and freedom. Hidden in this statement, for example, is a historically specific critique of Meiji modernization. In 1886, in response to cholera and other epidemic diseases, the police had been put in charge of enforcing all hygiene and sanitation regulations issued by the Home Ministry's Public Health Bureau. In 1893 they received complete jurisdiction over all health regulations—a responsibility they would keep until 1945. Tanaka's attack here is not (only) metaphorical. He is calling attention to the inability of the Home Ministry and the police, who had been ruthless (and ruthlessly effective) in the anticholera campaigns of the 1880s, to deal with the much more subtle, intractable problem of a polluted environment. He is calling attention to the specificity and fearsomeness of modern toxic threats—threats that are not discrete pathogenic sites, but are actively produced in the specific processes of a nature-society metabolism; threats that illuminate the porousness of the individual and social body and endanger the body's integrity as a stable locus of rights.

Tanaka does not fail to follow this logic to its apocalyptic conclusions. The major conceptual breakthrough in Tanaka's thought comes in this same petition from 1902, in which he grasps the fundamental change in the valley as a metabolic rift in human-nature relations. If human practice is not rectified, like a cancer that co-opts the body's own capacity for growth turning it against itself, an expanding doku can metastasize and consume the world: "If [the pollution] continues too long, the river's headwaters will trickle out from a poisoned mountain of foul rocks and polluted soil that wholly penetrates the water, forming a second [toxic] nature (*dai ni no tensei o nashi*); once this happens, there will be no saving anyone."[27] In many ways this statement was the culmination of the investigation of the 1890 floods by liberal activist groups such as the Shimotsuke Liberal League, which had noted that the age-old natural laws that people relied on in the production of daily necessities and the reproduction of their social existence could no longer be counted on. The mounting evidence that human practice was creating a second, toxic nature that menaced everyone marked the Ashio Incident as a historical rupture and metabolic rift in humanity's relations with the environment. And here with Tanaka we also have a conceptual rupture and the birth of an environmental politics. Humanity's unprecedented capacity to intervene in nature's flows, as revealed by Ashio, also meant that for the first time in history humans risked completely stopping nature's motion in the stillness of death (*yodomi*). Depressingly, it is not Tanaka's glorification of a preindustrial agrarian Japanese past that marks him as an environmental thinker; it is his modern vision of "ecocide," the possible extinction of a nature capable of supporting life and freedom.

Because doku is created from a systemic incompatibility—a result of the "way of humans" and the "way of nature" fighting each other—it is impossible to combat it from within the human realm of technological improvement. Instead, correcting it requires political and ethical renovation. Unlike the 1902 committee, Tanaka argued that dealing with pollution required remaking politics, not nature.

For Tanaka and many others, the Russo-Japanese War (1904–5) represented a congealing of the wayward path of Japanese modernity. The anarchist position on this will be discussed in more detail in the next chapter, but we should also note that not only was 1905 roughly the time when the assumed progress of social Darwinism was abandoned, but not coincidentally, it was also after 1905 that Julia Thomas found the emergence of a new right-wing identification of nature and culture.[28] Opposed to this right-wing exaltation of the Japanese land, for Tanaka, doku (understood broadly as pollution, war, imperialism, and social repression) had become the way Japan expressed itself at home and abroad. In 1904, in preparation for the construction of the flood-control reservoir, Yanaka village was legally obliterated, the levees intentionally cut, even as its sons were sent to fight the Russians in Manchuria. More than just linking Japanese environmental policy to the destruction of Yanaka, Tanaka went further and brought Japanese imperialism—from the Sino-Japanese War (1894–95) to the current conflict—into his emerging social ecology. In a 1905 pamphlet, Tanaka observed that more and more forests were being felled in service to the wartime state, and, like the deforestation of the Ashio hills in the 1880s, this caused erosion and flooding to increase. This connection allowed him to bring Meiji imperialism under the aegis of his environmental thought, creating an environmental rationale for pacifism: "After the war the floods will be worse than ever before. . . . Though we have gained the new territory of Taiwan, we continue to destroy our own. This time the forests of Tone county are being ruthlessly cut down. After this war is over the floods will be hundreds of times greater, worse than ever. All of this absolutely must be stopped."[29] While the focus here is on Meiji policies, far from some recent belief in the premodern Japanese past in tune with its environment or as the model of a sustainable society,[30] Tanaka continued pursuing this linking of environmental intervention and war preparation historically in criticizing the environmental practices of the Edo Era thinker Kumazawa Banzan (1619–91) for joining the Watarase and Tone Rivers. Kumazawa's project rerouted both rivers to flow into Zushi Bay in Ibaraki and no longer through Edo, thereby blocking a possible waterway invasion of the capital from Tōhoku.[31] This proved, Tanaka claimed, that the Watarase and Tone Rivers had never been managed according to nagare principles, but always according to narrow, doku-producing human projects: "In the Tokugawa period, for the benefit of the [shogun's] castle the watershed was unnaturally altered; today it is for the benefit of the mine."[32]

Because of the extraordinary power of doku in becoming a "second nature"—and thus making the world itself poisonous to humans—in these and other writings Tanaka had inverted the famous hierarchy of dangers outlined by a contemporary biologist, Oka Asajirō (1868–1944), who had popularized Darwinism in Japan. In Chūō kōron Oka observed that, in Japan's conquest of nature, nature was beginning to fight back. He explicitly cited polluted rivers and flooding. But Oka also concluded that the subjugation of nature was the prerequisite for "civilization" and that the alternative to this "progress" was colonization by a foreign power, something he judged "worse than Nature's revenge."[33] In this argument Oka was echoing Japanese thinkers from the seventeenth and eighteenth centuries, such as Kumazawa Banzan and Honda Toshiaki, as well as Meiji intellectuals like Fukuzawa Yukichi and most of the popular rights activists.[34]

Tanaka did not necessarily disagree with Oka's premise regarding the relations between "civilization" and "nature's revenge," but he clearly rejected the conclusions. In his criticism of the Russo-Japanese War, Tanaka went beyond a pacifist position, calling into question the entire civilization and enlightenment project. What he rejected was in many ways the fulfillment of the Meiji drive to great power status. Against the diplomatic and military triumphs of Japan's participation in global modernity, Tanaka contrasted the misery of Yanaka: "Soldiers are not representative of Japan. This is how my observations differ from all others. If we win in war, morality is not what wins it for us. So there is no gain. Be like Switzerland! If you want to know Japan look at Yanaka—it is enough to look at Ashikaga or Sano or the politicians of east Shimotsuke [who sold off public forests for private development and supported the reservoir]. . . . The nation (*kokka*) is dying on its own from within—only the soldiers are doing well."[35]

Doku's eradication, then, required not only a cessation of hostilities but a worldwide commitment to total disarmament. Together with anarchists and socialists from the journal *Shinkigen*, such as Ishikawa Sanshirō and Arahata Kanson, Tanaka drew up a list of "disarmament leaders," praising Tolstoy in Russia and the founder of the Salvation Army, William Booth, in England.[36] The entries for the United States, France, Germany, and Japan were left blank. The question of how and by whom the present would be redeemed was still undecided. But Tanaka's thoughts on nagare and doku, gleaned from his investigations, led him to conclude that the seizure and destruction of Yanaka village was *the* key to understanding Japanese modernity.

### The Destruction of Yanaka Village

Even more than the Russo-Japanese war, for Tanaka, Yanaka was ground zero of this wayward trend in Japanese modernity. The Russo-Japanese War was more likely the outward, international expression of the Yanaka Incident. If Yanaka could be made whole again, there was hope for the future; if not, there was not. As we shall see in the next section, just as water could not be made to answer to the Diet or the police, Tanaka believed he had found the human equivalent of nagare in the Yanaka residents who refused to be thrown from their homes by violence or artificial floods. For Tanaka, the Yanakans showed the way of true freedom, a freedom based not on human laws or on limited and partial (*ku ku taru*) political projects but on a holistic understanding of human embeddedness in an inescapable political ecology. Yanakans seemed to be answerable not to corrupt laws but only to nature's rules (*tensoku*). Aligning one's thought and practice with the "truth" of flowing water became the way to redeem the hell that Japanese political ecology had created in Yanaka.

Tanaka's move to Yanaka in 1904 should thus not be seen as a retreat from the politics and protest of the popular rights era or from the drama of the appeal to the emperor. Nor can it be consigned to the familiar "agriculture versus industry" debate. It was the logical move to the place where, more than any other, Japan was poisoning itself. Yanaka was where the state planned to create a site of *yodomi*—the complete absence of flow, the point at which doku so completely co-opts the power of nature that the whole system comes to a stop—the site of death itself. In contrast to an active village in harmony with nature's flows, the Meiji state planned to build a site completely devoid of life and movement in favor of a toxic pond of "dead water." For Tanaka, it would be the ultimate example of Matsumoto's "poison community" (see chapter 1). Yanaka was a village destroyed by the state in a futile war against the nagare principle of the river. The necessary failure required the repression of the antipollution petitioners, an escalating cycle of oppression ending in the destruction of a village. It was in Yanaka, whose sons were being killed in Manchuria while their parents were being dragged from their polluted homes in accordance with the state's rationalization and militarization of the Kanto plain, that it seemed clear to Tanaka, Shimada, Kinoshita Naoe, Ishikawa Sanshirō, and others that the Meiji state's projects were a massive machine dedicated to the production of doku. As Tanaka wrote in the preface to Arahata Kanson's *Yanakamura metsubōshi* (*The Extermination of Yanaka*, 1907), "The [Ashio] pollution problem has mutated; it has become the theft and destruction of homes."[37] A sense of Yanaka as a grand historical moment is explicit in Tanaka's diaries: "What sort of history begins in Yanaka in 1902? What sort of nation (*kokutai*) will it produce?"[38] Here we see Tanaka's focus on the Ashio/Yanaka problem as indicative of Japanese modernity itself: "Japan is a young country; and so Japan is the same as a child who contracts a disease. Though ill the child may still grow up. Japan too will grow older. [But] once grown it will be impossible to distinguish the disease [from Japan] (*miwakegatashi*)."[39] The fight over Yanaka forced a choice between salvation and "national death" (*bōkoku*). Whichever of the two rival processes of doku or nagare prevailed in Yanaka would reveal the path of Japanese modernity: "The problem of the five prefectures [Tochigi, Saitama, Ibaraki, Gumma, and Chiba] and Tokyo are concentrated here. In Yanaka they appear explicitly and openly. The problem is clearly not just Yanaka.... Yanaka is ground zero of disaster— [it is a] monstrous [place]."[40] The philosophy of nagare and doku allows this linking. Yanaka is the point of convergence of the two systems. Tanaka's philosophy insists on the unity of the ecological and the social, the defining characteristic of what I am calling the environmental turn. It is therefore no coincidence that the precise point where the state attempted to completely stop the flow of the river was also the point where the greatest oppression and human suffering occurred.

The importance of politics and power in the fate of Yanaka is explicit when we consider that originally, nearby Kawabe and Rishima had been chosen as possible locations for the reservoir. But in both villages a protest movement quickly formed, and the plan was dropped when the towns swore to withhold taxes and not submit to military conscription if the government persisted. In Yanaka, which had a very high percentage of absentee landlords (one-third), the protest movement was slower and smaller. In addition, in the 1890s pollution victims had received relief through a tax exemption for the damaged land. This meant that many residents had fallen below the minimum direct-tax requirements to qualify for suffrage: in 1902, of 1,202 adult males in Yanaka, only 2 had voting rights. This low level of suffrage also meant the mayor was not elected but appointed by the governor, and was therefore an agent of the state.[41] Yet even with these obstacles to legal opposition, the decision was autocratic. The final decision was made at an emergency, closed-door, midnight meeting of the Tochigi legislature in December 1904, guarded by a large group of police, at which the legislature allocated 480,000 yen[42] for the purchase of Yanaka.

In July 1906, after an initial round of buyouts plagued by corruption, rampant fraud, and coercion (including sabotage to the protective levees), Yanaka was officially assimilated into nearby Fujioka, ceasing to exist as an administrative unit. Of those residents who sold, many were relocated to Nasunohara in northern Tochigi, where they found that the land was nearly infertile without the application of chemical fertilizers, so farming here would require more cash. There was also limited opportunity to manufacture agricultural by-products, such as umbrellas or *minokasa* (straw raincoats), let alone operate fisheries. Worst of all, and to their horror, displaced Yanakans had sold out as owner-cultivators only to become tenant farmers.

In many cases their new landlords were Diet members, as Nasunohara was (and still is) a popular mountain retreat for escaping the Tokyo heat when the Diet was not in session. Given these grim prospects confronting the Yanaka residents, the government was successful in getting future sellers to join a Tochigi resettlement program in northern Hokkaido—an option heavily advertised during flood seasons. In a national settlement initiative from 1907 to 1912, many former Yanaka residents, together with other Tochigi farmers harmed by years of mine pollution and flooding, relocated to Saroma on the Sea of Okhotsk, across the straits from Sakhalin Island, the southern half of which had been ceded to Japan following the Russo-Japanese War of 1904–5. The Hokkaido settlement initiative was such a state priority that participants in the Ashio riot in 1907[43] were granted clemency if they relocated.[44] On top of this, public opinion turned against the Yanakans. In editorials and letters to the editor, the Yanakans were frequently denounced as "selfish" for standing in the way of progress by tenaciously clinging to their own narrow property rights and ignoring the national good.[45]

In 1906, faced with ever increasing flood damage, the Yanakans rallied support through lectures and editorials in the Christian socialist journal *Shinkigen* from sympathetic groups in Tokyo, raising enough money to add 1.5 *shaku* (about eighteen inches) to the height of their levees. In this way an instance of actual competing practices of nature became the site of the confrontation between Yanakans and the state. Though a proper restoration would have required the addition of 3 *shaku* rather than 1.5, the work saved close to half of that year's barley harvest and staved off starvation one more time. But this undertaking also caught the attention of the Tochigi and the national governments. The Yanakans' rebuilding of their levees was a violation of the 1896 River Law, which, as we saw, allowed for the transfer of jurisdiction of any of Japan's waterways from the local to the national level. Once invoked, the 1896 River Law gave the Home Minister authority over construction or demolition of all riverine or riparian structures. The villagers were informed that their levee repairs were a violation of the law, and they were given until April 27 to undo the repairs; if they did not do so by that date, the government would do it for them. Despite the worsening conditions, many refused to leave. Of the original 450 homes and 2,700 residents, nearly 70 homes remained. Those who remained tried to continue farming through an almost unimaginable process of digging many separate holes in their fields that they would then fill with poisoned topsoil in an effort to bring up pre-Ashio, unpolluted soil, a process they called "earth renewal" or "earth inversion" (*tenchigaeshi*). But with the levees in disrepair, this time-consuming and backbreaking project was only temporary, as each season's increasingly violent flooding would wash away the new topsoil, exposing the buried poisonous soil, and once again leaving even more toxins in its wake. In 1906 the entire village was declared subject to the 1896 River Law, making the remaining homes illegal structures.

On January 26, 1907, Home Minister Hara Kei of the Saionji cabinet announced the government's plans to invoke eminent domain to acquire the remaining households and begin the construction of the reservoir. On June 12 all remaining families were summoned to the Fujioka city office, where they were informed that they had until June 22 to sell; otherwise their homes would be destroyed and they would be billed for the destruction. Movement by nonresidents into or out of the village was prohibited. But the remaining residents had already decided to stay in Yanaka after the destruction. On the night of June 21 they gathered for a party to tell stories and drink sake to "the last night we'll eat with a roof over our heads." Tanaka reportedly quoted the Bible in calling for nonviolent resistance to the authorities when they came. During the party the police arrived to say that the date had been delayed five days but had not been canceled; on June 29, 1907, the police arrived at Sayama Umekichi's home.[46]

At 8 a.m. that day, sixty-seven workers accompanied by over two hundred police descended on Igeno hamlet on the east side of Yanaka village to begin forcibly dismantling the sixteen homes that residents had refused to sell.[47] Workmen entered Sayama's house and began removing all furniture and utensils, placing them in a pile outside. Once empty, the house was pulled apart, the poles and debris laid by the river and later moved to the former site of Nogimura's shrine as villagers, Tanaka, and newly arrived Kinoshita Naoe shouted, "Thief!" "Pirates!" at the officials present. That day this scene was repeated at Ogawa Chōzaburō and Kawajima Isegorō's homes. Ogawa delivered a blistering diatribe against the workmen destroying his home for adding extra harm to the day's violence, screaming, "This isn't even the proper way to destroy a house! The proper way is to take down a house according to its plans—numbering each piece for reassembly later. Why has the prefecture done it so violently? In such a way that it may never rise again?"[48]

The second day was even more emotional than the first. When they came to Moro Matsuemon's home, he refused to leave until he had first stripped naked and given a tear-choked apology to his family's ancestral tablets (*ihai*) for allowing their land and work to be lost forever on his watch. The apology was infused with rage, and he concluded by condemning the prefecture and its lackeys for this crime. Still refusing to leave, he was carried out by police. At the Watanabes' house, an old woman screamed, "If I were younger it would be different, but I no longer have the strength to kill." Even more disturbingly, her mentally ill daughter erratically circled the entryway mumbling and noisily beating the ground with a bamboo pole.

*Nihonjin* editor and Seikyōsha member Miyake Setsurei arrived to take photographs on day 3. Tokyo-based Christian activist Henmi Onokichi was there on day 4. Both had become Yanaka landowners in an effort to complicate its purchase by the state—a "one-*tsubo* movement." (This same sort of tactic would be duplicated in the postwar period in the "one-share movement," in which Minamata activists became shareholders in Chisso in order to gain access to annual meetings.) Though Miyake confronted the officials in charge of the project, saying, "If you are so sure this is legal why must it not be photographed?" for some reason Miyake acquiesced to the prefectural officials' requests and withheld publication of his photographs until a memorial exhibition of Tanaka's poetry in 1926, one year after the first volume of the *Gijin zenshū* appeared.

On day 4 Mizuno Riu, the twenty-two-year-old daughter of Mizuno Hikoichi, refused to allow the workmen into her father's home while he was away, staging a sit-in in her own home: "I am the eldest daughter, and while [my father] is gone I am in charge. You will not touch this house until he returns." When the workmen ignored her and entered the home to begin removing furniture, she reportedly screamed, "Stop!" (*Yame yo!*) so forcefully that they reportedly did so and the destruction was delayed until Hikoichi returned.[49] By July 5, one week after it had started, the destruction of Yanaka was complete.

And still all sixteen of the families subjected to the order collected the debris of their homes and began rebuilding. Shacks of little more than a few poles leaned against the remaining trees and hillocks would be their homes for the next five to ten years: the Takezawas' home consisted of no more than "one pillar of cedar and one pillar of hackberry (*enoki*); the rest is exposed."[50] Unable to salvage anything from his former home, Aoki Ichigorō lived on the Yanaka levees in a broken boat.[51]

Several weeks later, on August 24, the damaged levees failed to protect sixteen families from the backflow of the Tone, and the whole area was subjected to severe flooding. On August 27, the Tochigi government began to provide emergency rice for the Yanakans who were still living in their shacks on the levees. When the officials arrived to distribute the rice, Shimada Sōzo's father was there to meet them: "We are thankful for the rice in this awful time, but if you think about it, it is a very strange thing to offer, is it not? This flood damage, this flood, is bigger precisely because of what you built to prevent it. Offering this food in the middle of a flood you made takes us for fools. We wouldn't touch it if we were starving to death. Take it and get the hell out of here!"[52]

This was the same day that Tanaka's attitude toward the Yanakans underwent a change from teacher to admirer, a move that would eventually become Yanakagaku. A letter dated August 27 reads: "The Yanakans' perseverance exhausts our understanding—it comes from several places—it must be studied (*kenkyū, kenkyū*). It seems to all come down to this one character: 'shin' (belief). But just what kind of belief is this? It comes from their lives themselves. The power of this belief is enormous."[53] Yanakagaku, was an attempt to transform the doku cycle and revive the socio-ecological process of nagare. To cultivate the ecology of nagare in Yanaka, Tanaka immersed himself in the misery of the destroyed village, living with its residents from 1904 until his death in 1913.

### Yanakagaku

It was the Yanakan squatters' "shack life" (*kari koya seikatsu*) that demonstrated to Tanaka their seemingly superhuman capacity to resist and persevere. Shack life became for Tanaka a human expression of nagare. Like the Watarase itself, the Yanaka resisters could not be stilled by what he called "the techniques of contempt" of "the Ashio party" (*Dōzantō*). In Kinoshita Naoe's words on the first day of the destruction of Yanaka (echoing Tanaka), from now on the residents' "lives themselves" (*seikatsu sono mono*) must become the new model of modern social protest. This location of protest in daily life itself should not be underestimated. Life itself as a form of resistance to state power represented a major shift in the politics and ideology of social protest in modern Japan. As Ashio scholar Hayashi Takeji points out, this is not the spirit of the self-sacrificial, death-based protest of Japan's samurai tradition.[54] More specific to the Ashio and popular rights context, but making the same point, it is a rejection of the Sakura Sōgo model of protest that Tanaka had used in the appeal to the emperor just six years earlier.

Tanaka began his training in developing the Yanakans' abilities by immersing himself, often literally, in the wretched conditions of shack life, trying to achieve their ability to resist: "I've been in Yanaka, soaking wet, for twenty-six days straight. It's the first time in my sixty-seven years something's made me sick enough to lay me out for a whole day. This is my great foray in endurance so far [*watashi no jimanbanashi*]." The sense of training is so strong that Tanaka gives a list of witnesses who can attest to his story.[55] At this early stage in his training, shack life was all still a temporary hardship that needed to be endured (*gaman*). It had not yet become his "life itself": "The unpleasantness, the hardship (*tsurai*) of this shack life I felt just as they did, but I complained; for them, this is their lives. [I am convinced] it is precisely this hardship itself that is important. I get soaked, sleep in wet clothes, and complain. They do the same and seem fine, even peaceful. They have come close to *kami*—they have become *kami* and don't know it—but it's visible from a distance."[56] Achieving subjectivity beyond merely enduring hardship was necessary in order for the nagare of nature to unselfconsciously flow through the individual's body. If that could be done, one's movement would become the expression of nagare in daily life.

As seen in Tanaka's letter of August 27, 1907, the Yanakans' abilities seemed to be currently beyond the grasp of Tanaka and the Ashio activists. What was innate in the Yanakans would have to be actively cultivated in others if they too were to achieve oneness with water—if their very lives were to become a form of resistance. It would have to become a method. Because Tanaka and the others lacked the Yanakans' natural abilities to achieve a waterlike state, Yanakagaku required work. If the heart and mind were stilled, the spirit of nature would be expressed through one's body, flowing through one's own "arms and legs," and daily life would then become the embodiment of prayer.[57] In trying to extinguish ego (*jiga*), desire (*yoku*), and anger (*ikari*), and in attempting to cultivate the Yanakan consciousness in himself, Tanaka turned to the meditative method (*zazen*) of Okada Torajirō (1872–1920) and especially to the Meiji Swedenborgian Arai Ōsui (1846–1922).

Arai was born in Sendai in 1846 and schooled in the Confucian classics. During the Boshin War, Arai traveled to Hakodate with Enomoto Takeaki and the retreating shogunal forces, where he met Russian Orthodox missionary Father Nikolai.[58] After studying Russian Orthodoxy under Nikolai, in 1871 he traveled with future minister of education Mori Arinori (1847–89) to the upstate New York commune of Thomas Lake Harris (1823–1906),[59] where he remained for twenty-eight years, returning to Japan in 1899. Harris's mysticist commune, the Brotherhood of New Life, was part of a "new church movement," which pitted itself against institutional churches.[60] The new church movement was in fact divided into two factions: one looked to radical social reform and included Henry James, Robert Owen, and included the teachings of Charles Fourier and

Swedenborg; another was more mystical, striving for a systematization of angelic revelation and a complete integration of religion and science. The Harris commune was part of this latter faction, but a move to more social concerns did occur after Harris's visit to England in 1859,[61] where he was shocked by the social conditions, and on being introduced to socialist theory he concluded that England needed a spiritual revolution: "England requires to be convinced that no legal precedent, though of a thousand years standing, can convert a wrong into a right." It was also at this time that he developed the Swedenborgian concept of "spirit-ennobling labor" and "spirit-reducing labor." Much like Tanaka's fear of the implications for the Japanese spirit during the Russo-Japanese War, Harris saw the American Civil War as spirit-reducing labor.[62]

Unlike Protestant and Catholic Christianity, neither Russian Orthodoxy nor Swedenborgianism has a strong concept of humanity's original fall redeemed through Christ's crucifixion.[63] In the Swedenborgian tradition, Christ's death on the cross did not expiate humanity's original sin. Instead, it was an ongoing process for each individual to "take up the cross in daily life" with the goal of personally expiating sin, as Christ had done. Arai taught the Swedenborgian tradition that human practice alone was insufficient to overcome the inherited desire, anger, and ego. Each individual must work to align the inner Jesus nature with the outer divine presence and fight together to redeem an injured world (*banbutsu*).[64] This necessity of expanding the borders of the individual to the outside world was the point of contact between Arai's Swendenborg teachings and Tanaka's new politics based on the human body as necessarily implicated in nature's flows.

As Tanaka's thought developed in training with the Yanakans and Arai, free-flowing water became both the symbol of nagare and the ultimate ground of freedom: "The essence of water is honest; it flows true and even, taking this as its maxim (*shugi*). Regardless of the decisions of a Diet or the blustering swagger of legal argument or human cleverness, water does not subject itself to either law or contrivance.... [To these] water replies, 'I am free.'"[65] In contrast to the 1896 River Law, which allowed for nationalization and rationalization of rivers, Tanaka's "fundamental river law" (*konponteki kasenhō*) held that flowing water emerges as the ultimate ground of truth, existing above national laws and policies. Whereas politics could be corrupted by bribery and self-serving, twisted arguments, "the essence (*sei*) of water is honest.... Water does not harm people ... has no class distinctions ... is not false.... [And though] people may deceive each other, flowing water never deceives."[66]

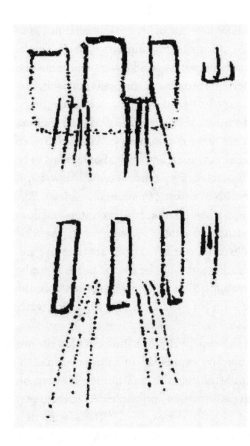

FIGURE 3.1. A sketch from Tanaka's diary, January 26, 1912. Tanaka's own caption reads: "These diagrams express the principle of nature (*tenchi*). River managers (*chisuika*) who understand the meaning of these images are truly rare." Source: Tanaka Shōzō, *Tanaka Shōzō zenshū* (Tokyo: Iwanami Shoten, 1977–80), 13:65.

But the natural freedom and equality of nagare, always present in nature, was everywhere confronted by the law-constructed obstacles that thwarted nature's inherent desire for beneficence. In his thoughts on water and nagare, Tanaka was fond of quoting the idiomatic expression "Water accommodates itself to a round bowl" (*mizu wa hōen no utsuwa ni shitagau*). But Tanaka claimed that this was true only of "dead water," water that had been artificially confined to such an extent that even regression was no longer possible and had become the complete absence of flow (*yodomi*, death). Tanaka saw the state's law as a constraining bowl, used to constrict the natural nagare of human freedom so that it too would be distorted, reverse itself, and, in extreme cases, result in death. If left unchecked, the growing constraints of the people by the law, too, would destroy Japan (and the world itself) and formed the basis of his quite literal "national death theory."[67] Rectifying ecological and social damage required smashing the bowl.

Completely reinterpreting the idiom in terms of his view of water not as as perfectly malleable and adaptable to any situation but as flow itself, Tanaka continued, "If the bowl were smashed," water would instantly become one with itself again and "immediately start to flow ... naturally following the principles [topography] of nature (*tenri*) [and not the artificial, confining bowl]."[68] While water may be formless, it is active and always in motion. There is no sense of balance or yin/yang dualism, only a choice between unrestricted flows and the stillness of an unnatural death. For humans to be free, then, they must reject all obstacles. They must become like water. If they can do so, they too will flourish in nature (*tennen ni tanoshimu*). Further, by doing so they will enter into a new relationship that fosters and does not fight the real powers of the land and water: "Flowing water (*chisui*) is the Way of Heaven. It does not exist for our benefit. We are to revere and not harm it. All I wish is that running water not be stopped; that it not be dirtied. ... With the hearts (*kono kokoro*) of all the villages, the states, the counties, all together in accord with it (*mizu ni shitagawaba*), this water only runs happily to the sea."[69]

Continuing his thoughts on the superiority of nature over law, in 1911 Tanaka articulated his most subversive expression of nature over nation: "We have a constitution. But unfortunately this constitution is based on Japanese principles, not on universal [natural] principles. As such, *even if Japan were to die, we are under no obligation to die with it.*"[70] This sentiment is possible because the land itself, the true source of freedom, will still exist. Both the Meiji constitution's "conferred rights," given to the people by the sovereign, and the liberals' natural rights, which exist within each individual and come together in the general will to form a national government, rely on the concept of the nation-state. Tanaka's conception does not. With these other state-based theories in mind, it is certainly not a stretch to call what Tanaka is talking about "environmental rights." Environmental rights based on the motion inherent in the healthy flows of nature itself are truly inalienable and could never be surrendered to a general will without the attendant distortion of regression and doku. Because they do not rely on the category of the nation, Tanaka's environmental rights exist above Japan— indeed, above all national subjectivities. A material nature as the ultimate source of freedom and the basis of what Tanaka began calling "the universal constitution" (*hiroki kempō, uchūteki kempō*) represents a complete rejection of the social Darwinist notion of nature as chaos tamed by state authority. It is also the culmination of the search for a guarantor of justice that began with the failed jikiso in 1901. This is not a cultural notion of a peculiarly Japanese relationship to nature. Here the land itself is not Japanese, and the nativists' mantra, "Japan is a divine country," is proscribed in this socio-ecological vision.

Tanaka's identification of water as the source of an original freedom initially suggests a Taoist understanding of the world and humans. But through contact with Arai's Swedenborgian theology and its teaching of taking up the cross in daily life, Yanakagaku moved beyond a negative definition of traditional Taoism, one that involves letting things be, or merely throwing oneself into a complete trust in nature. Instead Tanaka linked the Swedenborgian concepts of expiation of sin and "fighting together with God" to the ecological concept of extinguishing doku through the cultivation of the nagare ecology. In doing so, the Taoist *wuwei* ( J. *mui*), inflected by Arai's theology, became the transformative labor of Yanakagaku. This concept of rebirth and renewal, understood as "this worldly labor," allowed the conception of liberation *from within* the daily life of the Yanakan residents who defied the state's order to leave. The opening up to nature achieved through the perseverance of Yanakagaku was understood by Arai's Swedenborgian term "renew" or "open up to the new" (*kaishin*), at once a homonym of "reform" and explicitly coined to be distinguishable from the "opening up of things" (*kaibutsu*) of modern physics and the commercial exploitation of nature.[71] Arai's teaching on the embodiment of prayer in daily struggle stressed that through hard work and fighting together with God, eventually the "realm of the spiritual will open up," and from there things may be renewed. Daily practice, one's life itself, now also associated with the specific socio-ecology of the Yanakans, would become transformative, redemptive labor.

Importantly, and in contrast to other redemptive communities centered on a pure, unsullied nature, such as Mushakōji Saneatsu's Atarashiki mura, or the later agrarian fundamentalist versions, such as Tachibana Kōzaburō's Aikyōmura, or even Tanaka's friend and fellow antipollution activist Kinoshita Naoe's personal attempt to "seclude himself in the mountain," for Tanaka any redemption had to happen in Yanaka. A celebration of unsullied nature or wilderness was not only no longer possible in modern Japan; it was counterproductive. Tanaka explicitly criticized Kinoshita's attempt to drop out of the fight and retreat to this idealistic nature and mere personal cultivation. Tanaka's monism precluded the full separation of nature and society characteristic of later Taishō life philosophy and vitalism (*seimeishugi*). For him, the world was a single material economy of flows, not parallel processes that one could move in and out of at will. His appreciation for the strength of the expanding doku cycle (it had already spread from Ashio to Yanaka to Manchuria) taught him that doku must be turned back or it would create the "second [toxic] nature," making Kinoshita's flight to the wilderness and seclusion of his mountain retreat an impossibility. It was impossible to fight the doku cycle without first descending to the depths of poverty and pollution.

Before settling on "natural water management" (*chisui*), Tanaka experimented with defining his method in various ways, one of which he called the Three Nothings Church, his own version of a nonchurch church movement that went well beyond Uchimura Kanzō's more famous nonchurch church movement: "The Three Nothings Church (*san'mu kyōkai*): No selfishness, no prices, no literature (*bungaku*). From now on this is my religion."[72] Though defined negatively, the Three Nothings Church was an attempt to systematize Yanakagaku and rebuild a daily practice of nature based on a sense of value different from the nation, capitalism, or mere aesthetics. For this reason, Tanaka's privileged groups were not poets or artists. They were not the pure, but the wretched. Though Yanakans remained special in both the extent of their resistance and their location at the epicenter of the state's fight against nagare, Tanaka did look to other repressed groups within society; he increasingly included women as privileged seers. At talks to Tokyo's women's groups he warned women not to ignore the gift their status as victims gave them. He admonished them to resist the urge to become rich, even claiming that it was very dangerous for a woman to become rich, for money always seemed to cloud one's social vision. In his opinion, women had always both suffered more and seen the Ashio problem better. He noted that Furukawa Ichibei's wife had committed suicide after attending a Tokyo anti-Ashio rally where victims had described their suffering. Further, close to what today is called ecofeminism, Tanaka emphasized women's connection to healthful production, which he explicitly contrasted with the harmful production of men. In a side-by-side accounting, Tanaka listed the products of men: theft, murder, sake, tobacco (summed up as *kōgai*—one of the few times he used the term); and the products of women: weaving, textiles, paper maki, tea (summed up as *kōeki*).[73]

Like Ishikawa Sanshirō's unloved *domin* (土民) examined in the next chapter, modern Japan's despised populations, especially the water-like Yanaka "remainders," became what Žižek has called "the part of no-part" or the universal solvent of all social structures.[74] It was these oppressed groups, those that since the time of civilization and enlightenment had been rejected as the benighted, foolish masses (*gumin*), that Tanaka thought could see the true moral value that inhered in nature. They had grasped the truth—the revalorization of nature. This was their strength. Yanakans, he said, had lost everything but their "foolishness" (*gu*). There "is nothing left but to defend that foolishness."[75] Meiji rationalism had sought to sever the connection between the natural and human sciences, and it did so by divesting nature of all political and moral value. The long struggle against the Ashio pollution and later the flood-control plans relinked nature and politics. And it was the oppressed that could see it. If official knowledge could be transformed, it would be through the "foolishness" of the Yanakans: "Elementary school teaches geography well, foreign borders are known, but what of one's hometown's rivers? What and where is their source?"[76] It is therefore not too much to see the Yanakans as what contemporary radical ecology calls the ecological proletariat. This, I believe, is another reason Tanaka's environmental thought is expressed in the language of neo-Confucianism. In light of the unprecedented problems of the environmental crisis, neo-Confucianism's monistic language was one of the only languages available that could express the unity of the social and the natural in moral or political terms.

In his last years, Tanaka expressed some tantalizing thoughts regarding what an ecologically sane future society might look like. Through the practice of Yanakagaku and the resultant opening up to the world and value of nature, the powers of doku could be turned back and a new civilization based on nagare could be established. Tanaka called this new civilization "the civilization of rivers." In a critique of the hard engineering of the *fukoku-kyōhei* Meiji Era, Tanaka declared, "A civilization of rivers is not a civilization of roads!"[77] The exact meaning of "a civilization of roads" is not fully developed, but the language Tanaka uses to describe the two systems suggests that their respective attitudes toward nature are the key. The civilization of roads worships "straight lines," "hard corners," and "efficiency." Roads, of course, are by definition imposed on the land by humans and laid down by the needs of political economy. By contrast, the river follows the shortest path to the sea while respecting the topography. The active flow itself is determined by the real powers of the land. (Of course, the popular rights era struggle against Fukushima governor Mishima Michitsune's authoritarian politics and road-building projects is almost too perfect a metaphor for the governmental arrogance over nature and society of the early Meiji period.) In contrast to roads, a civilization of rivers must adhere to the limit of beneficial human agency toward nature; the humans in this civilization must be not subjugators or indiscriminate builders but managers of water.

If this were accomplished, the result would be the end of disasters and the restoration of nature so that it could function as the source of human life and rights in the form of the universal constitution. All self-cultivation was to be done in order to achieve an inner spirituality capable of managing the material and philosophical flow of water. Because they were situated at the site of the state's attempts to create "dead water" and the site of Japan's "act of violence since Meiji," Yanakans and those who grasped what they were teaching were uniquely qualified to see the truth and forge a new way as "natural *chisuika*." This Yanaka created by nature and cast aside by the river reforms already belonged more to the civilization of rivers than to that of roads. Anyone who wished to redeem Japanese modernity from "the toxic embrace of the Ashio faction" (which by now meant nearly all of modern Japanese politics and economics and even much public opinion) must practice Yankagaku. That person must embrace the "foolishness" of "vulgar learning on the path to achievement" ( *gegaku-jōtatsu*) until the world of nature opened up and he or she could become a water sage, naturally managing the flow of life through continuous hell-transforming labor.

As he grew older and sicker, Tanaka despaired of seeing the redemption of Yanaka. But he did find some areas of hope, especially in what he thought was a change in the next generation of Yanakans. He took heart in rumors that the younger generation was attempting to revive the *matsuri* in Yanaka's Osugi shrine, and he took even more pleasure in hearing that young men and women had begun meeting in the woods to "play" (*asoberi*) in nature. Play became for him a sign of a new practice of nature that could redeem the world: "The engineers' work is killing us. I wish they would stop working and start playing."[78] "Bringing in new soil is useless. We must stop the mine. DANCE!"[79] Here we have a new theory of the body and the human subject, one embedded in nature and in constant congress with its flows, a body that matches nature and the real power of the land and water in playful interaction, against the hard and ultimately futile "work" of trying to rebuild nature as a site of exploitable resources.

As shown in chapter 1, those who would cast Tanaka as an agrarianist place great emphasis on the first line of his autobiography of 1895, in which he states, "I am a peasant of Shimotsuke" (*Yo wa shimotsuke no hyakusho nari*). In chapter 2 I offered an alternative reading of this line and of the autobiography as a whole. But here, against the peasant consciousness theory and in light of Tanaka's thoughts on flow and playfulness, I think we can place much more emphasis on a later statement in Tanaka's diary: "I am an unleasher of flows" (*Yo wa nagare o nagasu mono nari*).[80] Despite his despair over the world, Tanaka felt that in Yanaka he had achieved something close to the innate, instinctual *mui* consciousness of the Yanakans and that he had been reborn as a water manager and unleasher of flows: "The Shōzō of today, the one who now exists according to the rules of *chisui*, he is not the Shōzō of old."[81] While I have been translating *chisui* as "river policy" or "water management," in light of Tanaka's "I am an unleasher of flows" declaration, the term must be read more broadly. It might best be translated as "managing the flow of nature" or even "managing the flow of life." Tanaka had completed his environmental turn.

As Tanaka explained, "Put simply, one must first become a sage in order to practice chisui."[82] One who studied "desktop chisui" would only produce more harm. Once developed, a natural chisui consciousness would be able to "know" water to such an extent that antagonism, exploitation, and manipulation would no longer be necessary. A different human-nature relationship would obtain: a sage in union with water would not constrict flow but achieve a mutual empathy. In Swedenborgian terms, both would have become of "helpful use" to each other. Thus Tanaka says, "We believe, if we say, 'Water! (*mizu yo!*), Fall not too much,' excessive rain will not fall. This is our truth. We believe that if we say, 'Water! Be still,' that the water will oblige."[83]

Both the emphasis on personal cultivation and the at times seemingly idealized nature echoed neo-Confucianism and brought Tanaka into close contact with the growing trend of Taishō vitalism. Some of his friends and mentors clearly belong in this increasingly depoliticized and mysticist movement. But as we saw, Tanaka criticized his fellow practitioner of the Okada *seiza* method, Kinoshita, for abandoning the world in pursuit of personal spiritual renewal. (Ishikawa Sanshirō criticized both Kinoshita and Tanaka for their dalliance with what he considered Okada's apolitical spiritualism.) Okada himself went much further in this direction, like many others, including Arai's teacher Harris, ultimately sliding from intense personalism into more right-wing vitalist movements.[84] Yet despite these points of contact with vitalism, Tanaka's vision always remained grounded in actual politics and centered on the very material practices of nature, society, and bodies in the destroyed Yanaka. It was of course Yanakans' resolve to resist the Pollution Prevention Committee through an alternative, everyday practice of nature by actually rebuilding their village on social and ecological principles that had sent him on the path to developing Yanakagaku in the first place. Thus, in Tanaka's natural chisui, self-cultivation maintains a constant and necessary connection to material nature, politics, and everyday life. For Tanaka, a destroyed Yanaka was the indispensable material base without which self-cultivation retreated into mere narcissism: "I've been struggling down here in the abyss of doku without reaching my goal. I have renewed my spirit—but this is not yet an occasion for praise."[85] Yanakagaku remains hell-transforming labor. Despite the transcendental language of the fundamental river law and its exaltation of a normative nature without humans, in a final inversion of Meiji's civilization and enlightenment, Tanaka's Yanakagaku remained socio-ecological to the end:

A True Civilization . . .
Does not crush its mountains
Does not destroy its rivers
Does not demolish its villages
Does not kill its people.[86]

# FOUR

# NATURAL DEMOCRACY

> But it will be said, bourgeois culture is suffering not from illusion but
> from disillusionment. . . . This is the very danger of its illusion, that it
> believes itself disillusioned . . . and because it is unaware of this illusion,
> and because this illusion is now stripped to its naked essence, it
> violently distorts the whole fabric of contemporary ideology.
>
> This illusion is that man is naturally free.
> —CHRISTOPHER CAUDWELL, *Studies in a Dying Culture*

If Tanaka Shōzō no longer represents Japan's peasant conscience and is recaptured as a Meiji liberal who became an environmental thinker, a vast and
vibrant tradition of prewar Japanese environmental thought emerges. In
fact, throughout the period from 1910 through 1950, many thinkers and activists continued working on the status of nature in industrial society. Two
important thinkers directly connected to Ashio and Tanaka, the anarchist
Ishikawa Sanshirō (1876–1956) and the founder of Snow Brand Dairy (Yukijirushi), Kurosawa Torizō (1885–1982), tried desperately to develop new
practices of nature that would undo past damage and foster human health
and freedom. Ishikawa is known, together with Kōtoku Shūsui and Ōsugi
Sakae, as one of Japan's leading anarchists. But unlike Kōtoku or Ōsugi, who
largely chose urban workers as the privileged subject of revolutionary transformation, Ishikawa stayed in the countryside, focusing on the environmental crisis as the most urgent issue of Japanese modernity. His social

ecology, what he called "dynamic social aesthetics" (*dōtai shakai bigaku*), was a major expansion of Japan's environmental turn after Tanaka's death and the "official" ending of the Ashio Incident with the flooding of the Yanaka reservoir in 1915. That much historiography on Japanese environmental politics seems to reach a dead end in 1913—only to be rediscovered by postwar people's historians (*minshūshi*) of the 1960s—is all the more striking given Ishikawa's long, deep links with Tanaka and the Yanaka struggles. Indeed, Ishikawa claimed that his "revolutionary baptism" came by witnessing the violence of the Meiji state's destruction of the Yanaka levees in 1906. So deep were the connections that fellow anti-Ashio activist Kinoshita Naoe even referred to Ishikawa as "Tanaka's child."

Ishikawa's thought and activism shows the deep connections between the environmental crisis and the "the social problem" (*shakai mondai*). In 1908, Ishikawa was jailed for participation in the anarchist protest known as the Red Flag Incident (*Akahata jiken*, 1908).[1] In prison he read widely on Western socialism and economics, establishing contact with two mentors: Paul Reclus, the brother of anarchist geographer Élisée Reclus; and the English social reformer, Fabian, vegetarian, and gay rights activist Edward Carpenter. Being in prison likely saved Ishikawa from being swept up in the Great Treason Incident of 1911, which claimed many leftists, including, of course, *jikiso* co-author Kōtoku Shūsui. Nonetheless, during the subsequent government repression of "dangerous" thought, the so-called winter period of the Japanese Left, Ishikawa fled to Europe, where he stayed until 1920. He initially sought passage to Europe legally, but when he was refused a passport by authorities in Yokohama, fellow activist Fukuda Hideko introduced him to a sympathetic Belgian consul, and Ishikawa was smuggled to Brussels posing as the attendant of the consul's wife.[2] From Brussels he went to London, where he was met by Carpenter, and the two traveled to Carpenter's Millthorpe cottage in Sheffield, where Ishikawa was introduced to the virtues of "the simple life" of rural retreat. After some time at Millthorpe, Ishikawa returned to Brussels to stay with Paul Reclus. There he worked as a decorator and painter, staying to care for the Recluses' home even after the Germans occupied the city during World War I.[3] Ishikawa later reunited with the Recluses, traveling with them to their homes in Dordogne and Morocco. It was in Dordogne that for more than five years Ishikawa practiced "the life of a part-time farmer" (*hannō seikatsu*), living by the motto "In sun, to the fields; in rain, to the books."

After returning to Japan in 1920, Ishikawa published countless articles and speeches in which he rejected all forms of open-ended development as a futile "pursuit of shadows," a pursuit that grew increasingly divorced from the essential conditions of life, especially the land itself. Throughout the 1920s, Ishikawa worked tirelessly to expose what he believed to be the hidden assumption of unlimited progress that lurked beneath the surface of nearly all modern ideologies: capitalism, socialism, Bolshevism, and evolutionism. In direct contrast to these ideologies of "cornucopianism"—the belief that nature was infinitely exploitable—Ishikawa argued for an "anti-cornucopian" view of the environment as a realm of human practice spatially and temporally bounded by an inescapable and historical materiality of inorganic, organic, and even cosmic processes. Unlike Second International socialism, which embraced Darwinian evolution—or Ōsugi, who adapted it to anarchist thought—Ishikawa rejected natural selection as an untenable thesis in the face of unprecedented disasters at Ashio and in World War I Belgium. Ishikawa's embrace of long-forgotten non-Darwinian thinkers has caused some historians to discount him as an anti-intellectual romantic or even as an irrationalist. But Ishikawa did not reject evolution from a romantic or even ethical standpoint. What marks him as a modern thinker of the environmental crisis is his skepticism toward the basic premise of Darwin's theory: the optimistic promise that organisms adapt to their environments. For Ishikawa, Ashio, Yanaka, and World War I proved that humanity and nature were not harmonizing, but diverging. As such, non-Darwinian theories of change better explained the apparent disconnect between society and nature—what recent Marxists have called the "metabolic rift" of capitalist modernity.[4]

In a speech in 1920, Ishikawa—under Carpenter's influence—coined the term *domin kurashī* (土民生活, "life of the people attached to the earth"; *chi ni tsukeru minshū*) as a translation of "democracy." Domin kurashī—or, using Ishikawa's gloss of domin as the Greek "demos," *demokurashī*—became the basis of Ishikawa's new vision of a society adequate to the metabolic rift of industrial production revealed in the Ashio crisis. Demokurashī was a return to the earth as a counter to the dangerous pursuit of shadows encouraged by modern life.[5]

Ishikawa is especially important because unlike his mentors Tanaka, Reclus, and Carpenter, he lived to see the fascist inflection of the "back to the land" ideology of the 1930s. In a self-published journal he called *Dynamique* (*Dinamikku*), Ishikawa struggled to distance his own thought from the "extreme" nature of the agrarian fundamentalists' native village, which he saw as a static, constraining place. But in rejecting the extreme nature of the fascists, Ishikawa was also forced to reject the ultimate "authority of the soil" that could be the source of authentic human life he had preached in the 1920s. In *Dynamique* he combined Carpenter, Reclus, and Comte into his own social ecology, a dynamic social aesthetics (*dōtai shakai bigaku*) that sought to integrate external stimulation, conscious choice, the material environment, and history (evolution). As the human subject moved within a world of vibrating matter, this movement—daily life itself—could create resonances with the world around it, a "cosmic symphony" in which each individual contributed a melody but never disappeared into the whole. In dynamic social aesthetics, Ishikawa proposed a dispersed and diffused social ecology of overlapping, temporary alliances between all living things that rose up and dissolved again before they could harden into hierarchies of domination and control.[6] Decades before Deleuze and Guattari, he opposed Japanese industrial modernity with his "complex net-form social organization" based on the rhizome. His inclusion of biology as on par with the other social sciences of history, economics, sociology, and psychology, like Tanaka's monism, betrayed a sense of indeterminacy between first and second natures, the clear separation on which both Meiji rationalism and agrarian fundamentalism's Japanized nature was built.[7] During the Fifteen-Year War, Ishikawa attempted a social aesthetics reading of the East-West conflict, an ambitious effort to debunk the very notion of race by showing that the history of all peoples was nothing more than countless, temporary constitutions and reconstitutions with no center or origin.[8]

From 1920s demokurashī to wartime criticism to postwar utopian cooperative thinking, Ishikawa's lifelong struggle to build natural and social relations that would thwart authoritarian structures and guarantee health and freedom for all life shows just how problematic the concept of nature can be once it is fully integrated into human history. His dynamic social aesthetics was the search for a political and scientific vocabulary adequate to a material nature that had lost its autonomy but not its agency. In many ways his dynamic social aesthetics anticipated the recent neo-Lamarckian "epigenetic revolution" and the current call to consider humanity's unprecedented ability to intervene in its environment a geological force that defines our age.[9] Further, his not always successful attempt to resist the equally oppressive determinisms of sociobiology and the romantic identification with the national soil not only reveals the metabolic rift as a deep current in Japan's modern intellectual and social history; it also suggests environmental history's strong potential to go beyond merely supplementing national narratives, turning environmental history into a surprisingly rich source of political, social, and cultural critique.

## The Break with Socialism and Demokurashī

In the early 1900s, Ishikawa was active in the Yanaka struggle both on-site and as an editor of the *New Era* (*Shinkigen*), a Christian socialist journal that succeeded the *Heimin shinbun* after the latter was closed for its opposition to the Russo-Japanese War (1904–5). *Shinkigen* published articles and sponsored Tokyo speeches by Tanaka. It also pioneered the "one-*tsubo* landowner" movement, in which activists and urban sympathizers purchased small plots in Yanaka both as financial aid to the villagers and to complicate the state's acquisition of the land.[10] It was in Yanaka that Ishikawa claimed to have been awakened to a concept of revolution based in daily life and ecological practice when he witnessed Tanaka and the Yanaka residents rebuilding part of the state-destroyed levees in the summer of 1906. Standing on the levees with Kinoshita Naoe and Henmi Onokichi in March 1906, as he watched the Yanakans work in a heavy rain, Ishikawa came to see the Meiji state as a destroyer of both people and nature: "We walked the levees and everywhere I could see the violence of our government in the remains of wrecked homes, with no green sprouting anywhere." He returned on April 28, the deadline for the Yanakans to remove the rebuilt levees. He had come to witness the anticipated clash with police, but none came that day. (The levee was cut a day later, at night, to avoid just such a confrontation.) The next day Ishikawa stood witness as Tanaka led the Yanakans in the rebuilding of the levees in the middle of yet another downpour. The Yanakans' resistance inspired him to an almost religious fervor, and he "could no longer sit by, and jumped onto the levees[,] delivering a lecture on class war." But as he later states, he was the one being educated as he watched the Yanakans rebuild their village:

> After hurrying for two miles or so I climbed one of the levees to
> where I could see the whole of a vast Yanaka. Up there on that levee
> I could not hold back the tears and "Revolution!" welled up from the
> depths of my breast. . . . These Yanakans who have shed tears of
> blood to rebuild the levees destroyed by the state. . . . Here starts the
> revolution. . . . This Yanaka, my Yanaka—Tanaka's Yanaka—the
> lessons I received there were many. Yanaka is my benefactor, my
> mentor (*onjin*). . . . If I am to go on to be a revolutionary, it must be
> said I received my revolutionary baptism in Yanaka. . . . To see the
> countless threats and dangers ceaselessly visited upon this place by
> the state, . . . I could neither stop my blood from boiling nor my tears
> from flowing.[11]

It was precisely during this period, from his first meeting with Tanaka to the destruction of Yanaka, that Ishikawa, in a debate with Sakai Toshihiko, began to develop his idea of social revolution by means other than formal worker-capitalist class war.

The proximate cause of the debate was Ishikawa's refusal of Sakai's invitation to join the newly formed, and immediately banned, Japan Socialist Party (Nihon shakaitō). The dispute officially began when Sakai published a critique of Ishikawa's views on class war (*Kaikyō sensō ron*) that had appeared in the May 10, 1906, issue of *Shinkigen*. Ishikawa had argued for a spiritual socialism to precede or at least parallel any proletarian revolution as a means to avoid merely replacing capitalist selfishness (*riyoku*) with worker selfishness. Mirroring anarchist-socialist debates in Japan and the West, Ishikawa's social view began from the question "What is the life of society?" (*shakai no seimei*), to which he answered, "The world of work lived by the workers." This perspective, which was part of a much larger Japanese anarchist valorization of the actually lived world of the people (*heimin*) over formal subjects (*kokumin*), led him to see the capitalist class as an exterior shell to the inner world of work.[12] It further suggested that the goal of revolution was not reachable through class war. Instead it required developing this actually existing "world of work," making it "wider, higher, deeper, stronger." Ishikawa cited Tanaka's move into Yanaka as an explicit example of how this might work in practice. For Ishikawa, immersion in the world of work would provide almost infinite possibilities for deepening and enriching the life of society. Contra Sakai, it followed that the formation of a party was antithetical to this broad field of resistance, because a party "is not a means to create [socialist] fervor or revolutionary feeling in the people, but a place to discipline people who already have that fervor." What was needed was something Ishikawa called the second path to socialism: [trans]mission (*dendō*). For Ishikawa, the danger of forming a party was that because of any party's disciplining organizational structure, its members would have fewer and fewer ways of fighting the class war. This could develop to the point where "it becomes too difficult to even think [class struggle, let alone practice it]. . . . That is why I don't see much practical difference between your [Sakai's] Japanese Socialist Party and Yamaji Aizan's National Socialist Party [which explicitly denied class war theory]."[13] Instead of being a class warrior, it was better to be a "transmitter" or "missionary" (*dendōsha*), outside any party apparatus, a single person—Tanaka had called this *tada no hitori*—working for freedom in a "free world" (*jiyū no tenchi*). The Yanakans' seemingly inexhaustible ability to resist the combined violence of the Meiji state and the Furukawa zaibatsu now appeared as an expression not only of Tanaka's *nagare*, but also of Ishikawa's struggle of daily life to deepen the world of work. Unlike the socialists who saw the Yanaka struggle as a peasant throwback, for Ishikawa the Yanakans' ends and means were aligned, so their struggle was modern and pure, grounded in their daily lives.

The Ishikawa-Sakai dispute was part of a much larger split in the Japanese Left in 1907, the year of both the destruction of Yanaka and—in February—the Ashio miners' riot. The internecine dispute also led to the breakup of the jikiso coalition that had come together from 1900 to 1901. Though increasingly distanced from each other both physically and ideologically, Tanaka and anti-Ashio protesters focused on Yanaka had managed to collaborate with those moving to a model of liberation based on the industrial proletariat. *Shinkigen* was itself a product of this collaboration. But as we saw, for Tanaka the redemption of Yanaka was by 1907 *the* struggle opened up by industrial society. Socialists, too, were refining their position. Jikiso author Kōtoku Shūsui's speech at the Socialist Party annual meeting a few weeks after the Ashio riot was explicit in rejecting the path of Tanaka and instead focusing attention on the privileged actor (the Japanese proletariat) and method (class war) that would come to dominate Japanese socialism: "Tanaka Shōzō is a man of admirable character, and we could not hope for a better one in the Diet if we waited a dozen years. But what has Tanaka accomplished in twenty years of crying out in the Diet? He couldn't lay a finger on Furukawa's mine, Gentlemen! But look what the Ashio laborers did in only three days. Didn't they terrify the privileged class! Violence is bad, but you must admit that three days of action did more than twenty years of parliamentary talk."[14] Kōtoku's relocation of struggle from the Yanaka levees to the mine is obvious and strident. But rather than an "expected" turn to "true socialist" positions,"[15] the differences between Tanaka and Kōtoku come down to differing positionalities toward nature. For his part Tanaka was sympathetic to socialism in most instances, declaring, "Socialism is the vitality of our times."[16] But he differed on his relationship to nature as seen in the Yanaka problem: "Socialists say that if we rationalize economics, industrialize production, and share the proceeds equally then we can enjoy a relaxed life without the drudgery of work today. But this is a future ideal. The revival of nature and the ability to once again grow rice and barley in a Yanaka destroyed by an artificial (*jin'i*) flood is what is important now."[17] To look for "true socialist" categories risks losing not only the still significant points of contact with heimin ideology but also the trauma of Marx's "metabolic rift" and Tanaka's understanding of the prior rupture of society and nature so that a co-opted *tennen* is now producing *doku*. Furthermore, as we saw in chapter 3, Kōtoku was wrong. With the failure of the jikiso, Tanaka and the antipollution movement had moved beyond parliamentary protest in favor of a monistic social ecology based on a material economy of flows that could be organized for healthful or harmful effects.

In Yanaka, too, a similar debate over tactics had unfolded on day 4 of the destruction. A young activist from Tokyo, Endo Tomojirō, had criticized Tanaka and Kinoshita's policy of nonviolent resistance, arguing that it was clearly not preventing the dismantling of Yanaka. Kinoshita and Shimada Sōzo, whose home already had been destroyed the day before, relayed the criticism to Tanaka. Shimada reports that Tanaka replied,

> That is the advice of a young man and very dangerous advice at that. Whoever takes that road goes to jail and can no longer do anything to help [rebuild Yanaka]. Look at what happened at Kawamata [the protestor-police clash in 1900]. The people were arrested, charged, and tried. Every day [for over a year] police were in and out of the villages, forcing everyone to live in fear inside their homes—just like the dead. It was a huge mistake. We don't fight violence. Until the very end we work for the realization, the actualization of the Constitution and Law, never straying from the recovery of Yanaka—of all the poisoned lands.[18]

Already wary of Sakai and the Japan Socialist Party's methods and theory, Ishikawa eventually made a full break with socialism, namely over the reembrace by socialists of a technocratic promise of the future subjugation of nature and the elimination of disasters. The debate played out in the pages of *Shinkigen*, such as in the 1906 editorial titled "Natural Calamities and Social Troubles": "Natural calamities are mostly beyond our control at present, but our knowledge is advancing so steadily and rapidly that the time will surely come when science can make the mysteries of the universe plain to us and will enable us to conquer and subjugate all these unavoidable disasters."[19] Rather than the subjugation of nature through technological and scientific progress, anarchists such as Ishikawa sought an accommodation with the material realities of the "real powers of the land and waters" by aligning human thought, practice, and social organization with nature. Japan's environmental turn was born with the realization that disaster was not something that came from the outside, that it was instead actively produced in an ill-defined socio-ecological site that had yet to be worked out politically, socially, economically, or even existentially. Ishikawa was one of the most interesting, and frustrating, thinkers who tried to work out the maddening details of an active nature increasingly subsumed under industrial capitalist relations.

In the following years, the site of Ishikawa's confrontation with socialism moved from a debate over revolutionary tactics to the role of nature, namely the status of Darwinian evolution. In Europe, Ishikawa argued that both the optimism of liberal modernizers and the mechanistic teleology of Second International socialists were exposed by the horrors of World War I. Ishikawa came to see both theories of mechanical progress as harmful fantasies, no different from the arrogant faith in material progress that led the Meiji state to destroy Yanaka. "Darwinism is a religion now . . . an authoritarian dogma. . . . It's not any different from the elderly believers in the Pure Land of the Western Paradise."[20] Ishikawa traced the basis of Darwinism and socialism in a long discussion of the history of progressive thought (*shinpo shisō*) from Montesquieu to Turgot and Condillac, from there to Spencer and Proudhon (both of whom he saw as tainted by this tradition), and finally to Darwin and Marx. For Ishikawa, the failure of this tradition at Ashio and Verdun also meant the failure of the socialist vision: "Without an absolute, automatic, natural evolution, socialism loses its foundation."[21] In several texts from the 1920s Ishikawa denounced the metaphysical pieties of modern progressive thought that underwrote Second International socialism and its faith that historical forces would inevitably lead toward the collapse of capitalism and the triumph of socialism. Under the influence of Carpenter and Reclus in Europe, he continued the move toward a much more reciprocal understanding of the human-nature relationship.

Immediately upon his return to Japan in 1920, Ishikawa founded a Japanese Fabian Society and announced his theory of "natural democracy" (demokurashī) as a cure for the ills of Japanese modernity. Like contemporary founders of redemptive communities such as Mushakōji Saneatsu and Shirakaba group members Yanagi Sōetsu and Shiga Naoya, Ishikawa, too, in his writings on World War I, built a hierarchy of nature over society.[22] And, in the 1920s at least, like these others he located true freedom in nature, identifying society with empty, vague appetites (*mumei no yoku*), an ultimately suicidal "pursuit of one's own shadow." For Ishikawa such a pursuit was a quest that ended in tragedy, for the only moment when the shadow was grasped came as one inevitably collapsed from exhaustion, falling to the ground in death. The main theme of Ishikawa's demokurashī of the 1920s indicted the pursuit of open-ended gain as a metaphysical dogma imposed on the world by humans. Such endless acquisitiveness, he argued, was not found in nature itself.

As mentioned, Ishikawa's demokurashī was really a domin kurashī, a return to the earth as a counter to the dangerous pursuit of shadows encouraged by modern life. In a speech given in 1920 shortly after his return to Japan, Ishikawa explained that his neologism had been inspired by a discussion with Carpenter at Millthorpe in 1913:

> I remarked how the kind of democracy developed in *Towards Democracy* [1883] was such a shocking twist on the normal use of the word. As I was saying this, [Carpenter] pulled a Greek dictionary from the shelf and explained to me that the original meaning of "*demos*" meant "a people attached to the soil" (*chi ni tsukeru minshū*). This meaning has been lost in today's usage . . . lost in the vulgar use by the Americans. And so, this "*demos*" I render as "*domin*" (土民)and "-*cracy*" as "*kurashī*" (生活). . . . In other words, *domin kurashī* [土民生活] expresses the true meaning of democracy.[23]

Ishikawa's understanding of demokurashī is clear: it is "*the life of* a people attached to the soil*.*" Personal autonomy requires a definite and active relation to the ultimate means of production, the land itself. But from Yanaka to World War I Belgium it seemed to him that those who lived in the world of commerce and in the city were alienated from the necessities of life, namely food, clothing, and shelter. The extreme deprivation they suffered when these phantom creations were destroyed in moments of crisis proved how precarious modern life had become:

> [With the war] one could see the truth, see human life in all its nakedness. . . . [The war] destroyed the empty, false life, the pursuit of shadows. It revealed the truth that no one is as strong as the farmer (*hyakusho*). It was then I understood that a farmer was one who stood tall with feet firmly planted on a strong earth. . . . All who lived by means of power and [political] organizations had lost their footing and fallen into abjection. But the farmers could still rely on their newly revealed powers. . . . And so I saw the truth: live by your own means within nature, make the sun, earth, trees, grass and birds your partners.[24]

Ishikawa likened the societies these acquisitive dogmas produced to a Tower of Babel, built so high that it was out of all proportion—an overdevelopment—to the basis of life, the land itself. World War I in Europe, like the Russo-Japanese War or the Yanaka Incident for Tanaka, was a moment of crisis that exposed the true nature of society. For Ishikawa, the crisis of World War I had "stripped European society to its core," revealing two competing sources of life.

Ishikawa took this original disconnect of life from its natural base as the origin of countless other discontinuities between means and ends: "The nation and society are now faced with the crisis that comes with the end of its disillusionment (*genmetsu*); in other words, a great change is at hand." This original crisis of separation from the land was everywhere manifested in the disconnect of means and ends that rippled throughout society. The army founded at the start of the Meiji period to secure the communal livelihood of the citizens did so by attacking the liberty and independence of brothers in neighboring countries. The circulation of goods meant to bridge the gap between individuals and regions and harmonize income instead resulted in the creation of barriers and the monopolization of national income. The police meant to preserve the people's freedom from threat and violence themselves became practitioners of oppressive violence. In short, all of society had been chasing an illusion of its own creation, a "modern-day Tower of Babel" built by science and industry.[25] Only agriculture existed in a seemingly unmediated relationship with the essentials of life and could continue providing when social, cultural, diplomatic, and economic relationships had broken down. Against open-ended temporalities of accumulation exposed by the crises, Ishikawa called for a return to the land and its cyclical temporalities of day, night, and the seasons. He claimed that the simple fact of the earth's rotation would create centrifugal forces that would topple the Tower of Babel humans had built on it.

Ishikawa's embrace of cyclical temporalities came from Élisée Reclus, who in his six-volume opus *L'homme et la terre* (1905–8) had made the natural rhythms of (earthly) rotation and (solar) revolution the basis of his own theory.[26] These temporalities were at once the most local and intimate—manifested in daily life experience of night and day and the changing seasons—and the most cosmic. Rotation and revolution thus sought to unify daily life with the universal, as close to the infinite as finite human beings could get. But Ishikawa went beyond merely translating Reclus. Reclus had criticized modern social organization, but he did believe in a behind-the-scenes operation of progress that was improving humanity in general. Ishikawa's anti-cornucopianism is clear when we notice that though he took these temporalities from Reclus, in the demokurashī speech,

Ishikawa argued for a much more delimited temporal theory of preservation and cultivation (of an original health and freedom). In place of Reclus's *time of spiraling progress* we have Ishikawa's *space of cultivation*. The Reclus that emerges from Ishikawa's introduction and translation of *L'homme et la terre* has also lost his faith in generalized progress and become an Ishikawa anti-cornucopianist.[27]

Ishikawa concluded the demokurashī speech by calling for the reorganization of all industry around the concept of cultivating the earth: "All industry, trade, politics, and education should be done in the service of cultivating the earth (*chi o tagayasu*). This is our ideal society—an industry of agri-cultivation (*kōjijigyō*, 耕地事業). This is demokurashī." The characters he chose for "cultivation" used the Chinese pronunciation for cultivation of the soil, *chi o tagayasu*—*kōji*—making it a homonym for and alternative to the standard phrase "(machine) industry" (*kōjijigyō*, 工事事業). As opposed to the building of enormous but unstable towers, what was needed was depth, "deep cultivation" (*fukaku tagayasu*) of the earth.[28] Cultivating the earth was the way to put humans in touch with authentic growth.[29] In his speech, Ishikawa read from his diary of 1917, written while he was working as a part-time farmer at the Recluses' home in Domme. His language fuses Reclus's cosmic temporalities with Carpenter's vitalistic images of bursting buds, seeds, and chrysalises in *Towards Democracy*: "Buds are born. . . . Yesterday's heat was oppressive. All had seemed ready to wither and die, even the seeds below ground were likely struggling. But hot days bring dewy nights. And that silent dew replenished the earth [so today the field is green]. . . . The buds grow on their own (*mizukara o nobashieta*). . . . Last night as we humans slept, [the buds] pierced the earth's surface and appeared before us." The self-starting moments of individual resistance that Ishikawa had first glimpsed in Yanaka were here elevated to a theory of all life as it struggles to express itself, even "in the face of tyrants [here, the oppressive heat] . . . even in troubled times. . . . Happy are those who plant seeds."

With production redefined as cultivation of the earth, the reward for this new form of production would be to achieve the ultimate goal absent in the socialist focus on class struggle, the unification of ends and means in daily life. This in turn would reveal earth's beauty and poetry of motion, making work and art one.[30] Only in this way would humans be able to avoid a repeat of the social and ecological disasters of the first quarter of the twentieth century. In the end, Ishikawa's theory might best be considered neither a rejection of evolution nor a retreat to a static equilibrium. As rotation and

revolution replace the progress and accumulation of linear time, his becomes a theory of constant variation that may or may not be conducive to
(individual and social) health and freedom.

Ishikawa tried to re-create this life attached to the soil in March 1927
when he moved to the village of Chitose, west of Tokyo. There he began
holding study sessions on Reclus and Carpenter, while also undertaking
experiments in small-scale farming and nudism as a way to get in touch with
authentic human life. In 1927, in preparation for this move, he published *The
Authority of the Soil* through his own "common studies press" (*kyōgakusha*)
and "for the benefit of the Farmers' Autonomy Association (*Nōmin
jichikai*)."[31] As we shall see below, with the rise of agrarian nationalism,
Ishikawa was later forced to further refine his theories of authority, a deep
process of self-reflection that eventually became his extraordinary, antiau-
thoritarian social ecology called "dynamic social aesthetics." To understand
how he was able to simultaneously criticize mechanistic theories of progress yet maintain a material theory of the body-in-environment that brought
him close to, but ultimately able to critique fascist visions of, the agrarian
fundamentalists (*nōhonshugisha*), we must first look closely at Ishikawa's
theory of life.

### Land, Life, and Lamarck

Although Ishikawa's privileging of nature over society superficially resem-
bled vitalism's romantic, spiritualist, even irrationalist rejections of modern
life, there was a robust view of material and *biological* life behind Ishikawa's
rejection of progress. It is true that Ishikawa did criticize Darwinian evolution's natural selection as (much like political parties' ideologies) a theory
of external determination that threatened to thwart and constrain the active
desire for freedom that existed within each living organism. It is also true
that Ishikawa was influenced by both European moral thought—Morris,
Carpenter, Ruskin, and Kropotkin—and the East Asian ethical tradition of
mutual aid (*tanomoshi kō*). But ultimately Ishikawa did not reject evolution
from an ethical position. Rather, I argue that the key to Ishikawa's social
ecology comes from his rejection of natural selection's optimistic promise
that organisms develop to fit into their environments. This rejection of natural selection made his views on evolution a bit different from many anarchists who largely followed Darwin but purged *Origin* of much Malthusian
and Spencerian struggle.[32] For Ishikawa, subjective, neo-Lamarckian theories of mutation—in which the organism is the *subject* of evolution rather

than the *object* of natural selection—better explained what he saw as the growing disconnect between society and nature. Though many Taishō vitalists did reject material civilization in favor of a spiritualized nature, and though Ishikawa did include a neo-Lamarckian subjective moment that culminated in what he saw as an emancipatory new mode of production, like Tanaka's use of neo-Confucian language to talk simultaneously of politics and nature, Ishikawa's inclusion of a subjective moment of choice was an extended interrogation of the "natural" part of natural selection, and a way for him to begin theorizing the recent rupture he saw between nature and society.

A suspicion of natural selection was in no way confined to Japan. Prior to the synthesis of Mendelian genetics and Darwinism in the mid-twentieth century, non-Darwinian models were not an unreasonable theory on a purely scientific basis. Indeed, across the scientific community, the 1890s to the 1910s was a period that historian of science Peter Bowler has called the "eclipse of Darwinism."[33] During this crucial period, natural selection as the mechanism of evolution was seriously challenged by various neo-Lamarckian and other vitalist theories of internal drives. According to non-Darwinian theories of evolution, it was these internal drives—especially the desire for life—and not natural selection that grounded a more individualized, "creative evolution." Darwin himself at times fostered this view. Despite his famous marginalia in his copy of *The Vestiges of Creation* promising never to use the terms "higher" or "lower," the later Darwin occasionally did include teleological language promoting a trend toward perfection, even adding neo-Lamarckian elements to later editions of *The Origin of Species*.[34] In Ishikawa's France of the 1910s, Darwinism and natural selection were even weaker, as Lamarckian evolution had been a feature of French scientific life for decades prior to Darwin's *Origin*.[35] Ishikawa's rejection of mechanical progress was part of this tradition.

With his gaze firmly set on the darker moments of recent history at Ashio and Verdun, Ishikawa also rejected the optimistic trends of much neo-Lamarckian theory in favor of pessimistic, more ominous theories of decline.[36] Theories such as Theodor Eimer's internally driven "overdevelopment" or Edward Drinker Cope's orthogenesis seemed to provide a better explanation for the apparent suicidal pursuit of industrial progress that produced the modern rift between humanity and the natural world. Orthogenesis, a theory of *nonadaptive*, even *maladaptive* variation, directly countered the Utilitarian thesis at the basis of Darwin's natural selection. Orthogenesis's enormous popularity was strengthened by paleontologists, such as the

American Henry Fairfield Osborn, who believed they saw in the fossil record long-range nonadaptive trends—indeed, trends that seemed to be actively harmful, occasionally even leading to a species' extinction. (Of course,
there is a way to reconcile these developments and even extinction with
Darwinian evolution, but we should remember that much of what was
called Darwinian evolution in those years, especially in prewar Japan,
was in fact much closer to more mechanistic theories of progress coming
from Spencer.) Famous examples of maladaptive overdevelopment leading to extinction included the enormous antlers of the Irish elk and the
oversized canines of the saber-toothed tiger. By apparently showing that
traits originally evolved for a purpose could at some point become antithetical to a species' continued existence, these cases of excessive growth
suggested an anti-utilitarianism at work in species development. Within
the orthogenesis community itself the theories were often decidedly pessimistic, leading some, including Eimer, to develop ominous concepts such
as "racial senility." Though Ishikawa rejected this grim logic, armed with
Eimer's and Osborn's theories he had a scientific basis for his criticism of
vague, open-ended yearning, and the "overdevelopment" signified in his
Tower of Babel metaphor from the demokurashī speech in 1920, allowing
Ishikawa to argue that Ashio and World War I could be early warning signs
of a future extinction if the human species could not change its internal
drive toward endless accumulation.

In order to escape the mechanical inevitability of decline preached by
some theories of orthogenesis, Ishikawa was also drawn to the "constancy"
or "preservationist" theories of the French biologist René Quinton. Quinton's theory, too, did include an organism's struggle with the environment,
but this struggle was a conservative one meant only to preserve the original
balance that existed between an organism and the earth's environment at
the moment of that species' emergence. Under Quinton's theory, because the
individual body was permeable and required constant interaction with the
outside, drastic changes in the environment would have a harmful effect on
the health of the organism. According to Quinton's 1904 *L'eau de mer, milieu
organique: Constance du milieu marin originel, comme milieu vital des cellules, à
travers la série animale*—a text Ishikawa quoted at length in *On Evolution*
(*Shinka to wa*, 1923), *Evolution and Socialism* (*Shinkaron to shakaishugi*,
1924), *Return to the Golden Age* (*Genshi ōgonjidai no kaiko*, 1925), and *Anti-
Evolutionism and Human Life* (*Hishinkaron to jinsei*, 1933)—all organisms
struggled to preserve the proper, healthful relation between internal and
external environments, most importantly salinity, freshwater ratios, and

temperature differentials. Ishikawa called these goals the "three great preservation/conservation principles."

For Quinton and Ishikawa, the maintenance of these healthful relations with the environment—and not progressive evolution or open-ended development—was essential for human health. According to Quinton's theory, individual cells regulated their relation to the external environment by effecting changes within its plasma. This plasma contained—in its temperature, salt, and freshwater ratios—its original relation to the original environment, the sea. So sure was Quinton of this original relation to the sea that he even conducted experiments by bleeding dogs and replacing the lost plasma with his own invention, a product derived from seawater that debuted in 1907, Plasma de Quinton. Ishikawa cites this experiment, repeating Quinton's own claims that the dogs not only recovered but eventually had more energy than before the procedure. Something of this tradition continues today. Online one may still purchase new versions of Plasma de Quinton: Quinton®Hypertonic and Quinton®Isotonic. The latter promises "the revival of the metabolic functions of the organism by correcting any deficiency in mineral salts and trace elements."[37] Ishikawa's attachment to Quinton's constancy theory was part of his theory of variation within rotation and revolution that must come to replace open-ended development.

Ishikawa also believed that Quinton's theory disproved the teleological claim, shared by Darwinism and contemporary socialism, that humans were the product of a long development toward perfection. The basis of Quinton's claim was the common belief that the earth had been cooling continuously since its separation from the sun. While it was soon overturned with the theory of solar radiation, this thermodynamic explanation for the earth's age is found in countless theorists, from seventeenth-century astronomer and paleontologist Nicholas Steno to Cuvier to Kant. A cooling earth meant organisms could be dated by their internal temperatures, as a species that had appeared in a cooler world would have needed to compensate with a higher internal temperature. Because humans and mammals had internal temperatures several degrees higher than reptiles, this suggested that they appeared later. But a human's internal temperature is in turn lower than that of most birds, meaning that under the thermodynamic theory birds emerged later than humans. Given these assumptions, this theory undermined the anthropocentric triumphalism of mechanistic Darwinism. Ishikawa therefore claimed that, in order to be consistent, Darwinists should regard birds as "higher" forms of life than humans. Inaccuracies of the chronology of species aside, the point was to denounce the qualitative language of "higher and lower" and "complete and incomplete" as unjustified impositions of linear temporality and particularist cultural values onto nature: "Humans call that which is close to themselves high, and that which is far, low. Whites believe themselves to be the best in the world, and so when they see blacks they assume them to be inferior savages. . . . Just what is completion or perfection anyway? By what standard is it judged? . . . A duck is not a less perfect, less complete crane because its legs are shorter." Later he concluded, "The idea that we are more advanced than previous peoples is a mere self-conceit of modern thinkers."[38] Even if it was eventually overturned, theories such as Quinton's rejection of the pure bodies of liberalism in favor of a permeable body whose health and prosperity depended on proper interactions with the outside gave Ishikawa the intellectual space for the questioning of the cult of progress *from within* natural science.

Quinton's theory helped to explain the dire threat to human life that would arise if the outside environment were altered too much from original conditions. In direct contrast to the Meiji germ theory of the body as an autonomous entity in danger of contamination from without—a *capacity for disease* that required quarantine—Quinton's plasma theory gave the cell an important capacity to resist and regenerate in conjunction with the outside—an active *capacity for health*. In Quinton, Ishikawa had a theory of *individual* health, but one necessarily tied to proper and direct relations with the outside world. Further, by acknowledging the permeability of the human body we saw exposed by Matsumoto Eiko's reporting (and in perfect contrast with the tradition of Tiegel's experiments on clothing in the 1870s), Ishikawa advocated constant contact with nature—sandals, sunbathing, river bathing, and even nudism—as a cure for modern illnesses, both individual and social.[39] Against Tiegel's clothing that crucially separated the subject from his or her environment, for Reclus clothes had been "nests of germs that cut us off from the pure air and light, make us sickly and uncoordinated, turn our skin pale and cover it with ulcers." Clothing constituted a repression of the body; it denied the metabolism between it and nature, pretending as if the body had "no longer any organs"[40] with which to interact with the outside world. For both Reclus and Ishikawa the benefits of nudism were both physiological and social. Because nudism also removed the outward signs of cultural, class, and political difference, Reclus had made nudism one of the main ways to restore both biological health and political freedom. Nudism was something Ishikawa would practice after his move to Chitose mura in 1927 and continue into the postwar period.

For Ishikawa the constant interaction between internal and external natures was a universal condition of existence that even applied to the earth itself. The productive capacity of a healthy earth was originally located in the sun, which had infused the earth, like a womb, with what Osborn called "chromatins." Again, although today no one would talk of chromatins, how different is it, really, from the contemporary view that all of the earth's energy (coal, oil, natural gas, solar, photosynthesis) originated in and is in some way tied to past or present solar energy?[41] Like eighteenth-century Tokugawa thinkers such as Goi Ranjū and Yamagata Bantō, Ishikawa formed his appeal to universal scales in such a way that he could relativize all local forms of power.[42] Tying the "authority of the soil" to a complex interaction with the solar system became an increasingly important relativizing move in the 1930s and 1940s, when Ishikawa's faith in the redemptive potential of agriculture was confronted with cultural nationalists' appeal to the divine land of Japan.

### Dynamic Social Aesthetics

While theories of nonadaptive change such as orthogenesis liberated Ishikawa from the benefits of acquisitive greed and the teleology of Second International socialism, they only raised the further problem of explaining the mechanism by which an initially positive trait could become negative.[43] Within the strict confines of natural science, this remained a problem until the discovery of genetics. By contrast, following Carpenter, Ishikawa escaped this aporia by including a conscious moment into his theories of social and natural change. This important move in turn brought natural science and biology out of the pure sciences and into the much murkier realm of social and historical study. Though Ishikawa's insistence on a conscious, subjective moment in development did bring him dangerously close to the irrationalist tradition of Bergson, Tanabe Hajime, and Watsuji Tetsurō, it also promised a unification of the natural and social sciences.

Interestingly, Ishikawa's chosen term for this conscious moment in evolution was "aesthetics." His later theory of dynamic social aesthetics (dōtai shakai bigaku) began with Carpenter's theory of emotional stimulation or the primacy of internal feelings that precede actions. Internally produced senses that were then acted on enabled the escape from the devolutionary conclusions of Eimer's orthogenesis by injecting a desire for life that could open a new path of action. The goal then became to make one conscious of the messages of the external stimulation so that one could choose a salvation from the toxic, alienating pursuit of shadows that was killing both humanity and nature. To put it in terms not used by Ishikawa, if at least part of human evolution were a conscious choice, then the incredible capacity for industrial capitalism to alter nature had made not natural but "artificial selection"—the model for Darwin's own natural selection—the dominant form of selection. To put it in Marxist terms (which Ishikawa did not), the new nature-society relation could be described as the real subsumption of nature under capital—a turning point in the form of capital accumulation that occurs when, with the aid of technological advances, capital extends itself into nature itself, remaking it into a resource more conducive to capitalist exploitation.[44]

Beginning in 1929 and continuing through the mid-1930s, writing in a personal monthly journal called *Dynamique* (*Dinamikku*), Ishikawa combined Carpenter, Reclus, and Comte to develop his dynamic social aesthetics. Of these, Carpenter was the key intervention. Carpenter's theory of "desire" as a higher form of all life's internal drive for self-actualization formed part of Ishikawa's theory. Carpenter's *Civilisation: Its Cause and Cure* (1889) had located civilization's cure in a neo-Lamarckian consciousness involved in synthesizing, understanding, yearning, and revelation. In this text, Carpenter transmuted Lamarck's concept of an inner need into inner desire, a vitalist understanding of an internal life energy, one that could change itself and thereby regulate its own healthful relation with nature. Carpenter's *Towards Democracy*, with its language of buds, seeds, and chrysalises bursting into bloom—a "Whitmanite 'exfoliation'"[45]—is even more explicit in locating each organism's potential for development within itself. The external environment is the stimulus for the individual's inner drive for life and self-actualization. Practice, then, is external materiality mediated by a desiring self. As Carpenter put it: "Facts are at least half feelings."[46]

But Ishikawa's project in Chitose was much more than a growing trend of dropping out of the hectic life of the city to become a gentleman farmer. For all his aristocratic poetry on the simplicity of rural life, Carpenter never denied the complex ecologies of the material world; he only sought to unify them with a thinking, feeling, aesthetic subjectivity. Unification of human and natural science is the theme of the opening pages of Carpenter's *The Art of Creation* (1907): "It is sufficient to see that on the very lowest rung of the ladder of life, and at a point where it is difficult to distinguish its laws from those of chemistry, such words as we are forced to use—words like Attraction,

Repulsion, Affinity—have a double meaning, covering both material and mental, external and internal, affections. Even the word 'motion' itself passes easily into E-motion."[47] Under this understanding of the human relation to nature, Ishikawa's rejection of Darwinian evolution in favor of a dynamic social aesthetics must be read as a search for a vocabulary adequate to humanity's recent and unprecedented ability to intervene in the environment.

Ishikawa's first issue of *Dynamique*, in November 1929, was a manifesto for a "liberation dynamics" (*kaihō no rikigaku*), a new theory of nature, self, and society that took as its point of departure the internal desire for life present in all living beings: something Ishikawa called the *idée force* (*ide forusu*). After announcing the "age of dynamism" (*dinamikku no jidai*) and introducing anarchist thought from Max Stirner, Reclus, and Carpenter, Ishikawa declared: "True ideals are the direct self-expression and expansion (*hyōgen kakujū*) of the *idée force*."[48] Ishikawa believed that recognition of the idée force of all living things had been intuited by the pantheism of ancient peoples but had been lost in both bourgeois and Bolshevik ideologies.[49]

Ishikawa announced his social model in *Dynamique* in March 1932, the same month agrarian fundamentalists, inspired by Gondo Seikyō, assassinated former finance minister Inoue Junnosuke, the head of the Mitsui zaibatsu Dan Takuma, and others in the Ketsumeidan jiken. This long issue, entitled "Anarchisme as Social Aesthetics," opened with the line "No movement is possible without aesthetic stimulation."[50] Ishikawa argued that aesthetic stimulation was key to anarchism and that it was from this sense of beauty that society must be critiqued. Further, he was quick to point out that this use of aesthetics was a question not of art or artists but of a fundamental way of living in the world. This theory of bits of vibrating matter operating on each other was characteristic of both aesthetics and evolutionary theorists' attempt to restore relations between people and things that had been erased by the abstractions of modern economic relations and early ecology.[51] The problem for Ishikawa, as for early aestheticians such as the Earl of Shaftesbury, was how to take that which was seemingly grounded only in subjective aesthetic judgment and make it social.

Ishikawa begins with a discussion of Benedetto Croce in which Ishikawa acknowledges the individual nature of aesthetic judgment. But though intuition and aesthetic contemplation are personal, they must go beyond mere personal sensation by acknowledging that sensation itself first requires the existence of the object of individual contemplation. This move introduces the material exterior into the discussion of aesthetic judgment. Ishikawa further glosses Croce's "our impressions" as "our lives" (*seimei*), our emotions moved by contact with the external object. This emotion is the object imported, objectified, and now a direct stimulus to our hearts: "the stimulation of beauty (*bi*)." But something as abstract as society may not be emotionally objectified in such a way, forcing Ishikawa to concede: "In this strict sense there can be no establishment of a social aesthetics." How then can it be established? His answer is "Indirectly." Paraphrasing the French scholar Jean-Marie Guyau, he states, "Beauty is already actualized good. The moral good is actualized beauty in both the individual and human society." For Ishikawa, the aesthetic stimulus of a healthful society is the felt harmony of the individual and the social: "This felt harmony, this stimulus that occurs within us, is the vibration [resonance] that occurs when the object confirms the movement of life, when it touches our fundamental selves. . . . It is therefore not a direct sensation of intuition; it is a kind of intuition passed through a synthetic ideal (綜合的観念). It is the meaning of this object of intuition, interrogated as much as possible by a social, composite ideal, that I call social aesthetics."[52] Ishikawa does not immediately address the problem of what grounds or authorizes society's synthetic ideal.

From here the discussion turns to Comte. Examining Auguste Comte's role in Ishikawa's thought further develops the material base of his social ecology and likely prevented him from following the idealist and rightist slide into pure interiority (of the self, or later of cultural hermeneutics) of most life philosophy in Japan and the West. Crucially, and unlike phenomenological and hermeneutic strategies, Ishikawa maintained links both to the material world beyond human consciousness and to actual social problems. I believe Comte's appearance at this point in Ishikawa's construction of his dynamic social aesthetics holds the key to determining society's synthetic ideal, against which subjective judgment is in turn judged. Indeed, it was precisely during this period in which he was developing his dynamic social aesthetics that Ishikawa took on the enormous task of translating Comte's *Cours de philosophie positive* (*Jissho tetsugaku*, 1928–31). Though now Comte is remembered or caricatured as a mechanistic positivist, here we would do well to recall Comte's role in a nearly wholly forgotten tradition of scientific thought. The discourse on the human being since the late Renaissance that culminated with Comte goes back to the seventeenth-century discourse on "fiber economies," the study of organic responses to external stimuli. Throughout the eighteenth century the medieval model of the human based on the body-soul problem was increasingly adapted to new models of organic order. According to the historian of science Tobias

Cheung, this early tradition culminated around 1800 in the rise of physical anthropologies such as those developed in Pierre-Jean-Georges Cabanis's *Homme physique et moral*. Comte's work came at the end of yet another transformation of this discourse. His *Cours*, like the work of Henri de Blainville's before him, was the synthesis of philosophy and physiology in a new regime of knowledge of the human body based not on the body-soul problem, but on the more materialist and ecologically friendly "organism-milieu" interface.[53] Indeed, when it first appeared as *organismus* in 1684, the term "organism" did not refer to an autonomous individual or subject; rather, it referred to a particular *organization* of powers and motive forces.[54] Just as early aesthetics was an attempt to reincorporate the body's relation to the world and society, Comte's theory posits that the body is an entity embedded within a field of action—a milieu. In our own more explicitly ecological terms, it is close to the body-in-environment. Ishikawa's social ecology sought to capture these healthful organizations at the cellular, bodily, social, and even cosmic level. Ultimately, the full self-actualization of the various life forces of society emerges as the synthetic ideal by which an aesthetic judgment would itself be judged. Further, Comte had also demonstrated the historical aspects of sciences intimately connected to daily life, especially biology. Early aesthetics, too, had a more material history that sought to account for an external stimulation on the organism as it moved through the world. The inclusion of Comte and the use of aesthetics then is made more clear because in Ishikawa's theory the external environment was the stimulus for the individual's inner drive for life, making aesthetic stimulation a (neo-Lamarckian) point of contact between the individual nervous system and the outside world.

### Ishikawa's Rhizomatic Critique of Japanism

The aestheticization of society and politics was of course also key to the discourse of cultural nationalism in the 1930s, especially after the Kwantung Army engineered the Manchurian Incident in September 1931, beginning the Fifteen-Year War (1931–45). For influential cultural philosophers such as Watsuji Tetsurō or Tanabe Hajime, the synthetic ideal that grounded individual aesthetic judgment stemmed from a cultural hermeneutic of the imperial house located in literature and arts going back to the eighth-century imperial genealogies, the *Kojiki* and the *Nihonshoki*. By contrast, I argue that despite the slippery nature of the category of aesthetics itself, Ishikawa's system escapes from fascist inflections by basing itself on the materiality of the body and that body's material exchanges with the environment. Unlike the turn to philology and hermeneutics of a Japanized nature that the Marxist critic Tosaka Jun labeled "the Japanese ideology," Ishikawa's fundamental ground was the material self-actualization and freedom of all living things. Specifically, (social) aesthetic intuition would be judged beautiful or good to the extent to which a given social organization fostered this self-actualization and freedom. Here Ishikawa remained true to his roots in the Ashio and Yanaka struggles. We should not forget that the point of departure for him was an attempt to develop a theory of society and action that could roll back the violence of industrial pollution that he witnessed there. By maintaining a focus on the actual practices of nature and not just on its conceptualization, Ishikawa's materialist aesthetics tied Guyau's "actualized good," the moment of beauty in aesthetic perception, to the material, physical health and freedom of organisms and society. Thus Ishikawa's system was continually tested against relations with the environment that either foster or hinder individual self-expression—not only in the mind, but "in the [actual] relations" within society, putting him where he always claimed to be, in the realm of science.

In maintaining this materialist moment in judging society, he came much closer to the Marxists than he was perhaps aware. Tosaka Jun's critique of Watsuji Tetsurō's *Fūdo* began from the materiality of a world of nature outside consciousness and culture. For Tosaka it was Watsuji's denial of the materiality of daily life that allowed him to fully Japanize his ethics. "Climate," as a combination of place and ethics—indeed, a place-based ethics—is an expanded version of the Heideggerian conception of nature as a human construction, but one much more rigorously tied to, even identified with, a particular nature. Tosaka argued that when the study of nature is nothing more than the self-contemplation of the (group) self, hermeneutics (not science) becomes the model of all knowledge.[55] Likewise, if divorced from Ishikawa's materialist "synthetic ideal" of the subject's relations with the outside, Watsuji's synthetic ideal becomes self-grounding, a closed loop or hermeneutic circle of cultural idealism.

To Tosaka, the cult of the divine land of Japan promoted by the agrarian fundamentalists Gondo Seikyō and Tachibana Kōzaburō—inspirations for the failed putsches in spring 1932—was precisely such a phenomenological enforcer. For Ishikawa, the nature of the agrarianists was a static place of the ethnic nation that constrained the inherent diversity and motion of the myriad idée forces. To make an analogy that Ishikawa did not, much like the Yanaka reservoir had stilled an inherently active nature—allowing industrial toxins to precipitate, forming what Tanaka called a "great lake of regression"—the nature of the agrarian fundamentalists was where the harmful absolutisms of emperor, capital, and race could congeal and accumulate. For Ishikawa, *physical* dynamism, not idealism, remained the key to a healthful social ecology. As Ishikawa put it elsewhere, "The problem is that contemplation cannot be made dynamic."[56]

In September 1932, Ishikawa responded directly to the fundamentalists with *Agrarian Fundamentalism and Domin Thought* (*Nōhonshugi to domin shisō*): "Recently there has been a lot of talk about agrarian fundamentalism. Twenty years ago I felt great happiness with the trend of getting 'back to the land' (*tsuchi ni kaere*). But the way I have tried to think about and practice demokurashī . . . is very different from today's agrarian fundamentalism, and so I must explain." Like early Ishikawa, Gondo and Tachibana imagined their projects as being national renewal literally from the ground up, with the farmers themselves as the agents of national renovation.

Unlike the fundamentalists, however, Ishikawa's frequent calls to return to the land or even return to a golden age represented not a cultural atavism or pathological antimodernism, but a return to mutually beneficial relations between humans and environment that he felt had existed in premodern peoples—before the runaway growth of modern industrial society. Growth per se was not proscribed, but he felt it must be aligned with the maintenance of healthful interactions between organisms and nature so as to preserve the original relations. This was the closest Ishikawa came to a theory of industrial society as a historically specific rift in human-nature relations. In his search for a golden past of nature-society relations, Ishikawa both followed Reclus's work on prehistorical peoples and anticipated Murray Bookchin's social ecology, which praised premodern societies for precisely this reason. The point of *Return to the Golden Age* (1925) was to give a historical counterexample to the contemporary nature-society metabolism.[57] He also reversed Meiji liberalism's separation of the human subject from its environment by reconnecting changes in the land to the fate of humanity. (He did so using the same term, *tenpen chii*, that Obata Tokujirō had used to announce the apolitical qualities of nature and natural disasters in 1868; see the introduction). But Ishikawa also saw that it was not a simple relation to a simple nature that was necessary, criticizing the easy escape from hierarchy in William Morris and Edward Bellamy: "They call for each of us to be fully wrapped in nature. But this is not enough, for there are severe relations in nature, too. Anarchists must never forget this."[58]

But most critically, Ishikawa's analysis of agrarianism showed the necessary inclusion of hierarchy in the seemingly compassionate doctrine: "In *nōhonshugi*, the rulers (*jisha*) take great care of both the imperial jewel (*Ōmitakara*) and the people (*tamigusa*), bathing them both in imperial authority. Agrarianism itself seems to exude this feeling (*kibun*)." Using Gondo Seikyō's own *Jichi minpan* (1927), Ishikawa argued that agrarianism's fundamental principle, Emperor Sujin's (r. 97?–30 BCE) declaration that "agriculture is the basis of the realm," was merely the first sentence of a political hierarchy that expressed a love of the farmers, but only from the perspective of the rulers and exploiters (*shiboritori mono*) of those subjects. Ishikawa realized that no matter what degree of "loving caress" (*aibuteki, aibushugi*) the imperial state offered the farmer, this theory was still subsumed under paternalistic system of ruler and ruled (*onjōshugi*), so for the farmers themselves it represented their alienation from the land and from each other. It was therefore "not an emancipatory project." Worse, Ishikawa continued, because the agrarianists merely imagined a harmonious social order within an actually existing class-conflict-ridden society, they merely repeated the mistaken visions of the nineteenth-century utopian socialists "some one hundred years ago."

The combination of a paternalistic, exploitative ideology with the denial of that exploitation set up some interesting interpretations. Here again Ishikawa moved closer to Marx, who in the *Economic and Philosophical Manuscripts* of 1844 had written of the partial alienation of the people from the land in precapitalist societies:

> In the first place, feudal landed property is already in essence land which has been sold off, land which has been estranged from man and now confronts him in the shape of a handful of great lords. In feudal landownership we already find the domination of the earth as of an alien power over men. . . . [But] there is still the appearance of a relationship between owner and land which is based on something more intimate than mere *material* wealth. The land is individualized with its lord, it acquires his status. . . . It appears as the inorganic body of its lord. . . . Similarly, the workers on the estate are . . . partly the property of the landowner, as are serfs, and they are partly linked to him through a relationship based on respect, submissiveness and duty. His relation to them is therefore directly political and even has an *agreeable* aspect.[59]

Over the next decades, in the *Grundrisse* and in *Capital* Marx would historicize the alienating relations of the 1844 manuscripts. Unlike Marx or

Tosaka, Ishikawa did not develop a full theory of ideology, but he clearly understood agrarian fundamentalism as an ideology that misrecognized the real relation of humans to nature and to each other. Stressing the vague mood or feeling (*kibun*) of empathy that characterized agrarian fundamentalism, Ishikawa sought to reveal this constantly repeated sense of love for one's subjects as a pretension that veiled the hierarchical, constraining nature actually at work. Because he saw that the love and harmony of the agrarianists was an appeal to harmony within an unequal social structure, he concluded that whatever else, agrarianism's love existed as mere feeling.

If the agrarianists were right, and if, as Marx stated, material nature as the source of human sustenance and autonomy is identified with the "inorganic body of the lord," this combination would set up a loop—Watsuji's imperial hermeneutic circle—whereby the Japanese agricultural laborer's own subjectivity is ultimately derived from the emperor. To go even further, the co-opted wartime Hōtoku movement of "repaying virtue" back to the land that sustains human life—so different from its Tokugawa version of local mutual aid—is easily transmuted into a repayment of virtue to the emperor for providing that life. In short, accepting the agrarianists' position on the divine soil means the emperor could indeed appear to be the source of all Japanese life and freedom.[60] Further, we can already see the problem of incomplete development of individual self-consciousness that the postwar scholar Maruyama Masao saw as the cause of an aborted Japanese modernity (see the conclusion).

But it can get still worse. In 1844 Marx was writing about feudal land ownership. He continued his examination of the body of the lord quoted above by concluding that, unlike the capitalist, the feudal lord "makes no attempt to extract the maximum profit from his property." One hundred years later, despite the agrarianists' wish to go back to a pre-Meiji, precapitalist past, in the industrial capitalism of 1930s such a call remained just that, a wish. Ishikawa criticized the agrarianists' belief that agriculture was the only source of value. This meant they did not reflect on the "organic relationships" between agriculture and other industries. Thus anything short of a regression to the state of primitives meant that the end result "would necessarily be the mere mechanization of agricultural labor" and therefore not, as in demokurashī, a centering of all industry around agriculture to "cultivate the entire earth (*chikyū*)."[61] This was not far off the mark. Tachibana's fundamentalist manifesto, "Nihon aikoku kakushin hongi" ("Fundamental Principles for the Patriotic Reform of Japan," 1932), called for a "reversal of the [current Western/capitalist] value system" by a valorization of agrarianism as a gift from the gods. Once the values of the Japanese village were held in the hearts of all Japanese, Tachibana's system would reestablish heavy industry and the market.[62] But to Ishikawa, if the imagined harmonious relationship of repaying virtue to the land—now understood as repaying virtue to the imperial house—is combined with the actual social relations of capitalism, then the imperial ideology is merely a new form of endless accumulation, another form of *mumei no yoku*, and the agricultural production of the Japanese feudal village becomes the alibi of (national) capital accumulation. The result is a fascistic, aestheticized capitalism demanding endless labor servicing an unrepayable debt to the lord.[63] To take one famous example, consider Tanabe Hajime's notorious address "Death/Life" ("Shi sei"), in which he argues that the ultimate unification of the individual with the Japanese "species" is achieved only in death on the battlefield in service to the emperor.[64] Is this not merely a grotesque, nationalized expression of Ishikawa's early belief that the capitalist "pursuit of shadows" was ultimately suicidal, ending only when the exhausted subject collapsed to the ground, dead —then, and only then, "grasping" his or her own shadow?

In 1938, the year after the full-scale Japanese invasion that began with the Marco Polo Bridge Incident, Ishikawa made a radical move in identifying the Chinese as the archetypical domin, even claiming that a new emancipatory society could be built on their relations to the land. Ishikawa listed the long, familiar way in which invaders such as the recent Manchus had themselves been assimilated by the Han. For Ishikawa, the Chinese were a domin society that could never be contained by external authority. In this, he said, they were like the loess sludge that made up the Yellow River: if inundated, it flowed; if dried, it dispersed in the wind. But it never stopped moving, nor did it submit to control, despite the efforts of emperors or engineers. Ishikawa warned of the implications that this domin quality of resistance would have for the newly invading Japanese—who themselves had been caught off guard and were stunned by the tremendous power of the Yellow River as it changed course after the levees were cut by retreating Chinese Nationalist forces.[65]

Tragically, this view of the Chinese as possessing an almost infinite capacity for hard labor was also the basis for Japanese imperialists' plans for economic exploitation of the continent. Mark Driscoll's brilliant examination of the Japanese exploitation of China and Korea, *Absolute Erotic, Absolute Grotesque* (2010), quotes several Japanese imperialists who marveled at the ability of the "coolie" to work—to death, if necessary. In his *Manchuria: A Survey* (1925) Adachi Kinnosuke was clear as to the economic basis of the

Japanese project in Asia: "[The coolies'] one passion seemed to be patient, eternal toil. Nothing stopped them in their work. And in that manner they laid the foundation of economic and financial power. . . . The history of the development of Manchuria is the story of the Shantung Coolie, nothing more."[66] Ishikawa saw this, too. In both "Gangs" ("Gyangu," 1932), written in response to the Manchurian Incident, and "Let's Clean Up the Water of the Yellow River" ("Kōga no mizu o mo jōka seyo," 1938), written in response to the full invasion of China, he openly feared what would happen if "machine production" and capitalism seized the power of Chinese nature and Chinese bodies. If that were to happen instead of a new emancipatory project based on the Chinese people's domin relation to the land, he foresaw an unprecedented "hell of exploitation." To use Driscoll's terms, Ishikawa explicitly saw and feared the capitalist "grotesqueing" of Chinese labor and Chinese nature by Japanese imperialism. The title "Gangs" was not metaphorical. Driscoll shows that it was indeed black marketeers, pimps, and gangsters who were the backbone of the Japanese seizure of labor power in Asia. Recalling Tanaka's doku, which was in Driscoll's language a "grotesqueing" of a healthy nagare, Ishikawa feared that under Japanese rule China would become the grotesque expansion and intensification of the doku cycle exposed so horribly in Yanaka and World War I Europe. Ishikawa made just this claim himself in a 1932 article in *Sekai Ōrai*, calling the global depression and the rise of fascism the price the world had to pay for not heeding "Tanaka Shōzō's Warning" (Tanaka Shōzō no Yogen).[67]

For Ishikawa, the actual existence and growing power of hierarchical and authoritative social relations of industrial capitalism required a combative theory of the domin, completely at odds with the passive repayers of virtue imagined by the agrarianists. Until the "iron cage" of capitalism "with its machine guns and bombers" was destroyed, the domin must resist. Opposing both middle-class farmers (*nōmin*) and the abiding folk (*jōmin*) of the Japanese ethnic nation, Ishikawa made his domin eternal resisters. While maintaining the domin's attachment to the soil, now demokurashī was just as often lauded for its relation to frequent unrest and in struggles against outside landlords in Japanese history: *domin okoru*. To be a domin meant to be a resister (*hangyakusha*). In place of the purity of the fundamentalists' farmer, the domin came to stand for the unruly surplus populations on the margins of the cultural and political nation, "those who fight any and all who would subjugate them . . . the barbarous, the heathen, the ignorant and the disorderly. . . . Domin implies none of the affection and warmth of love. The

FIGURE 4.1. Ishikawa Sanshirō's August 1, 1931, issue of *Dynamique*: "National Honor Strides Forth: The Man-Kan Two Step." The cartoon was quite prescient, because the following month the Kwantung Army engineered the Manchurian Incident, which began the Japanese takeover of Manchuria. Source: Ishikawa Sanshirō, *Ishikawa Sanshirō Chosakushū* (Tokyo: Seidosha, 1977), 3.

domin are precisely those who are not loved. . . . A domin is not a nōmin. Blacksmiths, carpenters, plasterers, all can be domin."[68] Alternatively called "barbarians," "the ignorant," or "the unruly rabble" (*jūjunna senmin*), the domin for Ishikawa, like the Yanakans for Tanaka, were the foundation on which to rebuild society. Ishikawa's domin were the ones who fought against those who would subjugate people and nature, against those who would thin the soil and prevent the organizing of society around the cultivation of the earth. Against the hierarchical vision of agrarianism, what was required was an organic life centered on the earth, together with organic social relations between individuals in a complex federated network of solidarity.

Though the idée force was intensely individual, one of its fundamental aspects was to be constantly in motion and therefore in constant congress with other "subjects" driven by their own idée forces. This constant motion of all meant that the human subject (or any life-form) moved within a world of vibrating matter (*biburashon*). This vibration—daily life itself—could create resonances with the world around it, a "cosmic symphony," in which each individual contributed a melody but never disappeared into the whole. As with Tanaka's nagare, the idée force in all living creatures could be hindered or allowed free play, resulting in harmonies or dissonances in the cosmic symphony. The goal was to discover a social organization that fostered rather than fought this capacity for creative movement within daily life itself.

"If there is one fundamental principle of social aesthetics it is 'the many ingredients of the single flavor' (多趣の一味)." This phrase appears over and over again in Ishikawa's writings on dynamic social aesthetics. He often illustrates the concept by discussing soy sauce, miso, or bonito (*katsuo*) stock, in which each ingredient maintains its own unique character yet contributes to something more complex and new. Occasionally paired with a similar understanding of a symphony, in which each instrument contributes its own tones, the preservation of individuality and singularity within a society formed the basis for his concept of social cooperation and represented the ideal organization of the activity of all living things. It was the essence of Ishikawa's anarchism.

Ishikawa looked to a cooperative nature of his own experience and that described by Kropotkin, the bacteriologist Ilya Mechnikov, and the entomologist Jean-Henri Fabre as a model for a new society that would thwart the formation of all hierarchies. Most of all, he looked to the rhizome as a centerless, dispersed, horizontal organization of healthful symbiosis. Society was to be reorganized as a federated network that included consumers and producers from all industries and lifestyles. In such a dispersed form of social organization any individual, by means of the diversity of his or her very life, would constantly move in and out of different spheres and come into contact with countless groups, themselves implicated in multiple affiliations. This mutual determination and diversity would "prevent the emergence of power from within."[69] In his discussion of the division of labor, which Ishikawa concedes is characteristic of capitalist exploitation, he claims that a complex network that fosters an individual's inherent diversity of interests would result not in a *social* division of labor but in a division of labor *within each individual,* as each person was allowed the freedom to pursue any of his or her interests and talents. (This too was a social expression of anarchist science coming from Ilya Mechnikov, who had shown the functioning of symbiosis within the human body as essential to survival.)[70] In this way not only would sideline, part-time work proliferate, but the strictures of cultural, class, or ethnic identities would also weaken, by further expanding the individual's implication in more networks. This theory was also Ishikawa's theory of national defense. For him, violence and war had brought previous empires low. This was "the lesson of five thousand years of history." The only enduring basis of world peace and national security was to have friends for neighbors. The complex net must operate at the global scale as well, and this, not empire, should be the goal of Japanese diplomacy and international relations.[71]

The rhizome was the mirror image of the infinity of the cosmos, an enormous, absolute expanse that had no center, making all earthly concepts by definition limited and relative. As in his writings on Comte and on the pantheistic vision of premodern peoples, rebuilding society along rhizomatic, cooperative lines would put the social organization (*shakaikan*) in line with the universal (*uchūkan*). Like the infinity of space, which does not, cannot have a center and in which everything is relative, the microscopic level of the rhizome fostered the diversity of the natural world. The complex cooperative network was not in pursuit of rural development. It was a total social vision in which the eternally resisting domin moved in and out of federations with nature and others. In Ishikawa's vision the domin is the universal solvent with no firm place in any social order, whose very movement through his or her daily life dissolves all would-be hierarchies, becoming what Slavoj Žižek has called "the part of no-part."[72]

With his organic or metabolic understanding of the social and natural relations of modernity, in many ways Ishikawa was back where he started, in Yanaka and the daily resistance of life itself. Much in the same way that Tanaka had founded a life based on the nagare ecology, Ishikawa offered his domin lifestyle as an alternative ecology to the "iron net" of militarist and capitalist ecologies. Both thinkers saw that capitalism and nationalism existed simultaneously as political theories and distinct ecologies. It was on the level of ecology, where thought, morality, and economics became instantiated in the material exchanges (metabolisms) of daily life, that they chose to resist.

Throughout the 1930s and 1940s Ishikawa tried to develop a theory of Japanese ethnicity viewed from the cosmic and rhizomatic perspective. While he joined the pro-state Oriental Culture Research Institute (Tōyō bunka kenkyūjo), his explicit goal in *One Hundred Lectures on Oriental Culture* (1939) was to show that all modern peoples had multiple origins and therefore were cosmic brothers, not national subjects or ethnicities: "The blood of all humanity from every corner of the globe flows in our veins." Since his anti-Darwinian-evolution days in the 1920s, Ishikawa had insisted that the concept of species itself was a contradiction to the cult of open-ended progress. Further, the concept of evolution and progress itself should be antithetical to a static, reified notion of "species," a category created by repetition, accumulation, and stagnation. From a cosmic perspective, any notion of race or species was necessarily relative. In its place, he argued, there were only temporary historical instances of societies that consciously built relations, for better or worse, with the land. To ossify it into a hard metaphysical concept and preclude its implication in other groupings was not only to reify it. Flattening the inherent diversity of existence into the hard certainties of race and cultural hermeneutics also removed the possibility for the "aesthetic stimulation" that comes from a constantly moving creative subjectivity within an open-ended social network. A lack of aesthetic stimulation is precisely how he described the social vision of the agrarian fundamentalists in 1932. (This notion of static elements of race, class, and ethnicity that compete against each other is the "struggle school" of sociology that nearly all anarchist social thought sought to combat.)[73] Even within this conservative discourse on race and species, Ishikawa was able to present some rather subversive material—though often only in *Dynamique*—including claiming that the rise and fall of the totalitarian (and agrarian fundamentalist) Qin Empire (221–206 BCE) had an uncanny resemblance to both contemporary Japan and Bolshevism.[74]

During the war years he refused rations and continued to farm and live off those proceeds. Against the state he was relegated to negative, nonparticipatory forms of resistance, such as his refusal of governmental food rations in an attempt to become a mere single farmer, echoing Japanese anarchism's base as "little men doing" and Tanaka's "single individual" (*tada no hitori*) who fights with life itself.[75] In practical terms, Ishikawa stayed in Chitose, lecturing on Reclus and Carpenter, practicing nudism, and developing his own life as "originally as possible." As he had written back in 1927: "If it were possible I would love to go deep into the mountains, casting off the world of people, and cultivate some land." But he immediately acknowledged that in his present-day Japan that was impossible: "I cannot [enter the mountains] and so I write. Working means working under a capitalist system. As I do not want to be a capitalist, I work to make my life as original (*genshiteki*) as possible. I work to live by my own means (*jikyū-jitoku*). But I can't do it alone. I need allies and so we work together in this. This is my social movement (*shakai undō*). . . . It is a life in search of truth. It is a living movement (*kurashī undō*)."[76] The inescapability of authoritarian and capitalist relations was also the reason he criticized both Tanaka and Kinoshita Naoe, who had claimed to find salvation in the purely contemplative method of Okada Torahiko's *seiza* method of personal renewal (see chapter 3).

Ishikawa's war resistance may seem a weak form of resistance when contrasted with the massive hell of exploitation he clearly saw and denounced at work in the empire. But it was consistent with his theories of life and struggle, and this view too was based on his theory of biological life. Ishikawa believed his individual daily struggle was paving the way for a true and lasting revolution of daily life. In "Social Mutation: A New Way to Revolution" (1930) Ishikawa had rejected the notion that social change must precede individual emancipation. Again he looked to non-Darwinian thought to support his social vision, this time to the Dutch cellular biologist Hugo De Vries (1848–1935) and his theory of cellular mutation. De Vries held that with the build-up of small changes within an individual cell, when a certain point was reached—as with Carpenter's chrysalis or Tanaka's thoughts on water—accumulated minor changes would burst out of their container and emerge as a new form. Hence Ishikawa's emphasis on producing a division of labor within each individual and not at the supra-individual, social level. De Vries's cell mutation theory was the scientific grounding of Ishikawa's attempt during the war years "to live as originally as possible." Ishikawa saw himself slowly accumulating changes within himself that promised a future political, social, and cultural revolution once they gained critical mass and exploded out into the world. He constantly repeated this claim when, as with his refusal to join the Japan Socialist Party in 1906, he resisted invitations to join agrarian and farmers' organizations. For him, the goal was to change the rhythm of life at the cellular, bodily, social, and cosmic level, not the farmers' organizations' desire to create an "agrarian middle class."

Regardless of his relative lack of success in stopping the war, the extraordinary events of 1946, during which workers themselves seized control of production outside of state or party control (and even formed federations of cooperatives between themselves), seemed to Ishikawa the "Whitmanite 'exfoliation'" of all the accrued minor, daily life changes he had been practicing since the start of his "part-time farmer's life" in 1927.

## The Two Hakone Conferences on Japanese Modernization

As we have seen, Ishikawa did more than merely resist the ideological conversion (*tenkō*) to the war goals of so many other Japanese leftists. Nonetheless, even though his project was prompted by what seemed a recent break in nature-society relations, his emphasis on cyclical temporalities of rotation and revolution over historical thinking, so vital for his social ecology, also meant that all human history was a replay of transhistorical power plays. This was clear in his writings on demokurashī, in which Carpenter's rural retreat was given the same status as the ancient Greek demos. This emphasis on analogy and repetition reappeared in the 1930s and 1940s, when Ishikawa equated the Qin Empire with Cromwell's revolution or Peter the Great's centralization of Russia. Indeed, the Qin's centralizing efforts were for Ishikawa the birth of centralized modernity. Ishikawa's weak historical sense caused him to greatly overestimate the ease with which the weight of history could be ignored and great events could produce completely "fresh starts." Already in June 1944, with the war rapidly turning against Japan, Ishikawa was looking forward to a fresh start, telling Tanaka's former river pilgrimage partner and Yanaka resident Shimada Sōzō that when the war ended and the Americans came, they must remember "to thank them" for creating "a chance to reflect on ourselves."[77] In an unpublished essay from February 1946, "An Anarchist Manifesto," Ishikawa criticized the Japanese Communist Party for their eagerness to blame the war on their enemies instead of pointing out the great opportunity for reflection signaled by the end of the war. In this text Ishikawa declared that the long nightmare of vain pursuit of false goals led by the military was finally over. The Japanese had been stripped down to their essentials by the war, and they could now emerge as their true selves for the first time in modern history:

> The emperor, with his radio address, has taken all of the evils of the military and the bureaucracy, all the wrongs that have happened since the Manchurian Incident [1931], all of the accumulated wrongs of the Japanese political system since the Meiji period, onto himself—to give us a fresh start. It is therefore our great duty to humanity to protect this [human, personal] emperor (*konjō tennō*, 今上天皇). . . . Events since the Manchurian Incident and the actions of the military faction (*nihon gunbatsu*) were not based on the Japanese Spirit, nor can it be said they were based on the spirit of the West. In truth, it was none other than a thin, Western veneer of imperialism. And so this

lost war is the loss of that Western veneer. . . . Japan's true self is allowed to appear by virtue of the emperor's declaration ending the war—the true Japanese spirit is now able to shine. . . . We built on this small island a huge Tower of Babel. . . . It is gone. People run around urging us to fix the election law, to revise the constitution, when in fact well below all of that, an earthquake has destroyed the foundation. The tower has fallen before the *kokumin*'s eyes.[78]

As optimistic as it is, this piece comes dangerously close to a *tenkō* for the absurd and creepy reason that this emergence of true democratic democracy is due to none other than the same emperor to whom the fascists had pledged allegiance just months earlier. Still, in this vision, all the trappings of the runaway pursuit of shadows embodied by the empire were gone, but the "cosmic, universal constitution" (*uchū no kempō*) and "the laws of nature" (*shizen no tensoku*) remained. Ishikawa may be forgiven for wanting to exhale after the horrors of the Fifteen-Year War, and no doubt the end of the war was an opportunity for the Japanese to reflect on themselves. But just as in his thoughts on the pure status of the farmer revealed in the collapse of society in World War I Europe, his language describing the complete stripping down to a historical, cultural, and political year zero is clearly overdone. Further, there is the dubious and politically dangerous periodization of true selves eclipsed by the Meiji Revolution, just as there is an identification of true democracy with "this emperor." As we saw in chapter 1, nature-society relations in the Tokugawa period, too, had been changing rapidly toward more capitalist forms of reification and accumulation. No matter how bare the life of the immediate postwar period seemed, the issues and problems that empire had so brutally attempted to solve remained the issues of postwar Japan as well. Perhaps Ishikawa sensed this, and that is why he never published the "Manifesto."

The language of race and emperor in the "Manifesto" are real problems that cannot be fully explained away by noting Ishikawa's lack of historicity. But if Ishikawa built upon the person of the emperor in the "Manifesto," in another work from 1946 he completely undid the wartime emperor system and laid out an ambitious plan for a democratic, cooperative postwar organization meant to replace empire. In many ways, *Japan, Fifty Years On* (*Gojū nen go no nihon*), with its bodies, nature, dispersed relations, federations, and even chromatins, is the culmination of Ishikawa's social ecology. Compared to the "Manifesto," *Japan*—like William Morris's *News from Nowhere*—shows a very different and surprisingly concrete and plausible path to a postwar global social ecology. Set in 1996, the text is a visionary piece recalling in great detail the way in which a cooperative society was created. In this text a 120-year-old Ishikawa, slightly hard of hearing but still robust, receives visitors at his mountain hut, regaling them with stories of the beginnings of the current peaceful world of federated global cooperatives that began at a conference at a large hot-springs resort in Kowakidani, Hakone, in autumn 1946.[79] One of the visitors is a young anthropologist (specializing in Southeast Asia) named Michel Roux, the grandson of Ishikawa's friend, the French anthropologist Jean Roux. He has traveled to visit Ishikawa on the eve of another grand anthropological conference at Hakone. He has come to Japan after doing research in the anthropology and ethnography of Hanoi and Haiphong. Here Ishikawa uses the obsolete term for ethnography, *dozokugaku* (土俗学), which, like his reading of *demos*, stresses a connection to the land. (It has been replaced in contemporary ethnography by the purely ethnic *minzokugaku*, making the distinction even clearer.) Prior to his studies in Vietnam, Michel had been to the Philippines, Taiwan, Tsingtao, Okinawa, and elsewhere, traveling on a new vehicle for developing ties, Japan's "Floating University" (洋上大学船), a sort of semester at sea.

As one might expect, Ishikawa explains how the current world was built on an aesthetic revolution in 1946 that penetrated down into daily life, consolidating an earlier economic revolution. Ishikawa tells his visitors how in the agitation of the immediate postwar, though "democracy" (not demokurashī) was a constant slogan, "it meant no more than mere voting. What was needed," he tells his visitors, "was a nonviolent, constructive movement under the banner of *anarchisme*, [a movement that enacted] the truth that a free society must be free at the level of daily life and lifestyle for it to have any meaning." The cultural cooperative that his listeners have come to Hakone to participate in is, in fact, the linking of many minor revolutions. The economic revolution started with the runaway inflation of the immediate postwar years, leading to a complete loss of faith in the government, the bureaucracy, and the political parties. Ishikawa lays out a very specific account of how with the collapse of the existing monetary system, cooperative bank currency gradually became the sole medium of exchange between producers and consumers. With the failures of the US-led Supreme Commander for the Allied Powers (SCAP) and the central government to provide even a semblance of security in daily life (food, housing, transportation), a cooperative bank in Yamanashi, in an effort to rebuild the regional economy, began issuing its own bills of exchange (交換券). Build-

ing on this initial success, again in Yamanashi, a mutual insurance cooperative was begun. This spread to other cooperative movements, encompass-
ing regional production, consumption, and even cultural production under
a generalized cooperative union (綜合的協同組合). The first move toward a
society of federated cooperatives came with the linking of rural farming cooperatives and the largely urban producers of fertilizer—a giant step in
overcoming the separation of town and country, and one that was part of
Ishikawa's social ecological vision from the beginning. From here, not only
did production increase and consumption become rationalized, but also, he
claims, the traditional antagonism between labor and capital naturally and
gradually disappeared. As Ishikawa further explains, this new beginning
was based on a direct relation to the land and its productive capacities. But
the new social model required domestic and international peace and therefore required a cooperative of the import/export and communications
(diplomatic) unions. In an effort to expand and consolidate the revolution
of daily life begun in Yamanashi, the call went out for a grand conference of
cooperatives from all of Asia Pacific.

The opening ceremony included Ishikawa's own poem:

The chromatins living in the earth
Chromatins, breathed deeply by the earth's womb
The offspring of this chromatin soil, Demos
Bathed in the light of spring, all things awaken
The call of the skylark, the rustle of the barley in the southern wind
This earthly Demos comes alive
In the cool of autumn, even the colors of the waters and forests soften
With Heaven our father and Earth our mother, here
we gather, the cosmic family[80]

To underscore the relativity of national identity vis-à-vis a universal nature, the meeting of representatives from around the world at the Hakone
hot springs was held in the nude, each member's nakedness a symbol of a
new beauty tied not to culture or wealth, but to the equal and free relations
of humans to each other and to nature. "The nakedness of the attendees in
the *onsen* reminded them that they were a single family (brothers and sis-
ters) mediated by their relation to the sun and cosmos—the true source of
life and equality embodied in the chromatins in the earth's womb."[81] With
this insight into their interrelatedness, the conference attendees decided to
reject all central bank notes and use cooperative-bank-issued notes interna-
tionally. We can see here Ishikawa's attempt to reincorporate both Japan and

the former colonies of the empire into a new mode of production based on broad, deep cultivation of the earth, which would replace finance capitalism (imperialism). This was, of course, the vision he had glimpsed in his writings on the Chinese as a modern domin society.[82] Further, the friendly federation of regional unions would fulfill Ishikawa's theory of national security by making true friends of one's neighbors. While clearly utopian, building as it does on trade unions by former enemies, this vision is not terribly different from that of Robert Shuman, the French foreign minister who in 1950 declared that the path to peace in Europe would start with a Franco-German industrial cooperative established through the pooling of French and German coal and steel production in order to create a "de facto solidarity" that would grow over time. In Ishikawa's vision, as the net of federated cooperatives gradually expanded, the five unions—agriculture, trade, communications, industry, and accounting—were in turn federated with the cultural union. Each year the six unions would meet in the old Diet building to plan the year.

Despite the obvious utopianism of *Japan, Fifty Years On*, it is shocking how closely Ishikawa's text was in capturing and expanding upon the extraordinary situation on the ground. In the chaos of food shortages, destroyed infrastructure, and explicit hoarding and market manipulation by the state and the zaibatsu, local and regional cooperatives did step in, flourishing throughout 1945 and 1946. A Home Ministry survey of town and village cooperatives in the spring of 1946 found more than two hundred thousand of them. Tetsuo Najita's recent work on grassroots economic practices in Japan shows that it was local cooperative banks, which had grown out of Tokugawa village practices, that kept functioning and prevented a total social collapse when the zaibatsu banks stopped working.[83] While many had been part of the wartime mobilization, in the absence of state and zaibatsu oppression temporarily prevented by SCAP (just as Ishikawa might have predicted), the cooperatives quickly took on new forms. As this was happening Ishikawa published another *Study of Evolutionary Theory* (*Shinkaron kenkyū*), once again marshalling Lamarck, Darwin, Mechnikov, and Jean-Henri Fabre to the cause of anarchist renewal of daily life. Further, local cooperatives were spreading, forming connections with each other, all without state, SCAP, or even Japanese Communist Party control. This process in the countryside was matched by the equally extraordinary phenomenon of workers themselves banding together to continue production in the face of a capital strike in the winter of 1946 by seizing control of key industries and running the factories themselves. These events became known as the production control (*seisan kanri*) movement.

In 1945–46, faced with extreme uncertainty as to their fate under SCAP, the zaibatsu made the economically rational decision to cease investment and even production, instead contenting themselves with the enormous profits to be had by provisioning the black markets with military rations looted from military stockpiles (with the consent of the Suzuki cabinet) in the last days of the war.[84] Ishikawa's too-neat separation of "the world of work" from capitalist relations caused theoretical and analytical problems at times, but in 1946 it could only have seemed to confirm his beliefs. Here the world of exchange value did indeed seem to be an unnecessary shell constraining "the world of work." Put simply, while there was simultaneous generalized hunger and idled industrial capacity, production stopped for the simple reason that there was no way for the zaibatsu to extract surplus value from that situation. Here the workers' production control movement took over in the name of the delivery of use-values. The movement started at the *Yomiuri shinbun* and quickly spread to mass mobilization at Toshiba and Japan Steel Tube. By January 1946, production control already involved nearly thirty thousand workers, often including Japanese side by side with Chinese and Koreans who had been brought to Japan as forced wartime laborers. As in Ishikawa's vision, a breakthrough occurred with the collaboration of a Mitsui chemical company in Niigata, Tōyō Gōsei, and the fifteen-thousand-member Niigata farmers' associations. Starting in March 1946, a production control movement at the Mitsui company began converting the plant to the production of chemical fertilizers. To pay for the conversion it contracted with another production-control-held company in Tokyo to sell three hundred thousand yen of methanol in the union's name.[85] The movement eventually linked up with Edogawa Manufacturing in Tokyo and created alliances with farmers in Tōhoku and Hokkaido and coal miners. By linking rural food production with urban industry, moves like this threatened to make the production control movement self-sustaining, raising the possibility that the seized firms might never return to their capitalist owners. When workers at Keisei Electric Railway (called the "hunger railway" because it was the train used daily by Tokyo residents to go into the countryside in search of food) began using the train fares to pay wages, it signaled a direct, and illegal, assault on the institution of private property.[86] As is well known, the combined might of the conservative retrenchment and the wrath of a communist-fearing SCAP brought the brief period of liberalization to an end with the famous "reverse course" in February 1947. Joe Moore's excellent analysis of the production control movements shows clearly that, more than the threat of communism in Asia, it was this assault on the foundations of Japanese capitalism by workers themselves that triggered Gen. Douglas MacArthur's intervention on behalf of the zaibatsu already in the winter of 1946.[87] The extraordinary moment and opportunity for a cooperative social ecology that opened briefly in 1946 had closed. By the time of the actual Hakone conference on Japan's modernization in November 1960, the chance for a cooperative democracy had been lost between the false dichotomy of Maruyama Masao's rigorously "autonomous" individual and modernization theorists' conservative systems theory. As much fun, or not, as it may be to imagine the attendees of the 1960 conference in the nude discussing their value-free functionalism, in the end the history of the two Hakone conferences must be written as tragedy.

Even though Ishikawa's thoughts on the end of the war were not as atomistic as the "radical democracy" of Maruyama Masao's autonomous subject, his belief that the war had stripped life to the bare essentials shows far too little sense of the historical continuity between pre- and postwar forms of capital accumulation. This position likely comes from his belief, going back to the early 1900s, that capitalism was but a veneer covering the real world of work. Thus a great calamity such as the war would not so much permanently alter these things as reveal them, allowing them to emerge in their true form. Here Ishikawa's disdain for teleological and deterministic theories, from Second International socialism to the arrogant triumphalism of social Darwinism, was similar to the vitalist aim to separate the "living" from the "moribund" of modern life.[88] Nonetheless, Ishikawa made tremendous strides and must be commended for avoiding the rightist pitfalls of the mystification of nature that seduced so many of his contemporaries. While he had high praise for Max Stirner's *The Ego and Its Own*, counting it as an anarchist text,[89] his dynamic social aesthetics insisted on placing the individual within a vibrating cosmos of other idée forces; he did not follow Stirner into the apotheosis of one's own ego as the only one.[90] Likewise, he refused to follow the imperial nature of people like Watsuji, who eventually brought every aspect of the external world under the aegis of consciousness. These were important achievements of Ishikawa's thought and kept him from complicity with the wartime state. But the wariness of large social models that had served him so well, helping him avoid the mechanism of the 1910s and 1920s and allowing him the intellectual space to envision a socially and ecologically sustainable mode of production based on a direct relation with nature, here failed him. His lack of a theory of the historical specificity of industrial capitalism's social and natural relations of production blinded him to the deep continuities within Japanese and global capitalism, which survived the war intact.

As for his positive programs, Ishikawa's faith in this elemental and ahistorical idée force as the basis on which to build a new society through individualized creative evolution (à la De Vries) meant he could put tremendous faith in extremely local—indeed, individual—anarchist practices as the solution to the global disaster of the 1930s. But the scale of the solution would ultimately prove inadequate to the scale of the problem. Even beyond his separation of the world of work from the world of capitalism, at its core Ishikawa's social theory relied, in the end, on a rather ahistorical concept of "life." In dynamic social aesthetics the life drive at the basis of every individual organism exists sui generis and with a teleological goal to fully realize itself. This individual "life" remained the touchstone of the whole theory even when Ishikawa's own evolutionary thought was arguing for something closer to Tanaka's thoughts on a fatal mutation leading to a toxic "second nature." As Tanaka and Matsumoto Eiko documented in their ethnographies of the polluted watersheds, through constant mutual penetration of the body and nature, the bodies of the pollution victims themselves—their biological, social, and ecological selves—were altered by greater processes. Ishikawa's theory was in this sense a type of materialism, but an ahistorical one.

Ishikawa's dynamic social aesthetics allows for influence from the outside, but his theory of resonances and vibrations was more metaphorical than material, and often stopped short of actual penetrations. The vibrations occur between two interacting but ultimately discrete entities. In this sense, it recapitulated, in a higher, more nuanced form, the individual subjects of liberalism. The coevolution of body and environment we have followed so far suggests instead that an individual life must be seen as the *product* of history, not its starting point. What is needed is a historical materialism.

Latour's theory requires simultaneously seeing each local site not just as itself, but also as the end point or result of another process. Marxian analysis goes even further, showing how merely setting a price for land or natural resources alters the metabolism between actors and those sites by mediating them through the laws of private property and the extraction of surplus value. Further, the idea that through natural selection organisms adapt to fit into their environment reproduces the logic of the market as two independent entities—organism and environment—interact to achieve an equilibrium. In contrast to this, the Marxian notion of subsumption of nature under capital comes much closer not only to describing Tanaka's monism or Ishikawa's neo-Lamarckian unification of individual and environment. It also seems to better grasp the status of nature given the unprecedented ability of industrial society to mold the natural world in its image. These social relations are not grasped by Ishikawa's internal idée force—or anarchism's communes, or Heidegger's life in the provinces, or Murray Bookchin's libertarian municipalism, or any social ecology so radically individualized and localized. These all fail to sufficiently historicize the materiality of the body and the soil, not to mention their historically specific interactions under capitalism. In *The German Ideology*, a text in which he and Engels also severely criticize the ahistorical "life" of Ludwig Feuerbach and Max Stirner, Marx talks about the necessity of seeing the individual as a historical product: "The real production of life appears as non-historical, while the historical appears as something separated from ordinary life, something extra-superterrestrial. With this the relation of man to nature is excluded from history and hence the antithesis of nature and history is created."[91] Dealing with an abstraction like money or capital as a constituent element of soil fertility was a major concern for Marx. It was also a crucial matter for the founder of Snow Brand Dairy and another follower of Tanaka, Kurosawa Torizo, examined in chapter 5.

Without this historical moment, Ishikawa's "living" (*kurashī, seikatsu*) became something much closer to the vitalist's "life" (*seimei*). Indeed, Ishikawa died in 1956—the same year scientists identified the cause of Minamata disease as methylmercury poisoning. The economic, natural, social, and ecological relations that combined to become Minamata disease spanned continents and decades of the pre- and postwar periods, and over the next decades, victims of Minamata disease would be sacrificed to the postwar economic miracle lorded over by "this human emperor," whom Ishikawa lauded in 1946. The maimed, crippled bodies of the Minamata victims surely attests to them not as isolated beings, but as the end point of some process that relied on distant mountains and rivers.[92]

# FIVE

# THE ORIGINAL GREEN COMPANY
## Snow Brand Dairy

Industry is the real historical relationship of nature, and hence of natural science, to man.　—KARL MARX, *Economic and Philosophical Manuscripts*

If you fertilize with money, the soil thins.
—TANAKA SHŌZŌ, *Tanaka Shōzō senshū*, vol. 4

### Hokkaido Elegy

With major scandals in 2000 and 2002 involving *E. coli*–infected meat and the sale of reprocessed, spoiled milk, Snow Brand Dairy (Yukijirushi) has lately made news as a lesson in corporate greed and callous decision making. After yet another scandal stemming from the relabeling of imported Australian beef as supposedly mad-cow-free Japanese meat, Snow Brand Foods was dissolved. In 2003 the parent company Snow Brand itself merged with agricultural conglomerates Zennō and Zenrakuren to form the enormous dairy corporation MegMilk. While this merger may have temporarily improved the balance sheet, Snow Brand could not avoid becoming a symbol of the rapacious pursuit of profit over human life at the end of Japan's "lost decade."[1]

Snow Brand's demise is all the more tragic when one reads it against the history of its founder, Kurosawa Torizō (1885–1982), for in fact Snow Brand

Dairy was founded as an ecologically and socially progressive cooperative designed explicitly to heal the natural and social degradations of the Ashio Incident. A sixteen-year-old Kurosawa was one of the many volunteers who flocked to Tanaka after his appeal to the emperor in December 1901. He worked as Tanaka's assistant in Tokyo for years, until a family illness and growing police surveillance sent him back to his home in Ibaraki. From there, with help from Tanaka, Kurosawa moved to Hokkaido, where he discovered what he considered the solution to the environmental crisis: small-scale dairy farming. In Hokkaido, Kurosawa created an especially ecological interpretation of Tanaka's theory of "national death" (*bōkokuron*), embedding human health and freedom in a reciprocal relationship with a living but vulnerable national soil: "healthy soil, healthy people" (*kendo-kenmin*, 健土健民).

Like his fellow activist and Tanaka follower Ishikawa, Kurosawa believed Ashio had exposed the extensive but fragile connections between the environmental and the social in modern Japan. More specifically, he saw the source of the pollution victims' plight as their necessary reliance on the whole social ecology of the Kanto basin, from the Watarase headwaters all the way to Tokyo and the halls of the National Diet. Their extreme social and political vulnerability to the power of the state and the Furukawa zaibatsu required finding a new relationship to nature that could become the basis of autonomy and security. As Kurosawa himself put it in a postwar speech, this meant a search for a self-sufficient, self-sustaining socio-ecological model that did not "rely on distant mountains and rivers" for its success.[2] He believed he had found this magic mode of production in dairy farming. The dairy farm, with its "reciprocal method" of household production, in which the domestic animals' manure fertilized the fields that in turn fed the livestock, seemed to promise a personal ecology shielded from the harmful interventions of outside politics and outside capital, thus preventing a repeat of the Ashio experience. For these reasons I call Kurosawa's vision of the dairy farm an ecology of autonomy. In its own way, then, Kurosawa's household dairy can be seen as a concrete vision of Ishikawa's "cultivation of the earth" (耕地事業), a healthful mode of production that would replace industrial capitalism (工事事業).

But unlike Ishikawa, who rejected open-ended accumulation in all forms, Kurosawa located the problem plaguing the dairy household much more narrowly—especially in the influence of outside capital. Kurosawa's dairy model was not a return to peasant subsistence, or to Ishikawa's self-sufficient "reap only what one sows" (*jikyū-jitoku*) mantra, but an ecologically informed attack on merchant capital. Taking inspiration from the model of household production and producers' cooperatives in Denmark and northern Germany, Kurosawa and his partner, Utsunomiya Sentarō, in 1913 created Japan's first dairy producers' cooperative in Hokkaido as a way to pool, market, and sell their milk. In 1925 this cooperative became the Hokkaido Federation of Production and Sales Cooperatives (Hokkaido seiraku hanbai kumiai rengōkai), often referred to as Rakuren, the precursor to Snow Brand. Throughout the 1920s and 1930s, dairy farming became a total social vision of national renovation built on this healthy and healthful mode of production, when with help from the Hokkaido government, Rakuren set out to make Hokkaido "the Denmark of Japan."

Yet despite the appeal to complete self-sufficiency, Rakuren's milk remained a commodity that needed to be sold. This reliance on the market meant the environmental could not be so easily individualized, and the organic relations of ecology were increasingly required of human society as well. This required a coordinated agriculture program. While a national agriculture policy allowed for much more detailed plans than Ishikawa's visionary anarchism, it also made Rakuren vulnerable to co-optation by the national mobilization of farming villages by the wartime state. If the ultimate source of the environmental crisis was the mere inclusion of outside capital, there was the danger that once outside capital was removed, the initial insight into the historicity of the soil might be lost in favor of an eternally fertile nature seen once again as a resource for exploitation. Indeed, in 1940 Kurosawa was the Hokkaido representative to Konoe Fumimaro's Imperial Rule Assistance Association (IRAA; Taisei yokusankai), becoming head of nearly all Japanese dairy production through leadership of the newly formed Hokkaido Dairy Promotion Company (Hokkaido kōnō kōsha). From its beginnings as a small producers' cooperative in 1913, operations expanded in Japan and later included major holdings in the empire in Korea and Manchuria, becoming so large it would be targeted by SCAP under anti-zaibatsu directives in 1948. In this way, over time, the ecology of *personal autonomy* blurred into the ecology of *national autarky*.

Like so much of the wartime economy, Snow Brand's project, minus the imperial metaphysics, transferred easily to the high-growth period. In fact, the two companies created in 1950 from the breakup of the Hokkaido Dairy Production Company—Snow Brand and Hokkaido (later Clover) Butter[3]—reemerged in 1958 on the eve of Prime Minister Ikeda Hayato's "income-doubling" plans for the 1960s. Kurosawa never wavered in his belief that the cause of socio-ecological crisis was speculative merchant capital. As in the war years, this thin theorization of the natural and social relations of capitalist production allowed him to preach the ecology of autonomy in high-growth Japan even long after dairy farming itself had moved from its labor-intensive origins to become the capital-intensive industry it is today.[4]

Yet despite these shortcomings, Kurosawa also never gave up preaching his central insight that had led him to unite ecological and social health (*kendo-kenmin*). By singling out dairy production as the way to national health and autonomy, Kurosawa and Snow Brand crucially acknowledged that not all contact with nature was necessarily conducive to health and freedom, and that the particular form of the material exchange instantiated in production produces not only commodities and wealth, but also a specific social form. That vision continues at Rakunō gakuen daigaku in Ebetsu, Hokkaido—the successor of Rakuren's first rural school founded in 1933 and today a research and technical university specializing in organic farming, alternative energy, and the nature-society metabolism.

### Tanaka Shōzō on Agriculture and Capital

Practically Tanaka was unable to resurrect Yanaka; theoretically what Tanaka left unfinished, another tantalizing part of his thought, was the relation of nature to capital. Though Tanaka did not develop a systematic critique of the commodification of nature, he had clearly been aware of the problem of competing systems of valuation between nature and money. The antagonism between these two value systems had been part of his thought ever since the era of "condolence payments" (*mimaikin*) and the permanent contracts promoted by the Ashio officials and the prefectural authorities in the first part of the crisis in the mid-1890s. Then, in an attempt to dissuade farmers from signing the contracts, Tanaka wrote in 1896: "Maguro is only found in Meguro. The solution to the mine pollution is only found in the engineers. Wealth is only found in [mine-owner] Furukawa [Ichibei]. These are all errors. [The solution] is in [finding] volunteers to fight the government. There is wealth throughout the land; there is wealth in the fields; there is no wealth in Furukawa."[5] And, as we saw, "no prices" had also figured highly in his Three Nothings Church. This kind of thinking has led some to ascribe Tanaka's protest to an "agriculture versus industry" dispute attendant on any modernization program. As we saw, this likely wasn't true even in 1896, at the height of Tanaka's liberal period. It was even less the case with Tanaka after his environmental turn in 1902. Later aphoristic musings on the relationship of land and capital are even more suggestive of a new valorization of the environment: "Today, both fish and people may be bought with money"; "Farmers use soil for food, clothing—they eat the soil, breathe its vapors like an earthworm [breathes earth]. If you trade earthworms for money, the soil dies."[6] Likewise, "If you fertilize with money, the soil thins."[7]

It requires only a bit of effort to translate Tanaka's thoughts on money and soil into a Marxian understanding of social and natural relations of town and country or metropole and colony—issues that Tanaka took on in his criticism of the Russo-Japanese war and issues that became explicit in Ishikawa and Kurosawa's continuation of Tanaka's project. By translating Tanaka's language into the language of capital accumulation we can see how Tanaka had begun to engage the problem of the commodification of nature's productive capacity. Commodification of nature is made explicit in several places in his diary, such as when he declares the wide productive powers of nature, or, rather, the "fundamental rules [constitution] of a nature in motion" (tenchijunkan no kenpō), which "must never be allowed to be owned and monopolized by any [one] individual." Drawing on Christianity, socialism, and the ecology of doku, Tanaka developed an ecological base for social relations in declaring that endless consumption and its attendant doku ultimately undermine not just the actual victims but also the conditions of human life itself, thus undermining the victimizers as well: "If the strong kill the weak and exterminate a productive nature, they also kill themselves. . . . [When] an insect feeds on a plant's leaves . . . the plant soon dies. And then, when the leaves have all been eaten, the insect dies, too."[8] These musings occasionally ended with the biblical phrase "a rich man through the eye of a needle . . . (iu, iu)."[9] In chapter 2, we saw how Tanaka grasped the depredations of the Ashio crisis through his theory of "national death" (bōkokuron), in which the victims existed outside the protections of the law and even the nation, such as the horrific abandoned villages documented in Matsumoto Eiko's reporting. As with Ishikawa's denunciation of "the pursuit of shadows," for Tanaka "national death" followed as selfishness took over people's hearts and, underwritten by a competitive individualism and nationalism based on social Darwinism, pursuit of money threatened to become the only form of morality. In this theory, money as the new measure of value destroyed or at least veiled true morality—human solidarity and cooperation with nature: "Today there is no society, no nation, no constitution, no people (jinmin), no rivers, no mountains. [Everywhere one looks] there is only selfishness and personal gain."[10]

Kurosawa's understanding of ecology over economy was also a critique of bourgeois individualism's open-ended accumulation and its relation to an alienated nature. Ishikawa had located the social and ecological crises in the existence of hierarchy itself. He did not therefore develop a specific critique of capitalism and nature. Kurosawa did. And for him the particular social ecology of family dairy farms promised a solution to the problem that could redeem both a society and nature in decline.

### Dairy and the Ecology of Autonomy

Kurosawa Torizō was born in 1885 in Mito, Ibaraki, near the famous Shōkōkan, where he claims he was brought up on the Wang Yang Ming philosophy of the "unity of thought and action."[11] Inspired by Tanaka's dramatic appeal to the emperor in 1901, he joined a student tour of the Watarase valley led by Uchimura Kanzō, Kinoshita Naoe, and Shimada Saburō, a group of over fifteen hundred that also included future Marxist Kawakami Hajime. Moved by the wretched conditions of the valley and its residents, Kurosawa and a friend did not return to Tokyo with the group; instead they extended the day trip to more than a week. In 1902 he helped form a small "youth action brigade" that toured the poisoned lands, organizing farmers in an attempt to eliminate the pre-Meiji attitudes toward authority—in his words, to smash faith in the power of others (tariki) in order to cultivate a faith in oneself and one's fellow farmers (jiriki). These organizing actions increasingly brought Kurosawa into trouble with the police. In 1905, when Kurosawa's mother died, he left Tanaka to return home to Ibaraki to deal with family business and to take care of his brother and sister. After a short stint selling used books from a cart in Ibaraki, he left for Hokkaido with legal and financial help from Tanaka.

Shortly after his arrival in Hokkaido, through connections at the Methodist church in Sapporo (he was baptized in 1910), Kurosawa met Utsunomiya Sentarō (1866–1940), a dairy farmer and disciple of Fukuzawa Yukichi. Prior to moving to Hokkaido, Utsunomiya had managed livestock at the new experimental farms set up by the Meiji government near Tokyo in Magome. In 1885 Utsunomiya was invited by the Hokkaido Development Agency (kaitakushi) to Hakodate, where he studied under "the father of Hokkaido agriculture," Edwin Dun (1848–1931).[12] In 1887, after two years under Dun, Utsunomiya left to study livestock agriculture in the United States, first in Seattle and then at the University of Wisconsin, where he was introduced to dairy farming.[13] When Kurosawa met him in the summer of

1905, Utsunomiya taught his eager younger colleague "the three virtues (*santoku*) of dairy farming":

1  A dairy farmer never has to bow his head before the officials (*yakunin*);
2  A dairy farmer does not have to lie;
3  Milk is good for the human body.

To Kurosawa, these virtues appeared to promise a way out of the defeats suffered by the pollution victims at the hands of Furukawa and the Diet: "The Ashio struggle taught me the value of the first virtue. But my career in [used book] sales had taught me lying was essential. [But then Utsunomiya reminded me], 'Cows don't respond to tricks or flattery—only to hard work.'" What most attracted Kurosawa was dairy farming's internal production of the conditions of future production, namely the production of future soil fertility through manure. This self-sufficiency seemed to point the way to a return of the autonomy that had been taken from the Ashio and Yanaka victims as their efforts were constantly undermined by distant actions taken by the Furukawa mine and Diet politics. The apparent internal production of fertilizer should not be underestimated, because during the Ashio crisis the mine not only polluted the rivers; it also deforested the mountains that had been the source of green fertilizer in the Watarase and Tone watersheds. As we saw in chapter 3, relocated pollution victims were often forced into purchasing fertilizer by the need to replace the compromised green fertilizer, which was either polluted or inaccessible after the state's reengineering of the Watarase and Tone watersheds.[14] Dairy farming's use of animal manure to fertilize a farm's fields of side-crops, which in turn fed both the cows and the household, seemed to promise a self-sufficient, self-sustaining model that did not "rely on distant mountains or rivers for its success":[15] an "ecology of individual autonomy" (see fig. 5.1).

The dairy model thus not only insulated the household from increasingly polluted mountains and rivers, but also eliminated the need to purchase fertilizer, which left the farmers vulnerable to merchant capital and created a constant need for cash and debt. Further, this model's use of multiple crops expanded the self-sufficiency of the owner-cultivators beyond what had existed in the polluted regions. There the model had largely been, or was seen by Kurosawa to have been, monoculture (rice or mulberry) supplemented by side industries such as the manufacture of straw raincoats, sandals, and other such items. But here, there is almost no need for supplementing from outside the family's own plots. As is immediately

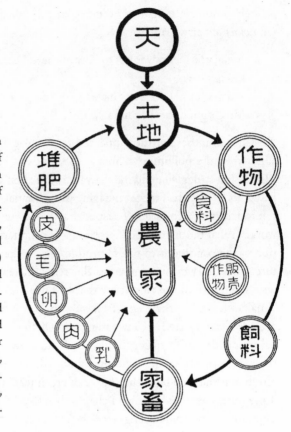

FIGURE 5.1. Kurosawa Torizō's "Ecological Cycle of Dairy Farming." 天: Heaven (top); 土地: Earth (top of circle); 農家: Farmhouse (center). Moving clockwise, the circle shows agricultural products (作物), food (飼料) for livestock (家畜), and manure for fertilizer (堆肥). Pointing inward toward the farmhouse: food and agricultural products for sale, as well as milk, meat, eggs, wool, and hides. Source: Kurosaw Torizō, *Nōmindō* (1937).

clear from the diagram, the model is not merely a scientific endeavor but also a social one.

After working in dairy farms around Sapporo for a few years, Kurosawa had saved enough to purchase his own cows. In 1909, just as he was getting started in his life as an independent dairy farmer, Utsunomiya returned to the University of Wisconsin, where he met the cofounder of Wisconsin's College of Agriculture and the school's first professor of agricultural economics, Dean Henry C. Taylor (1873–1969). Utsunomiya arrived in 1909, coincident with the establishment of the Department of Agricultural Economics. Like the future coop that would become Snow Brand, the program at Madison, too, began with a vision of social equality. Taylor had written a dissertation titled "The Decline of Land-Owning Families in England" for his degree from the General Economics Department at the University of Wisconsin in 1903. And it was under Taylor that the Wisconsin Union of the

American Society of Equity was founded in 1906. This society was responsible for marketing farm products and establishing farm supply cooperatives, livestock shipping associations, cooperative grain elevators, and equity exchanges (farm supply purchasing cooperatives). Like Rakuren's later policies against merchant capital, these dairy cooperatives were designed as an attack on the "cheese trusts" that controlled the state's agricultural product.[16]

Taylor's project was thus an attempt to restore self-determination to Wisconsin's dairy farmers that formed the political and ideological background for Taylor's influential speech "Agriculture Must Take Denmark as Its Model" ("Nōgyō wa denumaaku o kihan to seyo"), which Utsunomiya attended. Beyond the formal reorganization of production and distribution by cooperatives outside the Wisconsin cheese trusts, the specific ecology of dairy cooperatives promised much more than freedom from predatory capital. Indeed, dairy was seen as the way to avoid national ruin. It even represented the path to rejuvenation. According to Utsunomiya and Kurosawa, Taylor's speech was a polemic against what they called the "pillaging form of agriculture" (ryakudatsu nōgyō)—large-scale cereal monoculture and beef production that had been imported to Hokkaido by the Hokkaido Development Agency (kaitakushi) in the early Meiji years.[17] As Brett Walker has shown, in the early Meiji years it was the production of beef, not dairy, that drove the Hokkaido Development Agency's policy to modernize and colonize Hokkaido: "In the eyes of Meiji officials and their Western counterparts, ranching was progressive and scientific, and it produced the primary cuisine of modern nations—beef." Much of this was done under the guidance of Edwin Dun. Dun had been hired in 1873 by Albert Capron, son of the Hokkaido Development Agency adviser Horace Capron, to direct the beef cattle experimental farms in Hokkaido. Ninety-one head of cattle were imported to Hakodate from the Chicago stockyards, and a ten-year plan was begun to improve the existing stock by importing heifers and calves to an experimental ranch run by the Hokkaido Development Agency. Rational, large-scale cattle ranching in pursuit of beef production would remain the focus of Hokkaido development policy until the agricultural crises of the late Meiji and early Taisho periods.

Kurosawa and Utsunomiya's use of the term ryakudatsu needs to be understood literally as the "pillaging" of nitrogen from the soil, which slowly eroded the soil's productive capacity. By time Kurosawa arrived in Hokkaido in 1905, Meiji scientific agriculture had produced an exhausted soil and a disastrous surplus in dairy that led to extreme hardship for the region's farmers, threatening the collapse of the industry. The new need for maximum exploitation of the soil that came with the emergence of capitalist agriculture both in Japan and in the West meant that the earlier ways of replenishing the soil—fallowing and three-field crop rotation—had become a barrier to increased production. With capitalist development of agriculture, the need to somehow apply the productivity gains of the industrial sector to the lagging agricultural sector created a frantic search for new methods adequate to the need for constantly expanded production and capital accumulation. If this could not be done, the two sectors of the economy would only continue to diverge as investment abandoned agriculture for the gains available in industrial production. This search into the conditions required for expanded agricultural production culminated in soil chemist Justus von Liebig's (1803–73) "law of the minimum," which stated that soil fertility was limited by the nutrient (phosphorous, potassium, or nitrogen) in least supply. In nearly all cases across the globe, the limiting nutrient was nitrogen.

Prior to the discovery of the commercially viable Haber-Bosch process for making synthetic nitrogen in 1913, lack of organic nitrogen was the greatest limit to expanding agricultural production and crop yields, and throughout the nineteenth century this limit seemed to augur the Malthusian immiseration of humanity. Before the Haber-Bosch process, atmospheric nitrogen was "fixed" to the soil either by necessarily unreliable lightning or by the workings of certain soil bacteria.[18] Other remedies, such as night soil, were quickly outrun by the demands of large-scale capitalist agriculture and the growing divide between town and country in the nineteenth century.[19]

The initial response to the soil fertility crisis of nineteenth-century Europe was the massive importation of guano, the nitrogen-rich droppings of seabirds. The first shipment of Peruvian guano arrived in Liverpool in the 1820s. As the century wore on, the demand continued to grow. Great Britain's monopoly on Peruvian guano islands forced other nations, including the United States, to scramble to secure the scattered rocks, reefs, and atolls loaded with guano, creating a process that was called "guano imperialism." In the United States, guano imperialism was legalized through the Guano Islands Act of 1856, which allowed the seizure of guano deposits by any US citizen: "Whenever any citizen of the United States discovers a deposit of guano on any island, rock, or key, not within the lawful jurisdiction of any other government, and not occupied by the citizens of any other government, and takes peaceable possession thereof, and occupies the same, such island, rock, or key may, at the discretion of the President, be considered as appertaining to the United States." Over the second half of the nineteenth century, the United States seized ninety-four "islands, rocks, and keys" and claimed sixty-six of them, including Midway Island. Nine of these are still US possessions. The demand for nitrogen was so intense that European farmers raided the battlefields of Austerlitz and Waterloo for bones.[20] Elsewhere, the desperate search for nitrogen even included the raiding of catacombs and Egyptian mummies. In his famous chapter on the Parisian sewers in *Les Misérables*, Victor Hugo contrasted Paris's waste with the Chinese night soil industry, which returned to the countryside the alienated elements of soil fertility, and Marx himself mocked the London bourgeoisie as those who "can do nothing with the excrement produced by four and a half million people [other] than pollute the Thames with it, at monstrous expense."[21]

The growing demand for nitrogen was so intense that even the Peruvian guano boom was quickly exhausted, as guano mounds that had taken millennia to accumulate were depleted in fifty years. A switch from guano to sodium nitrate even led to the 1879 War of the Pacific between Peru, Bolivia, and Chile. And still supply was not enough to satisfy demand.[22] Of course, for our interests here, it should also be mentioned that production of synthetic nitrogen fertilizer is the origin, and the name, of the company responsible for Minamata disease: Nihon Chisso.[23] Neither guano imperialism nor catacomb raiding was available to Kurosawa and Utsunomiya, who were desperate to rebuild Hokkaido's exhausted soil.

The Denmark model of small-scale dairy farming was seen as a remedy to this crisis. In addition to providing food for livestock, the "reciprocal method" of deep-rooting legumes such as sugar beets, turnips, and safflower helped "mine" soil nitrogen, preventing it from being lost to groundwater and making more of it available for cultivation. Legumes have access to nitrogen that other crops, such as cereals, do not.[24] In the Denmark model that Kurosawa and Utsunomiya wished to import into Hokkaido, the nitrogen-mining legumes (turnips and beets) would not only increase the available nitrogen but would also feed the household and provide feed for the domestic livestock, and the livestock itself would lead to a further increase in manure and (nitrogen-rich) urea. The Denmark model would therefore keep capital, labor, and the fertility-restoring by-products of production local, "returning to the soil" (*kangen*, 還元) the elements of future production.

Inspired by Taylor's work on dairy cooperatives, in 1915 Kurosawa and Utsunomiya formed the Dairy Sales Union (Rakunō hanbai kumiai; the name was later changed to Sapporō rakunō kumiai), a producers' cooperative and the first of its kind in Japan. The union purchased milk not used for drinking, pooled it, and began condensed milk production on new equipment financed by the sale of cooperative stock. Before this, dairy farmers had worked door-to-door in the towns around their farm using horse-drawn carts in the summer, but Hokkaido's winters made roads impassable, so farmers carried their products by hand. The goal of the sales union was to revive the condensed milk industry, absorbing the surplus milk and converting it into a product that could be shipped outside Hokkaido.

Like the previous change from cereal production to beef, the move from "American-style pillaging agriculture" to the Denmark model was made with government cooperation. Just as Edwin Dun had worked with then Hokkaido governor Kuroda Kiyotaka, Rakuren gained an ally with the transfer of Miyao Shunji from Aichi in 1921. "Miyao agricultural policy" (*Miyao nōsei*) sought a "rationalization" of Hokkaido agriculture by "going one step beyond" the American livestock (pillaging) system to the (northern) German and Denmark system based on the three pillars of dairy cows, crop rotation, and (nitrogen-mining) sugar beet production. Based on his own observations in northern Germany and Denmark in 1903, Governor Miyao and his staff considered five domestic animals per household to be the ideal ratio, and two to three animals the minimum, for practicing intensive mixed agriculture. But when he arrived from Aichi in 1921 there were 180,712 households with 179,820 horses and 23,346 cows, a mere 1.12 per household. To bring the ratio to sustainable levels, the Miyao administration hired dozens of German and Danish agricultural experts and began an ambitious "1 million cows and horses" campaign, designed to turn Hokkaido into "the Denmark of Japan." The campaign offered subsidies and transport costs to anyone who would import cows or horses from outside Hokkaido; constructed an import office; established breeders' cooperatives; and built a processing facility for powdered milk. Miyao also strove to pair the mixed agriculture/livestock method with a mixture of forests and fields, a process he had begun in Aichi to restore water quality. In the event, Miyao was transferred to Tokyo to help rebuild after the 1923 earthquake, and later to the Colonial Development Corporation (Tōyō takushoku kabushiki gaisha). The ambitious "1 million cows and horses" mark was never reached, but by 1936 the campaign had achieved a tripling of cows to over 76,000 and a near doubling of horses to 290,000. In 1939, of 200,514 households, over 25,000 raised cows and 143,00 kept horses. Many of the households already had the two to three domestic animals considered the minimum for practicing the model.[25]

But the model was as much social as scientific. Beyond merely alleviating the economic pressures of dairy production and sales, Kurosawa saw Denmark not merely as an example of a superior agricultural economics, but more importantly as a nation that had brought itself back from the brink of "national death," in this case depleted soil and social crisis brought on by war and cereal monoculture.[26] Fifty years earlier Denmark had been a social, political, and economic basket case. A disastrous war with Bismarck had ended in the loss of the rich agricultural lands of Schleswig and Holstein in 1864, further damaging an industry that was already feeling the effects of the entry of Argentina, the United States, and Canada into the international grain markets. Forced to rebuild, the engineer Enrico Dalgas founded the Danish Heath Society (Det danske Hedeselkah) in 1866 to reclaim the barren heath country of Jutland north of the territories recently lost to Prussia. Over the next decades, farmers organized themselves into cooperatives and retreated from the production of grain. The first cooperative was founded in 1882, and by 1903 cooperatives handled milk from 80 percent of the dairy cows in Denmark. In turn, Danish eggs, butter, and bacon had come to be known as the highest-quality products in Europe.[27]

With the recognition of a combined social and agricultural crisis in late Meiji interest in Denmark was widespread. Another Ashio activist, Uchimura Kanzō, had also praised the Denmark model. In 1911, just after Utsunomiya and Kurosawa started implementing the Danish model they had learned at the University of Wisconsin, Uchimura delivered a speech to the Bible Lecture Hall (Seisho kōtō) entitled "The Story of Denmark: A Tale of National Salvation through Faith and Forestry" ("Denmaruku koku no hanashi: Shinkō to jumoku to o motte kuni o sukuishi hanashi"). In this speech, Uchimura stressed the union of religious faith and the environment in rebuilding Denmark. He spent considerable time explaining how the reforestation started by Dalgas and the Danish Heath Society had increased humidity and rainfall, which allowed the expansion of cooperative dairy cultivation in the previously barren heath lands. Uchimura concluded by likening Denmark's rejuvenation to the blossoming of the desert in Isaiah 35:1–2.[28]

Thus because Denmark had survived "national death," its social and educational institutions were of particular interest to Kurosawa. Like many others at the time, Kurosawa believed that the ground had been prepared for

Denmark's miraculous national salvation by the tradition of the rural folk schools begun in 1844 by the Danish social reformer and educator Nikolai Frederik Severin Grundtvig (1783–1872). In the mid-nineteenth century, Grundtvig had rebelled against the traditional educational system of memorization of the "dead languages," Latin and Greek, as well as against the domination of German language and science: "Education is never neglected in Denmark . . . but it has hitherto clearly been on the wrong track . . . attempting to teach all of us every bit of German knowledge about the heavens and logic . . . but no common sense about what lies nearest to us: about our own nature, conditions in the fatherland, and about what is best for the common interest. . . . [It teaches us nothing about this] one needful thing."[29] For Grundtvig, the end result was that these schools "have been at work for hundreds of years, widening the gulf between life and learning."[30] The foundation of Grundtvig's pedagogy was the so-called three loves philosophy (san'ai shugi): "Love God, love the people, love the soil." Kurosawa believed that it was the universalization of Grundtvig's three loves in the nineteenth century that had saved Denmark from the catastrophic failure of its society.

Tanaka's views on education likely linked the two "national death" thinkers in Kurosawa's mind, for Tanaka, too, had criticized the Ministry of Education for its inability to teach the things nearest and most important. For Grundtvig it was the patrie. For Tanaka it was the environment, especially the complex interactions with the individual and social body, that in the Ashio case had come together and created social and individual pain: "Elementary school teaches geography well. The foreign borders are known. But what of one's hometown rivers? What, where is their source? Where is the town's pain coming from? . . . This education is not reality; it cannot see the pain and damage staring it in the face (me no mae higai)."[31]

Thus in 1933, using Rakuren funds, Kurosawa established a dairy farming school, Rakunō gijuku (today's Rakunō gakuen daigaku), just outside Sapporo in Ebetsu, Hokkaido. Like the Danish folk schools it was modeled on, Rakunō gijuku was designed to "raise the spirit of the farmers, teach on-site dairy farm management, and promote production cooperatives (sangyō kumiai shugi)":[32] it was intended to educate the young from the villages so that they could, upon graduation, return home and farm in the method of the "three loves" of Grundtvig. Grundtvig had fostered pride in Danish farmers by emphasizing solidarity and nationalism through the teaching of Nordic myths, putting an emphasis on the awakening of the students' spirit and on the love of land that sustained them, instead of on the rote memorization of facts. Kurosawa's vision remained more focused on the nature-society metabolism created at the moment of production, with some exceptions we will examine later. To this day, attached to Rakuno gakuen daigaku in Ebetsu is the Towanomori Three Loves High School and Experimental Farm, and the philosophy and Kurosawa's calligraphy of the "three loves" continues to figure prominently throughout Rakunō gakuen's campus and website.

## Personal and Imperial Ecologies

For Kurosawa and Rakuren, the economic and ecological solutions to the environmental crisis dictated both the kind of agriculture (dairy/mixed) and the social organization within which it was to take place (cooperatives/planning). Done correctly, the specific socio-ecology of small-scale dairy farming emerged not just as the guarantor of personal autonomy but as the path to social and national rejuvenation. As the global economy was shaken by World War I and then by the Great Depression (in Japan the agrarian depression began by 1926), Kurosawa and Utsunomiya's project seemed to only grow more urgent.

Both Miyao and Rakuren had seen the deplorable state of the impoverished farmer and the impoverished soil as traceable to the pillage form of agriculture. This form encouraged not "real development" but "speculation in land."[33] They both also thought that in the Hokkaido ravaged by the pillage method, the community ties were missing and the land and people suffered as the potentially healthful mutual relations between the two were severed, regressing to a primitive individualism under the rule of speculative capital, absentee landlords, and open-ended production. A major part of Miyao nōsei, then, was the breakup of the large "American-style" farms employing large numbers of tenant farmers so as to make way for owner-cultivators who would have a felt connection to the land they worked. This connection between cultivator and land could then be the basis for a new community (kyōdōtai). Miyao and his 1939 biographer, Kurotani Ryōtarō, emphasized that only American-style agricultural calculations had been imported to Hokkaido; the kyōdōtai of the Japanese village that existed on the mainland (fuken) had not survived the crossing from Tōhoku. In a similar but not identical way, Kurosawa and Utsunomiya saw the Hokkaido method as a potentially and infinitely expandable quantity of food that would at the same time refound and rebuild the nation on sound socio-ecological principles—a healthy soil in a mutually beneficial relation with a healthy people (kendo-kenmin).

Of course, the ecological cycle of dairy farming was not wholly self-contained. The products of the cycle needed to be sold on the market in competition with other commodities. And in the market the important and progressive conditions of production would not reappear or influence their success in a market driven overwhelmingly by price. The cooperative model did provide some relief from the demands of maximizing profit and protecting small producers against the economies of scale that reigned once one left the confines of the dairy farm. Limiting capitalism to merely the presence of outside capital led Kurosawa and Rakuren to believe that they had discovered an agricultural model that could be infinitely expanded without somehow reproducing the ills of the pillaging form. As I will show, this meant that despite continued talk of a reciprocal relationship between nature and society, as long as they kept outside capital out, they had effectively assumed an ahistorical model of an infinitely fertile soil capable of infinite exploitation. It was precisely this conception of an ahistorical and infinitely fertile nature that would become the point of contact with the cultural metaphysics of the wartime state—and even the scandals of 2002–3.

But importantly—and this is what I believe ultimately saves Kurosawa's vision from complete subsumption under the wartime cultural metaphysics—Kurosawa's wartime writings of the 1930s and 1940s in fact rely on two separate and not necessarily compatible anticapitalist logics. First, there is the specific physical ecology of small-scale dairy farming against the pillaging form of capitalist agriculture. But there is also this second metaphysical appeal to the mystical relations obtaining between the farmers and the divine land of Japan. Realizing that there are in fact two separate value systems sitting side by side is important to understanding Rakuren's expansion into the empire. As we shall see, the existence of two systems also played a role in the postwar establishment of Snow Brand.

In texts from this period, especially *The Way of the Farmer* (*Nōmindō*, 1937) and *Imperial Way Agriculture* (*Kōdō nōgyō*, 1944), Kurosawa called for national integration centered on the land and on the farmers themselves in order to meet the crises of global depression and war. In *The Way of the Farmer*, Kurosawa established what he now took to calling the "Hokkaido method" of ecologically informed agricultural production as anticapitalist. It was Utsunomiya and Kurosawa's explicit belief that through the particular self-reinforcing ecology of dairy farming, production itself could enrich the national soil (*kokudo*) and simultaneously eliminate the need for investment by (merchant) capital[34]—a process that expanded in *Imperial Way*

*Agriculture*, which makes the transition from an ecology of individual autonomy to an ecology of national autarky.

As in Lukács's writings on labor, in *The Way of the Farmer* and *Imperial Way Agriculture* the reproductive capacity of the earth is reified and asked to stand outside (merchant) capitalist forms of reproduction. This vision of agriculture made it a mirror image of the equally reified money form of capitalist reproduction, in which money (such as bank interest) seems to create more money all on its own: Marx's M–M'.[35] The Hokkaido method was seen to be another form of value-creating "productive consumption," in which consumption of the fruits of the agricultural production process (animal power, labor, and fertilizer, seeds) itself produces soil fertility (use-value) and the conditions for future production. In other words, the production and consumption itself are self-sustaining—and therefore also, when combined with an improving technology also considered largely independent of agricultural production, infinitely scalable. Contrast this with the "productive consumption" described by Marx, in which the capitalist uses money to purchase the workers' labor power, which he then consumes in the production of surplus value, a surplus value that is temporarily stored in particular commodities (use-values) and then released or realized through sale and reconversion into money.[36] This criticism of capitalist accumulation based solely on money is explicit in Kurosawa. His proposed new economy promises to eradicate the social evils that result from the commodification of the national soil: "Humans' value cannot be measured with money, neither can the value of the soil. . . . The soil has a quality that cannot be measured by money."[37] The power of this nature-based cooperative was in itself supposed to be enough to counter any capitalist intrusions and thereby allow the soil to emerge in its true (productive) form.

It was precisely here that Rakuren's exclusive focus on merchant capital as *the* problem of capitalist agriculture opened the way to a Japanization of its vision. Like other non-Western countries, Japan did not have to repudiate a long mechanistic tradition; Japan seemingly only had to repudiate a rationalism now coded as Western, so the rejection of merchant capital as the abstract source of wealth in favor of the concrete productive capacities of the soil *could also appear to be an especially cultural turn*. Because the productive capacities of nature and human labor are the two things prior to capitalism and the two things capital is unable to produce itself, they can appear to be its Other. So even though the Denmark method was attempted in countless forms and places throughout the early twentieth century, if refounding national production on nature was now seen as anticapitalist, in

Japan it also could appear to be a return to native sensibilities. These supposed native sensibilities would include traditions that do indeed appear in postwar environmental ethics, such as the long neo-Confucian tradition of, in Mary Evelyn Tucker's words, "the philosophy of ch'i" seen in Kaibara Ekken, Kumazawa Banzan, Itō Jinsai, Miura Baien, and countless others.[38] What I believe this shows is that Kurosawa's collapsing of capitalism to the mere absence or presence of outside merchant capital (a tendency also found in many other wartime thinkers, such as economic historian Ōtsuka Hisao) is the key not only for giving an *account of* the Japanization of the land, it can also *account for* that move itself.

The rejection of speculative capital can also appear as a return to the divine soil of Japan itself. Agricultural labor thus becomes a dialectic of an infinitely fertile soil and human labor. And as we shall see, it matters little whether the inexhaustible soil fertility is imagined as resulting from the absence of corrupting merchant capital or from the divine properties of the *musubi no kami*.[39] Both models are ahistorical models of the environment that ignore the vulnerability (subsumption) of nature to human practice and thereby fail to unify nature and society in the historically specific act of production.

Indeed, we can see the convergence of divine soil and the Hokkaido method happening in writings from the 1930s and 1940s. Kurosawa began and ended *The Way of the Farmer* with invocations of the (dairy) farmers' special relationship to the imperial land and to Japanese traditions of honesty, frugality, and reverence. These three agricultural virtues were made analogous to the three imperial regalia of the mirror, the jewel, and the sword—and stand in contrast to the much more democratic and material three virtues (*santoku*) of dairy farming that Utsunomiya taught Kurosawa in 1905. Indeed, *The Way of the Farmer* was itself meant to be a five-point rescript complementary to the 1882 Imperial Rescript for Soldiers and Sailors.

1 The farmer (*nōmin*) is sincere and honest;
2 The farmer follows the movement of heaven and earth (*tenchi no keirin ni shitagae*);
3 The farmer loves the soil;
4 The farmer respects toil and keeps to frugality;
5 The farmer bands together with others (*kyōryoku itchi seyo*).[40]

The controlling dichotomy now emerges: production based on the *ecology of the national soil* emerges as the Other to production based on the *economy of global money.* In other words, national policy may be based either on national soil-enriching dairy production or on national soil-withering merchant capital. Both *The Way of the Farmer* and *Imperial Way Agriculture* are built on this dichotomy. Like Ishikawa's rejection of endless accumulation in favor of the concrete value of the soil, the result is a refounding of Japanese national production based on agriculture as a perceived alternative to early Meiji (now glossed as "American" and capitalist) production (*ryakudatsu nōgyō*).

Against an economy of money, the wartime state in the 1930s and 1940s appeared to emerge as a manager of an economy of concrete use-values based on the soil itself. In this ideological context, the state can emerge as the call to open-ended production previously represented by mere capital accumulation. And this is precisely what happened. By the time the war was over, nearly every one of Kurosawa's early tenets of sustainable, individual ecology had been sacrificed to mobilization of people, animals, and land for the war effort. And this was directly traceable to the narrow focus on merchant capital, a focus that would blind Rakuren to other forces calling for open-ended production—namely, the nation and total war. In the process the specific ecology of the production of dairy that had formed the basis of Kurosawa's initial socio-ecological vision in the Ashio crisis was (mostly) lost.

So the Hokkaido method expanded side by side and in cooperation with Japan's growing Asian empire and the production demands of total war. No longer the profit motive of speculators, the war effort now was the unanswerable call to increased production. Just months after the Marco Polo Bridge Incident in January 1938, Kurosawa chaired a meeting to respond to the increased demand for casein, a protein-based glue made from dairy products and essential for 1930s wooden aircraft production, such as the Mitsubishi Type 13 Carrier Attack Craft, the Taka-type Carrier Fighter, and, perhaps the most famous, though not Japanese, the British de Havilland Mosquito. Utsunomiya and other company officials lobbied the Colonial Development Corporation for state support for the expansion of the Hokkaido method, not only for national soil renewal, but also for the expansion of casein production. Indeed, in 1933 he had made a similar appeal simultaneously to the army, navy, and agriculture ministers. In this appeal, "Petition on National Independence in Casein Production" ("Kazein kōgyō kokusan dokuritsu ni kan suru seigansho"), Utsunomiya argued that with proper state support, Japan could in ten years become self-sufficient in casein and therefore not beholden to an increasingly hostile and dysfunctional global market system. In 1933 Japan was importing nearly 95 percent of its casein;[41] it is surely no coincidence, therefore, that this plan came at the height of the dispute with the League of Nations over the recognition of Manchukuo and the threat of international sanctions to cripple the development of Japanese air power. In 1933, casein was such a critical strategic resource that Rakuren officials had been prevented from observing the separation machines in the United States and Europe, but they were finally able to see one in New Zealand.[42]

With the outbreak of war, production on the farms would be switched to increase output for the military, beginning with canning operations for military rations. Correspondingly, in their role as essential members of the total war effort, the farmers would double down on their natural tendency toward frugality. But on an even deeper level, 1937 signaled more than a change in the form of social distribution. With the outbreak of total war in 1937, the military's seemingly insatiable need for casein required a fundamental change in the social ecology of the Hokkaido method. In 1905, Kurosawa's original vision had built up from the specific socio-ecological form of production to a subsequent form of distribution and consumption. Now the process reversed. The increased consumption of casein and other agricultural products demanded by the war reached back down to the production process and reorganized the socio-ecology of production to suit the demands of the total war state. Now the state, as the manager of a total war economy, made its entry into even the bodies of the people, animals, and the earth itself. The result was a truly imperial ecology. In an effort to satisfy the military's enormous demand for casein and lactose, there was a reorganization of the dairy farm to increase the fat content of Hokkaido's dairy cows. Milk fat that previously had been returned (*kangen shiteita*) to the household cycle as nutrients was now to be removed and collected for appropriation by military casein production facilities. In place of locally produced nitrogen-mining crops that fed the cows, now soybeans (from Manchukuo), oats, potatoes, and flaxseed were to be imported as fat substitutes in the calves' diet. I do not think it is an exaggeration to say that this new model essentially recruited not the whole domestic animal, but its digestive tract, to war production, in the process reengineering the physiology of the cow and the socio-ecology of the farm.[43] We see here how the mere absence of outside capital is not enough, as the total war state achieved the same kind of reorganization of labor and the environment not through economics, but through politics as the permeable body reappeared, this time permeated and physically transformed by the socio-ecology of empire and war.

By the end of the war the reengineering of the bodies of livestock became explicit in texts such as Kurosawa's *Certain Victory in Food Provisions
and the General Mobilization of Animal Power* (*Shokuryō hisshōsen to chikuryoku sōdōin*, 1944), a title using the same word for mobilization, *sōdōin*,
used in the 1942 General Mobilization Law that provided the social basis for
total war.[44] Thus the military's need for casein became a major reason for
the rationalization of all Japanese dairy production. Kurosawa became one
of the appointed members of Konoe Fumimaro's Imperial Rule Assistance
Association (IRAA), accepting nomination for the 1942 general election. In
1940 he had had already been selected as one of the "twelve model farmers"
brought together to consult on increasing agricultural production. In this
capacity he was also named head of the newly formed Hokkaido Dairy Promotion Company (Hokkaido kōnō kōsha), an enormous control group
(*tōseikai*) created by the integration of Rakuren, Meiji, and Morinaga dairy
companies. Being head of the Hokkaido Company put him in charge of
nearly all dairy production in the empire. As the call to produce for the war
reached down into the component digestive and circulatory systems of people, animals, and the soil itself, "imperial way agriculture" here emerged as
what it really was, the socio-ecological foundation of total war—a radical
form of open-ended accumulation nearly identical to its supposed opposite,
the pillaging of the capitalist form.[45] From here, the road is wide open to
Mark Driscoll's exposure of the fascist inflection of capitalist accumulation—
its tendency to completely consume all that get caught in its machinery.[46]

By the 1940s, the Hokkaido Dairy Promotion Company encompassed
the whole of Hokkaido and much of Japan and had expanded into the Japanese empire, with significant holdings in Korea and Manchuria. As the logic
of total war increasingly overshadowed the original ecological vision of the
ecology of autonomy, the intimacy of the state, war, and the Hokkaido
method could grow with no restraints. After Kurosawa's appointment to
Konoe's IRAA (an appointment that would get him purged by SCAP), the
Hokkaido method fitted easily with the state's own Healthy Citizens Movement (*kenmin undō*), a massive social engineering project ranging from the
establishment of physical exercises to the use of hot springs.[47] In this context, almost inevitably, "healthy land, healthy people" was transformed into
"healthy land, healthy soldiers" (*kendo-kenpei*). And showing just how far
from Tanaka's vision of the real powers of the land and waters Kurosawa had
strayed, he also called for a massive reengineering of all of Manchuria—
draining the boggy North and irrigating the dry South. Kurosawa hoped
that this project, together with the Hokkaido method, would renew the soil

enough that it could absorb up to 2 million Japanese colonists—in other words doubling the state's proposed 1 million settlers. While some of the earlier focus on pride of production and individual autonomy is present when Kurosawa argues that the Hokkaido method in Manchuria can allow a single household to cultivate up to 100 or even 150 *chōbu*, whereas even 10 *chōbu*[48] was seen as overwhelming in Japan, it is a decidedly Japanese production.[49] The cultural particularism appears here in obvious form when Kurosawa points out that this large-scale production can be done not only without the input of merchant capital, but also without the use of (increasingly uncontrollable) colonial labor. The Koreans, Chinese, and Manchurians are completely absent, by design, from this vision of Japanese colonists' autonomy.[50]

But just like Ishikawa, when confronted with the unvarnished fascist version of his return to the soil, Kurosawa did not go all the way to pure cultural theory, but held on to at least a sliver of the materialist ecology he began with. Though it was veiled by the imperial metaphysics of the divine soil and the three farmer's virtues, Kurosawa's focus on the specific form of the material exchange between humans and nature remained fundamentally materialist and ecological. Competing contemporary theories of the imperial way make the particularity of Kurosawa's vision easier to see. The very title *Imperial Way Agriculture* signals that Kurosawa had entered into a debate on the meaning and content of the imperial way itself—especially as it pertains to the empire, regional integration, and the Greater East Asia Co-Prosperity Sphere. The first part of *Imperial Way Agriculture* is a long explanation of the mutual production of a land and its people (*minzoku*). It is important to keep in mind that the two mutually produce each other. As such, unlike in the State Shintoist theories he was arguing against, there was in fact no necessary relationship between the form of agriculture and Japanese culture—with Kurosawa the two logics were juxtaposed, but were never integrated. There is no question that his was an imperial project, but as we shall see, the specific material base of that project mattered for both wartime and postwar politics.

In short, *Imperial Way Agriculture* and *The Way of the Farmer* are schizophrenic texts, desperately trying to suture the metaphysical appeal to the divine soil onto the physical ecology of dairy farming. As a material production, and as we saw, the Hokkaido was really the Denmark method and therefore a method open to all. By contrast, a fully cultural model such as Watsuji Tetsurō's hermeneutic is completely closed to non-Japanese people.[51] Likewise, other Shinto-inspired theories of regional integration, such as those of Imaizumi Sadasuke (1863–1944) or Hoshino Teruoki (1882–1957), rely exclusively on the metaphysics of cultural practice to sanctify practices of nature. Imaizumi's theory of the imperial way took "Japan," not the material productive capacity of the land, as the root of all things. Hoshino's theory of ritual as an integrating practice is even more unyielding. According to Hoshino's theory, rice, emperor, and the Japanese folk are completely identified. But they become one not through the material metabolic processes of bodies, society, and nature, but through the ancient *Shinjōsai* (*Ni'inamesai*) imperial ritual, in which the emperor would taste and dedicate the first rice harvest to the gods. For Hoshino, this ritual was the basis of all production. It not only produced food; it also produced the community, so much so that Hoshino explicitly argued against the expansion of the empire into regions where the climate could not support rice or millet cultivation, because this would mean they "could not thereby provide rice to [complete] the ritual." As non–rice producing, the regions could not be covered by the blessings of Amaterasu. Karafuto, or Sakhalin Island, under these terms, was not suitable for inclusion in the Co-Prosperity Sphere.[52] Integrating people into this cultural/racial model thus requires not so much teaching them sustainable agricultural techniques as teaching them to become "Japanese" as seen in the *kōminka* movement and the forced adoption of Shinto shrines and Japanese names. This culturalization was not part of Kurosawa's vision.

The unidirectional nature of the cultural model—up from the divine soil to the Japanese subject who merely receives the blessing and gives thanks (*hōtoku*)—is clear in another thinker influenced by Tanaka Shōzō, Eto Tekirei, whose "Chi kara wakeru kashoku nōjō no tanemomi" includes Eto's "mandala of the agricultural vehicle [to enlightenment]." The details of this fantastically esoteric diagram have been lost, if they were in fact ever fully worked out.[53] But what is clear is that Eto believes the source of life "bubbles up from the earth" (*chi kara uwaku*). This is symbolized by the *V* for *Vitalität* at the center (fig. 5.2). Eto looked to Tanaka as one of the great "four farmers," a group that also included Andō Shōeki, Ninomiya Sontoku, and Satō Nobuhirō. Originally influenced by the simple piety of Tolstoy, based on the belief that farming was less a nature-society metabolism than a form of prayer, Eto increasingly moved toward a theory of the divine land (*kokutairon*) based on a mix of Bergson, Nietzsche, Dōgen, and the eighth-century imperial genealogy the *Kojiki*. A full examination of this fascinating image is beyond the scope of this discussion, but the mandala forms a good pictorial contrast to the circulatory (and in comparison decidedly historical

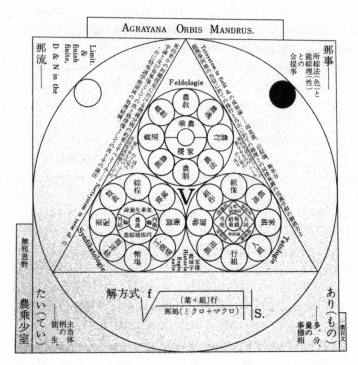

FIGURE 5.2. Eto Tekirei's "Mandala of the Agricultural Vehicle [to Enlightenment]" ("Nōjō mandara"). The majority of the meaning of this diagram has been lost, but the *V* at the center stands for the *Vitalität* (vitality) of the soil. Source: Eto Tekireikai, ed., *Eto Tekirei senshū* (Tokyo: Ie no hikari kyōkai, 1979), 2:90–91.

and materialist) vision in Kurosawa's diagram of the "Ecological Cycle of Dairy" (fig. 5.1).

With Eto we here again see the dialectic of an infinitely fertile divine land and faithful "repayment" of the blessings of the earth. In fact, Eto's mandala combined the divine land of Sato Nobuhirō with his own religious meditation of agricultural practice (*gyō*, 行) and, like early Kurosawa, household management (*kashoku*, 家稷), the last two concepts adapted from Dōgen, the founder of the Sōtō Zen school.

Though Kurosawa and others in the Hokkaido Company frequently appealed to the uniqueness of Japan, elsewhere at key moments Kurosawa's theory of regional integration explicitly refused to rely on a culture.[54] Unlike Hoshino, who made extensive use of traditional rituals, Kurosawa felt that culture needed to give way to material, ecological logics. The controlling concept of Kurosawa's vision for global production is his belief in a large coordination of mutually reinforcing production zones practicing ecologically appropriate production (*tekichi-tekisaku*, 適地適作): "No amount of diligence or knowledge can make bananas grow in Hokkaido."[55] These zones would produce for themselves and then harmoniously trade the surplus with one another—a vision, granted, that when not carefully maintained, easily cooperated with and even seemed synonymous with the Greater East Asia Co-Prosperity Sphere.[56] Nonetheless, the basis of this regional integration was ecologically appropriate production, or, to use the contemporary phrase coined by Misawa Katsue, "climatic production" (*fūdo sangyō*).[57] In *The Way of the Farmer*, each region was to produce the goods appropriate to its own ecological niche; then, after having produced all that it needed, it would trade only the surplus with other ecological regions. If this approach had actually been implemented, it would have gone a long way toward realizing ecologically sustainable global production. Of course, the vision put forward in this 1937 text was already jumbled together with the supposed Japanization of the farmer and his three virtues. Further, as we saw, with the outbreak of total war in 1938 this vision of producing for use was immediately compromised: Manchurian soybeans were needed as a replacement for the milk fat that was no longer returned to the local household ecology but was instead appropriated by the state for military production.

### Postwar Changes and Continuities

A schizophrenic appeal to two different value systems in Kurosawa's wartime writings is essential for understanding the history of Snow Brand in the postwar period, for what essentially happened during the occupation was the stripping out of the imperial metaphysics from Japanese thought and society. While this was fatal to the Shintoists, the Hokkaido Dairy Promotion Company and Kurosawa could fall back on their original cooperative vision. And this is precisely what they did. In fact, the divine metaphysics are almost already completely absent from *Total Mobilization of Animal Power*, which appeared during the desperation of 1944 and called for a nationally coordinated farm system of innovation and increased efficiency.[58] But this is not to say that the war ended, or that postwar civil society solved, the environmental crisis that had begun with the decade of leaks in the 1890s. Here we see clearly the inadequacy of Ishikawa's belief in a "fresh start." Following the story of how Hokkaido kōnō kōsha became

Snow Brand Dairy has much to tell us about not only the continuities of Japanese pre- and postwar history, but also about our own environmental crisis.

In the postwar iteration of the Hokkaido Dairy Promotion Company, Snow Brand Dairy, the ecological vision begun with Tanaka and Ashio was co-opted not by state capitalism or by the Co-Prosperity Sphere, but by a national rebuilding effort based on a new cooperative national capitalism—a postwar version of what Harootunian and Žižek have called *gemeinschaft capitalism*, capitalism without capitalism, or capitalist production (supposedly) without antagonistic class relations.[59] In this postwar formulation, the ecologies of the wartime *production* are the same; only the form of *distribution* has changed. In other words, from the standpoint of the society-nature metabolism, it matters little whether the milk, butter, lactose, or casein is destined for distant markets or distant battlefields. What matters is that a nearly unquenchable drive to extract more in order to produce more is not based on Kurosawa's initial vision of the complex socioecological interactions that produce the commodities; rather, those social ecologies are themselves organized according to the demands of (capital) accumulation. Indeed, like so much of the postwar global economy, it was the fascist period of the total war states on all sides of the conflict that fundamentally changed the nature of countless industries.[60] In the case of Snow Brand, it was the drive to increase the fat content that transformed the dairy industry from the small-scale, labor-intensive household model to the large-scale, capital-intensive industry it is today. But this postwar continuation was not a completely smooth transition.

Despite the enormous success that lay ahead in the high-growth period, the immediate postwar years of occupation were not kind to Kurosawa or the Hokkaido Dairy Promotion Company. Though SCAP did not dwell on the metaphysics of imperial way agriculture or on the Hokkaido Company's extensive holdings in the empire—all of which were obviously lost before SCAP took over—it did order the breakup of the company under the 1947 Excessive Concentration of Economic Power Law, an anti-zaibatsu initiative. Prior to this, the Hokkaido Company had tried to recapitalize itself as a more private business, and it had changed its name from Hokkaido kōnō kōsha to Hokkaido rakunō kyōdō kabushiki gaisha (Hokkaido Cooperative Dairy Joint-Stock Company). It further split itself into the Hokkaido Cooperative and the Hokkaido Agricultural Tools Manufacturing Company. Nonetheless, when the Holding Company Liquidation Committee (HCLC) investigated it found that Hokkaido Cooperative Dairy Company (Rakunō), yet another postwar renaming of Hokkaido kōnō kōsha, had in 1947 collected and processed 63.3 percent of all milk produced by Japan's dairy farms. It occupied an even larger market share in butter (78.2 percent) and cheese (84 percent). The increased production of cheese was in fact a postwar consumer legacy of the push for fattier milk for the production of casein and lactose for the military. It held 51 plants: "42 dairy products plants, 1 penicillin plant, 1 leather plant, 1 meat processing plant, 1 feed-seed plant, 1 lactoloid plant, and 4 butter packing plants." The HCLC also found evidence of restrictive arrangements (collusion) between Meiji and Morinaga dairy companies from 1931 and 1941. Officials with SCAP also claimed that the Hokkaido Cooperative routinely underreported the fat content in milk bought from farmers by 2 to 4 percent, resulting in a "great underpayment to producers, actually amounting to 6–8 percent loss."[61]

Kurosawa also seems not to have helped himself or his company in the deconcentration review. He and six others active in Rakunō had been previously purged for their participation in Konoe's IRAA yet were still involved in the company's day-to-day operations. In several places in his SCAP file, Kurosawa is reported to have flaunted the purge orders. The file even includes a rumor that he was bribing officials: "Although purged, he operates openly with six other purgees on his board of directors. When asked by local officials as to whether or not his company would be affected by the Anti-Trust Law he replied that after spending ¥5,000,000 in the right spots in Tokyo, he hardly thought so. Questions as to the most influential person in Hokkaido invariably bring forth his name."[62]

The history of Snow Brand and Kurosawa in the occupation years illustrates almost perfectly both the promise and the loss of a democratic postwar Japan from the initial flourishing of democracy in politics and economics to the reverse course and the rehabilitation of industrial capitalism to meet the perceived threat of Asian communism. Once again, the schizophrenic nature of *Imperial Way Agriculture* was essential. In the occupation, the "imperial way" side of the equation was dropped. Since it had never really been essential to the initial dairy model, the ecology of autonomy could reemerge, at least rhetorically, as a manifestation of SCAP's interest in developing a democratic Japan of small business owners and independent, small-scale Jeffersonian farmers. Because of this, too, Kurosawa was able to emerge as one of the reluctant pragmatists of the war years, rather easily shedding his own imperial metaphysics. There is no question that much of this rehabilitation of both Kurosawa and Snow Brand was explicit marketing designed to play on the Americans' fear of communism. In his 1950 rehabilitation hearing, Kurosawa submitted nearly a dozen statements attesting to his reluctance to accept a nomination to the 1942 Diet that established the new economic order and passed the legislation essential to prosecuting total war, notably the General Mobilization Law. Further, his defense team was led by the attorney who had previously defended Prime Minister Hideki Tōjō, who, at key points in the testimony, would personally attest to the contrast between the militarist Tōjō and farmer Kurosawa.

The split between the materialism of Kurosawa's vision and the idealism of the divine soil came up explicitly as well. To establish his distance from the fanatics, Kurosawa submitted a 1931 letter from Onomichi Yōichi, director of the Hokkaido branch of the ultranationalist Dainippon Kokusuikai, denouncing the "million horses and cows" campaign and Rakuren's dealings with the foreign company Nestlé. Onomichi had tied development of Hokkaido to the blessings of Emperor Meiji, who had opened the territory to the *minzoku*—nearly identical language to Kurosawa's own preface to the Hokkaido method in *Imperial Way Agriculture*. But to be fair to Kurosawa, and in what could only help distance Kurosawa and Rakuren from the virulent nationalism of the militarists targeted by SCAP, Onomichi continued his attack on foreign commerce, arguing that it "has always resulted in the oppression of Japanese industry. We suspect that there is a Jewish influence [behind it],—the influence of the Jewish people planning for . . . worldwide revolution for their sake."[63] Kurosawa's statement further claims that both he and Utsunomiya were physically assaulted by Kokusuikai thugs at a train station in Sapporo over this issue.

In Kurosawa's own rehabilitation statement, the five tenets of *The Way of the Farmer* are not renounced, but repeated. And though the three virtues of the farmer are decoupled from the three imperial treasures, they are, in turn, cited as an example of frugality and modesty consistent with Christianity. Even after the end of the occupation, Kurosawa and Snow Brand maintained this focus on the social ecology of dairy farming. Denmark once again became the model of a less ambitious, content, and sustainable Japan that had renounced "great power" status. Kurosawa returned to Denmark and wrote a new book, *Denmark, the Agricultural Nation* (*Nōgyōkoku denmaaku*), published in 1952, on the eve of Japan's regaining of national sovereignty.

The early and crucial postwar debate over the form of Japanese economy and society can be read out of the hearings as well. Included in the exhibits was a showing of support for both Kurosawa and for the cooperative model of production—occasionally moving toward a more collectivized organization of production than SCAP would have liked. Though the SCAP land reform had in common with Kurosawa and Governor Miyao a desire to emphasize the creation of owner-cultivators against absentee landlords,[64] there is a real sense of tension between the vision of SCAP and that of dairy farmers, who were arguing for the cooperative, not entrepreneurial individuals, to be the basis of postwar Japanese capitalism. One memorandum from July 1949 submitted by the Hokkaido rakunō kyōdō labor union to HCLC warned of harm to both the farmers and the public if Rakunō were dissolved. The memo includes an extended section titled "Comparison of Differences in Characteristics of the Corporation and the Cooperative." Cutting right to the chase, item 1 of this section, "The Aim of Business," contrasts the corporation's "Profit Aiming" with the cooperative's "Improvement of Agriculture." Other key differences recall the early modern tradition of mutual aid societies and rural cooperatives recently explored by Tetsuo Najita.[65] Under the heading "Accumulation of Capital" the petition declared that the corporation accumulates "not for the Agricultural Villages," putting it at odds with the planning and management of cooperative capital accumulation "made [to prepare] for [times of] depression." Further democratic aspects of the cooperative form include dealing with panic (crises), for which the corporate model has "no remedy . . . and [the pain] will be shifted to the farmers." Against this the mutual aid traditions of the cooperative claimed that "the burden will be borne evenly by all the parties concerned so that the surplus fund will be used for group insurance." Finally, the memo foresees the reproduction of the farmers' loss of autonomy in the corporate model: "It is difficult to become independent owing to the fact that the right of management and the power of capital belong to the company, so the farmers will become more dependent."

But, of course, by 1949 the SCAP reforms neither would nor could go all the way to complete democratization. Production and private property were not to be socialized. With the rise of Mao in China and Kim Il Sung in Korea, rebuilding a capitalist, pro–United States Japan was the key. In this context the early postwar cooperative movement was sacrificed to the Cold War. Some of this, to be sure, was internal to the politics of the cooperative movement itself. Other appeals to maintain the wartime managerial apparatus in agriculture came both from the *toseikai* technocrats and conservatives and from the farmers themselves. Both groups would occasionally offer the cooperative model as insurance against the Japanese Communist Party (JCP), as the corporate model, they said, was necessarily antagonistic between labor and management, thus providing an in for the communists.

In this largely conservative view, a cooperative that maintained the wartime organization would make sterile ground for JCP agitation.

In the event, Rakunō was broken into two companies, Snow Brand Dairy and Clover Butter.[66] Further, and with clearly disingenuous claims of being victims of the 1940 creation of the Hokkaido Company, officials from Meiji and Morinaga dairy companies appealed for a return of their market share and of processing capabilities that had been so unjustly taken from their entrepreneurial enterprises and forced to serve the wartime state. The result was that Meiji Dairy was granted a milk-processing facility in Hokkaido— undoing a collusion between Meiji and Rakuren from 1931 whereby Rakuren would get Hokkaido and would not compete in the Osaka region.

When one follows this complicated story of mergers and breakups engineered by SCAP, it becomes clear that SCAP's "freedom" emerged as Meiji Dairy's "reasonable expectation of profit" at a new processing center in Hokkaido, and the farmers' "freedom" became the freedom to sell milk to at least two different processors. As such, HCLC's breakup of the wartime concentrations did nothing to alter the fundamentally changed nature of the dairy industry from small-scale, labor-intensive household farming to the mechanized, capital-intensive industry. This immediately complicated the early SCAP planners' vision of a Jeffersonian democracy of middle-class owner-cultivators that would rebuild Japan into a postwar agricultural producer, without heavy industry (read: war-making capabilities). The high barriers to entry caused by the capital-intensive nature of the postwar dairy products even led one former cooperative member to renounce his support for agricultural cooperatives, at least until the economics of dairy production could be changed to benefit small-scale farms once again. They never were.

Perhaps most importantly, the postwar reorganization of Japanese agriculture enshrined dairy as just another commodity—a good produced for sale in the pursuit of capital accumulation.[67] This in turn necessarily also meant that Snow Brand's postwar milk, cheese, and butter were commodities like any other, reified and divorced from the web of socio-ecological relations that produced them. It should come as no surprise, then, to learn that Snow Brand's project transferred easily to the income-doubling and "GNP First" ideologies of the postwar period. In 1970, Kurosawa described dairy production as "the power of chemicals plus the power of human labor plus the [reciprocal] method [mixed livestock / side fields] that combine to create prosperity." Further, this belief was the basis for his position papers arguing against the liberalization of the dairy industry in 1968–69. He was especially adamant about the exclusion of the American company Kraft from the Japanese cheese market. Again, the appeal is to the specific soil-enriching ecology of dairy production: imported cheese would enrich the national soil of the producing country but would have harmful social effects in the destruction of domestic dairy employment and would have a withering effect on the national soil, as the reciprocal method was replaced by pillaging forms of production.[68] These appeals again argued that with proper state support, self-sufficiency in this crucial mediation between a healthy soil and a healthy people was still a possibility.

But perhaps just as importantly, insulation from speculative capital also remained part of Snow Brand's self-image even in the postwar period. As late as 1970, Kurosawa claimed that even though Snow Brand was organized as a joint-stock company, all members were dairy farmers themselves, ideally managing their households according to the ecological cycle, and thus they were not capitalists even when stock prices increased. "In those [early] days there was not a single capitalist in Snow Brand. I say to you today still there is not a single capitalist in Snow Brand. We are not a mere sales company. Big does not equal capitalist."[69]

Snow Brand's postwar failure to address the source of the environmental crisis—located in the specific moment of production, when labor transforms nature—counts as a missed opportunity. But it is an interesting one, for in the process of tracing the continuities between the pre- and postwar incarnations of Snow Brand, our true enemy has now revealed itself: the real subsumption of nature under capital, or, in other words, the active manipulation of nature by humans to produce a nature most conducive to capital accumulation—at the expense of all other possible valuations of nature.[70] This is the story of Snow Brand. With Snow Brand's product defined as merely one more commodity, like the pure body of the Meiji subject, a supposedly discrete and autonomous entity that bore no outward sign of its complex socio-ecological conditions of production and circulation, the integrated socio-ecology of Kurosawa's early vision is lost. And from here the road to the scandals of 2002–3 is wide open.

The postwar Kurosawa was fond of a poem by the Tang poet Du Fu (712–70), particularly a line the poet Matsuo Bashō had quoted to describe the North Country to which Kurosawa had devoted his life: "Nations may fall, but the mountains and rivers remain" (*Kuni yaburete yama kawa ari*). A collection of Kurosawa's postwar lectures bears this as its title. While this sentiment does recover some of the "nature over nation" focus on the environment going back to Kurosawa's mentor, Tanaka Shōzō, it is also clearly ahistorical and therefore too optimistic. The next line of Du Fu's verse is "When spring comes to the ruined castle, the grass is green again." But here is the problem, for the sure return of spring is precisely what is no longer promised to us in industrial capitalism. As Tanaka saw in 1902 when he developed the concept of doku, the mountains and the rivers are not necessarily still there. Even if they are, as the inhabitants of the Watarase and Tone valleys in 1890s and the poisoned communities documented by Matsumoto Eiko discovered, the mountains and rivers can be so transformed by the politics of the castle that we can no longer rely on them to provide green grass in the spring.

A tapestry with an updated version of Kurosawa's "Ecological Cycle of Dairy Farming" (fig. 5.1) still hangs in Kurosawa Memorial Hall, on the campus of the school he founded in Ebetsu in 1933, Rakunō gakuen daigaku. And it is important that it remains there. In this later version of the 1937 diagram, the Chinese character for Heaven is retained, but it is glossed as the materiality of the environment: rain, sun, and so on. In turn, in the center the farmhouse has been replaced simply with the character for people (hito). The tapestry is an essential reminder that despite the false steps, Kurosawa glimpsed the essence of the environmental crisis as the unreliability of the natural world under capitalism. Partly due to the political situation and partly due to his thin conception of capitalism as merchant capital, Kurosawa's early ecological vision was unable to fulfill its emancipatory promise. But like the tapestry, that promise is still there. The promise remains in his focus on production—on the specific form of the material exchange between society and nature—as our real relation to nature and productive of a particular social form. Production is the site and moment of the subsumption of labor and nature and must therefore form the ground of any aesthetic, moral, or political vision we may wish to build.

# BAD WATER, A THEORETICAL CONSIDERATION

## Bad Water Reloaded

It is often lamented that much of the misery and suffering of Ashio was repeated with the outbreak of Minamata disease (methylmercury poisoning)
in the postwar period. But given the history recounted here, such repetition
should not be so surprising. Indeed, the explicit purpose of postwar
policy—from the US-led Supreme Commander for the Allied Powers
(SCAP) to Japanese liberals such as Maruyama Masao and even the two-
stage revolution policy of the Japanese Communist Party (JCP)—was to
reconstitute both industrial capitalist production and liberal subjectivity.
We have seen how early SCAP tolerance of the production control movement allowed Ishikawa's hopes for a cooperative-based production to
briefly bloom, only to be quickly crushed in the counterattack of the old
guard and the "reverse course" in Allied policy with the onset of the Cold
War. We saw also how Kurosawa's essential ecological insight into the

particular nature-society metabolism—the ecology of autonomy at the heart of his dairy farm model that had been previously sacrificed to total war—was quickly co-opted by Cold War policy. As the reverse course gained steam, the postwar model of freedom narrowed to become some minimal sense of economic choice within capitalist production: at key moments during the breakup of the Hokkaido Company, the Meiji Dairy Company's freedom became an "expectation of reasonable profit," and the dairy farmers' freedom was limited to having a choice of two dairy-processing companies to which they could sell their milk. (As in the vertical organization of American beef processing, this often harms the individual cultivator, as the risks associated with weather, disease, and the like are borne only by the producer, leaving the processor insulated from the vagaries and risks of production.) Just as important as these political and economic repetitions, the autonomous liberal subject, too, was returned and asked once again to stand alone as the sole arbiter of judgment.

Politically, in the immediate postwar SCAP, the JCP, and most liberals located the cause of the recent disaster somewhere in the 1930s, when Japan had abandoned its Meiji and Taishō liberal economy and politics.[1] H. D. Harootunian has written about the repetition of these problematic political forms after the war:

> This theory of a second start was based on a misrecognition of the thirties conjuncture and an inflated investment in the powers of a heroic bourgeois individualism gendered as male. Its greatest mistake was to think it could wish away fascism as a historical moment and aberration that had passed now that Japanese (and we, I must add) had lived through its inaugural forms. Despite the promise of social democrats (the so-called modernizers or party of the enlightenment gathered around Otsuka Hisao, Maruyama Masao, and Kawashima Takayoshi) to formulate a conception of society based on a rational, autonomous, and responsible subject, the putative site where meaning is produced, . . . postwar Japan seemed to overlook the problematic of the 1930s. . . . [It turned instead to] the desire to restore a truer liberalism or a liberal order where one allegedly had not existed or had been aborted.[2]

Throughout this book, I have tried to show in a similar way that a return to liberalism and the liberal subject, with its imagined autonomous bodies, while perhaps understandable in the immediate postwar moment, was also a problematic solution to the environmental crisis. Once again, just as in the writings of Nishi Amane, Inoue Enryō, and others in the 1870s, in order to prevent an invasion of the individual as the locus of rights by the wartime and postwar state, the liberal subject had to be completely severed from the outside, and the individual consciousness had to be imagined as sui generis. Grand thinkers of the postwar period such as Ienaga Saburō and Maruyama Masao thus explicitly went back to the popular rights and liberty movement of the 1870s looking for indigenous traditions on which a democratic postwar Japan could be built. In Maruyama's case this impulse began a reconnection with the thought of Fukuzawa Yukichi. And so, like the 1870s, the postwar period saw the return of the Kantian divide between mind and body, individual and state, culture and science, nature and society.

And just as in the 1870s, prior to the environmental turn the specificity of modern toxic threats was lost as pollution became just another proxy for representative politics. Such a belief in local or national representative politics as the solution to the environmental crisis appears in the postwar writings on Minamata, Yokkaiichi asthma, *itai-itaibyō* (cadmium poisoning; literally, "It hurts, it hurts disease"), and countless other cases of postwar toxic events. As we saw in chapter 1, a faith in the extension of representative democracy had been the position of the Shimotsuke Liberal League in the early moments of the Ashio crisis as well. Timothy George's otherwise excellent study of the Minamata struggles, *Minamata: Pollution and the Struggle for Democracy in Postwar Japan*, occasionally succumbs to this faith in representative politics as the solution to the environmental crisis.[3]

If it is not done carefully, treating the environmental crisis as a metric for measuring levels of political participation can come close to reproducing the "transition" or "incomplete modernity" thesis of modernization theory, the other dominant trend in postwar scholarship on Japan. At its worst, and just as Obata had done, modernization theory's developmental telos eliminates even actually existing disasters from the historical experience of modern Japan. For example, Barbara Molony's *Technology and Investment: The Prewar Japanese Chemical Industry*—a history of Chisso, the company responsible for Minamata disease—completely ignores the social and environmental misery, offering instead a smooth narrative of technocracy gone right.[4] In short, as the history explored here shows, if liberalism has a built-in blind spot when it comes to environmental problems, then the solution to the pollution problem cannot be more liberalism. This was precisely what Tanaka Shōzō and Kōtoku Shūsui realized in 1901 when they pushed liberal politics and liberal subjectivity to their final limits in their failed appeal to the emperor. In this light, the dominant trends of today's global environmental citizens' movements based on individual consumption (like Ishikawa's) hold little hope for success.

Indeed, just what was the original issue that triggered the search for new social forms and practices of nature that we have been studying? Clearly, as Meiji liberals and soil scientists and muckraking journalists discovered, the relevant variables and actors need to be expanded beyond the individual human subject. A nature that has lost its autonomy but not its agency needs to be adequately accounted for in theory and practice. In the following, I would like to use the Marxian category of subsumption to see whether, first, a dialogue and can be deepened between *Capital* and actor-network theory (ANT) and science, technology, and society studies (STS). Second, continuing in a Marxian vein, I would like to see whether the history of Japan's and our own environmental crisis might be made more amenable to analysis and practice.

Expanding the list of relevant actors is precisely what ANT and STS have been trying to do for some time. I have learned a great deal from this creative and provocative tradition and used it throughout this book, especially Bruno Latour's work on networks and "actants." In Jane Bennett's words, an actant is "a source of action that can be either human or nonhuman; it is that which has efficacy, can do things, has sufficient coherence to make a difference, produce effects, alter the course of events," "a competence deduced from performance."[5] In this book I have tried to trace the way in which not only people, but also water, copper, smoke, fish, nitrogen, money, property laws, committees, and countless other actants, participated in and altered events. I have also tried to see how those actants' activities came together to form a social totality that was expressed in and by politics. In other words, after the rich description of the multiple actants, I reconstructed how they come together in a historically specific modality of power relations. It is at these times that I think Latour and ANT can be helpfully supplemented with the Marxian analysis of capital accumulation, especially the concept of subsumption, that is, "the variations which can occur in the relation of supremacy and subordination" of various practices.[6] This is not to say there is no theory of power relations in Latour. He is clear on this: "It's not that there is no hierarchy, no ups and downs, no rifts, no deep canyons, no high spots. It is simply that if you wish to go from one site to another, then you have to pay the full cost of relation, connection, displacement, and information."[7] This is absolutely true. The move from the abstract social level must be grounded in the interactions of all actants in daily life; otherwise it becomes a social or cultural metaphysics—a free-floating "context"—that posits what it should explain. Further, Latour's concept of "centers of calcu-lation" also includes a power dynamic and hierarchies: "No place can be said to be bigger than any other place, but some can be said to benefit from far safer connections with many more places than others."[8] Given these similar goals, why does Latour reject Marxian categories? I think much of the reason comes from Latour's admirable goal of not positing a stable "social," and this means he is justly wary of appealing to the capitalism of capitalist society to explain the effects of his actors and actants without rig-orous grounding in material practices. But seeing capitalism as just such an ungrounded "famed 'context'" that Latour rejects seems less suggestive of Marx's own description of the specific production of value in capitalist society that results from the material practice of commodification and pro-duction of surplus value than of a Weberian social context constituted by a "spirit of capitalism." I would agree with Latour that both Weber's Protes-tant ethic and the "iron cage" of rationality "[render social] interaction pos-sible by bringing on the scene most of its necessary ingredients, but that this something is at once present behind and much too abstract to do any-thing."[9] But I do not follow Latour in also ascribing this kind of ungrounded ideological "context" to Marx's own understanding of capitalism.

Latour's challenge here seems to me quite similar to Marx's own call to ground in daily life any scientific critique of social or religious forms: "It is in reality, much easier to discover by analysis the earthly kernel of the misty creations of religion than to do the opposite, i.e. to develop from the actual, given relations of life the forms in which these have been apotheosized. The latter method is the only materialist, and therefore the only scientific one."[10] Just as Latour critiques the assumption of a social framework that can serve as the basis of analysis, Marx has rejected positing a social framework or context that explains daily life and instead favored tracing up from the ac-tual practices.

Another common critique and possible source of distance from Marxian analysis—one that comes from even sympathetic ANT and STS theorists who are working to include nonhuman actants into social theory—is Marx's supposed humanist reductionism, a humanism that seems to remove all agency from the nonhuman. In *Vibrant Matter: A Political Ecology of Things* Bennett takes issue with Marx's concept of the fetishism of commodities because for her it seems to erase all "thingly" agency in a misrecognition of human processes behind everything. Her correct concern with losing the specificity of the material exterior, the thing-ness of things, leads to a call to be careful with the demystification at the heart of Marx's critique of the fetishism of commodities: "Demystification should be used with caution and sparingly, because demystification presumes that at the heart of any event or process lies a human agency that has illicitly been projected into things." Marx's fetish "[shows commodities] to be invested with an agency that belongs to humans."[11] This is all true—to a point. It is true of only one side, the value side, of the commodity, but Marx makes clear that the commodity form has two sides that come together to create a contradictory whole. Bennett's criticism does not hold for the material "use-value" side of the commodity. For Marx, the use-value of a commodity comes precisely from the specific materiality of the commodity's physical body. The fact that Marx did not talk about the details of use-value does not mean that he was uninterested in them. In chapter 1 of *Capital*, he explicitly states that use-value is always present but is the subject of different investigations— precisely because of a commodity's materiality. Lukács has zeroed in on the disavowed reification at the heart of the theory of marginal utility, which imagines itself to have abandoned Marx's value and recaptured material utility:

> Marx acutely summed up this situation with reference to economics when he declared that "use-value as such lies outside the sphere of investigation of political economy." It would be a mistake to suppose that certain analytical devices—such as found in the "Theory of Marginal Utility"—might show the way out of this impasse. It is possible to set aside objective laws governing the production and movement of commodities which regulate the market and "subjective" modes of behaviour in it and to make the attempt to start from "subjective" behaviour in the market. But this simply shifts the question from the main issue to more and more derivative and reified stages without negating the formalism of the method and the elimination from the outset of the concrete material underlying it. The formal act of exchange which constitutes the basic fact for the theory of marginal utility likewise suppresses use-value as use-value and establishes a relation of concrete equality between concretely unequal and indeed incomparable objects. It is this that creates impasse.[12]

Thus Bennett's criticism does not hold for the material "use-value" side of the commodity. The commodity's materiality retains its irreducible agency even as how, where, and why it moves through space and time becomes increasingly dictated by (subsumed under) its value side—for it is the abstract amount of socially necessary abstract labor time congealed in the value side of the commodity that is expressed as money and is thus the source of capitalist wealth and capital accumulation.[13] The key thing to keep in mind is that the commodity always simultaneously has both value and use-value sides that come together in a contradictory whole. In fact, the constant tension and antagonism between these two sides of the contradictory whole are the key to exploring the place and agency of the human and nonhuman actants, as I will show shortly. Capital, as Marx called it, is a self-valorizing value and a social abstraction; it famously functions as an analogous force to Hegel's *Geist* as the self-moving substance that is subject and driver of history. It is thus not caused by Latour's "homunculus CEO" or even humans in any conscious or individual sense. Capital is decidedly supra-individual; and in that both laborers and capitalists are less ontological categories than roles, or the "bearers" of capitalist social relations, capital, far from a deep humanism, is more properly understood as antihumanist. Like Pierre Bourdieu's concept of a structuring practice that in turn structures practice, capital can be seen as the cohering through practice of the movements of actants in a relation that itself can become active and hypostasized as another kind of actant, so to speak.

So, contrary to some in ANT, STS, and radical ecology who see Marx as overly humanist, I treat capital as a nonhuman subject that does have objective and coercive social power capable of explaining the drive toward the increasing unification and simplification of natural and artificial systems that Brett Walker has shown breaks down barriers and more efficiently moves toxins through the ecosystem and the embedded bodies that inhabit them. That subject is capital itself. The process described by Walker is capital's attempt to remake the world in its own image, according to its own accumulation requirements. But far from a free-floating "context," it is also a force whose interactions and material expressions can be traced. Below I will offer an exploration of the specific production process of capitalist production as a metabolic process between labor and the material environment undertaken in pursuit of capital accumulation in a way that will "pay [Latour's] full cost of relation, connection, displacement, and information" of the actants, human and nonhuman alike. Foucault too, like ANT and STS, has done a great deal of important work focusing on the laboratory and other sites as powerful centers of calculation in the creation of knowledge and power.[14] I will argue that Marx had already described such a place, a center of calculation that gathered multiple other sites to itself to become *the* site to begin an analysis of capitalist society, making it time for us to "leave this noisy sphere, where everything takes place on the surface and in full view of everyone, and follow them into the hidden abode of production."[15]

## Welcome to the Desert of the Real

*Capital* describes production this way: "Labour is ... a process between man and nature, a process by which man ... mediates, regulates and controls the metabolism between himself and nature."[16] Capitalist production, which Marx diagrams as M–C ... P ... C'–M', involves the purchase with a sum of money (M) both human labor power and raw materials (C). These are then employed in the production (P) of a qualitatively different commodity (C'), which is then (hopefully) sold for a quantitatively higher amount of money (M'), after which the process (again hopefully) repeats on an expanded scale. Capitalist production thus aims for the creation and capture of surplus value—or unpaid labor time above and beyond the socially necessary labor time needed to reproduce the worker him- or herself, this socially necessary labor time is what is expressed in wages. The value side of a commodity is a quantitative magnitude that includes both as little necessary labor time as possible and as much surplus labor time as possible. Competition between capitals takes place in this ratio between necessary and surplus labor time embedded in the commodity during the production process. Through competition between capitals the production process is constantly being speeded up and compressed to reduce the amount of labor time embedded in the commodity (thus allowing for the capitalist to undersell the competition). Competition also takes place in the ratio between necessary and surplus labor time, and this is called relative surplus value.

As such, the abstract temporality of capital accumulation is the goal. But, importantly, the use-value side, especially as relates to human life and a nature understood ecologically, has its own temporalities of metabolism, reproduction, maturation, and countless others. As Massimiliano Tomba has recently shown, the self-expansion of capitalism takes place on the basis of the socially necessary labor time that disciplines and reorganizes other competing temporalities.[17] We saw this in chapter 5, where we saw how millennia of guano were depleted in mere decades. Tanaka, too, spoke of the antagonism between the "time of humans" and "the time of heaven (nature)" when he warned that a better-than-expected harvest after an enormous flood in 1902 was no cause for celebration, explaining that the erosion had been so massive and went so deep that it reached down to and deposited relatively unpolluted soil dating back to the pre-Meiji period; accordingly, he further warned that worse pollution would follow this one-time event—and that is precisely what happened. We saw another version of this process in chapter 5 when the time required for the soil to replenish the elements of future production, especially nitrogen, came into conflict with the accelerated temporality of capital accumulation. In short, fallowing was too slow and therefore too costly, yet not fallowing a field quickly depleted soil fertility. The result was a series of methods—night soil, nitrogen-mining legumes, guano imperialism, and finally the commercialization of synthetic nitrogen with the Haber-Bosch process—that could bring agricultural rhythms more in line with the requirements of capital accumulation, in the process reorganizing the soil itself. The reorganization of the elements of production (labor and nature) to suit the needs of capital accumulation is what Marx called the "real subsumption of labor [and nature] under capital." When capitalist production is understood this way, the central antagonism between the (material) use-value and (abstract) value side of the commodity form is thus expressed as an antagonism of the temporalities of the two sides. Another way of expressing the conflict is between the limits (finitude) of nature and the limitlessness of capital.

As we saw in Ishikawa's critique of natural selection in chapter 4, the idea that through natural selection organisms adapt to fit into their environment reproduces the logic of the market as two independent entities—organism and environment—that interact to achieve an equilibrium. A major problem for taking nature as an outside to capital is introduced with the concept of real subsumption. With real subsumption we can no longer be certain that we are dealing with two independent variables. As Marx showed with the concept of relative surplus population, with respect for the demand for labor, capital operates on both sides of the supply and demand equation. In this game, as he puts it, "The dice are loaded" (*Les dés sont pipés*).[18] A similar process is under way in the real subsumption of nature under capital.

We saw real subsumption in the massive reengineering of the Tone and Watarase Rivers and watersheds; the domination of a particular temporality aims at reorganizing and remaking spatial configurations as well. As Brett Walker has shown, the rationalization of natural systems speeds up the flow of all materials through space and time, often leading to massive, indigestible, unmetabolizable amounts of elements, toxins, and even nutrients, which in the wrong amounts can become "matter out of place" and, like Tanaka's "second nature," can turn harmful; another example is the damage to the Gulf of Mexico by the huge amounts of fertilizer carried from farmland by the Mississippi River, which cause hypoxic dead zones.[19]

In short, capital seeks the complete reorganization of the world, seeks to remake the world—time, spaces, and bodies[20]—in its own image. But the attempted completion of the commodity relation, the real subsumption of labor and nature under capital, while logically possible using only the abstract value-side of the commodities of human labor power and nature, is constantly thwarted by the material, use-value sides of these same commodities. This is, I argue, precisely what Tanaka's "second nature" is describing. It is also in Ishikawa's extended interrogation of the "natural" part of natural selection. And this ultimate aporia between value and use-value sets up the central dynamic tension that characterizes the environmental crisis of capitalist industry. Which is to say, as Gavin Walker's work on Uno Kōzō has recently shown, that the *logical* completeness of the commodity relation is constantly at odds with its *historical* production.[21] This makes telling the history of capital's own life process a critical task.[22]

Thus capital immediately confronts a problem, for the two constituent elements of the production of surplus value, human labor-power and nature, are forever external to capitalism itself. Nonetheless, a capitalist society, if it is to maintain a smooth functioning and assure its own reproduction, must constantly ensure that these two elements are always readily available for new cycles of production. The ideal situation for capital would be to fully and forever be able to produce within itself all the elements necessary for its future reproduction—thereby becoming a closed, self-sufficient system, and completing the commodity form represented by the most fetishized form of capital accumulation where money appears to make more money on its own: M–M'. Building on the logically and historically prior formal subsumption of labor, the real subsumption, reorganizes the labor process itself to the one most conducive to the production of surplus value. An example would be the difference between the formal subsumption of labor in artisanal labor, which remains the same as before but with the surplus now appropriated by a capitalist, and the deconstruction of the constituent elements of the artisanal process into assembly-line production in the factory. We saw this in the cooptation of dairy cows' digestive tracts for expanded fat production. I believe, therefore, that it is possible to trace from the supremacy and subordination of multiple temporalities by capital accumulation all the way from the trading floor to the digestive tracts of dairy cows in Hokkaido or Manchukuo. Thus a social totality may come to be centered on the production of surplus value across multiple sites and disciplines without resorting to a Weberian free-floating "capitalism" context and so also rising to Latour's challenge to "pay the full cost of relation, connection, displacement, and information" across sites and processes.

But while the attendant deskilling of labor (and cows) in machine production renders labor more amenable to commodification, it fails to fully and completely appropriate the "industry" that produces labor power, or the very capacity to labor. As Gavin Walker's work shows, labor power, the human capacity to create, is an input to the capitalist production process. But it is not an output. The "industry" that creates labor power is the "substratum of physical-bodily energy itself, the concrete field of corporeality, of life. . . . That is, the zone of energy that reprocesses life-practices and forms them into sequences, is not itself 'appropriated' by capital."[23] This is true of nature's fertility processes, and its countless metabolic processes, human, bovine, or rhizomatic. Consequently, real subsumption realized in the commodity relation can never actually be achieved. Uno Kōzō's work centers on this ultimate and inescapable impossibility of completing the commodity relation. It shows that, despite what many Marxists think, crisis is not merely a *possibility* in the future, but an *inevitability* repeated at every cycle of production. Because nature and human labor power cannot be *directly* produced by capital; they must be produced *indirectly*. In the case of labor power, the inevitable repetition of crises is partially ameliorated with the administration of the "population" of surplus labor that must be maintained and made ready for commodification when needed, providing the point of contact between the value relation at the heart of the commodification of labor power and Foucault's biopolitics, as recently shown by Ken Kawashima.[24] As we saw in the case of the Meiji state's civil engineering projects of the Watarase and Tone watersheds, an inherently active nature is also targeted for real subsumption in order to make it behave more like an inanimate resource ready to hand for incorporation in capitalist production. But despite these juridical and engineering technologies, nature—the materiality and dispersed ecologies of Deleuze and Guattari's "and . . . and . . . and"—remains outside capitalist production proper. The inherent productive capacity of nature is precisely what was captured in Tanaka's theory of *nagare* and *doku*. Further, the case of biotechnology's "terminator seeds," which become sterile after one season, shows both the competing temporalities of capital accumulation and biological reproduction and the indirect attempt by capital to subsume the seeds' reproductive capacities without allowing those capacities to develop on their own to the point that they might become the basis of noncapitalist production.

Acknowledging the impossibility of completing the relation is important because without it we risk acquiescing to capital's own narrative of itself as both logically and historically closed. The alternatives would become not the struggle against the constantly repeated subsumptions, but resources and valuations imagined as outside of and incorruptible by the commodity relation, such as we saw with the cult of the divine soil in agrarian fundamentalism. Indeed, is this not precisely what happened in much of what is called Western Marxism when that tradition, particularly the Frankfurt School, adopted Weber's pessimism of the closed loop of the iron cage of rationality and thus looked to art for salvation from industrial society? The same process, I think, is clearly at work in much radical ecology that looks to an impossible and ahistorical "wilderness" ethic.[25] As mentioned, I also completely disagree with the exaltation of an untrammeled, unpeopled nature at work in Deep Ecology. This represents nothing more than the overcoming of the crisis merely in thought, in individual consciousness. Indeed, just what is "non-egotistical mountain climbing," and how in the world can the environmental crisis be solved by Deep Ecology's call for more of us to engage in it?[26] For these reasons, I am wary of Bennett's own wariness of demystification and sympathy for a reenchantment; like Ishikawa, she urges us to once again allow ourselves to be moved and "shocked" by the thingliness of things. Such neovitalism not only runs the risk of turning reactionary in the same way the original iteration did; it also ascribes to capital too much stability and naturalness. Understood as a historically specific metabolism between nature and human labor subsumed under capital, environmental history can become not only a rich narrative of human and nonhuman actants, but also a critically charged moment of political intervention. Such was the discovery of the politicality of nature I believe began in Japan with the environmental turn in the years after 1900.

Capital's attempted but ultimately futile flight into pure autonomy should sound familiar. In many ways it is attempting to repeat the flight from interrelatedness and mutuality of the liberal subject. We should be cautious of other similarities and accommodations between the two, indeed of any approach to the environmental crisis that relies on a methodological individualism. An example of this can be seen in the marketing of recycling as the most important thing one can do for the environment. Rising especially in the 1990s United States during the proliferation of antipublic, market-based solutions and rhetoric, recycling rests on a faith in personal solutions to a global problem. Recycling as an answer seems to smoothly and directly link the personal to the global, completely bypassing and further veiling the already "hidden abode of production." Thus recycling ignores much of the source of the problem while delivering a therapeutic sense of consumers, far from needing protection from the market, but actually empowered by it.[27]

While I believe, like Ishikawa and Tanaka, that the concept of real subsumption does point the way toward a federation of environmentalists and labor, the disconnect between material wealth and capitalist wealth presents problems here. Namely, the removal of parts and practices of nature from capitalist exploitation is necessary, but this removal will have a negative economic effect (in the narrow capitalist sense of the accumulation of value) that will likely reverberate negatively on the labor movement, leading to friction. Nonetheless, this is all the more reason to focus on the invisible hand of relative surplus value, so as not to misrecognize the causes. In the end, something like a union of "the dispossessed," as David Harvey has called for, is probably necessary. Such a reconciliation is surely possible as both nature and labor are joined and disciplined, in the subsumption of their own life processes, to the requirements of capital accumulation instantiated in the moment and site of the production process.

This focus on the value-producing labor also allows a direct criticism of actually existing socialist production regimes, including Stalin and Mao, for the interpretation offered here clearly shows that the form of labor itself must be overcome and that new forms of labor, relations to nature, and subjectivity are necessary. In short, contrary to the Soviet Union and other examples, to overcome the subsumption problems analyzed here, the political goal cannot be the universalization of proletarian labor, but must be its elimination and transcendence.[28] Further, workers are very often those most affected by and aware of the use of environmentally and socially dangerous production methods, storage, and distribution. Given that the subsumption of labor and nature often, but not always, occurs in the same sites and moments, the split between the Ashio miners and the Watarase farmers needs to be, and can be, undone.

Based on this idea, and following the insight of ANT and STS, what likely needs to happen is that Foucault's biopolitics needs to be expanded to include nature's productive capacity as much as it already deals with labor and population. Shall we call such an expansion of biopolitcs "environmentality"?[29] Indeed, while many environmental concerns can be traced to older methods of extracting and capturing from nature the resources for expanded production (such as hydrofracturing), there is also the more frequently attempted capture of the cognitive, creative, and metabolic processes of labor and nature themselves—agriculture itself is such a capture. As Gavin

Walker has shown, this "requires us to look at labor power not simply as a self-evident and available 'living labor capacity,' but also in its most contemporary sense: as many theorists have argued, today the primary concern of capitalist innovation is not discovering new ways of increasing the stock of fixed capital for the next cycle, but is precisely the transformation of the creative capacity and private cultivation of the *qualitative* dimensions of labor power."[30] In the end, Tanaka was correct: there is only motion, and we have to decide whether that motion will be the accumulation of life and freedom of nagare, or the debilitating and ultimately fatal motion of doku, ending in *yomi* (the complete stillness of death).

## We Are All Wired into a Survival Trip Now

In the 1870s, Nishi Amane tried to carve out space for human practice by separating the principles at work behind good government and falling rain. It is ironic and more than a little tragic to see how, less than 150 years later, with our coal-plant-produced acid rain, global warming's newly powerful floods and droughts, and of course the black rain over Hiroshima, falling rain and good government are once again united in a single system.[31] The dominant response to the metabolic rift of modernity by environmentalists in both Japan and the West has been either simple reformism or an attempted leap to an idealized nature, free as much as possible from human history, a wild space of true freedom. Both must be rejected. From our perspective in the midst of a global environmental catastrophe, where even the weather is a dependent variable of $CO_2$ production, we can no longer afford such illusions. In our age we know nature is no longer able to "commensurate the incommensurable,"[32] and though Nietzsche's sea may have been infinite, "eternally flooding back," his optimistic promise that "the sea may cast it up again"[33] becomes a warning when we consider our material sea of oil spills, red tides, mercury-laden fish, and at least two circulating systems of waste that make up the Great Pacific Garbage Patch—the smaller of which is twice the size of Texas. Just as early Ashio activists realized, the history traced in this book constantly demonstrates that nature itself has fundamentally changed. People, nature, society, and economy may no longer be thought of as discrete entities. To move forward at all requires their reincorporation into a continuing production of an increasingly toxic totality. It requires no less than the reintegration of the natural and social sciences. Unlike the infinitely fecund nature of *shizenron* of the Tokugawa period, so often appealed to as a model of an ecologically sustainable society, or the abstract space of (neo)liberal political economy, our nature is not infinite. It is not even nature. A recognition of nature subsumed under capital takes down with it the central illusion at the heart of all deep ecologies, an essential mystic fallacy: the desperate assumption that in the end nature will be there to save us—from ourselves.

APPENDIX

## Tanaka and Kōtoku's Appeal to the Meiji Emperor (1901)

Your lowly and humble subject, Tanaka Shōzō, in fear and trembling, reverently and respectfully submits this appeal. Humbly, even though a mere commoner, this subject dares to transgress the boundaries and break the law by approaching the imperial carriage, a crime punishable by death. Yet, resigned to this, and mindful only of the plight of the nation's people, it is suddenly clear that the current state of affairs can no longer be endured.

Humbly, I beseech you, in your majesty's profound benevolence and boundless compassion, have pity on this subject's great transgression, and deign to grant the reading of this appeal.

Respectfully, forty *ri*[1] north of Tokyo lies the Ashio Copper Mine. For some time, the exploitation of this mine has caused poisonous waste to fill the valley and flow in its waters, joining the Watarase River and continuing downstream so that nothing living along the banks escapes its disastrous effects. Together with increased mining, the poisonous flow has worsened; last year forests at the river's source were recklessly felled by toxic emissions so that now the river runs red with the poisoned earth of the bare mountain. The river has been drastically changed, so filled with poisonous sediment that water levels have risen, and frequent floods inundate the land, spreading poison in every direction, down into the four prefectures of Ibaragi, Tochigi, Gumma, and Saitama, and continuing on into tens of thousands of *chōbu*[2] in the watershed below. Entire species of fish have died out and the countryside lies ruined. Tens of thousands have lost their health and livelihoods: unable to work, hungry without food, sick without medicine, the old and the children lie dead by the roadside; the young men are forced to

1  Approximately one hundred miles. One *ri* is 2.44 miles.
2  One *chōbu* is 2.45 acres.

leave the villages for other lands. In this way, in the last twenty years, as far as the eye can see the once fertile land has been reduced to a wretched sea of withered yellow reeds and white rushes.

This subject has witnessed the dire straits of the people suffering under an ever-present destruction that knows no bounds. Feeling their anguish, I could no longer merely sit idly by. Elected to the House of Representatives, I questioned the government on this problem in the second session. In every session since, nearly screaming, I demanded relief measures. It is now ten years later, yet the government officials persist in vague, noncommittal responses and have taken no appropriate remedies whatsoever. Worse, even the regional authorities have shown no concern, so the people, no longer able to endure their suffering, band together and petition for their preservation; yet the officials order the police to slander the people as rioters and throw them in prison. Such is the awful state even today; it is no exaggeration. As a result, the public treasury has been reduced by hundreds of thousands of yen due to lost taxes from the barren land, this is sure to be millions more in the future. And so the people have been robbed of their rights as citizens. Countless towns and villages have thus lost their autonomy. The people die amid poverty, disease, and poison. The number of the dead grows with each passing year.

And so, to my mind, let the unbroken tradition of the imperial house's morality go out to all of Japan; do so and the people will surely honor you. Even now, not far from here can be seen hundreds of thousands of the desperately poor crying to the skies, requesting the blessing of your benevolence. Ah, must we not say that this is a stain on your enlightened rule? But in truth, it is the government officials who have neglected their office as leaders.

The land of the four prefectures, is it not of your majesty's house? The people of the four prefectures, are they not your majesty's children? The government officials have cast your majesty's land and people into this horrible condition. Though falling into this sad state, the government has not even begun to reflect on this matter, so this subject can no longer remain silent.

I believe the government officials carry the blame for this, so there is nothing left but for your majesty to unleash the great blessing and morality of the imperial house. The water of the Watarase River must be made pure again; that is first. The damaged areas of the river must be repaired and the river itself must be restored to its former state; that is second. The severely poisoned earth must be removed; that is third. The bountiful living things of the riverbanks must be restored; that is fourth. The many degraded towns and villages must be rebuilt; that is fifth. The polluting mine must be closed so that the issuance of poisoned waste and poisoned water may be once and for all stopped at its source; that is sixth. In this way countless souls will be saved from a death sentence; their populations restored, the villages may escape extinction by death and emigration. Only then shall we see the full realization of the laws and constitution of our Japanese Empire, only then shall we ensure the rights of its citizens and end the loss of limitless wealth and power, the very foundation of the nation's future strength. Yet if nothing is done and all is surrendered unto the flowing poison, this subject fears a disaster of immeasurable proportions.

The subject is in his sixty-first year and senility fast approaches. My days on this earth are numbered. So if by any chance this appeal is successful there can be no thought of my personal gain. It is for the cause that this subject risks death by beheading; with tears flowing and words failing, he earnestly beseeches your majesty to use your sagely wisdom to grasp the true meaning of this plea. This subject entreats you to end the suffering.

December the tenth, the thirty-fourth year of Meiji;

In fear and trembling, the lowly subject, Tanaka Shōzō.

1. This chapter covers such phenomena as swamp gas, phosphorescent light, and foxfire, phenomena that produce the appearance of a flame in the absence of heat. See Obata Tokujirō, "Tenpen chii."

2. One ken equals 1.99 yards.

3. Obata, "Tenpen chii," 36–38.

4. This turn toward certainty following a period of chaos is also the basis of Stephen Toulmin's explanation for the eclipse of Renaissance humanism and rise of Cartesian rationalism after the Thirty-Years War. See Toulmin, *Cosmopolis*.

5. Thomas, *Reconfiguring Modernity*, 62. The "just laws of nature" have also been translated as "according to international usage": see Tanaka, *New Times in Modern Japan*, 9.

6. This line of thinking applies to even the most "nature as subject" theorists of Meiji liberalism, such as Ueki Emori. While in Ueki's thought nature grants humans with rights (*tenpu jinken*), those rights are explained as objective and indifferent to human values or abilities: "The rights of nature (*ten*) are possessed by everyone . . . whether rich or poor, strong or weak, all men are the same under heaven." Ueki Emori, quoted in Reitan, "Ethics and Natural Rights Theory," 12.

7. "It is remarkable how Darwin rediscovers, among the beasts and plants, the society of England with its division of labour, competition, opening up of new markets, 'inventions' and Malthusian 'struggle for existence.'" See Marx and Engels, *Karl Marx, Frederick Engels: Collected Works*, 41:380.

8. Obata, "Tenpen chii," 40.

9. The protagonist in Obata's example from Vesuvius does not survive.

10. Obata's theory of earthquakes was the then current belief that they were the result of surface water trickling down through cracks in the earth's surface and coming into contact with a hot core, at which point the resulting steam, having nowhere to go, shook the earth. When the steam was able to make it to the surface, the result was a volcanic eruption, meaning that earthquakes and volcanoes are merely different expressions of the same principle. This steam theory of earthquakes

also implied that earthquakes were as predictable as volcanic eruptions. This theory of earthquakes was taught by, among many others, John Milne, professor of geology and mining at Imperial College in Tokyo, and it also appeared in an article by Tsuda Mamichi in the *Meiroku zasshi*. Tanaka, *New Times in Modern Japan*, 45–48. See also Tsuda in Braisted, *Meiroku zasshi*, 219–20.

11. Obata, "Tenpen chii," 39.

12. The journal was immediately banned. Kawashima had already predicted this move in the journal's last pages, which called on others to take up the fight.

13. Tochigikenshi hensan iinkai, *Tochigikenshi shiryōhen kingendai 9*, 461.

14. For Tanaka's quote see *Tanaka Shōzō senshū* (7 vols., 1989), 4:137–38. For ecocide see Davis, "Ecocide in Marlboro Country," in *Dead Cities*, 33–63.

15. Kurosawa, *Rakunō gakuen no rekishi to shimei*, 8–9.

16. Murakami, *Ashio dōzanshi*.

17. But even when these petitions called for the closing of the mine during sensitive periods of the agricultural cycle, this question of personal freedom was not part of their political economy or their political rhetoric. See Andō, *Kinsei kōgaishi no kenkyū*. For other projects see Sippel, "Chisui"; Shimoda, "Bad Sushi or Bad Merchant?"; Kelly, *Water Control in Tokugawa Japan*; McCormack, "Modernity, Water, and the Environment in Japan."

18. Totman, *The Green Archipelago*; Walker, *The Conquest of Ainu Lands*; Howell, *Geographies of Identity in Nineteenth-Century Japan*. See also Marcon, *The Knowledge of Nature and the Nature of Knowledge in Early Modern Japan*.

19. Totman, *The Green Archipelago*.

20. Meiji voting rights were dependent on paying above a certain threshold of national taxes, meaning that when pollution relief took the form of tax relief, victims often fell below the suffrage threshold and lost their voting rights.

21. Indeed, John Stuart Mill's famous *On Liberty* (1859) begins to waver on the question of whether or not the individual be allowed the freedom to buy poison.

22. Marx, "Economic and Philosophical Manuscripts" (1844), in *Karl Marx: Early Writings*, 328. More recently, John Bellamy Foster has brilliantly excavated the works of Marx to illuminate Marx's ecological thinking. Foster argues that Marx's writings show his awareness of capitalism as a new epoch in the human relation to nature. Historical epochs may be grasped by different modes of what Marx calls the nature-society metabolism, or the material exchange (*Stoffwechsel*) between humans and nature, mediated by the mode of production. Capitalism therefore has its own particular form of this nature-society metabolism. Under Marx's understanding, the separation of city and country is marked by a plundering of the countryside's fertility by exporting, and not returning, the produce of the soil to the great industrial city centers. The result, says Marx, is a "metabolic rift" of capitalism that fundamentally alters the nature-society exchange. Foster, *Marx's Ecology*.

23. Walker, *Toxic Archipelago*.

24. Quoted in Guattari, *The Three Ecologies*, 76n1.

25. Thomas, *Reconfiguring Modernity*, 159.

26. Foster, *Marx's Ecology*, 252.

27. Totman, *A History of Japan*; Totman, *Pre-Industrial Korea and Japan in Environmental Perspective*.

28. Latour, *The Pasteurization of France*.

29. See, for example, Manning, *Against the Grain*.

30. Murphy, *Sick Building Syndrome and the Problem of Uncertainty*.

31. See "Formal and Real Subsumption of Labour under Capital, Transitional Forms," in *Karl Marx, Frederick Engels: Collected Works*, 34:93–121, and "Results of the Immediate Process of Production," in *Capital*, 1:1019–38. Formal subsumption is the process in which existing social, cultural, and economic forms are largely left intact but their produced surpluses are captured by capital accumulation processes. Real subsumption is the reflexive moment when the demands of capital accumulation reflect back into the social, cultural, and economic processes reorganizing them from the beginning into forms more conducive to accumulation. The example given in *Capital* is the difference between the formal subsumption of handicraft work versus the real subsumption of the emergence of large-scale machinery and the factory form. Both forms may be simultaneously present, though Marx notes that real subsumption presupposes the existence of formal, whereas formal does not require real. In Marxian theory, each form roughly has its own form of surplus value, where formal produces absolute surplus value, and real produces relative surplus value.

32. Lukács, *History and Class Consciousness*.

33. There is an enormous literature on this subject. See, for example, Tsurumaki, *Kindaika to dentōteki minshū sekai*.

34. Harvey, *Justice, Nature, and the Geography of Difference*.

35. Further, as will be made more explicit in the conclusion, a focus on the value form and capital accumulation provides for a critique of actually existing socialist practices from within a Marxian analysis by focusing on the particular aspects of capitalist production that remained even within these self-professed socialist regimes. For a study of how the assumed differences between capitalist and socialist systems do not appear in the relation to industrialization and nature, see Josephson, *Industrialized Nature*. There is also a large, if largely unknown, literature on this subject. See for example Marcuse, *Soviet Marxism*, and Postone, *Time, Labor, and Social Domination*. There is also, of course, Stalin's own claim, in *Economic Problems of Socialism in the USSR* (1952), that the value form did not apply to the Soviet Union. For a critique of those elements of capital accumulation that remained within Stalin's vision see Mao, *A Critique of Soviet Economics*. And for a further critique of how Mao's own system also failed to rid itself of basic capital accumulation strategies and forms see Meisner, *Mao's China and After*, and Shapiro, *Mao's War against Nature*.

1. See, for example, Nakamura Mitsuo: "If we see the second decade of the Meiji period as one of turbulence, the third was one of unification and stability." Quoted in Karatani, "The Discovery of Landscape," 37.

2. Notehelfer, "Between Tradition and Modernity"; Gluck, "'Meiji' for Our Time."

3. This ideology of national project was hardly less a part of the "opposition" liberal parties than of the early Meiji oligarchs. Even the famous Osaka conference of 1875 was centered on how best to cultivate a sense of nationalism in Japan's newly liberated commoner population. Essentially, Meiji liberals felt that representative government best bound the people's hearts and minds to the state—more so than the more autocratic methods favored by Meiji conservatives. That there was real antagonism and real violence between the two groups should not blind us to their similarities. See Kanai, "'Tōyō minken hyakkaden' ni miru 'kindai' teki ningenzō," and Howland, *Personal Liberty and Public Good*.

4. See, for example, Karatani's discussion of Kunikida Doppo's stories "Musashino" or "Wasureenu hitobito" or Shiga Shigetaka's *Nihon fūkeiron* (1895) in "The Discovery of Landscape."

5. Thomas, *Reconfiguring Modernity*, 159, 177.

6. Thomas, *Reconfiguring Modernity*, 159.

7. Tanaka, *New Times in Modern Japan*, 56.

8. Thomas, *Reconfiguring Modernity*; Walker, *The Lost Wolves of Japan*.

9. Massive protests throughout the 1870s succeeded in reducing the tax to 2.5 percent. For a good study of the protests against the new cash tax see Tsurumaki, *Kindaika to dentōteki minshū sekai*. See also Steele, "From Custom to Right."

10. In the June 1875 issue of the Enlightenment journal *Meiroku zasshi*, the great systematizer of Meiji knowledge, Nishi Amane, created modern definitions of "knowledge" (*chie*), "wealth" (*tomi*), and "health" (*mame*), identifying them as the "Three Human Treasures" by which Japan would achieve Mill and Bentham's "greatest happiness." For the English translation see Braisted, *Meiroku zasshi*, 462–67. Narita Ryūichi calls health, wealth, and knowledge the fundamental values of the *bunmei kaika* period. See Narita, "Shintai to kōshu eisei," 379.

11. Anderson, "Excremental Colonialism," 645.

12. As Tetsuo Najita has shown, the concepts of prevention and sanitation in the fight against cholera were part of the Tokugawa discourse, but the epistemology of "public health" as social policy instituted by Nagayo Sensai and Matsumoto Ryōjun went beyond the Tokugawa understanding. See Najita, "Ambiguous Encounters," 235.

13. For bourgeois property relations as the apotheosis of alienation of land see Marx, "Economic and Philosophical Manuscripts," 318–21.

14. Totman, *The Green Archipelago* and "Preindustrial River Conservancy."

15. Marcon, *The Knowledge of Nature and the Nature of Knowledge in Early Modern Japan*.

16. Fukutō et al., *Kegare no bunkashi*; Namihara, *Kegare no kōzō*.

17. See Kakimoto, *Kenko to yamai no episuteemee*, 101–2; Sugiyama, "Korera sōdōron"; Jannetta, *Epidemics and Mortality*.

18. See Abe, "Yōjō kara eisei e," 58–59.

19. Najita, "Nature Is the Source of Rights, but Nature Has No Rights," 181–99.

20. Matsumoto, "The Idea of Heaven."

21. Stallybrass and White, *The Politics and Poetics of Transgression*, 93.

22. Reitan, *Making a Moral Society*, 77.

23. This, of course, was how Mill himself saw his *Logic* in relation to Comte's social physics. See Comte and Mill, *The Correspondence of John Stuart Mill and Auguste Comte*.

24. See, for example, Suzuki Noboru, "Nishi Amane tetsugaku no ninchitaikei to tōitsu kagaku"; Sato Tatsuya, "Nishi Amane ni okeru 'saikorogii' to 'shinrigaku' no aida"; or Havens, "Comte, Mill, and the Thought of Nishi Amane in Meiji Japan," 217–28.

25. For more examples, see Reitan, "Ethics and Natural Rights Theory," 8.

26. Reitan, *Making a Moral Society*.

27. Fukuzawa's *Outline of a Theory of Civilization* (1875), too, claimed that a foreign navy may be defeated with force but that a military is useless against the chains of debt. Not coincidentally, one of his first best-sellers was a bookkeeping textbook—another favorite of Tanaka Shōzō. See chapter 2.

28. The translated title of *Saikoku risshi hen* is essentially "The Secret of the West's Success."

29. Figal, *Civilization and Monsters*, 50.

30. Figal, *Civilization and Monsters*, 40–41. For similar examples, see also Tanaka, *New Times in Modern Japan*, 72.

31. Figal, *Civilization and Monsters*, 43. See also Tanaka, *New Times in Modern Japan*, 72.

32. Narita, "Teito Tokyo," 180. Of course, in the wake of Saigo's rebellion, Ueno park would once again fight this battle in the decision to have Saigo's statue face the imperial palace and not his native Kyūshū. See Fujitani, *Splendid Monarchy*, 124. Ian Miller has recently problematized this clean separation in his excellent study of the "ecological modernity" of the Ueno Zoo. See Miller, *The Nature of the Beasts*, 2–8.

33. See Tiegel, *Eisei hanron* (1879), and Rogaski, *Hygienic Modernity*, 150–51.

34. Pettenkofer was so sure of the miasmatic, as opposed to germ, sources of cholera that he famously drank a vial of cholera slurry to prove it. He survived, but his theory did not.

35. For a nearly identical move made in the West, see the excellent history of disease, bodies, and landscapes by Nash, *Inescapable Ecologies*, especially 84 and 90.

36. Tiegel, "Ifukuryō shinkensetsu," 297.

37. Tiegel, "Ifukuryō shinkensetsu," 297.

38. Rogaski says of "Ifukuryō shinkensetsu," "Tiegel subjected Japanese objects to the laboratory scrutiny of Pettenkofer's scientific hygiene. He tested the ability of Japanese textiles to keep out harmful drafts, and examined Japanese straw sandals to see if they could prevent the harmful pollutants of the earth from reaching the

Japanese foot." The focus throughout this pre–germ theory idea of disease was on maintaining the body's vital temperature within healthful ranges. This view of the body included experiments on textiles and straw sandals (*waraji*) by soaking them in water to see how fast they were able to dry out. Tiegel did criticize the *waraji* for shrinking after repeated dousings and dryings and thereby cramping the foot. Further, as a miasmist, he was especially interested in various forms of footwear and their capacity to produce bad smells. Rogaski, *Hygienic Modernity*, 151.

39. Tiegel, "Ifukuryō shinkensetsu," 308.

40. There is large body of work in both English and Japanese on the creation of the new discipline of public health, and I cannot retrace all or even most of it here. In English, see, for example, Rogaski, *Hygienic Modernity*; Janetta, "From Physician to Bureaucrat"; Najita, "Ambiguous Encounters"; Johnston, *The Modern Epidemic*; in Japanese, Abe, "'Eisei' to iu chitsujo"; Kakimoto, *Kenko to yamai no episuteemee*; Sugiyama, "Korera sōdōron"; Narita, "Shintai to kōshū eisei"; and numerous others.

41. This was a characteristic of Western medicine as well. See Nash, *Inescapable Ecologies*.

42. Nash, *Inescapable Ecologies*; Latour, *The Pasteurization of France*.

43. Kitasato Institute and Kitasato University, *Collected Papers of Shibasaburō Kitasato*, 361–77.

44. Waseda University has an 1814 copy of *Dandokuron* in its rare books collection.

45. See Yasuda, *Tsūzoku yōjōkunmō*, section 2. See also Narita, "Shintai to kōshū eisei," 381–82.

46. Narita, "Teito Tokyo," 183.

47. Kakimoto, *Kenko to yamai no episuteemee*, 156–57; Anderson, "Excremental Colonialism."

48. Abe, "Yōjō kara eisei e," 64–65.

49. Komori, "Sōsetsu," 5.

50. On the linking of cholera and the burakumin see Komori, "Sōsetsu." On the Chinese people and Japan's colonial possessions see Ijima and Wakimura, "Kinda ajia ni okeru teikokushugi to iryō."

51. See, for example, one of the largest—the "Shiba shiritsu eiseikai"—in Kikaku henshū kin-gendai shiryō kankōkai, *Kindai tōshi no eisei kankyō*, 43:77–105.

52. I am indebted to Richard Reitan's paper on the social mind for allowing me to make this connection. Reitan, "The Social Mind and the Body of the Crowd."

53. See, for example, Marran, *Poison Woman*.

54. In 1899 the state passed a law of inspection of ports for the prevention of epidemic disease. See Komori, "Sōsetsu," 41. Kitasato, too, saw these as the best way to prevent the infection of Japan by bubonic plague, even proposing a proactive, international expedition into India and China to treat the sources of plague with carbolic acid.

55. Contemporary narratives of the Ashio incident often date the trouble's beginning to 1880, when Tochigi governor Fujiwara issued an edict forbidding the sale or consumption of fish taken from the Watarase. However, this prohibition was in fact an antichol-

era edict issued during one of the worst outbreaks of the disease in the Meiji period. See Anzai, "Kaisetsu," in Tanaka, *Tanaka Shōzō senshū* (7 vols., 1989), 3:313 (hereafter cited as *TSs*).

56. Tochigikenshi hensan iinkai, *Tochigikenshi shiryōhen kingendai 9*, 449–50.

57. See Notehelfer, "Japan's First Pollution Incident," 353.

58. Shōji and Sugai, "The Ashio Copper Mine Pollution Case," 18–20.

59. Murakami, *Ashio dōzanshi*, 165–96; Sugai, "The Development Process of Mining Pollution at the Ashio Copper Mine"; Notehelfer, "Japan's First Pollution Incident," 352–61.

60. See, for example, "Kigyō orimono, senshoku ni kan suru chinjō," in *Tochigikenshi shiryōhen kingendai 9*, 837–40. The first part of the petition establishes the previously unknown connection of the upstream dyers to the Ashio mine. On the modern use of ecological tracers see Bocking, "Ecosystems, Ecologists, and the Atom."

61. *Tochigikenshi shiryōhen kingendai 9*, 461.

62. See "Tanban mondai—tai—Shimotsuke jiyū kōdōkai," in *Tochigikenshi shiryōhen kingendai 9*, 456–57. Shimotsuke is the former name of what is now southern Tochigi prefecture.

63. Itagaki, *Jiyūtōshi*; Bowen, *Rebellion and Democracy in Meiji Japan*; Irokawa, *The Culture of the Meiji Period*.

64. Kano Masanao, *Nihon no kindai shisō*, 90–100; Steele, *Alternative Narratives in Modern Japanese History*, 133–56.

65. *Tochigikenshi shiryōhen kingendai 9*, 456–57. The league member calls on the fellow patriots, using the *bakumatsu* word *shishi* (men of high purpose), to continue the work of the 1870s and 1880s in the fight against mine pollution. The sense of absolute will (*kesshin*) and sacrifice was a staple of the struggles of this period, during which blood oaths prevailed. See, for example, the use of such an oath in the Fukushima jiken in 1882, where the pledge was signed with blood and buried in the yard. Here and elsewhere in the movement, a cult of martyrdom in the name of liberty was common. See *Jiyūtōshi*, 254–55.

66. *Tochigikenshi shiryōhen kingendai 9*, 452–54.

67. *Tochigikenshi shiryōhen kingendai 9*, 464.

68. Tanaka, *TSs*, 3:5–8.

69. Murakami, *Ashio dōzanshi*, 201.

70. "Kōdoku yobōkōji meireisho," in *Tochigikenshi shiryōhen kingendai 9*, 814–16.

71. Walker, *Toxic Archipelago*. Similar arguments from Europe and the United States can be found in Latour, *The Pasteurization of France*, and Nash, *Inescapable Ecologies*.

72. *Tochigikenshi shiryōhen kingendai 9*, 450–61.

73. See, for example, the January 27, 1890, *Yubin hōchi shinbun* article on blue vitriol's effect on fish. This article mentions how "mysteriously" (*fushiginimo*) fish have died out with "the great Tokyo-merchant (*Tokyo no goshō*) Furukawa Ichibei's" takeover of the mine at the headwaters of the Watarase. In *Tochigikenshi shiryōhen kingendai 9*, 450.

74. *Tochigikenshi shiryōhen kingendai 9*, 467–69.

75. *Tochigikenshi shiryōhen kingendai 9*, 470–71.

76. See Ewald, "Two Infinities of Risk"; van Wyck, *Signs of Danger*; Beck, *Risk Society*; Erikson, *New Species*.

77. Ewald, "Two Infinities of Risk," 224.

78. Ewald, "Two Infinities of Risk," 222–23.

79. Van Wyck, *Signs of Danger*, 86.

80. Walker, *Toxic Archipelago*; Deleuze and Guattari, *A Thousand Plateaus*, 25.

81. Tanaka, *TSs*, 3:277.

82. Their results matched very closely a later official government investigation. The national averages were 3.21 births per 100 and 2.30 deaths per 100.

83. Matsumoto Eiko, "Kōdokuchi no sanjō (1902)," 30.

84. Matsumoto Eiko, "Kōdokuchi no sanjō (1902)," 62.

85. Matsumoto Eiko, "Kōdokuchi no sanjō (1902)," 31.

86. Nixon, "Slow Violence and Environmental Storytelling," June 13, 2011, on the Nieman Storyboard website, www.niemanstoryboard.org. See also Nixon, *Slow Violence and the Environmentalism of the Poor*.

87. Erikson, *New Species*. See also Nixon, *Slow Violence and the Environmentalism of the Poor*.

88. Matsumoto Eiko, "Kōdokuchi no sanjō (1902)," 31.

89. Erikson, *New Species*, 121.

90. Erikson, *New Species*, 121.

91. Matsumoto Eiko, "Kōdokuchi no sanjō (1902)," 112–13. This word, *urami*, using a different character, would be central to the Minamata protests of the 1960s and 1970s. See Smith and Smith, *Minamata*.

TWO. **Pollution and Peasants**

1. Approximately one hundred miles.

2. A full translation of the jikiso is in the appendix.

3. See "Jikiso ni tsuite 'kokkei shimbun' e no kisho," in Tanaka, *TSs*, 4:111–13.

4. Tanaka, *TSs*, 4:111–13.

5. Sakura Sōgo, sometimes Sogorō, is the name later attached to Kiuchi Sogorō. It may be written with various Chinese characters (佐倉宗吾・佐倉総五郎, etc.). There is only a single rice-levy register (*kokudaka*) with the name "Kiuchi Sogorō—village headman" to even suggest such a person existed. The register is on display at the Sōgo Reido in Narita city, Chiba prefecture. For a good summary of the Sakura legend and how it fits into the genre of tales of Edo Era peasant protest see Walthall, *Peasant Uprisings in Japan*, 35–75.

6. Most versions include a daughter who is spared death but married off into another domain.

7. In the kabuki versions of the Sakura legend Lord Hotta is haunted by the ghosts of Sakura and his wife not as retribution for their own executions, but only for the unjust executions of their sons. In the tradition of peasant tales the martyr is always consigned to death from the moment the decision to appeal or rebel is made. That so many

versions include Sakura's wife's execution is most likely a morality lesson on wives' filial piety duties to their husbands. It also resonates with the popular "love suicides" tale of Edo popular storytelling. Still, most Sakura legends include a scene where Sakura divorces his wife before his final decision to perform a jikiso in an attempt to take all the blame himself.

8. In many accounts of the tale, including the one translated by Walthall, Sakura, too, fails to place the petition into the shogun's hands but manages to get it into the hands of an attendant. It is later read and acted on by the shogun. Tanaka did not get even this far with his appeal, and there is no evidence that the Meiji emperor ever saw the text. Woodblock prints of the kabuki version of the jikiso event show Sakura getting his petition into the hands of the shogun by attaching it to the end of a split bamboo pole.

9. Almost all Ashio and Tanaka literature claims that Tanaka was branded as insane by the state as a way to discredit the antipollution cause. But research since the publishing of the zenshū in the 1980s has shown this was not true, overturning one of the major pillars of the "last peasant protest" ideology, where the new discipline of psychology pathologizes the peasant who is out of place and time in the Meiji present. In fact, for Tanaka, Kōtoku, Ishikawa Hanzan, and many others of the jikiso coalition, the indifference of the modern state was much more deflating.

10. It would be made illegal in 1917 as part of the process of State Shinto construction. This caused serious legal problems, as the only crime that came close to covering Tanaka's behavior was *lèse-majesté*, "lack of respect," which was clearly not applicable in this case that gave so much deference to the sovereign. For this debate see Fukawa, *Tanaka Shōzō to tennō jikiso jiken*.

11. See for example Hayashi, *Tanaka Shōzō*.

12. Traditional Tanaka historiography, based mainly on the *Gijin zenshū* (5 vols., 1925–28) and its emphasis on the heroic, assumes a continuity between the Sakura of legend and Tanaka's invocation in 1901. In short, Tanaka's jikiso is seen as the "last peasant protest," an example of Japan's repressed agrarian consciousness. Some historians conclude the incident with the formation of the Second Pollution Prevention Committee of 1902, some with the destruction of Yanaka village in 1907, and others not until the closing of the mine in 1987. But a 1991 *Yomiuri shinbun* shows that the mine continues to pollute, and activists centering on Tanaka Shōzō reading groups have followed the Furukawa company to the Philippines, which suffered its own copper mine pollution through the 1980s. The "last peasant protest" thesis is too simplistic and takes away from the relevance of Tanaka's later constitutional and political thought by removing him from the middle of the Meiji debate on the nature of rights and national identity.

13. In what will become a bigger influence on Tanaka's thought after 1902, the last entries do mention the autocratic road-building projects of governor Mishima Michitsune (1835–88) have adversely affected the river's flows (*chisui*). *TSs* 1:158–59.

14. Pyle, "Symposium: The Ashio Copper Mine Pollution Case," 347–50.

15. Tatematsu, *Doku*; Hayashi, *Tanaka Shōzō*; Gluck, "'Meiji' for Our Time," 19.

16. Notehelfer, "Between Tradition and Modernity." Something of this narrative continues in Timothy George's *Minamata: Pollution and the Struggle for Democracy in Postwar Japan.*

17. In other words, to paraphrase Bakhtin, "disparities in the [social] context are played out as heteroglossia in the text." See Hanks, *Intertexts,* 112.

18. *Osaka nippō,* June 9, 1878. See "Osaka Nippō 9 June 1878." With the executive and legislative powers monopolized by former samurai of Satsuma and Chōshū, the earliest Peoples' Rights activists focused on the courts as the only enlightened branch of Meiji government.

19. Makihara, *Kyakubun,* 6.

20. Fukuzawa, *An Encouragement of Learning,* 63–72.

21. Quoted in Makihara, *Kyakubun,* 7.

22. Kanai, "Kokkai kaisetsu seigan undō ni miru Matsuzawa Kyūsaku no shisō (1)."

23. See, for example, Howland, *Personal Liberty and Public Good.*

24. Ueno, "Jiyūminken ni okeru igirisu kōrishugi shisō no taishū," 35. For a discussion of the role of Utilitarianism in the thought of high minken figures such as Nakae Chōmin, Ono Azusa, and Itō Hirobumi see Uesugi, "Kindai nihon ni okeru kōrishugi seiji shisō no juyō."

25. Tawara Jirō quoted in Mizoguchi, *Ichigo no jiten,* 16.

26. Watanabe, *Higashi ajia no ōken to shisō,* and Mass, *Antiquity and Anachronism in Japanese History.* The use of the term *bakufu* was actually a rhetorical move by Edo Era nativists who sought to deny legitimacy to the shogun by highlighting the exclusively military, and therefore illegitimate, basis of Tokugawa rule.

27. Quoted in Thomas, *Reconfiguring Modernity,* 70–71.

28. In the preface to the first installment Komurō said that although he used the word *tōyō* (Asia, Orient) in the title, he did so in order to contrast it to *seiyō* (Western), and the title could just as well have used *nihon* (Japan). Komurō, *Tōyō minken hyakkaden,* 11. The work was published in three parts, and the title for parts 2 and 3 replaced the word *minken* with the word *gimin: Tōyō gimin hyakkaden* (peasant martyrs).

29. Constructing the Satchō batsu as a narrow, selfish tyranny is a major motif of the entire popular rights movement and forms the logic of Ueki Emori's "Minken jiyūron" and Nakae Chōmin's "Kokumin mezamashi" and "Kokkai mezamashi."

30. The phrase "Proclaiming peoples' rights" (*minken o tonaeru*) is in nearly all Meiji Sakura representations. A memorial stele donated to the Sōgo Reido in Narita City, Chiba prefecture, by activist Hoshi Tōru (1850–1901) contains a kanbun ode that begins with this phrase.

31. Glossed as "maruchirudomu" in katakana in Fukuzawa's text.

32. Fukuzawa, *Gakumon no susume,* 72. Emphasis added.

33. In contrast, compare this view of self-sacrifice with conservative ideologue Inoue Tetsujirō's interpretation of the Imperial Rescript on Education in 1891 and 1893 and its emphasis on necessary sacrifice for one's lord and nation.

34. Walthall, *Peasant Uprisings in Japan,* 21, 238n54.

35. See especially Arai, "Gimin to minken fokuroa."

36. The volume even includes two samurai biographies. See Kanai, "Tōyō minken hyakkaden' ni miru 'kindai' teki ningenzō."

37. Komurō, *Tōyō minken hyakkaden*, 11–12. *Jinjin gishi* is the same term we saw used by the Shimotsuke Liberal League and the early antipollution activists in the last chapter.

38. See Osamu, *Rongo*, 308.

39. See Jansen, *Sakamoto Ryōma and the Meiji Restoration*, and Harootunian, *Toward Restoration*.

40. Despite this conservative tendency, the potential for revolutionary action is not completely removed—Sasshin-jōjin is a major tenet of the Wang Yang Ming school of radical Confucianism. Stressing the identity of thought and action (*chigyō-gōitsu*), Wang Yang Ming eschewed the more official neo-Confucian emphasis on contemplation and the "investigation of things to learn their principles" (*kakubutsu-kyūri*) in favor of political activism. See Shimada Kenji, *Shūshigaku to yōmeigaku*. There is some evidence that Tanaka was schooled in or at least familiar with this tradition. Komatsu Hiroshi, *Tanaka Shōzō no kindai*, 681–702.

41. Ueki, "Discourse on Popular Rights and Liberty (1880)," in *From Japan's Modernity*, 50.

42. Arai, "Gimin to minken fokuroa," in *Kindai ikōki no minshūzō*. "Free speech" talismans produced at local shrines and temples are just one of the many important reminders of popular (*minshū*) participation in the entire movement, an aspect of the *jiyūminken undō* that could not have heartened the more rationalist bunmei-kaika advocates such as Fukuzawa.

43. Howland, *Translating the West*, 23; Stefan Tanaka, *New Times in Meiji Japan*.

44. See, for example, Strong, *Ox against the Storm*, and Hayashi, *Tanaka Shōzō*. See also George, "Tanaka Shōzō's Vision of an Alternative Constitutional Modernity for Japan."

45. See Komatsu Hiroshi, *Tanaka Shōzō no kindai*.

46. For the "unproblematic figure" quote see Komatsu Hiroshi, *Tanaka Shōzō: Nijū isseki e no shisōjin*, 6–7. For the gijin-shisōka quote see Yui, *Tanaka Shōzō*, ii–iii.

47. See Hayashi, *Tanaka Shōzō*.

48. Quoted in Sugawara, "Tanaka Shōzō no kōdō no ronri."

49. Letter to Kawamata Kyūhei in Tanaka Shōzō, *Tanaka Shōzō zenshū* (20 vols. 1977–80), 14:136–37 (hereafter cited as *TSz*).

50. See Komatsu Hiroshi, *Tanaka Shōzō no kindai*, especially chap. 2.

51. A source of major rural disturbance in early Meiji. Massive resistance by farmers across Japan resulted in a reduction of the land tax from 3 percent to 2.5 percent.

52. Yui, *Tanaka Shōzō*, 59–61.

53. Novelist and Tanaka author Wahei Tatematsu quoted this line as the key to all of Tanaka's thought on an NHK television program in November 2001. There is also, it seems, an anachronistic projection of his later thoughts on Yanakagaku and chisui (see this volume, chap. 3).

54. This is still the best work on Tanaka in English in the later chapters, even without the insight of the zenshū (1977–80). Using mainly sources from the Gijin zenshū,

Strong is able to go beyond this peasant thesis and make fruitful comparisons to Gandhi and Danilo Dolci.

55. Translation from Strong, *Ox against the Storm*, 31. See also George, "Tanaka Shōzō's Vision of an Alternative Constitutional Modernity for Japan."

56. See Shōji, "Shōzō no tochi hanbai 'sanzento en' no mōke ni gigi ari." See also Akagami, "Tanaka Shōzō mukashi banashi 'kasei no kempō' hyōkasetsu e no gimon," 43–70. Komatsu shows that it was likely impossible for Tanaka to have received help from the Tengutō rebels of nearby Mito during his fight with the house of Rokkaku as he had claimed. See *Tanaka Shōzō no kindai*, 681–702.

57. See, for example, the presentation of a very young Shibusawa Eiichi's likely apocryphal childhood skepticism of fox-possession exorcisms. Shibusawa, *The Autobiography of Shibusawa Eiichi*, chap. 1.

58. Other than becoming Sakura Sōgo there was probably no greater way to establish one's activist credentials than to run afoul of Mishima. The most highly praised incident in the history of the Liberal Party, the Fukushima Incident, recounts the hardships and imprisonment of Liberal members sworn to good government who were persecuted by Mishima. One of these members eventually achieved martyrdom when he died in prison from malnutrition and exposure. Mishima's methods are legendary. In his bid to bring civilization and enlightenment to Fukushima and Tochigi he extorted "donations" to pay for his road-building scheme, with dire consequences for those who refused to contribute. A current guidebook for sites of the Ashio Incident includes a stop at the former site of Kimura Asashichi's house near Ashikaga, Tochigi with poles marking how Kimura's house was cut in half by one of Mishima's roads—retaliation for Kimura's refusal to donate.

59. Tanaka, *TSz*, 1:24.

60. For a brief note on the relation of bad government to river management see the final sections in *TSs*, 1:158–59.

61. *Tochigikenshi shiryōhen kingendai 9*, 453–54.

62. Grimmer-Solem, "German Social Science, Meiji Conservatism, and the Peculiarities of Japanese History," 201.

63. Makihara, *Kyakubun*, 42.

64. Grimmer-Solem, "German Social Science," 215–16.

65. Winch, *Economics and Policy*.

66. See Tanya Maus, "Rising Up and Saving the World."

67. For the editorial see Ogura, *Can Japanese Agriculture Survive?*, 83. Emphasis added.

68. Tanaka, *TSs*, 3:44. Emphasis added.

69. In *Kyakubun* Makihara Norio has shown that in the Edo Era temple-school (*terakoya*) textbooks that served as education for the majority of the people, benevolent government meant not only reducing the rice-tax levy during hard times but also controlling the merchants' selfishness and greed (*shiyoku*).

70. Makihara, *Kyakubun*, 54–59. Makihara points out that these texts included concrete examples of bad government and thus were actually more democratic than their Meiji counterparts.

71. Williams, *Marxism and Literature*, 122.

72. Winch, *Economics and Policy*, 39.

73. Tanaka, *TSs*, 3:280–303.

74. Tanaka, *TSz*, 15:124–25.

75. Mencius, Wan Zhang A, no. 6, quoted in Zhang Dainian and Edmund Ryden, *Key Concepts in Chinese Philosophy*, 128.

76. See Matsumoto Sannosuke, "The Idea of Heaven."

77. Ishikawa Hanzan, June 8, 1901, quoted in Fukawa, *Tanaka Shōzō to tennō jikiso jiken*.

78. Tanaka, *TSs*, 4:46–48. Emphasis added. The invocation of Sakura Sōgo's embodiment of benevolent government in both rhetoric and practice expresses what Raymond Williams calls a "residual" cultural practice that tries to express something new using the resources of the past. "The residual, by definition, has been effectively formed in the past, but it is still active in the cultural process, not only and often not at all as an element of the past, but as an effective element of the present. Thus certain experiences, meanings, and values which cannot be expressed or substantially verified in terms of the dominant culture, are nevertheless lived and practised on the basis of the residue—cultural as well as social—of some previous social and cultural institution or formation." Williams, *Marxism and Literature*, 122.

79. Tanaka, *TSs*, 3:272–74. While the reference to Sakura Sōgo is explicit, the phrasing "born and sacrifice himself again seven times" is also highly suggestive of the Wang Yang Ming (Ōyomei) imperial activist Yoshida Shōin (1830–59), who ended his final text, *Ryūkonroku* (*Record of an Immortal Soul*, 1859), with a similar line: "Though I be reborn seven times, how should I ever forget my resolve to expel the barbarians?" Yoshida's text has the sense of inevitable victory in place of Tanaka's resignation and doubt. See Yoshida Shōin, "Ryūkonroku," in Najita, *Readings in Tokugawa Thought*, 271.

80. Matsuzawa Kyūsaku, "Kokkai kaisetsu o jōgan suru no sho," in Irokawa, *Meiji kenpakusho shūsei*, 6:20.

81. Kōno, "Kokkai o kaisetsu suru inka o jōgan suru sho," 282. Emphasis added.

82. Kanai, "Kokkai kaisetsu seigan undō ni miru Matsuzawa Kyūsaku no shisō (1)."

83. Kanai, "'Aiso' to iu shisō."

84. Ōmachi, *Jiyūminken undō to chihō seiji*.

85. This phrase was often used rhetorically in Diet debates, and Tanaka occasionally disagreed with the idea. In 1907 Tanaka rejected this belief in a letter to Noguchi Haruzō, stating, "Even today people hold onto this old teaching but today is different. Today there is a constitution and the prince (*kunshi*) is bound to rule by it. . . . Today, depending on the situation a prince's pronouncements can indeed by revoked (*torikeshi*)." See Komatsu Hiroshi, *Tanaka Shōzō no kindai*, 103.

86. The jikiso was written for Tanaka by Kōtoku Shūsui and then heavily edited by Tanaka. Fred Notehelfer's work reminds us that though eventually a full-fledged socialist, up to 1902 Kōtoku still believed in benevolent loyalism. See Notehelfer, *Kōtoku Shūsui*.

87. This language explicitly calling for the closure of the mine was the most important last-minute correction Tanaka made to Kōtoku's text.

88. Emphasis added.

89. See especially Fujitani, *Splendid Monarchy*.

90. Gluck, "'Meiji' for Our Time," 18.

91. Kinoshita, "Shakai kaigo no iro."

92. The first half of the essay condemns public sympathy for the samurai ethic of the man who assassinated former Liberal Party activist Hoshi Tōru for perceived profiteering and selfish excess in June 1901. Although Kinoshita condemned both the mine pollution and Hoshi Tōru, for Kinoshita these two examples were merely the unacceptable present attacked by the unacceptable past.

93. Kinoshita, "Shakai kaigo no iro," 6.

94. Arai Ōsui, "Ka o mite sono jin o shiru."

95. Mencius, "Kung-Sun Ch'Au, Part II, Chapter 4.3," 217–18.

96. Mencius, "Kung-Sun Ch'Au, Part II, Chapter 4.3," 218. See Matsumoto Eiko, "Kōdokuchi no sanjō (1902)," 53–54.

97. See Kanai, "'Aiso' to iu shisō," 195.

98. Of course the language is Irwin Scheiner's. See Scheiner, "Benevolent Lords and Honorable Peasants," 39–62.

99. See Vlastos, *Peasant Protests and Uprisings in Tokugawa Japan*. See also Bowen, *Rebellion and Democracy*.

100. For this debate see Fukawa, *Tanaka Shōzō to tennō jikiso jiken*. A jikiso was not illegal until 1917.

101. One point is interesting in light of later cultural nationalists' claims that the imperial house was identified with an indigenous nature in the 1930s: here the Meiji emperor himself is actually the one standing in the way of both social harmony and an environmental or nature ethic.

102. "Kakkoku kōshi ni chinjō kika no ken," in *Tochigikenshi shiryōhen kingendai 9*, 1030–33. Emphasis added.

103. Tanaka Shōzō, September 1904, quoted in Makihara, "Tanaka Shōzō," 88.


THREE. Nature over Nation

1. This had been a problem in 1896 as well. See Uchimizu, *Shiryō Ashio kōdoku jiken*, 21–28; see also Anzai, "Kōdoku chōsa iinkai—dai ichiji, dai niji—no setchi to Tanaka Shōzō," 395.

2. Put another way, the 1902 committee represents what Henri Lefebvre marked as a major change in modern society: from the production of things within space to the production of space itself. See Lefebvre, *The Production of Space*.

3. The 1902 project was the extension of the abstract, sterilized space of the Meiji public health campaigns to the countryside. As public health officials began a campaign in Tokyo on the virtues of the daily use of soap, in another branch of the Home Ministry the second Pollution Prevention Committee planned no less than the

complete remaking of nature in the Kanto plain, a nature that would behave. It should also come as no surprise that in yet another part of the Home Ministry this period also saw the establishment of the Local Improvement Movement (*chihō kairyō undō*). See Pyle, "The Technology of Japanese Nationalism."

4. Nimura, *The Ashio Riot of 1907*, 235n6.

5. *Tochigikenshi shiryōhen kingendai 9*, 990.

6. *Tochigikenshi shiryōhen kingendai 9*, 990.

7. *Tochigikenshi shiryōhen kingendai 9*, 1001.

8. *Tochigikenshi shiryōhen kingendai 9*, 998.

9. Andō, *Kinsei kōgaishi no kenkyū*.

10. There were countless other domain-level projects, such as Dazai Shundai's plan to monopolize the entire domainal product and use the trading receipts to strengthen the economic base of the samurai. The most famous and successful domainal plans were perhaps Satō Nobuhirō's capital accumulation strategies for Satsuma. See Marcon, *The Knowledge of Nature and the Nature of Knowledge in Early Modern Japan*.

11. Honda, "Keisei hisaku." There are still instances of this view of Japan as geographically and geologically handicapped. Programs like the Discovery Channel's *Extreme Engineering* often include Japanese projects; one such episode suggested that Tokyo's overcrowding could be alleviated by essentially inverting a mountain in Tokyo Bay, thereby creating new urban space. Former prime minister Tanaka Kakuei, too, vowed to destroy the mountains that seemed to leave his native Niigata a backwater of Tokyo. In the event, the result was the Jōetsu Shinkansen linking Niigata with Tokyo.

12. See Okuma, *Tonegawa chisui no hensen to suigai*, 112–14.

13. Chiba kenritsu sekiyadōjō hakubutsukan, *Shizen saigai o norikoete*; Fukawa, *Tanaka Shōzō to Tone, Watarase no nagare*; Komatsu Hiroshi, *Tanaka Shōzō no kindai*.

14. Purseglove, *Taming the Flood*. For the postwar continuation of this tradition see Dinmore, "Concrete Results?"

15. *Tochigikenshi shiryōhen kingendai 9*, 998. Emphasis added.

16. Latour, *Reassembling the Social*, 220.

17. Beck, *Risk Society*, 65. Emphasis in the original. See also Ewald, "Two Infinities of Risk," 223–24.

18. See Davis, *Dead Cities*, 33.

19. Morris-Suzuki, "Concepts of Nature and Technology in Pre-Industrial Japan"; Kaibara, *The Philosophy of Qi*; Ch'in-shun Lo, *Knowledge Painfully Acquired*.

20. This too continued the agronomic tradition that had said famine was not natural but the result of bad social practices.

21. Tanaka, *TSs*, 4:89.

22. Tanaka, *TSs*, 4:136.

23. Tanaka, *TSs*, 4:159.

24. Tanaka, *TSs*, 4:160.

25. Douglas, *Purity and Danger*.

26. Tanaka, *TSs*, 4:149–50. Emphasis added.

27. Tanaka, *TSs*, 4:137–38. Emphasis added. This recalls not only the reintegration of morality, politics, and nature of neo-Confucian language, but also the sense of excess turning deadly in the understanding of doku in Chinese medicine.

28. For the collapse of the social Darwinist and Hegelian theories of progress in favor of theories of retrogression see Konishi, *Anarchist Modernity*, 210. Also see Thomas, *Reconfiguring Modernity*, chap. 7.

29. Tanaka, *TSs*, 4:287.

30. There is a great deal of recent environmental history in Japan and the West that seeks to present Tokugawa Japan as a model of a "green" society. Of the many cases see, for example, Ishikawa Eisuke, *Ōedo risaikuru jijō*; Azby Brown, *Just Enough*; or more critically, McCormack, "Modernity, Water, and the Environment in Japan."

31. Tanaka, *TSs*, 5:280–82.

32. Tanaka, *TSs*, 7:88.

33. Oka, "Jinrui no seifuku ni tai suru shizen no fukushū."

34. Oka, "Jinrui no seifuku ni tai suru shizen no fukushū"; McMullen, "Kumazawa Banzan and *Jitsugaku*"; Honda, "Keisei hisaku"; Fukuzawa, *Outline of a Theory of Civilization*.

35. Tanaka, *TSs*, 5:8.

36. Tanaka, *TSs*, 7:38.

37. Arahata, *Yanaka mura metsubōshi*, 8.

38. In naming the year 1902 Tanaka refers to the Second Pollution Prevention Committee of 1902, the one that proposed the reengineering of the Watarase and Tone watersheds and the construction of the flood-control reservoir on the site of Yanaka village. See above. Tanaka, *TSs*, 7:136.

39. Tanaka, *TSs*, 4:228.

40. Tanaka, *TSs*, 6:243, 6:276.

41. Komatsu Hiroshi, *Tanaka Shōzō no kindai*, 476–78; Arahata, *Yanaka mura metsubōshi*.

42. Denied access to government levee-repair funds, Yanaka mayor Anjō Junshirō purchased a pump at personal cost but was able to convince villagers into guaranteeing the debt through annual payment in kind. When the pump proved useless against the increasing breaches in the disintegrating levees and barley production failed, the villagers were left with only the debt. Anjō was repaid from the 480,000 yen appropriated for the purchase of their homes. Arahata, *Yanaka mura metsubōshi*, 109–13.

43. In February 1907 Ashio workers went on a three-day rampage, terrorizing foremen and mine officials and destroying equipment. Nimura, *The Ashio Riot of 1907*.

44. For the relocation to Saroma see Yanaka mura to Moro Chikasuke o katarukai, *Yanaka mura sonchō*.

45. Miura Ken'ichirō, "Yanaka mura haison." There had been a brief period of improved yields in 1903, a year after the huge flooding of 1902. The improved yields coincided with the 1902 committee's announcement of the flood-control plan and seemed to support the committee's plans. Tanaka contended, however, that the 1902

flood had been so massive, taking so much sediment from the denuded hills upstream in the Watarase, that it had brought large amounts of unpolluted, pre-Ashio sediment. To him it showed the relative power of the slowly produced tennen against the frighteningly fast accumulation of doku. In his words the improved yields of 1903 merely showed that five thousand years of tennen was just barely able to combat five years of doku. The renewal of toxic flooding in 1907 and 1910 confirmed 1903 as a one-time event, consistent with Tanaka's analysis. Tanaka, *TSs*, 5:29.

46. Shimada Sōzō, *Tanaka Shōzō ō yoroku*, 1:111–13.

47. Three more homes remained outside the levees and thus were not subject to the order.

48. Shimada Sōzō, *Tanaka Shōzō ō yoroku*, 1:125–26.

49. Shimada Sōzō, *Tanaka Shōzō ō yoroku*, 1:131.

50. Tanaka, *TSs*, 7:41.

51. Tanaka, *TSs*, 7:56.

52. Shimada Sōzō, *Tanaka Shōzō ō yoroku*, 1:154.

53. Tanaka, *TSs*, 5:185.

54. Hayashi, *Tanaka Shōzō*, 26.

55. Tanaka, *TSs*, 5:186.

56. Tanaka, *TSs*, 5:188.

57. See "Michi o tsutaeru," in Arai Ōsui, *Arai Ōsui chosakushū*, 2:552.

58. Born Ivan Dimitriyevich Kasatkin, he traveled to Hokkaido after reading Vasilli Golovnin's *Memoirs of Captivity in Japan*. See Nakamura, *Senkyōshi Nikorai to meiji nihon*, 8–9.

59. Mori had met Harris during his time as a student studying abroad for Satsuma.

60. Schneider, *A Prophet and a Pilgrim*, xiv. The new church movement favored theocratic communities and became part of the Second Great Awakening in the United States in the mid- to late nineteenth century. A Calvinist until the age of twenty, Harris was active in the dynamic religious movements of the time, learning about Mesmerism from Andrew Jackson Davis. Later, after Davis's conversion to Swedenborgian Christianity, and following a dream in which he met Swedenborg and the medieval doctor Galen, Harris became a Swedenborgian himself. In the words of William James, Harris was "America's best-known mystic."

61. The centerpiece of the commune was the notion of mystical sexual union with celestial beings, above all a heavenly Queen Lily of the conjugal angels, who represented ideal womanhood and pure love, while maintaining celibate terrestrial marriages. Schneider, *A Prophet and a Pilgrim*.

62. But only for a time. Eventually, like many other Christian socialists and members of the Second Great Awakening, Harris became a virulent social Darwinist and white supremacist who believed monarchy was the way to cure the degeneracy of American democracy and give birth to a new time and a new life. He preached on the need for a pivotal, grand man (an idea also found in Swedenborg) to emerge and redeem the world. Increasingly Harris saw himself as a latter-day John of Patmos, author of the book of Revelation. In the end he claimed to have gone beyond the Judeo-Christian

tradition, saying that as his physical masculine flesh declined with age, his female side was emerging and he was becoming The Avatar, a Hindu Aryan mother deity. In addition, if God were to work in the world, he would have to work through an American empire "in the hands of a strong military dictator who will found a dynasty. . . . Better the sword with its morality than a system whose life is mere corruption." In a chapter titled "The Hell of American Democracy" he declared ruling men from below infernal and predicted that in the end "the Negro Race will disappear; the Jewish race will also disappear. Generally speaking the inferior races will disappear." Schneider, *A Prophet and a Pilgrim*, 290, 312. Despite spending nearly three decades under Harris's spiritual supervision in New York and California, Arai never seems to have adopted this level of social Darwinism, suggesting a stronger attachment with the socialism of the other wing of the new church movement.

63. The concept of redemption preached by Arai in Tokyo followed the Swedenborgian theology of teaching that God imparted a good nature (*sentensei*) to every person, but that through birth to an earthly mother that nature became flesh (*kōtensei*), and anger, desire (*yoku*), and ego became entangled with the original. How these evils did or did not develop depended on one's parents, the times, and the place. One's deeds and original nature coiled around each other to form the person.

64. Corl, "Arai Ōsui to jukyō o megutte."

65. Tanaka, *TSz*, 11:369–70.

66. Tanaka, *TSz*, 5:333.

67. Again we must not exclusively identify *doku* with the presence of copper, arsenic, or other chemicals in the soil or water but as a finite and possibly harmful natural world. As Tanaka's thought developed, the reversal of flow that brought harm to the physical, environmental, and social realms was increasingly indistinguishable from how he used *doku*.

68. Tanaka, *TSs*, 7:234.

69. Tanaka, *TSz*, 18:67.

70. Tanaka, *TSs*, 7:247. Emphasis added.

71. Marcon, *The Knowledge of Nature and the Nature of Knowledge in Early Modern Japan*, and Morris-Suzuki, "Environmental Problems and Perceptions in Early Industrial Japan."

72. Tanaka, *TSs*, 6:279.

73. Tanaka, *TSs*, 7:191.

74. Žižek, "Introduction: Robespierre, or, The 'Divine Violence' of Terror," xxviii.

75. Tanaka, *TSs*, 6:6.

76. Tanaka, *TSs*, 6:279. This could be seen as a precursor of Deep Ecology's "Where you at?" quiz, which asks students to identify the source of their water, the constituent parts of their breakfast, etc. The more immediate link, I believe, comes from the Danish founder of the rural folk schools, Nikolaj Frederik Severin Grundtvig (1783–1872), who criticized official Danish schooling as privileging Greek and Roman history while neglecting local conditions and ecologies. Grundtvig and Danish education and farming in general were discussed in Tanaka's circles. Grundtvig's folk

school model had a major influence on one of Tanaka's disciples, the founder of Snow Brand Dairy, Kurosawa Torizō. See chapter 5. For Grundtvig, see Grundtvig, *A Grundtvig Anthology*, and Borish, *The Land of the Living*.

77. Quoted in Komatsu Hiroshi, *Tanaka Shōzō no kindai*, 583.

78. Tanaka, *TSz*, 13:185.

79. Tanaka, *TSs*, 4:238.

80. Tanaka, *TSs*, 7:266. In the context of praising the Yanakans and the valorization of *gu*, he does state, "I am a small village farmer. I have become a fool among fools," which I think can be read more as the apotheosis of the "foolishness" of the Yanakans against the *fukoku-kyōhei* of the engineers than as a statement of continuity with his peasant past. Tanaka, *TSs*, 6:115.

81. Tanaka, *TSs*, 6:205.

82. Tanaka, *TSs*, 6:231.

83. Tanaka, *TSs*, 6:207.

84. Okada eventually claimed that the goal of seated meditation (*seiza*) was to come to perceive the underlying unity of Rousseau's confessional *Émile* and Plato's *Republic*. Georg Lukács has examined the rightist slide of vitalist thought (*Lebensphilosophie*) in Europe. In that tradition, the human/nature divide was maintained along largely neo-Kantian lines in the early periods. But later, rather than adapting personal politics to the material environment as Tanaka, Ishikawa, and Kurosawa did, nature itself was subjectified and mystified—the material environment was subsumed under the aegis of consciousness and thus disappeared as a basis for politics. Something very similar occurred in Japan in the thought of later thinkers such as Tanabe Hajime, Watsuji Tetsurō, and (as we shall see in chaps. 4 and 5) Tachibana Kozaburō. See Lukács, *The Destruction of Reason*.

85. Tanaka, *TSs*, 5:13.

86. Tanaka, *TSs*, 6:226.

FOUR. **Natural Democracy**

1. On June 22, 1908, following a meeting celebrating the release of the socialist Yamaguchi Kōken, several attendees marched through the streets with red flags bearing the slogans "Anarchism" and "Anarchist Communism." They clashed with police, and fourteen, including Sakai Toshihiko, Ōsugi Sakae, and Yamakawa Hitoshi, were arrested for violating the Peace Police Law.

2. Tsuzuki, "'My Dear Sanshiro,'" 5; Nozawa, "Ishikawa Sanshirō ni okeru Erize Rukuryu no shisō," 840.

3. Carpenter reports that Ishikawa was possibly part of a prisoner exchange with the German and Japanese governments, but this is unverified, and highly unlikely.

4. Foster, *Marx's Ecology*.

5. In some ways, the early Ishikawa could be considered a leftist version of Taishō "life philosophy" (*seimeishugi*). Growing from the same disillusionment that led to the collapse of Meiji liberalism, seimeishugi was in many ways a rejection of the liberal

order that separated human and nature in favor of a vitalist identification of "human life." Influenced by Tolstoy, Bergson, Nietzsche, Schopenhauer, and many others, seimeishugi grew to a deep and broad ideology of nature in the second decade of the twentieth century. But as seimeishugi slid into vitalism and became increasingly associated with an antimaterialist irrationality—including, in the 1930s, compatibility and complicity with fascism—Ishikawa was forced to reevaluate his position. This rethinking led him back closer to Tanaka's monistic philosophy of doku and nagare in focusing on the particular material relations between a body and its environment.

6. For the often intense debate between the competing visions of Deep Ecology and Social Ecology see Zimmerman, *Contesting Earth's Future,* chaps. 1 and 4; van Wyck, *Primitives in the Wilderness;* Devall and Sessions, *Deep Ecology;* and Bookchin, *The Philosophy of Social Ecology.* Put in the language of contemporary radical ecology, Ishikawa retreated from a deep ecological communion with premodern (and now Japanized) nature as the site of true freedom, to something closer to both Marx's and Murray Bookchin's Social Ecology. See Bookchin, *The Ecology of Freedom.* Like Bookchin, Ishikawa sought the elimination of all hierarchies over explicitly anticapitalist movements.

7. Not only is this group part of the history of the metabolic rift by virtue of the discovery of "landscape" in the 1890s in such works as Kunikida Doppo's 1898 works *Musashino* and *Wasureenu hitobito,* but one of the Shirakaba's founders, Shiga Naoya, was also active in the Ashio protests of the 1890s and part of the jikiso coalition of 1901.

8. As we shall see, he was adamant that the concepts of species and evolution were contradictory, especially as they were used in social Darwinism or Tanabe Hajime's "logic of species," where the species or races remained ideal categories perfecting themselves through time but never mutating into other species or races. As we saw in chapter 1, this was also true of the early liberals like J. S. Mill, who allowed evolution only *within* species and insisted that species remained a natural type. Rejecting this autonomy of a species opened the way to radical new forms of politics and ontology. Here, too, he was at the cutting edge of recent radical environmentalism that rethought the boundaries and even the category of the human being.

9. Carey, *The Epigenetics Revolution.*

10. This tactic appears again in Japanese protest such as the "one-share movement" by Minamata activists to gain entry to the Chisso shareholders' meetings, and another "one-tsubo movement" to fight the government's attempted acquisition of Sanrizuka farms to make way for Narita Airport in the 1960s and 1970s.

11. Ishikawa, *Ishikawa Sanshirō chosakushū,* 1:430–31. Hereafter cited as Ishikawa, *Chosakushū.*

12. For the polemic of heimin versus kokumin see Konishi, *Anarchist Modernity,* 160.

13. Ishikawa, *Chosakushū,* 1:129–30.

14. Quoted and translated in Stone, "The Vanishing Village," 177.

15. Notehelfer, "Between Tradition and Modernity."

16. Tanaka, *TSz,* 10:552.

17. Komatsu Hiroshi, *Tanaka Shōzō: Nijū Isseki e no shisōjin,* 195.

18. Shimada Sōzō, *Tanaka Shōzō ō yoroku*, 1:131–32.

19. Sumitani Mikio and Rōdō undōshi kenkyūkai, *Shinkigen*, 3:101.

20. "Shinka to wa" (1923), in Ishikawa, *Chosakushū*, 2:319, 2:340.

21. Ishikawa, *Chosakushū*, 2:347.

22. Suzuki Sadami, *"Seimei" de yomu nihon kindai* and *Taishō seimeishugi to gendai*; Brandt, *Kingdom of Beauty*, 33; Karatani, "The Discovery of Landscape."

23. "Domin kurashi," in Ishikawa, *Chosakushū*, 2:310. This makes *kurashi* both a transliteration and a reading for the *ateji*, 生活. For a discussion of the many variations of the translation of *demos* see Brown, "We Are All Democrats Now," 45–46.

24. Ishikawa, *Chosakushū*, 3:20–21.

25. Ishikawa, *Chosakushū*, 2:312.

26. Some of this text has been translated into English. See Reclus, *Anarchy, Geography, Modernity*.

27. Reclus, *Anarchy, Geography, Modernity*, 233. Here is Reclus on the Franco-Prussian war (1870) in his essay "Progress," the conclusion of his multivolume work *L'homme et la terre*: "Various geographical names will be erased from maps, but despite changes, the peoples encompassed by modern civilization . . . will certainly continue to participate in the material, intellectual, and moral progress of one another. They are in the era of mutual aid, and even when they engage in bloody conflicts with each other, they do not stop working in part for the common welfare. During the last great European war between France and Germany, hundreds of thousands of men perished, crops were devastated, and wealth was destroyed. . . . [But now] a thousand new . . . inventions have become the common heritage of the two neighboring nations . . . engage[d] relentlessly in broader work for the benefit of all men." Perhaps it was the difference in the mechanized slaughter of World War I against the Franco-Prussian war that caused Ishikawa to consistently write out Reclus's progressivism in favor of a bounded temporality of variation without upward development. It is also likely he had in mind Tanaka Shōzō's linking of the environmental degradation of the Ashio Incident and the Russo-Japanese war (1904–5), for Reclus lauded aspects of this war, too: "And in the Far East, one finds that the covert or overt war between Japan and Russia cannot stop the astonishing progress that is being accomplished in this part of the world through the sharing of human culture and ideals."

28. "Domin kurashī," in Ishikawa, *Chosakushū*, 2:315.

29. Ishikawa, *Chosakushū*, 5:279–81. Here again it is interesting to see in this now defunct language an early version of contemporary theories of life on earth as nothing more than some form of energy consumption that did, in fact, originate largely in the sun.

30. "Domin kurashī," in Ishikawa, *Chosakushū*, 2:315, 2:317–18.

31. Ishikawa, *Chosakushū*, 5:277.

32. What counted as Darwinism at this time was in reality mostly from Spencer, as Spencer's social Darwinism was popularized in Japan(ese) before Darwin's own texts. In fact, when Darwin's work itself became popular in Japan in the 1910s, it served as a criticism of what had to that time been called Darwinism. Golley, "Darwinism in

Japan." Further, and for the same reasons, anarchism nearly completely ignored Darwin's later *Descent of Man*. See Konishi, *Anarchist Modernity*, 317.

33. See Bowler, *The Eclipse of Darwinism*.

34. Foster, *Marx's Ecology*, 188–89.

35. See Bowler, *The Eclipse of Darwinism*, 109–10.

36. As we saw, neo-Lamarckian theories of evolution were a major part of the cult of progress of early Meiji liberalism. See chapter 1.

37. See, for example, www.quinton.ch/pro1.htm. Another page, www.quinton.ch, warns that neither hypertonic nor isotonic is approved for injection, only for drinking. (Accessed December 7, 2010.)

38. Ishikawa, *Chosakushū*, 2:323–24, 2:345.

39. Carpenter called this his "gospel of salvation by sandals and sunbaths." See Carpenter, *Civilisation*, 49.

40. Reclus, *Anarchy, Geography, Modernity*, 107.

41. See, for example, precisely this approach in periodizing Japanese history in Totman's textbook *A History of Japan*.

42. Najita, *Visions of Virtue in Tokugawa Japan*.

43. Bowler, *The Eclipse of Darwinism*, 142–43.

44. The real subsumption of nature under capital is thus a secondary revolution in nature-society relations. Prior to this is what Marx called the formal subsumption. Under formal subsumption nature itself and practices of nature that existed prior to capitalist development continue on as before but are now incorporated into a regime of surplus capture that goes to the newly created capitalists. An example would be the persistence of peasant agriculture on a given plot where the surplus of that endeavor, likely through the privatization of the land, accrues to the owners of capital as a private property right—as opposed to, say, seigneurial privilege or other direct forms of appropriation. Real subsumption alters the actual practices of the agricultural labor itself as a way to prepare the land for greater extraction of surplus value.

45. Rowbotham, *Edward Carpenter*, 146.

46. Rowbotham, *Edward Carpenter*, 147.

47. Carpenter, *The Art of Creation*, 2.

48. Ishikawa, *Chosakushū*, 3:117.

49. He did add, "Were Marx alive today he would not have stood for the way [these Marx Boys—*marukusu boi*] automatons (*kikai ningen*) had dirtied his name." Ishikawa, *Chosakushū*, 3:119.

50. See "Shakai bigaku toshite no museifushugi," in Ishikawa, *Chosakushū*, 3:190–206.

51. Eagleton, *The Ideology of the Aesthetic*, 31–69; Bowler, *The Eclipse of Darwinism*, 74.

52. Ishikawa, *Chosakushū*, 193.

53. Cheung, "How Humans Became Organisms."

54. Cheung, "From the Organism of a Body to the Body of an Organism."

55. Of course, hermeneutics had existed earlier, but it had always been purely subjective; it had never been grounded because it had never been able to overcome

"the fundamental thesis of materialism": the objective existence of an exterior nature that existed independent of human representation. Overcoming the fundamental thesis of materialism provided Watsuji and cultural history with a starting point for a worldview that required philological and hermeneutic interpretations in place of natural and scientific analyses. For more on Tosaka's critique of Watsuji see Stolz, "Here, Now."

56. Lukács has shown how the early neo-Kantian separation of nature and society was always illogical from the standpoint of consciousness as the sole arbiter of meaning in idealism. Eventually, he argues, this discrepancy was solved by bringing external nature, too, under the aegis of consciousness. Ishikawa never followed the complete subsumption of nature under consciousness or culture as Watsuji and so many others of the time did, enabling him to resist collaboration with the wartime state. See Lukács, *The Destruction of Reason*, 414.

57. Ishikawa, *Chosakushū*, 2:371.

58. Ishikawa, *Chosakushū*, 3:205

59. Marx, "Economic and Philosophical Manuscripts," 318. Emphasis in the original.

60. For the Tokugawa movement and its continuation into the present see Najita, *Ordinary Economies in Japan*. For the wartime uses see Iwasaki, *Nōhon shisō no shakaishi*, and Kerry Smith, *A Time of Crisis*.

61. This is the phenomenon Tosaka Jun called the "primitivizationism" (*genshikashugi*) of thought characteristic of Japanese fascism. Because no modern military could in fact go back to nonmechanized infantry units, the primitive, feudal aspects had to remain in thought though they would and did have real-world effects. See "The Fate of Japanism," chap. 10 of *The Japanese Ideology* (1935). Tosaka, *Tosaka Jun zenshū*, 2:322–27.

62. In his article Ishikawa emphasized the hierarchical nature of Tachibana Kōzaburō's commune by using Kropotkin's term "free commune" for the exclusionary and anachronistic medieval commune. Tachibana Kōzaburō, "Nihon aikoku kakushin hongi." Tachibana's essay was published in 1932 but had circulated in manuscript form for some time prior to that.

63. This is not all speculation on my part. Already in 1928 Ishikawa noted the strangeness of the Peace Preservation Law, which linked the imperial house (*kokutai*) with the system of private property (capitalism). In a short piece he went back to show that there was in fact no discrete body of law that dealt with crimes against property in the pre-Meiji history of Japan. There were, however, many laws dealing with crimes against nature, specifically about interfering with agriculture: "The social psychology and the human psychology of the period can be seen in its views of crime and pollution (*kegare*). And there is no instance of a crime against property. . . . If the punishment is a prayer or ritual for purification [and not punishment], can't we then say that there was no real sense of private property or ownership?" See "Shiyū zaisan to nihon no kokutai," in Ishikawa, *Chosakushū*, 3:318–19.

64. Sakai, "Subject and Substratum."

65. Ishikawa, *Chosakushū*, 3:474–83; Iwasaki, *Nōhon shisō no shakaishi*, 100–102.

66. Driscoll, *Absolute Erotic, Absolute Grotesque*, 25.

67. See "Tanaka Shōzō's Warning," in *Sekai ōrai* and also in "Our Pacifist History" (*Waga hisenronshi*). Ishikawa, *Chosakushū*, 3:358–63.

68. Ishikawa, *Chosakushū*, 3:98.

69. Ishikawa, *Chosakushū*, 3:135–46. Though he does not make it explicit, based on his views on nature as truth, his translation of "democracy" as *domin kurashi* is his attempt to provide the breathing space for part-time work. Support for this can be found in Kropotkin's "Anarchy: Its Philosophy, Its Ideal" (1896), where he began, "That a society restored to possession of all of the accumulated wealth within it, can largely provide everyone with a guarantee of plenty, in return for four or five hours of effective, manual toil at production each day, all who have reflected upon the matter are unanimously agreed with us." See Guérin, *No Gods, No Masters*, 324.

70. Konishi, *Anarchist Modernity*, 27.

71. See "Kokubō no dai ichi gi" (1932), in Ishikawa, *Chosakushū*, 3:349–52.

72. Žižek, "Introduction: Robespierre, or, The 'Divine Violence' of Terror," xxviii–xxix.

73. Konishi, *Anarchist Modernity*, 65.

74. Ishikawa, *Chosakushū*, 3:481, 3:383–84.

75. Komatsu Kōzō, *Okada Torajirō*.

76. Ishikawa, *Chosakushū*, 3:22.

77. Iwasaki, *Nōhon shisō no shakaishi*, 104–5.

78. Ishikawa, *Chosakushū*, 4:74–77.

79. See "Gojū nen go no nihon," in Ishikawa, *Chosakushū*, 4:87–117.

80. Ishikawa, *Chosakushū*, 4:105.

81. Ishikawa, *Chosakushū*, 4:104–6.

82. See "Gangs" (1932) and "Let's Clean Up the Yellow River" (1938), in Ishikawa, *Chosakushū*, 3:364–67, 3:474–83.

83. Najita, *Ordinary Economies in Japan*.

84. Joe Moore, *Japanese Workers*, 28.

85. Joe Moore, *Japanese Workers*, 156–58.

86. Joe Moore, *Japanese Workers*, 56–59.

87. Joe Moore, *Japanese Workers*.

88. Lukács, *The Destruction of Reason*, 26–28.

89. Ishikawa, *Chosakushū*, 3:230–40.

90. Tomba, *Marx's Temporalities*, 14.

91. Marx quoted in Tomba, *Marx's Temporalities*, 28. See also Lukács, *The Destruction of Reason*, 201–2. Marx talks about the necessity of seeing the individual as a historical product in *The German Ideology*, a text in which he and Engels also severely criticize Stirner: "The real production of life appears as non-historical, while the historical appears as something separated from ordinary life, something extra-superterrestrial. With this the relation of man to nature is excluded from history and hence the antithesis of nature and history is created." Quoted in Tomba, *Marx's Temporalities*, 28.

92. See Eugene Smith and Aileen Smith, *Minamata*, and Walker, *Toxic Archipelago*.

FIVE. **The Original Green Company**

1. Hokkaido shinbun shuzaihan, *Kenshō "yuki jirushi" hōkai*. Another merger with Japan Milk Net in 2009 has consolidated further under the new name Yukijirushi Meg Milk. Meiji and Morinaga remain the main Japanese competitors. See also Finkelstein, *Why Smart Executives Fail*, chap. 5.

2. Kurosawa, *Rakunō gakuen*, 8–9.

3. Morinaga and Meiji were also made independent in 1950.

4. See, for example, Adam Davidson, "Even Dairy Farming Has a 1 Percent," *New York Times*, March 6, 2012: "Milk went from a local industry to a national one, and then it became international. The technological advances that made the Fulpers more productive also helped every other dairy farm too, which led to ever more intense competition. But perhaps most of all, in the last decade, dairy products and cow feed became globally traded commodities. Consequently, modern farmers have effectively been forced to become fast-paced financial derivatives traders."

5. Tanaka, *TSs*, 3:35. The reference to Maguro above is a variation of the *rakugo* story "Sanma wa meguro ni kagiru." In the story, while exploring the commoner section of Meguro of Edo, a samurai develops a taste for the dish of Sanma (a Pacific saury)—a fish deemed unworthy of the ruling-class palate. Later, back home in his uptown *Yama no te yashiki*, he asks his cook to prepare it for him. The cook, wholly ignorant of the way to prepare such a common dish, botches the job and is rebuked by the samurai: "This is awful. Where did you get it?" When the cook replied that he got it from the sea, the samurai screams, "You idiot! Sanma doesn't come from the sea, it comes from Meguro! [*Sanma wa Meguro ni kagiru*]."

6. Tanaka, *TSs*, 5:198. It is entirely possible that farming in the Shimotsuke section of the Watarase valley was possible and even profitable without capital inputs. As all Ashio literature points out, pre-Ashio floods deposited green fertilizer in enough quantity that night soil and later chemical fertilizers were not needed.

7. Tanaka, *TSs*, 4:235.

8. Tanaka, *TSs*, 6:28.

9. Tanaka, *TSs*, 6:23.

10. Tanaka, *TSs*, 6:264–65.

11. There is also a tradition linking Tanaka with Mito philosophy and Wang Yang Ming idealism, even to the point of claiming that Tanaka had contact with the Tengu rebels in *bakumatsu* Mito. Komatsu Hiroshi has done extensive research on this subject, thoroughly debunking the Tengu connection and casting much doubt on Tanaka's formal training in Wang Yang Ming. See Komatsu Hiroshi, *Tanaka Shōzō no kindai*, 681–702.

12. See Walker, *The Lost Wolves of Japan*, especially chap. 4.

13. Kurosawa, *Utsunomiya Sentarō*.

14. Of course, this also replaced the nearly defunct night soil industry—but that was never an option in Hokkaido. See Hanley, *Everyday Things in Premodern Japan*, especially chap. 3.

15. Kurosawa, *Rakunō gakuen*, 8.

16. See Shaars, "The Story of the Department of Agricultural Economics, 1909–72," 29.

17. Walker, *The Lost Wolves of Japan*.

18. Leigh, *The World's Greatest Fix*.

19. On the use of night soil, see, for example, Howell, "Fecal Matters," and Hanley, *Everyday Things in Premodern Japan*, especially chap. 5.

20. Foster, *Marx's Ecology*, 149–50; Leigh, *The World's Greatest Fix*.

21. Quoted in Foster, *Marx's Ecology*, 163.

22. Leigh states that in 2000 Chile's entire stock of sodium nitrates was barely enough to supply one year of global demand. Leigh, *The World's Greatest Fix*, 86. See also Cushman, *Guano and the Opening of the Pacific World*.

23. The story of the discovery of synthetic nitrogen is a major drama itself. According to Vaclav Smil, fully two out of five people today owe their lives to Fritz Haber's discovery and Carl Bosch's commercialization. In 1918 Haber received the Nobel Peace Prize for this discovery. But this beneficial discovery was also fundamental in the production of ammonium nitrates for use in explosives; Haber himself went on to invent poison gases, including Zyklon B, the preferred gas of Nazis. And the same process that fixed soil nitrogen to increase yields was used by Timothy McVeigh in the Oklahoma City bombing in 1995. See, for example, Smil, *Enriching the Earth*.

24. This, too, was noticed by farmers in Europe for hundreds of years, going back to at least to "Turnip Townshend," or Charles, the second Viscount Townshend (1675–1738), known for developing the Norfolk four-crop rotation and emphasizing turnips as a feed for animals and humans. The details of this process were not worked out experimentally until the Hellriegel and Wilfarth experiment in 1886 in Germany. Leigh, *The World's Greatest Fix*, 66–67, 113–15.

25. Kurotani, *Miyao Shunji den*, 400–403; Yukijirushi nyūgyō kabushikigaisha, *Yukijirushi nyūgyōshi*, 25 (hereafter cited as *Yukijirushi nyūgyōshi*).

26. Kurosawa, *Rakunō gakuen*, 66. Kurosawa occasionally included Sweden and Norway, highlighting the absence of war in their histories: "Sweden has not had a war in 150 years, and Norway has not had any wars, even with Germany. Still every citizen is in the army; but this is for defense only." Kurosawa, *Rakunō gakuen*, 47.

27. Borish, *The Land of the Living*, 14, 202.

28. Uchimura, "Denmaruku koku no hanashi." See Isaiah 35:1–2 (New International Version): "The desert and the parched land will be glad; the wilderness will rejoice and blossom. Like the crocus, it will burst into bloom; it will rejoice greatly and shout for joy. The glory of Lebanon will be given to it, the splendor of Carmel and Sharon; they will see the glory of the Lord, the splendor of our God."

29. See Grundtvig, "The School of Life," in *A Grundtvig Anthology*, 77.

30. Borish, *The Land of the Living*, 177.

31. Tanaka, *TSs*, 6:280.

32. Kurosawa, *Rakunō gakuen*, 47.

33. Kurotani, *Miyao Shunji den*, 399.

34. As we saw, this was also a major part of the Ashio crisis that so influenced Kurosawa. Though often exaggerated in later postwar environmental literature on Tanaka and Ashio, the green fertilizer delivered by the Tone and Watarase Rivers did allow for agricultural production with minimal and occasionally no imported (purchased) fertilizer. The loss of this green fertilizer and the subsequent need to purchase fertilizer on the market was one of the leading causes of farmer impoverishment.

35. This is the fetishized M–M′ of Marx's formula in *Capital*.

36. This cycle is presented by Marx in volume 1 and again in more detail in volume 2 of *Capital*, where it is designated as M–C . . . P . . . C′–M′. See Marx, *Capital*, 2:109–10. Kurosawa did not explicitly make this argument, focusing instead on farmer autonomy against the depredations of merchant capital, but it nonetheless remains an important part of his total socio-ecological vision and a historical resource for possible new foundations of a new agriculture.

37. Kurosawa, *Nōmindō*.

38. Tucker, "The Philosophy of Ch'i as an Ecological Cosmology."

39. See Marcon, *The Knowledge of Nature and the Nature of Knowledge in Early Modern Japan*, especially the discussion of the divine soil in the thought and practice of *honzōgaku* by Satō Nobuhirō.

40. See the 1882 Rescript: "1. The soldier and sailor (*gunjin*) should take loyalty as their essential duty. 2. The soldier and sailor are to conduct themselves properly (*reigi tadashku subeshi*). 3. The soldier and sailor should esteem valor. 4. The soldier and sailor are to value highly faithfulness and righteousness. 5. The soldier and sailor should take simplicity as their aim."

41. *Yukijirushi nyūgyōshi*, 205–6. See also Utsunomiya, *Hikōki seisaku hitsuju genryō taru kazein kōgyō kokusan dokuritsu ni kan suru seigansho*.

42. *Yukijirushi nyūgyōshi*, 318.

43. *Yukijirushi nyūgyōshi*, 320–21.

44. Kurosawa, *Shokuryō hisshōsen to chikuryoku sōdōin*.

45. Here Kurosawa and Hokkaido Dairy Promotion Company were no different from other Control Bureaucrats (*tōsei kanryō*), such as the economist Ōtsuka Hisao. In trying to construct a model of a nonconflictual (that is to say nonrevolutionary, non-Marxist) theory of capitalist society, Ōtsuka turned to Weber's "spirit of capitalism," contrasting this against Brentano's "capitalist spirit," which was reducible to acquisitive greed. Against acquisitive greed Ōtsuka believed that the culturally concrete state had replaced abstract capital as the goal of labor and production. See Koschmann, "The Spirit of Capitalism as Disciplinary Regime."

46. Driscoll, *Absolute Erotic, Absolute Grotesque*. To Marx's formal and real subsumptions Driscoll adds a third "deformal" subsumption, a "necropolitical" economic regime in which the earlier capitalist concern with maintaining the land and the laborer so that both would be available for work in the future is gone and both are forced to produce to death. A third term seems unnecessary to me, for in *Capital* Marx explained that his assumption that the worker not be worked to death was an analytical tool temporarily adopted in order to allow a clear vision of the workings of surplus

value and capital accumulation. It was never meant to be an actual guide to actual capitalist practice. In fact, the pursuit of absolute surplus value already contains within it the potential for Driscoll's deformal subsumption: as absolute surplus value tends toward 100 percent of the value, the necessary labor required to keep the worker alive necessarily also approaches zero.

47. Technically the hot springs belong to the different but related public health movement. For both, as well as the truly strange "book reading movement" (*dokusho undō*), see Takaoka, *Shiryōshū*.

48. One *chōbu* equals 2.45 acres.

49. Kurosawa, *Kendo kokusaku to yūchiku kikai nōgyō*.

50. For much more on the plans for colonizing Manchuria see Young, *Japan's Total Empire*. For actual Japanese civil engineering projects see Aaron Moore, "'The Yalu River Era of Developing Asia.'"

51. For a brief discussion of Tosaka's critique see chapter 4. See also Stolz, "Here, Now."

52. Sano, "Ideologies of Integration Past."

53. This was the topic of some discussion at meetings of the Tekireikai I attended in 2001–2, but no one was able to give a full accounting of the mandala.

54. Given the unstable relation between the Denmark method and imperial metaphysics in Kurosawa's work, he does occasionally suggest that he "has some doubts about [how to incorporate] the tropics" into this system. See also Nihei, *Nanpō no inasaku to nōkigu*. Nihei states outright that because the Hokkaido method is inappropriate to the tropics, Japan's success will come from a mix of cultural relations and demonstrating the superiority of Japanese agriculture to the tropical members of the empire. For more on this tutelary function of the Japanese empire see Fujihara, *Ina no daitōakyōeiken*, and Aaron Moore, *Constructing East Asia*.

55. Kurosawa, *Nōmindō*.

56. Kurosawa, *Nōmindō*, 4–7.

57. Misawa, *Misawa Katsue chosakushū*, vol. 3.

58. Kurosawa, *Shokuryō hisshōsen to chikuryoku sōdōin*.

59. Harootunian, *Overcome by Modernity*.

60. For other examples, including aluminum manufacturing in the United States and Japan, see Yamanouchi, Koschmann, and Ryūichi, *Total War and "Modernization."*

61. Supreme Commander for the Allied Powers (SCAP), Staff Study of the Hokkaido Dairy Cooperative Joint Company, Headquarters Hokkaido Military Government District APO 468, November 15, 1948, 4.

62. Supreme Commander for the Allied Powers (SCAP), Staff Study of the Hokkaido Dairy Cooperative Joint Company, 2.

63. Supreme Commander for the Allied Powers (SCAP), "An Appeal to the People in Hokkaido Concerning the Move Made by the Nestle Company: Clarifying the Attitude of the Northern Japan Headquarters of the Kokusuikai," August 1931; SCAP translation. Item 27 at Kurosawa's rehabilitation hearing. See SCAP, *Kurosawa Torizō*, ARC Identifier 358041, Record Group 331: Records of Allied Operational and Occupa-

tion Headquarters, World War II, 1907–1966, Textual Reference (Military) (Rd-Dc-2-Mil).

64. This policy famously went wrong when many Ainu who had been prevented from selling their land by efforts to create an American-style reservation system became landlords: their poverty required them to rent the inalienable holdings, making them "absentee landlords" under the postwar reforms.

65. Najita, *Ordinary Economies*.

66. Initially Clover Butter was called Hokkaido Butter until a complicated trademark dispute between Rakunō and Meiji Dairy was resolved. Rakuren had owned the Clover mark for butter, limited to Hokkaido Butter. Meiji owned the name for all milk products but butter.

67. Kurosawa did seek to have milk designated a "staple food" and therefore eligible for government promotion and protection. Interestingly, this was deemed a political campaign by a purgee and harmed both his and Rakunō's cases in the eyes of the HCLC.

68. Kurosawa, *Sōgo nōsei ni kan suru ikensho* (1968) and *Sōgō nōsei to rankunō no kiki ni kan suru ikensho* (1969).

69. Kurosawa, *Rakunō gakuen*.

70. Once again, in Marxist terms this is the urgent pursuit of the particular form of accumulation called relative surplus value. See Marx, *Capital*, vol. 1, part 4.


CONCLUSION

1. Maruyama and other postwar liberals may be forgiven for focusing exclusively on democratic traditions that they felt were lacking in the Japanese past. Even the dominance of the "feudal remnants" thesis of immediate postwar and Comintern policy contributed to this moment, a moment when it seemed everyone—SCAP, Japanese liberals, and the JCP—were actively trying to re-create the liberal subject. This was one of the reasons the JCP was not only absent from the *seisan kanri* movement, but at times actively against it, believing that any move to a communist revolution in a still partially feudal Japan was unwise.

2. Harootunian, "The Execution of Tosaka Jun and Other Tales," 161. In his political critique of liberalism and fascism, *The Japanese Ideology* (*Nippon ideorogiiron*, 1935; in *Tosaka Jun zenshū*, 2), Tosaka Jun had already warned against these postwar plans, as had other contemporary theorists of fascism such as Hannah Arendt, in showing that there is not in fact a clean and comforting break between liberalism and fascism. Indeed, Tosaka strove to demonstrate the genealogical links and family resemblances between the two ideologies, showing how with the onset of a global crisis, the individual, negative freedoms of conscience could become without corruption (*sono mama*) the collective, positive freedoms of (national) culture.

3. George, *Minamata*.

4. Molony, *Technology and Investment*.

5. Bennett, *Vibrant Matter*, ix.

6. Marx, "Results of the Immediate Process of Production," in *Capital*, 1:1027.

7. Latour, *Reassembling the Social*, 176.

8. Latour, *Reassembling the Social*, 176.

9. Latour also rejected the dialectic as a method. But here I think he is on shakier ground, for he sees it not as perpetually open ended, but as a closed "circle," an indispensable "lasso used to draw paradoxical connections . . . [that] loses all its value when it's taken to be the relation of an actor 'inside' a system." A case for the dialectic as closed could at best be made for the most vulgar Hegelianism of *The Philosophy of History* but cannot be said to be shared by the overwhelming number of its practitioners, including Hegel, who regard movement, flux, and openness as fundamental aspects of the method itself.

10. Marx, *Capital*, 1:494n4.

11. Bennett, *Vibrant Matter*, xiv.

12. Lukács, *History and Class Consciousness*.

13. Marx, *Capital*, vol. 1, chap. 1.

14. Latour, *The Pasteurization of France*; Mitman, Murphy, and Sellers, *Landscapes of Exposure*; and of course Foucault, *The Birth of the Clinic, Discipline and Punish*, and *The Birth of Biopolitics*.

15. Marx, *Capital*, 1:279.

16. Marx, *Capital*, 1:283.

17. Tomba, *Marx's Temporalities*, xiv: "Capital, due to its indifference to different cultural horizons and social or familial structures, is able to functionalise different temporalities to the rhythm of socially necessary labor."

18. Marx, *Capital*, 1:793.

19. See for example, Brett Walker, *Toxic Archipelago*; Douglas, *Purity and Danger*.

20. Obvious and intended examples include the accelerated time to market for livestock and the chickens bred specifically to maximize breast meat at the expense of a bird viable outside the industrial factory. Unintended consequences would include all the material expressions explored in this book—disease, poverty, loss of suffrage, etc.

21. Gavin Walker, "The Absent Body of Labour Power."

22. In some ways we have another version of J. S. Mill's insistence that humans are not wholly reducible to natural relations; however, here there is the crucial difference that this power over nature is not a natural condition of humanity but the result of a historical process.

23. Gavin Walker, "The Absent Body of Labour Power"; see also Laibman, *Value, Technical Change, and Crisis*.

24. Kawashina, "Biopolitics and the Aleatory Event(s) of Capitalism" and *The Proletarian Gamble*, 204–15.

25. Devall and Sessions, *Deep Ecology*; Cronon, "The Trouble with Wilderness"; and van Wyck, *Primitives in the Wilderness*.

26. Devall and Sessions, *Deep Ecology*.

27. Dunaway, "Green Goes Mainstream." This has further moral and political implications and needs to be the source of much further analysis and critique. Under this neoliberal paradigm, we, as individuals, are in command of our lives and its

unfolding in the sense that "everyone is a shareholder," everyone is an owner or entrepreneur: this has powerful ethical and political consequences. Neoliberalism is essentially a moralizing force, for if everybody is an entrepreneur, then his or her indebtedness acquires a moralistic (Kantian) overtone and politically can become a new form of exploitation and control.

28. See, for example, Postone, *Time, Labor, and Social Domination*, 28–29, 355–57, and Gavin Walker, "The Absent Body of Labour Power."

29. Some have started this process, even using the term. See Goldman, *Imperial Nature*; Eckersley, *The Green State*; and McCully, *Silenced Rivers*.

30. Gavin Walker, "The Absent Body of Labour Power."

31. Parts of this paragraph refer to and are inspired by Hunter S. Thompson's *Fear and Loathing in Las Vegas: A Savage Journey to the Heart of the American Dream* (New York: Vintage, 1989).

32. Hardin, "The Tragedy of the Commons," 1244.

33. Guattari, *The Three Ecologies*, 4–5.

# BIBLIOGRAPHY

Abe Yasunari. "'Eisei' to iu chitsujo." In *Shippei, kaihatsu, teikoku iryō: Ajia ni okeru byōki to iryō no rekishigaku*, edited by Tsurumi Shunsuke, Saito Susumu, Wakimura Kōhei, and Ijima Wataru. Tokyo: Tokyo daigaku shuppankai, 2001.

———. "Yōjō kara eisei e." In *Kansei no kindai 2: 1870–1910*, edited by Komori Yōichi, 47–78. Tokyo: Iwanami shoten, 2002.

Akagami Takeshi. "Tanaka Shōzō mukashi banashi 'kasei no kempō' hyōkasetsu e no gimon." *Tanaka Shōzō to Ashio kōdoku jiken kenkyū* 12 (2000): 43–70.

Anderson, Warwick. "Excremental Colonialism: Public Health and the Poetics of Pollution." *Critical Inquiry* 21, no. 3 (1995): 640–69.

Andō Seiichi. *Kinsei kōgaishi no kenkyū*. Tokyo: Yoshikawa kōbunkan, 1992.

Anzai Kunio. "Kōdoku chōsa iinkai—dai ichiji, dai niji—no setchi to Tanaka Shōzō." In *Eiinhon Ashio dōzan kōdoku jiken kankei shiryō*, 393–415. Tokyo: University of Tokyo Press, 2009.

Arahata Kanson. *Yanaka mura metsubōshi*. Tokyo: Iwanami bunko, 1999.

Arai Katsuhiko. "Gimin to minken fokuroa." In *Kindai ikōki no minshūzō*, edited by Arai Katsuhiko. Tokyo: Aoki shoten, 2000.

Arai Ōsui. *Arai Ōsui chosakushū*. 6 vols. Edited by Arai Ōsui chosakushū henshūkai. Yokohama: Shunpūsha, 2001.

———. "Ka o mite sono jin o shiru." *Nihonjin*, January 1902.

Beck, Ulrich. *Risk Society: Towards a New Modernity*. Translated by Mark Ritter. London: Sage, 1992.

Bennett, Jane. *Vibrant Matter: A Political Ecology of Things*. A John Hope Franklin Center Book. Durham, NC: Duke University Press, 2010.

Bocking, Stephen. "Ecosystems, Ecologists, and the Atom: Environmental Research at Oak Ridge National Laboratory." *Journal of the History of Biology* 28, no. 1 (1995): 1–47.

Bookchin, Murray. *The Ecology of Freedom: The Emergence and Dissolution of Hierarchy*. Palo Alto, CA: Cheshire Books, 1982.

———. *The Philosophy of Social Ecology: Essays on Dialectical Naturalism*. Montreal: Black Rose Books, 1990.

Borish, Steven M. *The Land of the Living: The Danish Folk High Schools and Denmark's Non-Violent Path to Modernization*. Nevada City, CA: Blue Dolphin, 1991.

Bowen, Roger W. *Rebellion and Democracy in Meiji Japan: A Study of Commoners in the Popular Rights Movement*. Berkeley: University of California Press, 1980.

Bowler, Peter J. *The Eclipse of Darwinism: Anti-Darwinian Evolution Theories in the Decades around 1900*. Baltimore: Johns Hopkins University Press, 1983.

Braisted, William Reynolds, ed. *Meiroku zasshi: Journal of the Japanese Enlightenment*. Tokyo: University of Tokyo Press, 1976.

Brandt, Kim. *Kingdom of Beauty: Mingei and the Politics of Folk Art in Imperial Japan*. Durham, NC: Duke University Press, 2007.

Brown, Azby. *Just Enough: Lessons in Living Green from Traditional Japan*. North Clarendon, VT: Tuttle, 2013.

Brown, Wendy. "We Are All Democrats Now." In *Democracy in What State?*, edited by Amy Allen, 44–57. New York: Columbia University Press, 2011.

Carey, Nessa. *The Epigenetics Revolution: How Modern Biology Is Rewriting Our Understanding of Genetics, Disease, and Inheritance*. New York: Columbia University Press, 2012.

Carpenter, Edward. *The Art of Creation: Essays on the Self and Its Powers*. London: George Allen, 1907.

———. *Civilisation: Its Cause and Cure, and Other Essays*. New York: Charles Scribner's Sons, 1895.

Caudwell, Christopher. *Studies and Further Studies in a Dying Culture*. New York: Monthly Review Press, 2009.

Cheung, Tobias. "From the Organism of a Body to the Body of an Organism: Occurrence and Meaning of the Word 'Organism' from the Seventeenth to the Nineteenth Centuries." *British Journal of the History of Science* 39, no. 3 (2006): 319–39.

———. "How Humans Became Organisms: Some Reflections on the Transition from the Soul-Body Problem to the Organism-Milieu Interface." Paper presented at the University of Tokyo Center for Philosophy, Tokyo, December 7, 2009.

Chiba kenritsu sekiyadojō hakubutsukan. *Shizen saigai o norikoete: Tonegawa churyūiki no doboku isan kara mieru rekishi*. Noda (Chiba): Chiba kenritsu sekiyadojō hakubutsukan, 2008.

Clark, John P., and Camille Martin, eds. *Anarchy, Geography, Modernity: The Radical Social Thought of Elisée Reclus*. New York: Lexington Books, 2004.

Comte, Auguste, and John Stuart Mill. *The Correspondence of John Stuart Mill and Auguste Comte*. Translated and edited by Oscar A. Haac. New Brunswick, NJ: Transaction, 1995.

Corl, Daniel. "Arai Ōsui to jukyō o megutte." In *Shirarezaru inochi no shisōka: Arai Ōsui o yomitoku*, edited by Arai Ōsui sensei kenenkai, 80–100. Yokohama: Shunpūsha, 2000.

Cronon, William. "The Trouble with Wilderness: Or, Getting Back to the Wrong Nature." In *Uncommon Ground: Toward Reinventing Nature*, edited by William Cronon, 69–90. New York: Norton, 1995.

Cushman, Gregory T. *Guano and the Opening of the Pacific World: A Global Ecological History*. Studies in Environment and History. New York: Cambridge University Press, 2013.

Davis, Mike. *Dead Cities: And Other Tales*. New York: New York Press, 2002.

Deleuze, Gilles, and Félix Guattari. *A Thousand Plateaus: Capitalism and Schizophrenia*. Translated by Brian Massumi. Minneapolis: University of Minnesota Press, 1987.

Devall, Bill, and George Sessions. *Deep Ecology*. Salt Lake City: G. M. Smith, 1985.

Dinmore, Eric. "Concrete Results? The TVA and the Appeal of Large Dams in Occupation-Era Japan." *Journal of Japanese Studies* 39, no. 1 (2013): 1–38.

Douglas, Mary. *Purity and Danger*. New York: Routledge Classics, 1966.

Driscoll, Mark. *Absolute Erotic, Absolute Grotesque: The Living, Dead, and Undead in Japan's Imperialism, 1895–1945*. Durham, NC: Duke University Press, 2010.

Dunaway, Finis. "Green Goes Mainstream: The Visual Politics of American Environmentalism circa 1990." Paper presented at the American Society for Environmental History Annual Meeting, Toronto, Canada, April 4, 2013.

Eagleton, Terry. *The Ideology of the Aesthetic*. Oxford: Blackwell, 1991.

Eckersley, Robyn. *The Green State: Rethinking Democracy and Sovereignty*. Cambridge, MA: MIT Press, 2004.

Erikson, Kai. *A New Species of Trouble: The Human Experience of Modern Disasters*. New York: Norton, 1994.

Eto Tekireikai, ed. *Eto Tekirei senshū*. Vol. 2. Tokyo: Ie no hikari kyōkai, 1979.

Ewald, François. "Two Infinities of Risk." In *The Politics of Everyday Fear*, edited by Brian Massumi, 221–28. Minneapolis: University of Minnesota Press, 1993.

Figal, Gerald. *Civilization and Monsters: Spirits of Modernity in Meiji Japan*. Durham, NC: Duke University Press, 1999.

Finkelstein, Sydney. *Why Smart Executives Fail: And What You Can Learn from Their Mistakes*. New York: Portfolio Trade, 2004.

Foster, John Bellamy. *Marx's Ecology: Materialism and Nature*. New York: Monthly Review Press, 2000.

Foucault, Michel. *The Birth of Biopolitics: Lectures at the College de France 1978–9*. Translated by Graham Burchell. Edited by Arnold I. Davidson. New York: Picador, 2008.

——. *The Birth of the Clinic: An Archaeology of Medical Perception*. Translated by Alan Sheridan. New York: Vintage Books, 1994.

——. *Discipline and Punish: The Birth of the Prison*. 2nd ed. Vintage, 1995.

Fujihara Tatsushi. *Ina no daitōakyōeiken: Teikoku nihon no "midori no kakumei."* Tokyo: Yoshikawa kōbunkan, 2012.

Fujitani Takashi. *Splendid Monarchy: Power and Pageantry in Modern Japan*. Berkeley: University of California Press, 1998.

Fukawa Satoru. *Tanaka Shōzō to tennō jikiso jiken*. Utsunomiya: Zuisōsha, 2001.

————. *Tanaka Shōzō to Tone, Watarase no nagare*. Utsunomiya: Zuisōsha, 2004.

Fukutō Sanae, Kojima Naoko, Masao Shin'ichirō, and Togawa Tomoru, eds. *Kegare no bunkashi: Monogatari, jendaa, reigi*. Bunka no ekkyo 11. Tokyo: Shin'washa, 2005.

Fukuzawa Yukichi. *An Encouragement of Learning*. Translated by David Dilworth and Umeyo Hirano. Tokyo: Sophia University, 1969.

————. *Gakumon no susume* (Iwanami bunko). Tokyo: Iwanami shoten, 1978.

————. *Outline of a Theory of Civilization*. Translated by David Dilworth and G. Cameron Hurst. Tokyo: Monumenta Nipponica Monographs, 1973.

George, Timothy S. *Minamata: Pollution and the Struggle for Democracy in Postwar Japan*. Cambridge, MA: Harvard University East Asia Center, 2002.

————. "Tanaka Shōzō's Vision of an Alternative Constitutional Modernity for Japan." In *Public Spheres, Private Lives in Modern Japan*, edited by Gail Lee Bernstein, Andrew Gordon, and Kate Wildman Nakai, 89–116. Cambridge, MA: Harvard University Asia Center, 2005.

Gluck, Carol. "'Meiji' for Our Time." In *New Directions in the Study of Meiji Japan*, edited by Helen Hardacre and Adam L. Kern, 11–28. Leiden: Brill, 1997.

Goldman, Michael. *Imperial Nature: The World Bank and Struggles for Social Justice in the Age of Globalization*. New Haven, CT: Yale University Press, 2005.

Golley, Gregory. "Darwinism in Japan: The Birth of Ecology." Paper presented at the Association for Asian Studies Annual Meeting, Chicago, 2005.

Grimmer-Solem, Erik. "German Social Science, Meiji Conservatism, and the Peculiarities of Japanese History." *Journal of World History* 16, no. 2 (2005): 187–222.

Grundtvig, N. F. S. *A Grundtvig Anthology: Selections from the Writings of N. F. S. Grundtvig*. Translated by Neils Lyhne Johnson and Edward Broadbridge. Cambridge, UK: J. Clarke, 1984.

Guattari, Félix. *The Three Ecologies*. Translated by Ian Pindar and Paul Sutton. London: Athlone, 2000.

Guérin, Daniel. *No Gods, No Masters: An Anthology of Anarchism*. Oakland, CA: AK Press, 2005.

Hanks, William F. *Intertexts: Writings on Language, Utterance, and Context*. New York: Rowman and Littlefield, 2000.

Hanley, Susan B. *Everyday Things in Premodern Japan: The Hidden Legacy of Material Culture*. Berkeley: University of California Press, 1999.

Hardin, Garrett. "The Tragedy of the Commons." *Science and Its Conceptual Foundations* 162 (1968): 1243–58.

Harootunian, H. D. "The Execution of Tosaka Jun and Other Tales: Historical Amnesia, Memory, and the Question of Japan's 'Postwar.'" In *Ruptured Histories: War, Memory, and the Post–Cold War in Asia*, edited by Sheila Miyoshi Jager and Rana Mitter, 150–71. Cambridge, MA: Harvard University Press, 2007.

————. *Overcome by Modernity: History, Culture, and Community in Interwar Japan*. Princeton, NJ: Princeton University Press, 2000.

——. *Toward Restoration: The Growth of Political Consciousness in Tokugawa, Japan*. Publications of the Center for Japanese and Korean Studies. Berkeley: University of California Press, 1991.

Harvey, David. *Justice, Nature, and the Geography of Difference*. Cambridge, MA: Blackwell, 1996.

Havens, Thomas R. H. "Comte, Mill, and the Thought of Nishi Amane in Meiji Japan." *Journal of Asian Studies* 27, no. 2 (1968): 217–28.

Hayashi Takeji. *Tanaka Shōzō: Sono shō to tatakai no "konpongi."* Tokyo: Tabata shoten, 1980.

Hokkaido shinbun shuzaihan, ed. *Kenshō "yuki jirushi" hōkai: Sono toki, nani ga okotta ka*. Tokyo: Kōdansha (bunko), 2002.

Honda Toshiaki. "Keisei hisaku." In *Nihon shisō taikei 44: Honda Toshiaki, Kaihō Seiryō*, 11–86. Edited by Akihiro Tsukatani and Kuranami Seiji. Tokyo: Iwanami shoten, 1970.

Howell, David L. *Capitalism from Within: Economy, Society, and the State in a Japanese Fishery*. Berkeley: University of California Press, 1995.

——. "Fecal Matters: Prolegomenon to a History of Shit in Japan." In *Japan at Nature's Edge: The Environmental Context of a Global Power*, edited by Ian Jared Miller, Julia Adeney Thomas, and Brett L. Walker, 137–51. Honolulu: University of Hawai'i Press, 2013.

——. *Geographies of Identity in Nineteenth-Century Japan*. Berkeley: University of California Press, 2005.

Howland, Douglas. *Personal Liberty and Public Good: The Introduction of John Stuart Mill to Japan and China*. Toronto: University of Toronto Press, 2005.

——. *Translating the West: Language and Political Reason in Nineteenth-Century Japan*. Honolulu: University of Hawai'i Press, 2002.

Ijima Wataru and Wakimura Kōhei. "Kinda ajia ni okeru teikokushugi to iryō: Kōshū eisei." In *Shippei, kaihatsu, teikoku iryō: Ajia ni okeru byōki to iryō no rekishigaku*, edited by Tsurumi Shunsuke, 75–95. Tokyo: Tokyo daigaku shuppankai, 2001.

Irokawa Daikichi. *The Culture of the Meiji Period*. Translated by Marius B. Jansen. Princeton, NJ: Princeton University Press, 1985.

——, ed. *Meiji kenpakusho shūsei*. Vol. 6. Tokyo: Chikuma shobō, 1991.

Ishikawa Eisuke. *Ōedo risaikuru jijō*. Tokyo: Kōdansha, 1997.

Ishikawa Sanshirō. *Ishikawa Sanshirō chosakushū*. Tokyo: Seidosha, 1977.

Itagaki Taisuke. *Jiyūtōshi*. 3 vols. Tokyo: Iwanami bunko, 1957.

Iwasaki Masaya. *Nōhon shisō no shakaishi: Seikatsu to kokutai no kōsaku*. Kyoto: Kyoto daigaku gakujutsu shuppankai, 1997.

Janetta, Ann Bowman. *Epidemics and Mortality in Early Modern Japan*. Princeton, NJ: Princeton University Press, 1987.

——. "From Physician to Bureaucrat: The Case of Nagayo Sensai." In *New Directions in the Study of Meiji Japan*, edited by Helen Hardacre and Adam L. Kern, 151–60. Leiden: Brill, 1997.

Jansen, Marius B. *Sakamoto Ryōma and the Meiji Restoration*. New York: Columbia University Press, 1995.

Johnston, William. *The Modern Epidemic: A History of Tuberculosis in Japan*. Harvard East Asian Monographs No. 162. Cambridge, MA: Council on East Asian Studies, Harvard University, 1995.

Josephson, Paul. *Industrialized Nature: Brute Force Technology and the Transformation of the Natural World*. Washington, DC: Island, 2002.

Kaibara Ekken. *The Philosophy of Qi: The Record of Great Doubts*. Translated by Mary Evelyn Tucker. 1713. Reprint, New York: Columbia University Press, 2007.

Kakimoto Akihito. *Kenko to yamai no episuteemee*. Kyoto: Mineruba shobō, 1991.

Kanai Takanori. "'Aiso' to iu shisō: Kokkai kaisetsu kenpaku-seigan ni miru 'shūtai' no katei." In *Kindai ikōki no minshūzō*, edited by Arai Katsuhiko, 157–81. Tokyo: Aoki shoten, 2000.

———. "Kokkai kaisetsu seigan undō ni miru Matsuzawa Kyūsaku no shisō (1)." *Waseda seiji kōhōkenkyū* 50 (1995).

———. "'Tōyō minken hyakkaden' ni miru 'kindai' teki ningenzō." *Minshūshi kenkyū* 56 (1998): 17–34.

Kano Masanao. *Nihon no kindai shisō*. Tokyo: Iwanami shinsho, 2002.

Karatani Kōjin. "The Discovery of Landscape." In *Origins of Modern Japanese Literature*, 11–44. Durham, NC: Duke University Press, 1993.

Kawashima, Ken C. "Biopolitics and the Aleatory Event(s) of Capitalism." *positions: east asia critique*, forthcoming.

———. *The Proletarian Gamble: Korean Workers in Interwar Japan*. Durham, NC: Duke University Press, 2009.

Kelly, William W. *Water Control in Tokugawa Japan: Irrigation Organization in a Japanese River Basin, 1600–1870*. Cornell University East Asia Papers No. 31. Ithaca, NY: China-Japan Program, Cornell University, 1982.

Kikaku henshū kin-gendai shiryō kankōkai, ed. *Kindai tōshi no eisei kankyō: Tokyo hen*. Vol. 43, *Kindai tōshi kankyō kenkyū shiryō sōsho*. Tokyo: Kin-gendai shiryō kankōdai.

Kinoshita Naoe. "Shakai kaigo no iro." *Rikugō zasshi* 253 (1902).

Kitasato Institute and Kitasato University, eds. *Collected Papers of Shibasaburō Kitasato*. Tokyo: Kitasato Institute and Kitasato University, 1977.

Komatsu Hiroshi. *Tanaka Shōzō: Nijū isseki e no shisōjin*. Tokyo: Chikuma shobō, 1997.

———. *Tanaka Shōzō no kindai*. Tokyo: Gendai kikakushitsu, 2001.

Komatsu Kōzō. *Okada Torajirō: Sono shisō to jidai*. Osaka: Sōgensha, 2000.

Komori Yōichi. "Sōsetsu: Sabetsu no kansei." In *Kansei no kindai 2: 1870–1910*, edited by Komori Yōichi, 3–46. Tokyo: Iwanami shoten, 2002.

Komurō Shinsuke. *Tōyō minken hyakkaden*. Tokyo: Iwanami bunko, 1957.

Konishi Sho. *Anarchist Modernity: Cooperatism and Japanese-Russian Intellectual Relations in Modern Japan*. Cambridge, MA: Harvard University Asia Center, 2013.

Kōno Hironaka. "Kokkai o kaisetsu suru inka o jōgan suru sho." In *Jiyūtōshi jō*, edited by Itagaki Taisuke. Tokyo: Iwanami bunko, 1995.

Koschmann, J. Victor. "The Spirit of Capitalism as Disciplinary Regime: The Postwar Thought of Ōtsuka Hisao." In *Total War and "Modernization,"* edited by Yasushi Yamanouchi, J. Victor Koschmann, and Ryūichi Narita, 97–115. Ithaca, NY: East Asia Program, Cornell University, 1998.

Kurosawa Torizō. *Kendo kokusaku to yūchiku kikai nōgyō.* Tokyo: Nihon yūchiku kikai nōgyō kyōkai, 1943.

———. *Nôgyôkoku: Denumaaku.* Tokyo: Kawade, 1952.

———. *Nōmindō.* Sapporo: Hokkaido rakunō gijuku, 1937.

———. *Rakunō gakuen no rekishi to shimei.* Ebetsu: Rakunō gakuen, 1970.

———. *Shokuryō hisshōsen to chikuryoku sōdōin.* Tokyo: Hokkaido kōnō kōsha, 1944.

———. *Sōgo nōsei ni kan suru ikensho.* Sapporo: Chūō rakunōkai, 1968.

———. *Sōgō nōsei to rankunō no kikin ni kan suru ikensho.* Sapporo: Chūō rakunōkai, 1969.

———. *Utsunomiya Sentarō.* Ebetsu: Rakunō gakuen shuppanbu, 1957.

Kurotani Ryōtarō. *Miyao Shunji den.* Tokyo: Yoshioka kōzō, 1939.

Laibman, David. *Value, Technical Change, and Crisis: Explorations in Marxist Economic Theory.* New York: M. E. Sharpe, 1991.

Latour, Bruno. *The Pasteurization of France.* Translated by Alan Sheridan and John Law. Cambridge, MA: Harvard University Press, 1988.

———. *Reassembling the Social: An Introduction to Actor-Network-Theory.* Oxford: Oxford University Press, 2005.

Lefebvre, Henri. *The Production of Space.* Translated by Donald Nicholson-Smith. Oxford: Blackwell, 1991.

Leigh, G. J. *The World's Greatest Fix: A History of Nitrogen and Agriculture.* Oxford: Oxford University Press, 2004.

Lo Ch'in-shun. *Knowledge Painfully Acquired.* Translated by Irene Bloom. New York: Columbia University Press, 1987.

Lukács, Georg. *The Destruction of Reason.* Translated by Peter Palmer. London: Merlin, 1980.

———. *History and Class Consciousness: Studies in Marxist Dialectics.* Translated by Rodney Livingstone. Cambridge, MA: MIT Press, 1971.

Makihara Norio. *Kyakubun to kokumin no aida.* Tokyo: Yoshikawa Kobunkan, 1998.

———. "Tanaka Shōzō: Hijisha to jisha no hazama ni." In *Kansei no kindai 2: 1870–1910,* edited by Komori Yōichi, 81–114. Tokyo: Iwanami shoten, 2002.

Manning, Richard. *Against the Grain: How Agriculture Has Hijacked Civilization.* New York: North Point, 2005.

Mao Zedung. *A Critique of Soviet Economics.* Translated by Moss Roberts. New York: Monthly Review, 1977.

Marcon, Federico. *The Knowledge of Nature and the Nature of Knowledge in Early Modern Japan.* Chicago: University of Chicago Press, forthcoming.

Marcuse, Herbert. *Soviet Marxism.* New York: Columbia University Press, 1985.

Marran, Christine L. *Poison Woman: Figuring Female Transgression in Modern Japanese Culture.* Minneapolis: University of Minnesota Press, 2007.

Marx, Karl. *Capital: A Critique of Political Economy*. Vol. 1. Translated by Ben Fowkes. London: Penguin Books, 1976.

——. *Capital: A Critique of Political Economy*. Vol. 2. Translated by David Fernbach. London: Penguin Books, 1978.

——. "Economic and Philosophical Manuscripts" (1844). In *Karl Marx: Early Writings*, 279–400. New York: Penguin, 1992.

Marx, Karl, and Frederick Engels. *Karl Marx, Frederick Engels: Collected Works*. 50 vols. New York: International, 1975.

Mass, Jeffrey P. *Antiquity and Anachronism in Japanese History*. Stanford, CA: Stanford University Press, 1992.

Matsumoto Eiko. "Kōdokuchi no sanjō (1902)." *Tanaka Shōzō no sekai* 5 (1986): 29–116.

Matsumoto Sannosuke. "The Idea of Heaven: A Tokugawa Foundation for Natural Rights Theory." In *Japanese Thought in the Tokugawa Period*, edited by Tetsuo Najita and Irwin Scheiner, 181–99. Chicago: University of Chicago Press, 1978.

Maus, Tanya. "Rising Up and Saving the World: Ishii Jūji and the Ethics of Social Relief during the Mid-Meiji Period (1880–87)." *Japan Review* 25 (2013): 67–87.

McCormack, Gavan. "Modernity, Water, and the Environment in Japan." In *A Companion to Japanese History*, edited by William M. Tsutsui, 443–59. Malden, MA: Blackwell, 2007.

McCully, Patrick. *Silenced Rivers: The Ecology and Politics of Large Dams*. Enlarged and updated ed. New York: Zed Books, 2001.

McMullen, Ian James. "Kumazawa Banzan and *Jitsugaku*: Toward Pragmatic Action." In *Principle and Practicality*, edited by William Theodore de Bary and Irene Bloom, 337–73. New York: Columbia University Press, 1979.

Meisner, Maurice. *Mao's China and After: A History of the People's Republic*. 3rd ed. New York: Free Press, 1999.

Mencius. "Kung-Sun Ch'Au, Part II, Chapter 4.3." In *The Chinese Classics*, vol. 2, *The Works of Mencius*, edited by James Legge. Hong Kong: Hong Kong University Press, 1960.

Miller, Ian Jared. *The Nature of the Beasts: Empire and Exhibition at the Tokyo Imperial Zoo*. Berkeley: University of California Press, 2013.

Misawa Katsue. *Misawa Katsue chosakushū*. Vol. 3, *Fūdo no hakken to sōzō*. Tokyo: Nōsangyōson bunka kyōkai, 2009.

Mitman, Gregg, Michelle Murphy, and Christopher Sellers, eds. *Landscapes of Exposure: Knowledge and Illness in Modern Environments*. Chicago: University of Chicago Press, 2004.

Miura Ken'ichiro. "Yanaka mura haison." *Hakuō hōgaku* 18 (2001): 211–46.

Mizoguchi Yuzo. *Ichigo no jiten: Kōshi*. Tokyo: Sanshodō, 1996.

Molony, Barbara. *Technology and Investment: The Prewar Japanese Chemical Industry*. Cambridge, MA: Harvard Council on East Asian Studies, 1990.

Moore, Aaron Stephen. *Constructing East Asia: Technology, Ideology, and Empire in Japan's Wartime Era, 1931–35*. Palo Alto, CA: Stanford University Press, 2013.

———. "'The Yalu River Era of Developing Asia': Japanese Expertise, Colonial Power, and the Construction of Sup'Ung Dam." *Journal of Asian Studies* 72, no. 1 (2013): 115–39.

Moore, Joe. *Japanese Workers and the Struggle for Power, 1945–1947.* Madison: University of Wisconsin Press, 1983.

Morris-Suzuki, Tessa. "Concepts of Nature and Technology in Pre-Industrial Japan." *East Asian History* 1 (1991): 81–97.

———. "Environmental Problems and Perceptions in Early Industrial Japan." In *Sediments of Time: Environmental Society in Chinese History,* edited by Mark Elvin, 756–80. New York: Cambridge University Press, 1998.

Murakami Yasumasa. *Ashio dōzanshi.* Utsunomiya: Zuisōsha, 2006.

Murphy, Michelle. *Sick Building Syndrome and the Problem of Uncertainty: Environmental Politics, Technoscience, and Women Workers.* Durham, NC: Duke University Press, 2006.

Najita Tetsuo. "Ambiguous Encounters: Ogata Kōan and International Studies in Late Tokugawa Osaka." In *Osaka: The Merchants' Capital of Early Modern Japan,* edited by James L. McClain and Wakita Osamu, 213–42. Ithaca, NY: Cornell University Press, 1999.

———. "Nature Is the Source of Rights, but Nature Has No Rights: Rethinking Humanity in the Issue of Ecology." Paper presented at the Imminent Issues: Symposium in Honor of Masao Miyoshi, New York University, April 29, 2004.

———. *Ordinary Economies in Japan: A Historical Perspective, 1750–1950.* Berkeley: University of California Press, 2009.

———, ed. *Readings in Tokugawa Thought.* 3rd ed. Select Papers, Center for East Asian Studies, University of Chicago, Vol. 9. Chicago: Center for East Asian Studies, 1998.

———. *Visions of Virtue in Tokugawa Japan: The Kaitokudo Merchant Academy of Osaka.* Honolulu: University of Hawai'i Press, 1997.

Nakamura Kennosuke. *Senkyōshi Nikorai to meiji nihon.* Vol. 458, Iwanami shinsho. Tokyo: Iwanami shoten, 1996.

Namihara Emiko. *Kegare no kōzō.* Shinseban ed. Tokyo: Seidosha, 1988.

Narita Ryūichi. "Shintai to kōshū eisei: Nihon no bunmeika to kokuminka." In *Kōza sekaishi,* 375–401. Tokyo: Tokyo daigaku shuppankai, 1995.

———. "Teito Tokyo." In *Iwanami kōza: Nihon tsūshi 16, kindai 1,* edited by Asao Naohiko, Amino Yoshihiko, Ishii Susumu, Kano Masanao, Hayakawa Atsuya, and Yasumaru Yoshio, 175–214. Tokyo: Iwanami shoten, 1994.

Nash, Linda Lorraine. *Inescapable Ecologies: A History of Environment, Disease, and Knowledge.* Berkeley: University of California Press, 2006.

Nihei Teiichi. *Nanpō no inasaku to nōkigu.* Tokyo: Nihon yūchiku kikai nōgyōkyōkai, 1943.

Nimura Kazuo. *The Ashio Riot of 1907: A Social History of Mining in Japan.* Translated by Terry Boardman and Andrew Gordon. Durham, NC: Duke University Press, 1997.

Nixon, Rob. *Slow Violence and the Environmentalism of the Poor.* Cambridge, MA: Harvard University Press, 2011.

———. 2011. Slow Violence and Environmental Storytelling. www.niemanstoryboard .org.

Notehelfer, F. G. "Between Tradition and Modernity: Labor and the Ashio Copper Mine." *Monumenta Nipponica* 39, no. 1 (1984): 11–24.

———. "Japan's First Pollution Incident." *Journal of Japanese Studies* 2, no. 1 (1975): 351–83.

———. *Kōtoku Shūsui, Portrait of a Japanese Radical.* Cambridge: Cambridge University Press, 1971.

Nozawa Hideki. "Ishikawa Sanshirō ni okeru Erize Rukuryu no shisō: Sono juyō to sai." *Chirigaku hyōron* 79, no. 14 (2006): 837–56.

Obata Tokujirō. "Tenpen chii." In *Meiji bunka zenshū 24 kagaku hen*, edited by Yoshino Sakuzō, 33–44. Tokyo: Nihon hyōronsha, 1930.

Ogura Takekazu. *Can Japanese Agriculture Survive?* Tokyo: Agricultural Policy Research Center, 1980.

Oka Asajirō. "Jinrui no seifuku ni tai suru shizen no fukushū." *Chūō kōron* 27, no. 274 (1912): 13–20.

Okuma Takashi. *Tonegawa chisui no hensen to suigai.* Tokyo: Tokyo daigaku shuppankai, 1987.

Ōmachi Masami. *Jiyūminken undō to chihō seiji.* Utsunomiya: Zuisōsha, 2002.

Osaka nippō. "Osaka Nippō June 9, 1878." In *Wappa sōdō shiryō*, edited by Tsuruoka shishi henshūkai, 303–5. Tsuruoka (Yamagata): Tsuruoka shishi henshūkai, 1982.

Osamu Kanaya, ed. *Rongo (kaiban).* Tokyo: Iwanami shoten, 1999.

Postone, Moishe. *Time, Labor, and Social Domination: A Reinterpretation of Marx's Critical Theory.* Cambridge: Cambridge University Press, 1996.

Purseglove, Jeremy. *Taming the Flood: A History and Natural History of Rivers and Wetlands.* Oxford: Oxford University Press, 1988.

Pyle, Kenneth. "Introduction: Japan Faces Her Future." In "Symposium: The Ashio Copper Mine Pollution Case," special issue, *Journal of Japanese Studies* 2, no. 1 (1975): 347–50.

———. "The Technology of Japanese Nationalism: The Local Improvement Movement, 1900–1918." *Journal of Asian Studies* 33 (1973): 51–65.

Reclus, Elisée. *Anarchy, Geography, Modernity: The Radical Social Thought of Elisée Reclus.* Edited by John P. Clark and Camille Martin. New York: Lexington Books, 2004.

Reitan, Richard. "Ethics and Natural Rights Theory: Competing Conceptions of Nature during the Meiji Period." *Nenpō nihon shisōshi* 8 (2009): 1–28.

———. *Making a Moral Society: Ethics and the State in Meiji Japan.* Honolulu: University of Hawai'i Press, 2010.

———. "The Social Mind and the Body of the Crowd: Crowd Psychology in Early Twentieth Century Japan." Paper presented at the University of Tokyo Center for Philosophy, 2009.

Rogaski, Ruth. *Hygienic Modernity: Meanings of Health and Disease in Treaty-Port China.* Berkeley: University of California Press, 2004.

Rowbotham, Sheila. *Edward Carpenter: A Life of Liberty and Love*. London: Verso, 2008.

Sakai Naoki. "Subject and Substratum: On Japanese Imperial Nationalism." *Cultural Studies* 14, nos. 3/4 (2000): 462–530.

Sano Tomonori. "Ideologies of Integration Past: Universality, Revolution-Phobia, and Integration." *Asian Regional Integration Review* 1 (2009).

Sato Tatsuya. "Nishi Amane ni okeru 'saikorogii' to 'shinrigaku' no aida." In *Nishi Amane to Nihon no kindai*, edited by Shimane kenritsu daigaku Nishi Amane kenkyūkai, 217–50. Tokyo: Perikan sha, 2005.

Scheiner, Irwin. "Benevolent Lords and Honorable Peasants: Rebellion and Peasant Consciousness in Tokugawa Japan." In *Japanese Thought in the Tokugawa Period 1600–1868*, edited by Tetsuo Najita and Irwin Scheiner, 39–63. Chicago: University of Chicago Press, 1978.

Schneider, Herbert Wallace. *A Prophet and a Pilgrim, Being the Incredible History of Thomas Lake Harris and Laurence Oliphant; Their Sexual Mysticisms and Utopian Communities; Amply Documented to Confound the Skeptic*. New York: Columbia University Press, 1942.

Shaars, Marvin A. "The Story of the Department of Agricultural Economics, 1909–72." University of Wisconsin, 1972. http://www.aae.wisc.edu/pubs/AAEStory.pdf (accessed November 11, 2009).

Shapiro, Judith. *Mao's War against Nature: Politics and the Environment in Revolutionary China*. Studies in Environment and History. Cambridge: Cambridge University Press, 2001.

Shibusawa Eiichi. *The Autobiography of Shibusawa Eiichi: From Peasant to Entrepreneur*. Translated by Teruko Craig. Tokyo: University of Tokyo Press, 1994.

Shiga Shigetaka. *Nihon fūkeiron*. Tokyo: Iwanami bunko, 1995.

Shimada Kenji. *Shūshigaku to yōmeigaku*. Tokyo: Iwanami shinsho, 2002.

Shimada Sōzō. *Tanaka Shōzō ō yoroku*. 2 vols. Tokyo: San'ichi shobō, 1972.

Shimoda Hiraku. "Bad Sushi or Bad Merchant? The 'Dead Fish Poisoning Incident' of 1852." *Modern Asian Studies* 35, no. 3 (2001): 513–31.

Shōji Kichirō. "Shōzō no tochi hanbai 'sanzento en' no mōke ni gigi ari." *Tanaka Shōzō to Ashio kōdoku jiken kenkyū* 8 (1989): 61–109.

Shōji Kichirō and Masuro Sugai. "The Ashio Copper Mine Pollution Case: The Origins of Environmental Destruction." In *Industrial Pollution in Japan*, edited by Jun Ui, 18–63. Tokyo: United Nations University Press, 1992.

Sippel, Patricia. "Chisui: Creating a Sacred Domain in Early Modern and Modern Japan." In *Public Spheres, Private Lives in Modern Japan, 1600–1950*, edited by Gail Lee Bernstein, Andrew Gordon, and Kate Wildman Nakai, 155–84. Cambridge, MA: Harvard University Asia Center, 2005.

Smil, Vaclav. *Enriching the Earth: Fritz Haber, Carl Bosch, and the Transformation of World Food Production*. Cambridge, MA: MIT Press, 2004.

Smith, Kerry. *A Time of Crisis: Japan, the Great Depression, and Rural Revitalization*. Cambridge, MA: Harvard University Asia Center, 2001.

Smith, W. Eugene, and Aileen Smith. *Minamata: The Story of the Poisoning of a City, and of the People Who Chose to Carry the Burden of Courage.* New York: Alskog-Sensorium / Holt, Rinehart and Winston, 1975.

Stalin, Josef. *Economic Problems of Socialism in the USSR.* Peking: Foreign Languages Press, 1972.

Stallybrass, Peter, and Allon White. *The Politics and Poetics of Transgression.* Ithaca, NY: Cornell University Press, 1986.

Steele, M. William. *Alternative Narratives in Modern Japanese History.* London: RoutledgeCurzon, 2003.

———. "From Custom to Right: The Politicization of the Village in Early Meiji Japan." *Modern Asian Studies* 23 (1989): 729–48.

Stolz, Robert. "Here, Now: Everyday Space as Cultural Critique." In *Tosaka Jun: A Critical Reader,* edited by Ken C. Kawashima, Fabian Schäfer, and Robert Stolz. Ithaca, NY: East Asia Program, Cornell University, forthcoming.

Stone, Alan. "The Vanishing Village: The Ashio Copper Mine Pollution Case, 1890–1907." PhD diss., University of Washington, 1974.

Strong, Kenneth. *Ox against the Storm: A Biography of Tanaka Shōzō.* Kent: Japan Library, 1977.

Sugai Masuro. "The Development Process of Mining Pollution at the Ashio Copper Mine." *Project on Technology Transfer, Transformation, and Development: The Japanese Experience (JE)* (1983).

Sugawara Hikaru. "Tanaka Shōzō no kōdō no ronri." Unpublished essay.

Sugiyama Hiroshi. "Korera sōdōron: Sono kōzu to ronri." In *Jiyūminken to kindai shakai,* edited by Arai Katsuhiko, 147–75. Tokyo: Yoshikawa kobunkan, 2004.

Sumitani Mikio and Rōdō undōshi kenkyūkai, eds. *Shinkigen.* 8 vols. Vol. 3, *Meiji shakaishugi shiryō shū.* Tokyo: Rōdō undōshi kenkyūkai, 1961.

Supreme Commander for the Allied Powers. Economic and Scientific Section. Director of Production and Utilities. Industry Division. Industrial Production and Construction Branch. ARC Identifier 458432. *Hokkaido Co-operative Dairy Company Ltd (HCLC Matters).* Record Group 331: Records of Allied Operational and Occupation Headquarters, World War II, 1907–1966. Textual Reference (Military) (Rd-Dc-2-Mil). College Park, MD: National Archives and Records Administration, 1945–50.

———. Government Section. Administration Division. (10/02/1945–04/28/1952), *Kurosawa Torizo.* ARC Identifier 358041, Record Group 331: Records of Allied Operational and Occupation Headquarters, World War II, 1907–1966. Textual Reference (Military) (Rd-Dc-2-Mil). College Park, MD: National Archives and Records Administration, 1945–52.

Suzuki Noboru. "Nishi Amane tetsugaku no ninchitaikei to tōitsu kagaku—sōgōka e no kōzu o motomete." In *Nishi Amane to nihon no kindai,* edited by Shimane kenritsu daigaku Nishi Amane kenkyūkai, 282–323. Tokyo: Perikan sha, 2005.

Suzuki Sadami, ed. *"Seimei" de yomu nihon kindai: Taishō seimeishugi no tanjō to tenkai.* Tokyo: Nihon hōsō shuppankai, 1996.

———. *Taishō seimeishugi to gendai.* Tokyo: Kawaide shobō shinsha, 1995.

Tachibana Kōzaburō. "Nihon aikoku kakushin hongi." In *Gendai nihon shisōshi taikei*, vol. 31, *Chōkokkashugi*, 213–38. Tokyo: Iwanami shoten, 1964.

Takaoka Hiroyuki, ed. *Shiryōshū: Sōryokusen to bunka 2: Kōsei undō, kenmin undō, dokusho undō*. Tokyo: Otsukishoten, 2001.

Tanaka Shōzō. *Tanaka Shōzō senshū*. 7 vols. Edited by Anzai Kunio, Kano Masanao, Komatsu Hiroshi, Sakaya Junji, and Yui Masaomi. Tokyo: Iwanami shoten, 1989.

———. *Tanaka Shōzō zenshū*. 20 vols. Tokyo: Iwanami shoten, 1977–80.

Tanaka, Stefan. *New Times in Modern Japan*. Princeton, NJ: Princeton University Press, 2004.

Tatematsu Wahei. *Doku: Fūbun Tanaka Shōzō*. Tokyo: Tokyo shoseki, 1997.

Thomas, Julia Adeney. *Reconfiguring Modernity: Concepts of Nature in Japanese Political Ideology*. Twentieth-Century Japan No. 12. Berkeley: University of California Press, 2001.

Tiegel, Ernst. *Eisei hanron* (1879). Vol. 3. Translated by Ōi Gendō. Eisei hanron maku 1–2, *Kindai Nihon yōjōron eiseiron shūsei*. Tokyo: Ozorasha, 1992.

———. "Ifukuryō shinkensetsu" (1881). In *Kaseigaku bunken shūsei zokuhen Meiji 6*, edited by Chitako Tanaka, 297–314. Tokyo: Watanabe shoten, 1969.

Tochigikenshi hensan iinkai, ed. *Tochigikenshi shiryōhen kingendai 9. Tochigikenshi*. Utsunomiya: Tochigiken kyōiku kōhōkai, 1980.

Tomba, Massimiliano. *Marx's Temporalities*. Leiden: Brill, 2013.

Tosaka Jun. *Tosaka Jun zenshū*. 6 vols. Tokyo: Keisō shobō, 1966.

Totman, Conrad. *The Green Archipelago: Forestry in Pre-Industrial Japan*. Athens: Ohio University Press, 1989.

———. *A History of Japan*. Blackwell History of the World. Malden, MA: Wiley-Blackwell, 2005.

———. *Pre-Industrial Korea and Japan in Environmental Perspective*. Handbook of Oriental Studies / Handbuch Der Orientalistik. Leiden: Brill, 2004.

———. "Preindustrial River Conservancy: Causes and Consequences." *Monumenta Nipponica* 47, no. 1 (1992): 59–72.

Toulmin, Stephen. *Cosmopolis: The Hidden Agenda of Modernity*. Chicago: University of Chicago Press, 1990.

Tsurumaki Takao. *Kindaika to dentōteki minshū sekai: Tenkanki no minshū undō to sono shisō*. Tokyo: Tokyo daigaku shuppankai, 1992.

Tsuzuki Chūshichi. "'My Dear Sanshiro': Edward Carpenter and His Japanese Disciple." *Hitotsubashi Journal of Social Studies* 6, no. 1 (1972): 1–9.

Tucker, Mary Evelyn. "The Philosophy of Ch'i as an Ecological Cosmology." In *Confucianism and Ecology: The Interrelation of Heaven, Earth, and Humans*, edited by Mary Evelyn Tucker and John Berthrong, 187–207. Cambridge, MA: Harvard University Center for the Study of World Religions, 1998.

Uchimizu Mamoru, ed. *Shiryō Ashio kōdoku jiken*. Tokyo: Akishobō, 1971.

Uchimura Kanzō. "Denmaruku koku no hanashi: Shinkō to jumoku to o motte kuni o sukuishi hanashi (1911)." In *Kōsei e no saidai ibutsu-denmaruku koku no hanashi*, 71–87. Tokyo: Iwanami bunko, 2002.

Ueki Emori. "Discourse on Popular Rights and Liberty." In *From Japan's Modernity: A Reader*, edited by Tetsuo Najita, translated by Katsuya Hirano, 49–52. Chicago: University of Chicago Center for East Asian Studies, 2002.

Ueno Takashi. "Jiyūminken ni okeru Igirisu kōrishugi shisō no taishū—Mutsu Mumemitsu to Jierimi Bensamu." *Gendaishi kenkyū* 35 (1991): 35–50.

Uesugi Kentarō. "Kindai nihon ni okeru kōrishugi seiji shisō no juyō." In *Nihon bunka o yominaosu—shinpishugi to ronri*, edited by Uesugi Kentarō, 72–106. Tokyo: Hokue shuppan, 1991.

Utsunomiya Sentarō. *Hikōki seisaku hitsuju genryō taru kazein kōgyō kokusan dokuritsu ni kan suru seigansho*. Sapporo: Hokkaido seiraku hanbai kumiai rengōkai, 1933.

Van Wyck, Peter. *Primitives in the Wilderness: Deep Ecology and the Missing Human Subject*. Albany: SUNY Press, 1997.

———. *Signs of Danger: Waste, Trauma, and Nuclear Threat*. Minneapolis: University of Minnesota Press, 2005.

Virilio, Paul. "The Primal Accident." In *The Politics of Everyday Fear*, edited by Brian Massumi, 211–18. Minneapolis: University of Minnesota Press, 1993.

Vlastos, Stephen. *Peasant Protests and Uprisings in Tokugawa Japan*. Berkeley: University of California Press, 1986.

Walker, Brett L. *The Conquest of Ainu Lands: Ecology and Culture in Japanese Expansion, 1590–1800*. Berkeley: University of California Press, 2006.

———. *The Lost Wolves of Japan*. Seattle: University of Washington Press, 2005.

———. *Toxic Archipelago: A History of Industrial Disease in Japan*. Seattle: University of Washington Press, 2010.

Walker, Gavin. "The Absent Body of Labour Power: Uno Kōzō's Logic of Capital." In *Historical Materialism*. Forthcoming.

Walthall, Anne. *Peasant Uprisings in Japan*. Chicago: University of Chicago Press, 1991.

Watanabe Hiroshi. *Higashi ajia no ōken to shisō*. Tokyo: Tokyo daigaku shuppankai, 1997.

Watsuji Tetsurō. *Fūdo: Ningengakuteki kōsatsu* (1935). 38th ed. Tokyo: Iwanami bunko, 1999.

Williams, Raymond. *Marxism and Literature*. Oxford: Oxford University Press, 1977.

Winch, Donald. *Economics and Policy*. London: Hodder and Stoughton, 1969.

Yanaka mura to Moro Chikasuke o katarukai, ed. *Yanaka mura sonchō: Moro Chikasuke*. Utsunomiya: Zuisōsha, 2001.

Yasuda Keisai. *Tsūzoku yōjōkunmō*. Edited by Ōi Gendō. Vol. 4, *Yōjōdan, Tsūzoku yōjōkunmō, Eisei tekiyō, eisei yōron, Kindai Nihon Yōseiron Eiseiron Shūsei*. 1880. Reprint, Tokyo: Ozorasha, 1992.

Yasushi Yamanouchi, J. Victor Koschmann, and Ryūichi Narita, eds. *Total War and "Modernization."* Ithaca, NY: East Asia Program, Cornell University, 1998.

Young, Louise. *Japan's Total Empire: Manchuria and the Culture of Wartime Imperialism*. Twentieth-Century Japan: The Emergence of a World Power. Berkeley: University of California Press, 1999.

Yui Masaomi. *Tanaka Shōzō*. Tokyo: Iwanami shinsho: kiban, 1984.

Yukijirushi nyūgyō kabushikigaisha. *Yukijirushi nyūgyōshi*. Vol. 1. Sapporo: Yukijirushinyūgyō, 1960.

Zhang Dainian and Edmund Ryden. *Key Concepts in Chinese Philosophy*. New Haven, CT: Yale University Press, 2002.

Zimmerman, Michael E. *Contesting Earth's Future: Radical Ecology and Postmodernity*. Berkeley: University of California Press, 1994.

Žižek, Slavoj. "Introduction: Robespierre, or, The 'Divine Violence' of Terror." In *Virtue and Terror: Maximilien Robespierre*, edited by Jean Ducange, vii–xxxix. London: Verso, 2007.

dairy farming, 5, 161; as an ecology of autonomy, 160, 162, 185, 192; casein demand, 177–79, 185; as a commodity, 161, 174, 188–89, 235n4; Denmark model of, 169–71, 175, 186; markets, 174; virtues (*santoku*) of, 165, 176, 183, 186; wartime and postwar practices, 177–79, 183–85, 188–89; in Wisconsin, 167. *See also* Hokkaido Dairy Promotion Company; Snow Brand Dairy

Darwin, Charles, 4, 211n7, 231n32; *The Origin of Species*, 4, 129–30

Darwinism, 21–22, 98, 110, 132, 231n32; natural selection, 5, 27, 119, 129–30, 135, 157, 199–200

Davis, Andrew Jackson, 227n60

Davis, Mike, 94

death rates, 45–47

Deep Ecology, 202, 228n76, 230n6

Deleuze, Gilles, 19, 45, 120, 201

democracy, 152, 185, 193; American, 227n62; cooperative, 156; liberal, 64; "natural" (*demokurashī*), 119, 125–26, 128, 234n69; true, 80, 126, 151

Denmark: dairy farming model, 169–71, 175, 186; folk schools, 172, 228n76

desire: Carpenter's theory of, 135; for life, 134, 136

De Vries, Hugo, 149

Diet, 19, 51, 65; Tanaka's speeches/questions to, 38–39, 71, 94, 123

disasters, 43, 48, 124, 128, 193; artificial, 95

disease: cholera, 30–32, 97, 214n12, 215n34; epidemic, 23–24, 216n54; germ theory of, 22–24, 30–31, 133. *See also* Minamata disease

divine soil, 16, 142, 176, 180, 186, 202; Eto's mandala of, 181–82

*doku* (poison): cycle, 97, 106, 111–12, 144; eradication of, 100, 111; Tanaka's concept of, 15, 86, 92, 94–98, 204, 228n67; in Yanaka village, 100–102, 227n45

*domin*: Chinese society as, 143–44, 154, 231n23; concept, 119, 126, 144–45, 147. *See also* democracy

Driscoll, Mark, 143–44, 179, 237n46

Du Fu, 189–90

Dun, Edwin, 164, 167, 170

dynamic social aesthetics (*dōtai shakai bigaku*), 112, 120, 129, 134–37, 146, 156–57

earth: cooling of, 132; cultivation of, 128, 142, 145, 154, 160; rotation of, 127; solar energy and, 134, 231n29. *See also* Heaven and Earth

earthquakes, 2–3, 48, 211n10

"ecocide," 5, 98

ecological threats, 44, 54, 67, 93

ecology: of autonomy, 160–62, 165, 175, 179, 185, 192; capitalism and, 17, 147; of dairy farming, 173–74, 177, 189; Deep Ecology, 202, 228n76, 230n6; of *doku*, 163; inescapable, 6, 9, 12, 24, 44, 46, 93; materialist, 180; multiple interactions of, 95; of national soil, 176; politics/political, 44, 101; production and, 183; radical, 12, 22, 113, 230n6. *See also* social ecology

economic revolution, 152

Edo period. *See* Tokugawa (Edo) period

Eimer, Theodor, 130–31, 134

electricity (*ereki*), 2

emperor: criticism of, 80–81; end of war declaration, 150–51; "people's," 75, 77–78, 81; rituals of, 181. See also *jikiso*

Engels, Friedrich, 72; *The German Ideology*, 158, 234n91

environmental crisis, 6–8, 15–16, 190; benevolent government and, 71; of 1890s Japan, 5, 10, 21, 38, 87, 183; historicity of, 12; individualism and, 202; Meiji politics and, 54–55, 93; outside capital and, 161; representative politics as a solution to, 193; social problems and, 118

environmental politics, 118; emergence in Japan, 7, 12–14, 21, 54

Erikson, Kai, 48

erosion, 34, 99, 198

ethics: environmental, 23–24, 176; national, 26; place-based, 139

Eto Tekirei, 181–82

evolution, 9, 27, 119, 129–32, 148, 230n8. *See also* Darwinism

Ewald, François, 44, 66, 93

exploitation, 141, 241n27; Ashio mine, 7, 41, 52, 92, 207; capitalist, 135, 146, 203; Japanese, 143–44; of nature, 111, 119; of soil, 168, 174

extinction, 98, 131, 209

fascism, 6, 144, 192, 233n61, 239n2

fertilizers: green, 34, 48, 165, 235n6, 237n34; nitrogen, 168–69

humanism, 195, 197

human-nature relations: alienation, 22; beneficial interactions, 140, 173; coevolution, 27, 30; connection and reconnection, 9, 11, 13, 140; land connection, 9, 140–44, 152–53, 173–74; metabolic rift in, 98; mutual penetrations, 3–4, 11, 21, 45, 85, 157; nudism and, 133; pollution and, 97–98; separation/division, 3–4, 8, 12–13, 20–21, 25–26; texts/guides on, 24–25; transcendence in, 8, 15, 27; vulnerability of, 6; water and, 115

hygiene, 28–33, 215n38

Ibaraki, 14, 47

ideal, synthetic, 137–39

*idée force*, 136, 145–46, 156–58

ideological conversion (*tenkō*), 150–51

Imaizumi Sadasuke, 181

imperial house, 143, 224, 233n63; cultural hermeneutic, 138; morality of, 78, 208

imperialism: Japanese, 99, 143–44; Western, 56, 58, 90, 150

Imperial Rule Assistance Association (IRAA), 161, 179, 185

imperial way theories, 180–81

imperial will, 76–77, 79

indigo industry, 35

individual, the: autonomy of, 8, 14, 21, 25, 138; historical product of, 157–58; rights of, 57–58, 76; sense of right and wrong, 31–32

industrialization, 20, 67, 90; and nature, 40, 88, 213n35

Inoue Enryō, 26–27, 41, 193

Ishikawa Hanzan, 50, 74, 219n9

Ishikawa Sanshirō, 5, 16, 100, 118, 158, 229n5; on agrarian fundamentalism, 139–41; back to the land ideology, 119, 127, 140, 142–43, 152–53; cyclical temporalities, 127–28, 132, 150; on division of labor, 146, 149; *domin* concepts, 119, 126, 143–45, 147, 154; dynamic social aesthetics theory, 112, 120, 129, 134–37, 146, 156–57; *idée force*, 136, 145–46, 156–58; move to Chitose, 129, 134, 148; natural democracy theory (*demokurashī*), 119, 125–26, 128, 234n69; natural selection criticism, 5, 27, 119, 129–30, 135, 157, 199–200; nudism, 129, 133, 148; references to Quinton, 131–33; rejection of socialism, 16, 122–25; rhizomatic theory, 120, 146–47; species concept, 148; view of the

Chinese, 143–44; views on class war, 122–23; visit to Yanaka, 121

Ishikawa Sanshirō, works, 131; *Agrarian Fundamentalism and Domin Thought*, 140; "An Anarchist Manifesto," 150–51; *The Authority of the Soil*, 129; diary, 128; *Dynamique (Dinamikku)*, 119–20, 135–36, 148; "Gangs" ("Gyangu"), 144; *Japan, Fifty Years On*, 151–54; "Let's Clean Up the Yellow River," 144; *One Hundred Lectures on Oriental Culture*, 147–48; *Return to the Golden Age*, 140; "Social Mutation: A New Way to Revolution," 149; *Study of Evolutionary Theory*, 154

Itagaki Taisuke, 56

Japanese Communist Party (JCP), 150, 191–92, 239n1; cooperative model and, 187–88

Japanese Left, 118, 123, 150. See also socialism

Japanization, 175–76, 183

*jikiso* (appeal): coalition, 123; cultural form of, 81–82; failure of, 55, 72; Matsuzawa's, 76–78; Sakura's, 52, 55; Tanaka and Kōtoku's, 50–53, 76, 78–80, 93, 207–9; text, 54–55, 75–76

Kanai Takanori, 59–60

Kantian divide, 2, 26, 193

Kanto: people, 65; plain, 15, 90, 101, 160, 225n3

Katō Hiroyuki, 21, 27

Kawakami Hajime, 68, 164

Kawashima, Ken, 201

Kawashima Isaburō, 5, 35, 37, 212n12

*kegare* and *yomi*, 23–25, 97, 204, 233n63

Kinoshita Naoe, 46, 80, 82, 106, 118, 224n92; nonviolent resistance policy, 124; retreat to nature, 111–12, 115

Kitasato Shibasaburō, 30

knowledge, 139; Meiji, 3, 25, 214n10; social, 67

*kōeki*, 57, 112

*kōgai*, 94, 112

Komatsu Hiroshi, 62, 235n11

Komori Yōichi, 32

Komurō Shinsuke, 58–61, 220n28

Kōno Hironaka, 76, 79

Kōtoku Shūsui, 6, 117–18, 123; appeal (*jikiso*), 15, 50–53, 76, 78–80, 93, 207–9

Kozai Yoshinau, 41–42, 46, 88

Kropotkin, Peter, 129, 146, 233n62, 234n69

Kumazawa Banzan, 7, 34, 99–100

Kurosawa Torizō, 16–17, 92; dairy farming activities/philosophies, 164–66, 173, 188–89, 239n67; "Ecological Cycle of Dairy Farming" diagram, 166, 182, 190; establishment of Rakunō gijuku (school), 169–70; formation of Dairy Sales Union, 169–70; founding of Snow Brand Dairy, 5, 159–62; as head of Hokkaido Dairy Promotion Company, 179, 183–84, 237n45; participation in Konoe's IRAA, 179, 185; rehabilitation hearing, 185–86; and Tanaka relations, 159, 164

Kurosawa Torizō, works: *Denmark, the Agricultural Nation*, 186; *Imperial Way Agriculture*, 174–75, 177, 180, 184–86; *Total Mobilization of Animal Power*, 179, 183; *The Way of the Farmer*, 174–77, 180, 183, 186

labor: agricultural, 142, 176, 232n44; artisanal, 200; Chinese, 143–44, 155; demand, 199; division of, 146, 149, 211n7; redemptive, 111; reorganization of, 178; spirit-reducing, 108; time, 196, 198; value-producing, 203. *See also* subsumption of nature and labor

labor power, 144, 175, 201, 204; commodification of, 12, 200

Lamarck, Jean-Baptiste, 135. *See also* neo-Lamarckian theory

land and water, powers of, 124, 179; Tanaka's theory of, 15, 85, 96, 110, 113–14

landownership: feudal, 141–42; movement, 105, 121

land tax, 12, 63, 221n51

Latour, Bruno, 30, 197, 201, 240n9; actor-network theory (ANT), 11, 92, 194–95; rejection of Marxian categories, 195

lawlessness, 72

leaks: of Japan of 1890s, 21, 35, 183; language of, 11

Lefebvre, Henri, 22, 25, 224n2

Levins, Richard, 10

liberalism, Meiji, 7–8, 13–14, 21; activists/activism, 35–37, 63, 98; invocations of Sakura, 55–56, 58, 61, 223n78; laissez-faire ideal, 67; pollution problem and, 39, 54–55, 66, 193; of postwar Japan, 192–93, 239n1; tradition/modernity narrative and, 54; utilitarianism and, 56–57

Liberal Party (Jiyūtō), 36, 56, 222n58

liberty movement, 19, 36, 61, 193

life philosophy, 16, 111, 137, 229n5

lightning, 1–3, 41, 168

Lukács, Georg, 12, 196, 229n84, 233n56

Makihara Norio, 67, 222nn69–70

Manchuria, 144, 179–80, 183

Marcon, Federico, 23

Marshall, Alfred, 67, 71

martyrdom, 56, 58, 75, 82; peasant, 59–61

Maruyama Masao, 142, 156, 191–93, 239n1

Marx, Karl: on Darwin, 4; ecological thinking, 212n22; *Economic and Philosophical Manuscripts*, 141, 159; on fetishism of commodities, 195–96; on feudal landownership, 141–42; formal and real subsumption concepts, 11–13, 194, 199, 213n31, 232n44; *The German Ideology*, 158, 234n91; *Grundrisse*, 49, 141; humanist reductionism, 195; on the London bourgeoisie, 169; on nature, 8, 16, 142; on productive consumption, 175; on religion and science, 195; on use-value, 196. *See also Capital*

masses, 66, 112; foolish (*gumin*), 112–13; rural, 56, 62

materiality, 8; of the body, 12, 138–39, 158, 196; commodity's, 196; of daily life, 139; of the environment, 190; and nature, 26; of pollution, 11

Matsukata Masayoshi, 67

Matsumoto Eiko, 6, 14, 68, 92–93; move to California, 49–50, 85; *Sufferings of a Mine-Poisoned Land*, 21, 46–49, 72, 81

Matsuzawa Kyūsaku, 76–78

Mechnikov, Ilya, 146

medicine, 22–23

Meiji Dairy, 188, 192, 235n1, 239n66

Meiji period, 19–20; beef production, 167; Constitution, 38, 110; emperor, 51, 79, 82, 186, 224n101; enlightenment, 37, 60; government, 68, 164, 220n18; ideology, 20, 56, 70, 79; pollution problem, 36, 39, 46, 75; power, 100; revolution, 61; soil science, 41–44, 55; time and space ideologies, 21; voting rights, 212n20. *See also* liberalism, Meiji; rationalism, Meiji

Meiji state, 8, 36, 93, 101; control of rivers, 95, 102; reaction to environmental crisis, 87–88; violence, 114, 118, 121–22

Meiji subject, 4, 8, 13, 19–21, 189

STUDIES OF THE WEATHERHEAD
EAST ASIAN INSTITUTE, COLUMBIA UNIVERSITY

**Selected Titles**

*Beyond the Metropolis: Second Cities and Modern Life in Interwar Japan,* by Louise Young. University of California Press, 2013.

*Imperial Eclipse: Japan's Strategic Thinking about Continental Asia before August 1945,* by Yukiko Koshiro. Cornell University Press, 2013.

*The Nature of the Beasts: Empire and Exhibition at the Tokyo Imperial Zoo,* by Ian J. Miller. University of California Press, 2013.

*Reconstructing Bodies: Biomedicine, Health, and Nation-Building in South Korea since 1945,* by John P. DiMoia. Stanford University Press, 2013.

*Tyranny of the Weak: North Korea and the World, 1950–1992,* by Charles Armstrong. Cornell University Press, 2013.

*The Art of Censorship in Postwar Japan,* by Kirsten Cather. University of Hawai'i Press, 2012.

*Asia for the Asians: China in the Lives of Five Meiji Japanese,* by Paula Harrell. MerwinAsia, 2012.

*Lin Shu, Inc.: Translation and the Making of Modern Chinese Culture,* by Michael Gibbs Hill. Oxford University Press, 2012.

*Occupying Power: Sex Workers and Servicemen in Postwar Japan,* by Sarah Kovner. Stanford University Press, 2012.

*Redacted: The Archives of Censorship in Postwar Japan,* by Jonathan E. Abel. University of California Press, 2012.

*Empire of Dogs: Canines, Japan, and the Making of the Modern Imperial World,* by Aaron Herald Skabelund. Cornell University Press, 2011.

*Planning for Empire: Reform Bureaucrats and the Japanese Wartime State,* by Janis Mimura. Cornell University Press, 2011.

*Realms of Literacy: Early Japan and the History of Writing*, by David Lurie. Harvard University Asia Series, 2011.

*Russo-Japanese Relations, 1905–17: From Enemies to Allies*, by Peter Berton. Routledge, 2011.

*Behind the Gate: Inventing Students in Beijing*, by Fabio Lanza. Columbia University Press, 2010.

*Imperial Japan at Its Zenith: The Wartime Celebration of the Empire's 2,600th Anniversary*, by Kenneth J. Ruoff. Cornell University Press, 2010.

*Passage to Manhood: Youth Migration, Heroin, and AIDS in Southwest China*, by Shao-hua Liu. Stanford University Press, 2010.

*Postwar History Education in Japan and the Germanys: Guilty Lessons*, by Julian Dierkes. Routledge, 2010.

*The Aesthetics of Japanese Fascism*, by Alan Tansman. University of California Press, 2009.

*The Growth Idea: Purpose and Prosperity in Postwar Japan*, by Scott O'Bryan. University of Hawai'i Press, 2009.

*Leprosy in China: A History*, by Angela Ki Che Leung. Columbia University Press, 2008.

*National History and the World of Nations: Capital, State, and the Rhetoric of History in Japan, France, and the United States*, by Christopher Hill. Duke University Press, 2008.

COMPLETE LIST AT:

http://www.columbia.edu/cu/weai/weatherhead-studies.html